MW00534787

"After a desultory post–Cold War insider d
ment settled on an ambitious grand strategy to integrate states g
a US led liberal international order. Despite the poor performance of this grand
strategy for the last quarter century, particularly its propensity for war, advocates
continue to rely on a handful of key arguments as to why it is both essential and
doable. This book takes on these arguments one by one, and demonstrates their
weakness. The key elements of a new, more cautious, and more cost-effective grand
strategy-restraint are then systematically advanced and assembled into a coherent
whole. Those uneasy with the present US course of action, and hungry for an alternative, will find allies in these pages."

— Barry R. Posen, Massachusetts Institute of Technology, USA

"A. Trevor Thrall and Benjamin H. Friedman have assembled the intellectual
A-Team of national security analysts in *US Grand Strategy in the 21st Century*.
Covering the regional and functional waterfront, the authors of this timely and
compelling volume demonstrate that the American pursuit of global hegemony
over the past quarter century has been neither necessary nor realistic. The only
puzzle remaining after reading this essential corrective to America's collective
Liberal hegemonic delusion is why we fell for any alternative to restraint?"

— Michael Desch, University of Notre Dame, USA

"The essays in this volume shine a bright and skeptical light on America's global
military commitments, and make a compelling case for restraint in US strategy. The
book includes fruitful discussions of the social science literature bearing on various
strategic questions like nuclear proliferation, oil security, democracy promotion, and
military intervention. It offers superb dissections of the role of distance, national character, public opinion, and built-up military institutions in shaping national strategy.
The authors show, with keen argument and telling evidence, that restraint rather than
primacy offers a superior route to ensuring America's security, liberty, and prosperity."

— David Hendrickson, Colorado College, USA

"America's recent unhappy experiences in Afghanistan, Iraq, and Libya have caused
many Americans to question the basic contours of U.S. foreign policy, but they lack
the confidence to challenge these ideas directly, and they are uncertain about realistic
alternatives. This book helps fill in the details. It shows why warfare in the 21st century
is unlikely to produce desirable results at reasonable costs. It challenges the notion that
a forward-leaning U.S. military posture is required to produce safety and prosperity.
And it shows why a more restrained foreign policy would better align with classic
American values of limited constitutional government, individual liberty, free markets,
and peace. Taken together, the entries in this volume reassure readers that the United
States can remain engaged in a complex world without having to manage it."

— Christopher Preble, Vice President of Defense and Foreign Policy,
the Cato Institute, Washington DC, USA

US GRAND STRATEGY IN THE 21ST CENTURY

This book challenges the dominant strategic culture and makes the case for restraint in US grand strategy in the 21st century.

Grand strategy, meaning a state's theory about how it can achieve national security for itself, is elusive. That is particularly true in the United States, where the division of federal power and the lack of direct security threats limit consensus about how to manage danger. This book seeks to spur more vigorous debate on US grand strategy. To do so, the first half of the volume assembles the most recent academic critiques of primacy, the dominant strategic perspective in the United States today. The contributors challenge the notion that US national security requires a massive military, huge defense spending, and frequent military intervention around the world. The second half of the volume makes the positive case for a more restrained foreign policy by excavating the historical roots of restraint in the United States and illustrating how restraint might work in practice in the Middle East and elsewhere. The volume concludes with assessments of the political viability of foreign policy restraint in the United States today.

This book will be of much interest to students of US foreign policy, grand strategy, national security, and International Relations in general.

A. Trevor Thrall is a Senior Fellow in the Defense and Foreign Policy Department, Cato Institute, USA, and editor of *Why Did the United States Invade Iraq?* (Routledge, 2011) and *American Foreign Policy and the Politics of Fear* (Routledge, 2009).

Benjamin H. Friedman is a Foreign Policy Fellow and Defense Scholar at Defense Priorities and an Adjunct Lecturer at George Washington University's Elliott School of International Affairs.

ROUTLEDGE GLOBAL SECURITY STUDIES

Series Editors: Aaron Karp and Regina Karp

Global Security Studies emphasizes broad forces reshaping global security and the dilemmas facing decision-makers the world over. The series stresses issues relevant in many countries and regions, accessible to broad professional and academic audiences as well as to students, and enduring through explicit theoretical foundations.

Stable Nuclear Zero
The vision and its implications for disarmament policy
Edited by Sverre Lodgaard

Nuclear Asymmetry and Deterrence
Theory, policy and history
Jan Ludvik

International and Regional Security
The causes of war and peace
Benjamin Miller

US Foreign Policy Towards the Middle East
The realpolitik of deceit
Bernd Kaussler and Glenn P. Hastedt

North Korea, Iran and the Challenge to International Order
A comparative perspective
Patrick McEachern and Jaclyn O'Brien McEachern

US Grand Strategy in the 21st Century
The case for restraint
Edited by A. Trevor Thrall and Benjamin H. Friedman

US GRAND STRATEGY IN THE 21ST CENTURY

The Case for Restraint

Edited by A. Trevor Thrall and
Benjamin H. Friedman

Routledge
Taylor & Francis Group

LONDON AND NEW YORK

First published 2018
by Routledge
2 Park Square, Milton Park, Abingdon, Oxon OX14 4RN

and by Routledge
711 Third Avenue, New York, NY 10017

Routledge is an imprint of the Taylor & Francis Group, an informa business

British Library Cataloguing-in-Publication Data
A catalogue record for this book is available from the British Library

Library of Congress Cataloging-in-Publication Data
A catalog record for this book has been requested

ISBN: 978-1-138-08453-7 (hbk)
ISBN: 978-1-138-08454-4 (pbk)
ISBN: 978-1-315-11177-3 (ebk)

Typeset in Bembo
by Out of House Publishing

CONTENTS

FIGURES

TABLES

CONTRIBUTORS

Emma M. Ashford is a research fellow in defense and foreign policy studies at the Cato Institute, USA.

Alexander B. Downes is an associate professor of political science and international affairs at the George Washington University, USA.

David M. Edelstein is an associate professor in the Edmund A. Walsh School of Foreign Service and the Department of Government at Georgetown University, USA.

Benjamin H. Friedman was a research fellow in defense and homeland security studies at the Cato Institute, USA.

Eugene Gholz is an associate professor of political science at the University of Notre Dame, USA.

Brendan Rittenhouse Green is an assistant professor of political science at the University of Cincinnati, USA.

Jonathan Monten is a lecturer in political science and the director of the International Public Policy Program at University College London, UK.

John Mueller is a senior research scientist at the Mershon Center for International Security Studies and an adjunct professor of political science at Ohio State University. He is also a senior fellow at the Cato Institute, USA.

Patrick Porter is a professor of strategic studies at the University of Exeter, UK.

Edward Rhodes is a professor at the Schar School of Policy and Government at George Mason University, USA.

William Ruger is the vice president for research and policy at the Charles Koch Institute and a research fellow in foreign policy studies at the Cato Institute, USA.

Harvey M. Sapolsky is an emeritus professor of public policy and organization at the Massachusetts Institute of Technology, USA.

Joshua R. Itzkowitz Shifrinson is an assistant professor of international affairs at the Bush School of Government and Public Service at Texas A&M University, USA.

A. Trevor Thrall is a senior fellow in defense and foreign policy studies at the Cato Institute and an associate professor of political science at George Mason University, USA.

1

NATIONAL INTERESTS, GRAND STRATEGY, AND THE CASE FOR RESTRAINT

A. Trevor Thrall and Benjamin H. Friedman

Forging a coherent grand strategy is difficult. This is particularly true in the United States, where the separation of powers and the lack of direct security threats create discord about how to manage foreign policy. Nonetheless, in the wake of the Cold War, a grand strategy consensus arrived in Washington around "primacy" or "liberal hegemony." Both Democratic and Republican leaders see US military power as indispensable to stability everywhere. US military alliances, they agree, secure the peace between foreign powers, and armed interventions are needed occasionally to halt civil conflict abroad.

Partisanship masks this consensus. Political combat over issues like the Iran nuclear deal or Obama's "red line" in Syria can give the impression that the parties greatly differ on how to deliver national security. But the distinction is one of degree, not kind. Republicans complained about Obama's foreign policy because they wanted more of it—more energetic efforts to aid Syrian rebels, more troops in Afghanistan for longer, more Pentagon spending, and more vigorous efforts to demonstrate US fidelity to detering Putin through NATO. Most prominent intellectuals in Washington reflect these views. News reports, in turn, largely mirror the strategic consensus and the contours of elite discourse.

The consensus is unearned. There are a variety of feasible explanations for primacy's dominance in Washington, but neither American foreign policy performance over the past twenty-five years nor its intellectual superiority justify continued pursuit of primacy. Indeed, the obvious failures of US policy, especially in the Middle East, have spurred pointed challenges to the consensus. Growing numbers of experts, especially outside the beltway, argue that America's grand strategy is dangerous, costly, and counterproductive.

The case for restraint rests on three central arguments. First, the United States faces limited threats to its national security thanks to its geographic, economic, and military advantages. Military interventions, permanent alliances, and other military endeavors abroad are thus rarely needed to secure the nation. Second, the United States would derive significant benefits from a foreign policy involving fewer military engagements and commitments. Wars are costly and dangerous, and tend to produce unintended negative effects. Alliances entailing garrisons and defense commitments are costly to maintain, induce recklessness among some allies, and risk entangling the United States in avoidable conflict. Third, a grand strategy of restraint aligns with the values of the classical liberal tradition of the nation's founding. A more restrained foreign policy would help constrain excess government power and protect civil liberties at home.

A healthy debate now rages between advocates of restraint and the intellectual defenders of primacy and liberal hegemony. The outcome of the debate matters a great deal. Primacists and restrainers provide very different answers to key questions in American foreign policy, such as: Under what circumstances should the US use military force? Should the United States maintain alliances established during the Cold War? How should the United States deal with the rise of China? What should the size and composition of the military be?

The start of a new presidency is a good time to take stock of American grand strategy and foreign policy. The case for restraint draws on a vast array of political science for its core arguments, and there are various works making the general case, including Barry Posen's recent book (Ravenal 1973, Tucker and Hendrickson 1992, Nordlinger 1995, Gholz, Press, and Sapolsky 1997, Sapolsky, Friedman, Gholz, and Press 2009, Posen 2014). Still, the full brief has never been assembled in one place. This volume's purpose is to combine the most recent critiques of primacy with positive arguments in favor of restraint and analysis about how to implement it.

Alternative grand strategies

Restraint is a grand strategy. Grand strategies are theories about how states should secure themselves against threats (Posen 1986). Strategy is logic for choices among options; it prioritizes resources. Strategy is "grand" when it aims to guide other state security choices.

Grand strategy is inevitable in that it is present whenever states have security policies informed by causal ideas, which is virtually always. On the other hand, grand strategy is never fully realized in practice. Various organizations, interests, and goals within states means that grand strategies compete for dominance. That is especially true in democracies with powers shared by different branches of government (Jervis 1998).

Grand strategies are distinct from paradigms like liberalism, constructivism, and realism. Paradigms are descriptive explanations of how politics works. Grand strategies are prescriptive. They typically use descriptive ideas about politics, often gleaned from paradigms, to make suggestions about what policy should be.

Today, there is one dominant grand strategy in US politics, which is primacy, also known as liberal hegemony.[1] In Washington, among government officials and most foreign policy analysts, primacy is presented with limited theoretical backbone. The

United States' military endeavors are crucial to global stability, we are told, without much underlying causal logic explaining how that works exactly (Campbell and Flournoy 2007, Kagan 2012). A more fulsome statement of primacy's logic requires undergirding that argument with the works of its academic proponents.

That approach suggests that primacy has two components. One is geopolitical in its focus on the balance of power among states and trade. The other is liberal because it is concerned with the internal conditions of foreign states and the spread of liberal values, especially democracy.[2]

Primacy's geopolitical component holds that US military power is crucial to the maintenance of "the global order," which refers generally to peace among great powers, international commerce, and state cooperation through international organizations (Ikenberry 2011). Here primacy builds on hegemonic stability theory, a theory centering on the claim that the global order is a public good. As such, nations will try to enjoy it without contribution—free-riding—causing the order to atrophy, unless there is a state—the hegemon—that compels other states to protect it (Kindleberger 1973, Gilpin 1987). Primacy says that the United States provides this hegemonic leadership chiefly through its military commitments and deployments, which protect allies and their trade routes. Under US protection, states can worry less about their security and forgo balancing against rivals by forming alliances and increasing military capacity. That makes their rivals more secure and less prone to arming in response (Brooks, Ikenberry, and Wohlforth 2012). Also, because they fear attack less, states can trade freely without worrying much about enriching potential rivals (Krasner 1976). US leaders can also essentially trade protection for concessions, compelling allies to cut better trade deals and to be supportive of the global economic system (Brooks, Ikenberry, and Wohlforth 2012).

Without alliances backed by US military forces, three threatening results might occur, according to primacy. First, some aggression could go unchecked, as smaller states capitulate to stronger ones, either by conquest or by alliance formation. Powerful states like Russia or China would thus develop greater ability to directly attack or coerce the United States. Second, absent US protection, states might balance each other more—arming more heavily or allying to prevent aggression. Primacy sees such balancing as unstable because it produces security dilemmas—self-reinforcing dynamics of mutual alarm—which lead to war or tension disruptive to commerce (Brooks, Ikenberry, and Wohlforth 2012). Those risks, primacy reasons, are more costly to the United States than maintaining the alliances that mitigate them (Egel et al. 2016). Third, primacy says to worry that would-be allies deprived of US protection will become strong and independent and thus less inclined to accept US leadership, or will even become outright rivals to the United States (Principal Deputy Under Secretary of Defense 1992).

Twenty years ago, one could accurately describe primacy using only the geopolitical logic above (Posen and Ross 1996). Primacy's advocates focused on interstate relations, especially among big powers. Today, primacy has fused with what was a distinct grand strategy: cooperative engagement, sometimes called liberal internationalism, which centers on the need for multilateral cooperation to promote peace, democratic government, and free trade (Posen and Ross 1996).

The fusion was a long process but turned on two relatively recent developments. First, Democratic foreign policy elites grew more enamored of US military predominance. The difficulty of organizing multilateral actions in the Balkans and the failure to intervene in Rwanda boosted their enthusiasm for unilateral US action. The Cold War's end and the swift victory in the Gulf War encouraged their enthusiasm about the effectiveness of US military power. And with the Soviet Union gone, the possible uses for US force multiplied and overseas commitments needed new justifications. As a result, Democratic foreign policy elites became less enthralled with international institutions, more hawkish, and prone to celebrating the transformative virtues of US military power. As Clinton's secretary of state Madeleine Albright said in 1998, "If we have to use force, it is because we are America. We are the indispensable nation. We stand tall. We see further into the future."[3]

Second, the right became more liberal in its foreign policy thinking, particularly after the September 11, 2001, attacks. Republicans long had among their ranks those that shared the Wilsonian idea (named after President Woodrow Wilson) that the United States should use force not just to secure its citizens and interests but also as a means to redeem humanity by giving it liberal government (McDougall 1997). That thinking grew popular among Republicans as neoconservatives gained power starting in the 1970s. It bloomed into full flower after the 9/11 attacks. Much of the right saw the cause as disorder and illiberal governments abroad and the solution in forceful reordering and democratization (Schmidt and Williams 2008, Monten 2005, Desch 2007).

So Democrats grew more comfortable with the virtues of unilateral US military power as Republicans got more willing to use force to liberalize states' internal politics. As result, they joined in supporting a more muscular version of primacy (Posen 2014). Primacy's backers on the left and right still disagree on some things, especially whether international endorsement is a hindrance or a useful way to legitimize war. But they agree on far more. That includes the geopolitical component of primacy discussed above and an additional liberal component, which has three tenets.

First, states' internal conditions can be inherently dangerous to distant powers like the United States. State failure and civil war create wider danger by nurturing terrorists, destabilizing neighboring states, and resulting in losing track of weapons. States lacking democracy and the rule of law are inherently threatening because they are more aggressive, especially toward democracies, and prone to collapse.

Second, security is highly interdependent—insecurity anywhere is a threat everywhere (Posen and Ross 1996). Modern communications and transport technologies mean that people, resentments, and arms of growing deadliness travel easily across borders and oceans, so that geographic barriers aid defense less than they once did. Because security is interdependent, distinctions between moral and security goals collapse (Rice 2008, Slaughter 2011). Protecting civilians from mass killing is not just a humanitarian good but a way to limit threats from failed states.

Installing democracy, even by force, is not just a good deed but a way to make the United States safer.

Third, the United States and its partners have considerable ability to mitigate these dangers through military intervention. That includes multilateral state-building missions, capacity-building through military training, and airstrikes that threaten or decapitate the leadership of nefarious regimes, insurgencies, or terrorist organizations. The unhappy US experiences in Iraq and Afghanistan have shaken foreign policymakers' belief in the effectiveness of intensive state-building efforts but not their general conviction that US security requires US military efforts to reshape states' internal politics (Friedman and Logan 2012).

The geopolitical and liberal components of primacy create a capacious idea of US interests and thus threats. Primacy's advocates worry about the credibility of the many promises that the United States makes to defend allies. They fear proliferation of weapons technology, especially nuclear weapons, and believe that alliances prevent it by assuring allies and preventing security dilemmas (Brooks, Ikenberry, and Wohlforth 2012). Primacists tend to argue that internal conditions abroad (foreign civil wars, failed states, or illiberal governments) can easily undermine US global leadership, creating danger. These fears translate into heavy work for the US national security establishment. As a result, primacy favors high military spending and regular use of force—patrols, military-to-military training, deployments of forces, commitments to defend nations, or acts of war (Monteiro 2011).

Restraint is not the only alternative grand strategy to primacy. Selective engagement shares primacy's geopolitical logic to an extent, but sees the need for US commitments only in important regions where a rival might gather enough strength to threaten the United States (Art 1998). In these regions, selective engagement shares primacy's pessimism that the balance of power can contain the positional hegemon absent US military contributions. In practice, advocates of selective engagement tend to support occasional military efforts to contain illiberal regimes or stabilize failed states. That is probably because the strategy lacks clear selection criteria and is thus somewhat indeterminate as to when and where US forces should be employed (Posen and Ross 1996).

The grand strategy of offshore balancing is a close cousin of restraint. Offshore balancers share most of the objections to primacy discussed below in explaining the restraint strategy, but they share selective engagers' concern about the need for US forces to balance potential hegemons (Layne 1997, Walt 2005, Layne 2006, Mearsheimer 2014). They add a crucial caveat that US forces should be held in reserve—off-shore rather than garrisoned in allied nations—until a potential hegemon threatens. There is considerable variation among offshore balancers as to how likely that is. John Mearsheimer and Stephen Walt, for example, see the Chinese threat as sufficient to merit maintaining a large US military presence in East Asia (Mearsheimer and Walt 2016). Other offshore balancers see the threat of a hegemon as so remote that the US military can be shrunk considerably and built up only if a threat of that caliber re-emerges. That is a position essentially indistinguishable from restraint.

Restraint

The grand strategy of restraint takes its name from the idea that sound US foreign policy requires restraint against the many temptations to use force that great power affords.[4] Restraint starts with the assertion that the United States inhabits an extremely favorable security environment in the post-Cold War world. Thanks to its geography, friendly and militarily weak neighbors, large and dynamic economy, and secure nuclear arsenal, the United States faces very few real threats to its security (Ravenal 1973, Nordlinger 1995, Gholz, Press, and Sapolsky 1997, Preble 2009, Posen 2014). Thus the United States enjoys what Nordlinger called "strategic immunity"—most of what happens in the rest of the world is basically irrelevant to US national security. The outcomes of civil conflicts in the Middle East, the balance of power in Asia, or whether Russia annexes Crimea may be morally and politically significant for many reasons, but they do nothing to threaten the United States.

Restraint's relatively benign take on danger follows from two related insights. One is that the causes of the interstate peace that have prevailed for many decades are largely unrelated to the hegemonic provision of security by the United States. Restraint says the cause is instead a widespread realization among powerful states that wars against other powerful states do not pay (Mueller 1989). That calculation reflects several factors that make military aggression less profitable. Economic changes, including trade growth and the shift from heavy industry to human capital and information, have made economies harder to exploit by conquest. Nationalism has also increased the difficulties of military occupation. Finally, modern military technologies, especially nuclear weapons, give significant advantages to the defender (Jervis 1989, Kaysen 1990, Van Evera 1990, Liberman 1998, Hammes 2016). These shifts, enshrined by memories of the two world wars, are sufficiently appreciated to the make the world less prone to aggression, though obviously not free from it (Mueller 1989).

Second, restraint is far more optimistic about the stability of balances of power than primacy, which has faith in them only if hegemons are involved (Friedman, Green, and Logan 2013). Geographic barriers—especially large bodies of water—aided by defensive military technologies make security dilemmas far less frequent than primacy contends (Jervis 1978, Schweller 1996, Van Evera 1998). Even where security dilemma dynamics do occur, war remains unlikely because the advantages of surprise attack are generally limited (Reiter 1995, Trachtenberg 2003). According to restraint, these factors, rather than US military forces, are what allow states to worry less about security and trade more freely.

Restraint also denies that US military actions have net positive economic effects. American prosperity is the result of participation in, not control of, the international economic system, according to restraint. American military might is not required to ensure the ability of American companies to sell their goods around the world, not even to ensure the flow of oil on which much of its economy relies (Gholz and Press 2010). In peacetime, threats to trade for naval forces to protect against are virtually nonexistent. Even major wars do not disturb trade to the point that fighting to help end them is less costly than sitting out (Gholz and Press 2001). Rather than creating economic dependence that requires military protection, globalization creates supply options and thus reduces the need to militarily protect trade routes or stabilize supplier states (Sapolsky, Friedman, Gholz, and Press 2009).

It is true that the United States played the leading role in establishing the liberal institutions that make globalization possible. It does not follow, restrainers argue, that the United States must play the role of hegemon to maintain them. In any case, US wealth—potential access to its massive domestic market—is a stronger inducement to economic openness than military alliances (Friedman, Green, and Logan 2013).

Restraint rarely sees a security rationale for reshaping foreign nations. One reason is that security is divisible. Civil wars create tragic local results, but the costs they spill across borders rarely outweigh the cost of even their neighbors' intervention, let alone that of distant powers. Restraint's advocates generally agree that while illiberal states are on balance more trouble than liberal ones, those states rarely threaten the United States. Second, US military force is a decidedly poor tool for transforming states' internal politics. Spreading democracy, promoting liberal values, and "fixing" failed states by nation-building are beyond the capabilities even of a military as powerful as the United States'—at least at reasonable cost. With the right preconditions and planning, the brutalization of the local population, and decades of occupation, success might occur, as in post-war Germany and Japan. In most cases, however, the affront to liberal values and the human and financial costs will be politically unsustainable (Friedman, Sapolsky, and Preble 2008). Moreover, the places where the US forces fight are rarely good candidates for stability, let alone democracy (Downes and Monten 2013). And participation in distant civil wars creates civilian resentment toward the occupier that can create new security problems (Pape 2005).

Those same concerns apply to humanitarian military interventions, though restraint's advocates do not wholly reject them. Generally, they take the view that if the danger to people is high and the difficulty of intervention low, it is morally justified. But because these interventions are proposed chiefly in the midst of civil wars and tend to morph into costly state-building missions, few cases will qualify (Mandelbaum 1996, Luttwak 1999, Byman and Seybolt 2003, Pickering and Peceny 2006, Peic and Reiter 2011, Lynch 2013).

Restraint is then quite skeptical about the benefits of US military endeavors. Reinforcing this argument is the belief that military activism can easily make things worse by creating new enemies, by making large conflicts out of smaller ones, by drawing the US into more wars, and by necessitating the expenditure of large sums of national treasure (Mearsheimer 2014, Posen 2014, Gholz, Press, and Sapolsky 1997, Preble 2009, Bacevich 2009, 2016, Mandelbaum 2016). In particular, restraint sees costs in military alliances that primacy neglects (Beckley 2015). That includes moral hazard, where the ally behaves recklessly due to US protection (Posen 2014). In that sense, US forces can actually thwart the stabilization of relations among states in particular regions. Another danger is entrapment, where the ally pulls the United States into conflict or war that is otherwise remote from US interests (Carpenter 1992).

While restraint is deeply informed by structural realism, especially its defensive variant (Waltz 1979, Rose 1998), it shares classical liberalism's general skepticism about unchecked power, war, and ambitious efforts to control the course of international relations (Boucoyannis 2007). Attempts to micromanage other nations' foreign policies and the global order are like the famous fatal conceit where states disastrously think they can centrally plan economic activity (Hayek 1988). As formidable as the US military is, it remains a blunt instrument, not a precise tool that produces carefully measured outcomes. War tends to have tragic and unintended consequences, and primacy entails more of them than restraint, as recent US history demonstrates (Monteiro 2011). Some of primacy's academic backers try to disassociate the strategy from recent wars (Brooks, Ikenberry, and Wohlforth 2012). They see primacy as a low-risk strategy of alliance maintenance, which peacefully deters without requiring much war. But military alliances derive their utility from the believability of coercive threats, which logically must be exercised sometimes. Wars fought with forces that primacy demands and justified largely with its arguments, moreover, cannot be fully separated from the strategy.

The prospects for restraint

The preoccupation with primacy has not always been a feature of American foreign policy. In breaking with British rule, the Founders believed strongly in keeping America out of European politics. Not only did they worry about "foreign entanglements" potentially dragging the United States into war. They also worried about the corrosive effects of empire-building abroad on the nation's democratic system.

And though the 20th century saw the United States embrace a progressively more interventionist strategy, the early part of the 21st century may represent a turning point. For many academic and policy analysts, the costly failures of extended American military intervention in Afghanistan, the Middle East, and North Africa in the wake of 9/11 has sharpened the case against primacy. There also appears to be growing unhappiness among the public with primacy. Though majorities acknowledge the need to confront terrorism, especially the Islamic State, recent polls have also found historically high levels of people indicating a preference for stepping back from America's portfolio of foreign activities and focusing more heavily on domestic issues (Smeltz, Daalder, and Kafura 2014, Pew Research Center 2016).

Restraint advocates do not all agree on precisely what a belated return to a more restrained foreign policy would look like, but most would agree on the broad principles in at least three areas. First, the United States would resist calls for military intervention as a tool for counterterrorism, except in extreme instances, and would renounce nation-building as a viable foreign policy tool. Most obviously this first principle would call for an end to the use of drone strikes and for the eventual withdrawal of most US personnel from Afghanistan and Iraq. Additionally, a restrained foreign policy would reject military options in situations like the NATO intervention in Libya, the civil war in Syria, or the Saudi intervention in Yemen. Though these situations were (and remain) horrendous, American military intervention is the wrong tool for making them better.

Second, the United States would reduce its commitments to various Cold War allies like NATO, South Korea, Taiwan, and Japan. Not only are these nations wealthy enough to provide for their own defense, but continued US commitments raise the risk of becoming involved in conflict while doing almost nothing to enhance American security. This is not to say that the United States cannot work with or partner with these nations on security issues. Nor would it mean the United States might not decide to fight in defense of a former ally. It is simply to say that the United States is more secure when not making such commitments ahead of time and by avoiding a forward military presence that increases the risk of being dragged into war.

And finally, thanks to a strategy that eschews globe-straddling alliances and frequent military intervention, the United States would field a reshaped and significantly smaller military force. A strategy of restraint would take advantage of America's geographic advantages and give the Navy a larger share of the Pentagon's budget. Ships and submarines have access to most of the Earth's surface without needing basing rights. The Navy would operate as a surge force that deploys to attack shorelines or open sea-lanes, rather than constantly patrolling peaceful areas in the name of presence. In that role the Navy could still reduce the number of carriers and air wings it operates.

At the same time, restraint recommends cuts to the Air Force and to ground forces. Few enemies today challenge US air superiority, making it possible to handle most missions with drones and other non-stealth aircraft. Moreover, thanks to new technologies, each aircraft is far more capable than ever before. On the ground force side, there are simply few conventional war scenarios in which the United States would need to play a major role in the future. Large wars elsewhere should be fought by troops in the region. In addition, as noted, large armies are poorly suited to counterterrorism, stability operations, or nation-building. Beyond this, because restraint both requires less frequent deployments and reduces the emphasis on deployment speed, policymakers could also shift more personnel to the reserve and National Guard forces.

Though tangential to its strategic rationale, the strategy of restraint would allow vast savings in the defense budget. In real terms, Americans spend more on the military now than at any point during the Cold War except peaks during the Korean War and the 1980s. The United States spends more than double what Russia, China, Iran, and North Korea spend collectively on their militaries.

After a brief glimmer of hope during the presidential campaign, Donald Trump has slowly made it clear that a coherent foreign policy of restraint is not on the horizon. During the campaign Trump staked out several positions that suggested he might implement a more restrained foreign policy, at least relative to his predecessors. He broke with fellow Republicans by calling the invasion of Iraq a horrible mistake. He repeatedly declared nation-building to be a waste of money and contrary to US interests. He even warned that it was time to rethink NATO, and other US security guarantees to countries like Taiwan and Japan.

Now in office, however, Trump has shown little instinct for restraint. Instead, it appears that the driving forces of his foreign policy will be his hawkish inclinations on terrorism and his desire for the United States to look strong in the eyes of the world. Within his first two months in the White House Trump loosened the rules of engagement for US forces operating in the Middle East, gave the CIA greater authority to launch drone strikes, sent several hundred more US forces to aid the fight against the Islamic State in Syria, and proposed a significant increase to the defense budget. Trump may not wind up invading two nations as Bush did, or help topple a regime like Obama did, but it seems a fair guess that the Trump Doctrine will not be one of restraint.

Road map of the book

The first half of this edited volume assembles the case against the strategy of primacy. Chapters 2 and 3 take aim at primacy's faith in the US–alliance structure. Chapter 4 challenges the belief that oil security demands intervention, Chapter 5 casts doubt on the efficacy of regime change as a tool for promoting democracy, and Chapter 6 argues that despite technological advances, geography still favors the defender.

In **Chapter 2**, David Edelstein and Josh Itzkowitz Shifrinson challenge primacy's assumption that alliances do not entangle the United States in otherwise avoidable conflicts. That assumption, Edelstein and Shifrinson argue, follows from a superficial reading of the Cold War experience. Historically, allies have often roped the United States into costly foreign adventures by manipulating America's perception of foreign threats, exacerbating tensions with other states then relying on the US to mediate, and occasionally provoking crises that embroil the United States in would-be regional conflicts. These behaviors are increasingly part of today's foreign policy landscape and a cost that the US must address.

Brendan Rittenhouse Green confronts the argument that America's alliance structure prevents nuclear proliferation in **Chapter 3**. Green reviews the existing literature and then considers eight case studies. The chapter argues that the literature has largely undercut primacy's theoretical rationale for believing that commitments will reliably staunch proliferation. In practice, Green argues, while American military commitments have enjoyed some modest successes in restricting nuclear proliferation, they have just as often encouraged proliferation among friendly states, and are accompanied by serious strategic costs not accounted for by most advocates of primacy.

In **Chapter 4** Eugene Gholz challenges the idea that US military forces are needed ensure a stable supply of oil and thus American economic prosperity. Gholz argues that these arguments, which are prominent in the policy community's case for primacy, are built on a misunderstanding of the global oil market and American military capabilities. Under a grand strategy of restraint, he contends, the United States could still provide the relatively easy, low-cost protection for trade in the global commons, including energy trade, but would not intervene in specific oil-producing countries or use its military to try to influence their international political and military relationships with other consumers. Restraint would maintain US and global energy security while avoiding needless, costly international conflict.

Alexander Downes and Jonathan Monten, in **Chapter 5**, provide ammunition for restraint's skepticism about military interventions. They evaluate how successful states have been historically in using military force to promote democratization via regime change. Using a mix of quantitative and qualitative measures to improve on existing studies of the question, they find the answer is hardly successful at all. They discuss how recent US efforts at democratization—in Iraq, Libya, and perhaps Syria—have come in countries especially ill-suited to successful democratization and suggest that US policymakers must scale back their expectations that democratization naturally follows forcible regime change and leadership decapitation.

In **Chapter 6**, Patrick Porter attacks an underlying premise of primacy: the claim that advances in information, transport, and weapons technologies have destroyed the defensive utility of geography, leaving the United States and its allies more vulnerable to attack. Because distance, time, and borders no longer protect the United States, primacy says that global defenses are needed. Porter argues, however, that geography still goes far to protect the United States and its allies. He explains how recent advances in military technology actually aid defenders. Porter uses a possible conflict between Taiwan and China to make his case.

The second half of the volume discusses what restraint might look like in practice, the political changes that have caused primacy's rise at restraint's expense, and how that dynamic might shift. Chapters 7 and 8 consider the historical foundations of restraint. Chapters 9 and 10 examine what restraint might look like in modern practice, while Chapters 11 and 12 consider the political prospects for restraint.

In **Chapter 7**, William Ruger examines restraint's historical roots and the doctrine that underpins it, realism. Ruger shows how rather than being a modern import at odds with liberal values, realism was present at the founding of US grand strategy and served to protect liberal values. Despite considerable argument among early leaders, the United States followed a realist and classically liberal approach to foreign policy from the Revolutionary War through the Spanish-American War. Military interventions abroad in that period occurred primarily to protect trade and did not involve long land wars. Ruger argues that this approach was consistent with the US's limited security interests, and its liberal values—the fear that entanglement in foreign conflicts would centralize power and harm the nation's experiment in liberal democracy.

In **Chapter 8**, Edward Rhodes considers what changed the nation's approach to foreign policy in the early 20th century—how the nation's leaders went from generally seeing entanglement in the European balance-of-power system as a danger to liberty to believing that protecting liberty requires military involvement in distant controversies. Rhodes focuses on Theodore Roosevelt and the progressives, who saw a more imperial-style foreign policy as a way to restore republican *virtu* and protect national cohesion from the fraying brought on by industrialization.

In **Chapter 9**, Emma Ashford evaluates American involvement in the Middle East since the end of the Cold War. She argues that the massive US commitment to the region has improved neither American security nor regional stability. Some US allies in the region have meanwhile become a hindrance to US goals in the region. Ashford argues that the United States' limited interests in the region—preventing the rise of a regional hegemon, maintaining energy supply, and counterterrorism—require nothing like the current level of US military engagement there. A better approach would move forces offshore, enabling the US to achieve its limited security needs while minimizing involvement in the region's interminable civil conflicts and sectarian struggles. She argues for moving US forces offshore, enabling them to pursue the nations' limited security needs while minimizing involvement in the region's upheavals.

In **Chapter 10**, John Mueller offers a particularly restrained version of restraint. He argues that the United States is substantially free from threats that require a great deal of military expenditure or balancing behavior, and that keeping forces beyond what is necessary creates risk that they will be misused for foolish wars like Vietnam and Iraq. Mueller argues for keeping some rapid-response forces, a small number of nuclear weapons, and some capacity to rebuild quickly in the unlikely event that a sizable threat eventually materializes.

In **Chapter 11**, Benjamin Friedman and Harvey Sapolsky explain why the United States has embraced primacy despite its failings, and how circumstances might change to favor restraint. They argue that over time, relative power—wealth and military capability—concentrated the benefits of expansive military policies in the United States while diffusing the human and material costs of the strategy. The result is a strong support base for primacy, a public largely indifferent to its failings, and political support for primacy even though its costs to the nation outweigh its benefits. The chapter considers how leaders might change this outcome by concentrating primacy's costs so that interests in favor of restraint emerge.

Trevor Thrall assesses the potential public support for a strategy of restraint in **Chapter 12**. He finds that the "restraint constituency" is larger and more diverse than many imagine. Thanks to the emergence of the Millennial Generation, who have lived through fifteen years of futile US wars in the Middle East, Thrall finds a public that is becoming increasingly restrained in its attitude toward foreign policy.

Notes

1 This term is used to refer to an updated version of primacy in Posen (2014). A recent article making the case for primacy calls it "deep engagement" (Brooks, Ikenberry, and Wohlforth 2012).
2 Charles Glaser made this useful distinction in remarks during a conference discussing the draft of chapters in this book (Glaser 2016).

3 Quote originally said in an interview on NBC's Today show, reported in Herbert (1998).
4 That logic, evident in the title of the classic modern article on the subject, "Come Home America: The Strategy of Restraint in the Face of Temptation" (Gholz, Press, and Sapolsky 1997), is why we prefer "restraint" to "retrenchment," the term preferred by those arguing against the strategy (Brooks, Ikenberry, and Wohlforth 2012, Egel et al. 2016). We also reject "isolationism," (sometimes lightened by the prefix "neo") because it implies protectionism, nativism, and other isms that most modern advocates of restraint reject, and is often employed by them as a kind of ad hominem attack.

References

Art, R.J. 1998. Geopolitics Updated: The Strategy of Selective Engagement. *International Security* 23(3): 79–113.

Bacevich, A.J. 2009. *American Empire: The Realities and Consequences of US Diplomacy*. Harvard University Press.

Bacevich, A.J. 2016. *The War for the Greater Middle East*. Random House.

Beckley, M. 2015. The Myth of Entangling Alliances: Reassessing the Security Risks of US Defense Pacts. *International Security* 39(4): 7–48.

Boucoyannis, D. 2007. The International Wanderings of a Liberal Idea, or Why Liberals Can Learn to Stop Worrying and Love the Balance of Power. *Perspectives on Politics* 5(4): 703–727.

Brooks, S.G., Ikenberry, G.J., and Wohlforth, W.C. 2012. Don't Come Home, America: The Case against Retrenchment. *International Security* 37(3): 7–51.

Byman, D., and Seybolt, T. 2003. Humanitarian Intervention and Communal Civil Wars. *Security Studies* 13(1): 33–78.

Campbell, K., and Flournoy, M. 2007. The Inheritance and the Way Forward. June 27. Center for a New American Security. Accessed March 23, 2017, from www.cnas.org/publications/reports/the-inheritance-and-the-way-forward.

Carpenter, T.G. 1992. *A Search for Enemies: America's Alliances after the Cold War*. Cato Institute Press.

Desch, M.C. 2007. America's Liberal Illiberalism: The Ideological Origins of Overreaction in US Foreign Policy. *International Security* 32(3): 7–43.

Downes, A.B., and Monten, J. 2013. Forced to Be Free? Why Foreign-Imposed Regime Change Rarely Leads to Democratization. *International Security* 37(4): 90–131.

Egel, D., Grissom, A., Godges, J.P., Kavanagh, J., and Shatz, H. 2016. *Estimating the Value of Overseas Security Commitments*. RAND Corporation.

Friedman, B.H., and Logan, J. 2012. Why the US Military Budget is "Foolish and Sustainable". *Orbis* 56(2): 177–191.

Friedman, B.H., Green, B.R., and Logan, J. 2013. Correspondence: Debating American Engagement: The Future of US Grand Strategy. *International Security* 38(2): 181–199.

Friedman, B.H., Sapolsky, H.M., and Preble, C. 2008. *Learning the Right Lessons from Iraq*. Cato Institute Policy Analysis no. 610.

Gholz, E., and Press, D.G. 2001. The Effects of Wars on Neutral Countries: Why It Doesn't Pay to Preserve the Peace. *Security Studies* 10(4): 1–55.

Gholz, E., and Press, D.G. 2010. Protecting "the Prize": Oil and the US National Interest. *Security Studies* 19(3): 453–485.

Gholz, E., Press, D.G., and Sapolsky, H.M. 1997. Come Home, America: The Strategy of Restraint in the Face of Temptation. *International Security* 21(4): 5–48.

Gilpin, R. 1987. *The Political Economy of International Relations*. Princeton University Press.

Glaser, C. 2016. The Case for Restraint. Conference paper. Cato Institute, June 15. www.cato.org/events/case-restraint-us-foreign-policy.

Hammes, T.X. 2016. *Technologies Converge and Power Diffuses: The Evolution of Small, Smart, and Cheap Weapons*. Cato Institute Policy Analysis no. 786.

Hayek, F.A. 1988. *The Fatal Conceit*. University of Chicago Press.

Herbert, B. 1998. In America; War Games. *New York Times*, February 22.

Ikenberry, G.J. 2011. *Liberal Leviathan: The Origins, Crisis, and Transformation of the American World Order*. Princeton University Press.

Jervis, R. 1978. Cooperation Under the Security Dilemma. *World Politics* 30(2): 167–214.

Jervis, R. 1989. *The Meaning of the Nuclear Revolution: Statecraft and the Prospect of Armageddon*. Cornell University Press.

Jervis, R. 1998. US Grand Strategy: Mission Impossible. *Naval War College Review* 51(3): 22–36.

Kagan, R. 2012. *The World America Made*. Vintage Books.

Kaysen, C. 1990. Review: Is War Obsolete? A Review Essay. *International Security* 14(4): 42–64.

Kindelberger, C.P. 1973. *The World in Depression 1929–1939*. University of California Press.

Krasner, S.D. 1976. State Power and the Structure of International Trade. *World Politics* 28(3): 317–347.

Layne, C. 1997. From Preponderance to Offshore Balancing: America's Future Grand Strategy. *International Security* 22(1): 86–124.

Layne, C. 2006. *The Peace of Illusions: American Grand Strategy from 1940 to the Present*. Cornell University Press.

Liberman, P. 1998. *Does Conquest Pay? The Exploitation of Occupied Industrial Societies*. Princeton University Press.

Luttwak, E.N. 1999. Give War a Chance. *Foreign Affairs* 78(4): 36–44.

Lynch, M. 2013. The Political Science of Syria's War. POMPEPS Studies #5, December 13. Project on Middle East Political Science, George Washington University.

Mandelbaum, M. 1996. Foreign Policy as Social Work. *Foreign Affairs* 75: 16–32.

Mandelbaum, M. 2016. *Mission Failure: America and the World in the Post-Cold War Era*. Oxford University Press.

McDougall, W. 1997. *Promised Land, Crusader State: The American Encounter with the World Since 1776*. Houghton Mifflin.

Mearsheimer, J.J. 2014. America Unhinged. *The National Interest* 129: 9–30.

Mearsheimer, J.J., and Walt, S.M. 2016. The Case for Offshore Balancing: A Superior US Grand Strategy. *Foreign Affairs* (95): 70–83.

Monteiro, N.P. 2011. Unrest Assured: Why Unipolarity Is Not Peaceful. *International Security* 36(3): 9–40.

Monten, J. 2005. The Roots of the Bush Doctrine: Power, Nationalism, and Democracy Promotion in US Strategy. *International Security* 29(4): 112–156.

Mueller, J.E. 1989. *Retreat from Doomsday: The Obsolescence of Major War*. Basic Books.

Nordlinger, E.A. 1995. *Isolationism Reconfigured: American Foreign Policy for a New Century*. Princeton University Press.

Pape, R. 2005. *Dying to Win: The Strategic Logic of Suicide Terrorism*. Random House.

Peic, G., and Reiter, D. 2011. Foreign-Imposed Regime Change, State Power and Civil War Onset, 1920–2004. *British Journal of Political Science* 41(3): 453–475.

Pew Research Center. 2016. Public Uncertain, Divided over America's Place in the World. April.

Pickering, J., and Peceny, M. 2006. Forging Democracy at Gunpoint. *International Studies Quarterly* 50(3): 539–560.

Posen, B.R. 1986. *The Sources of Military Doctrine: France, Britain, and Germany between the World Wars*. Cornell University Press.

Posen, B.R. 2014. *Restraint: A New Foundation for US Grand Strategy.* Cornell University Press.

Posen, B.R., and Ross, A.L. 1996. Competing Visions for US Grand Strategy. *International Security* 21(3): 5–53.

Preble, C.A. 2009. *The Power Problem: How American Military Dominance Makes Us Less Safe, Less Prosperous, and Less Free.* Cornell University Press.

Principal Deputy Under Secretary of Defense. 1992. *FY 94–99 Defense Planning Guidance Sections for Comment.* Washington, DC. http://nsarchive.gwu.edu/nukevault/ebb245/doc03_extract_nytedit.pdf.

Ravenal, E.C. 1973. The Case for Strategic Disengagement. *Foreign Affairs* 51(3): 505–521.

Reiter, D. 1995. Exploding the Powder Keg Myth: Preemptive Wars Almost Never Happen. *International Security* 20(2): 5–34.

Rice, C. 2008. Rethinking the National Interest: American Realism for a New World. *Foreign Affairs* 87(4): 2–6.

Rose, G. 1998. Neoclassical Realism and Theories of Foreign Policy. *World Politics* 51(1): 144–172.

Sapolsky, H.M., Friedman, B.H., Gholz, E., and Press, D.G. 2009. Restraining Order: For Strategic Modesty. *World Affairs* 172(2): 84–94.

Schmidt, B.C., and Williams, M.C. 2008. The Bush Doctrine and the Iraq War: Neoconservatives Versus Realists. *Security Studies* 17(2): 191–220.

Schweller, R.L. 1996. Neorealism's Status-Quo Bias: What Security Dilemma? *Security Studies* 5(3): 90–121.

Slaughter, A. 2011. Interests vs. Values? Misunderstanding Obama's Libya Strategy. *The New York Review of Books*, March 30.

Smeltz, D., Daalder, I., and Kafura, C. 2014. Foreign Policy in the Age of Retrenchment. *The Chicago Council on Global Affairs.*

Trachtenberg, M. 2003. The Question of Realism: A Historian's View. *Security Studies* 13(1): 156–194.

Tucker, R.W., and Hendrickson, D.C. 1992. *The Imperial Temptation: The New World Order and America's Purpose.* New York University Press.

Van Evera, S. 1990. Primed for Peace: Europe after the Cold War. *International Security* 15(3): 33–40.

Van Evera, S. 1998. Offense, Defense, and the Causes of War. *International Security* 22(4): 5–43.

Walt, S.M. 2005. *Taming American Power: The Global Response to US Primacy.* W.W. Norton & Company.

Waltz, K.N. 1979. *Theory of International Politics.* Waveland Press.

PART I

The myths of liberal hegemony

2

IT'S A TRAP!

Security commitments and the risks of entrapment

David M. Edelstein and Joshua R. Itzkowitz Shifrinson

How likely is it that the United States will become entrapped by its alliances? The answer to this question is critical not only to international relations theory, but also to the conduct of US grand strategy. In this chapter, we argue that the risk is higher than many have assessed. Both the logic and the evidence supporting claims that entrapment is rare are flawed. A more restrained US grand strategy is the surest way to prevent America's entrapment in unwanted conflicts.

Since the Cold War, commitments to others in the form of both informal and formal alliances have been central to US grand strategy. Policymakers from across the political spectrum believe formal alliances in Western Europe and East Asia, as well as more informal commitments in the Middle East, serve as the clearest and most credible indicators of American interests. Conventional wisdom treats these alliances as crucial to the maintenance of international security and to the avoidance of the types of deterrence failures and insecurity spirals that often contribute to wars and crises. Simply put, the United States' extensive alliance commitments are believed to help states escape anarchy and its associated dangers. They are thought to be an essential tool for protecting America's interests as they allow the United States to signal its interests around the world (Clinton 1994; Goldgeier 1998; Bush 2002; Bush 2006; Obama 2015; Brooks, Ikenberry, and Wohlforth 2012).

Crucially, this perspective assumes that the political and military costs to the United States of maintaining these commitments are small, especially in comparison to the costs of war and instability that would attend any change in American policy. Despite the growth of regional tensions attendant on the rise of China and resurgence of Russia, advocates point to a body of research suggesting that alliances perform a security-dampening function: they allow the United States to reassure its partners and prevent insecurity spirals, while still affording the US exit options that limit the likelihood that it will be entrapped into conflicts it would rather avoid (Brooks and Wohlforth 2016; Beckley 2015; Kim 2011). Alliances, in short, function as a silver bullet that reassure friends, deter foes, and leave the United States unexposed.

Increasingly, however, skeptics question this conventional wisdom. Part of the case for a US grand strategy of "restraint" is that American security commitments risk entrapment (Posen 2014; Wright 2015). In this view, the alliance commitments of the US must involve *some* risk of war that is not purely in the United States' interest; otherwise, and as Thomas Schelling suggested long ago, American allies would have no reason to trust American security guarantees (Schelling 2008). Security commitments, in other words, cannot be unvarnished goods: for them to influence allies and adversaries, there must be some risk of the United States coming to allied assistance when, all things considered, it would prefer not to do so.

These contending arguments raise a number of questions: Is committing to various countries around the world in the United States' interest because commitment only requires burdens the United States will willingly accept? If not, is it time to pull back from committing to those who are now able to look out for their own security or which are so indefensible that the US runs great risks for uncertain benefits? More generally, when should *any* great power be worried about entrapment into others' conflicts – under what conditions do the risks of entrapment start to outweigh the value of the security commitments themselves?

In this chapter, building on the foundational work of Jack Snyder and Thomas J. Christensen (Snyder 1984; Christensen and Snyder 1990), we contend that the risks of entrapment for the contemporary United States are significant. More specifically, we make two arguments. First, much of the entrapment debate thus far has been a game of shadow boxing. As elaborated below, current efforts to study the frequency and risks of entrapment have virtually defined the problem away by treating entrapment as solely occurring when one ally goes to war for the sake of a partner when the first ally would prefer to avoid conflict. Although this is indeed the most concerning form of entrapment, it misses that entrapment does not necessarily manifest in an either/or choice in which a state clearly takes a step it avowedly prefers to avoid. Instead, entrapment can also manifest in critical decisions states make when confronting an adversary that involve the *timing* of confrontation, the *relative resources* contributed to the effort, and the *objectives* involved. These different decisions on the road to deterrence and reassurance – and war – are crucial, as they help explain why states can be entrapped even if they agree that confronting an opponent is generally in their "national interest."

Second, all forms of entrapment are more likely to occur in today's unipolar world, and to be especially prevalent if and when unipolarity begins to wane. This is significant because evidence that entrapment is uncommon – and thus current US grand strategy sustainable – has almost exclusively been drawn from the bipolar world of the Cold War. Yet, because the two great powers in bipolar systems do not *need* allies to establish a workable balance, the Cold War is among the least likely of all situations for entrapment to occur (Waltz 1979).

Instead, alliances in multipolar and unipolar systems are likely to carry greater entrapment risks. Multipolar entrapment is easily understood (and much studied) – needing allies for a workable balance of power, states are entrapped into costly foreign adventures out of fears of being isolated and left strategically vulnerable. Studies of Europe's pre-World War I system make this point (Snyder 1984: 471–483; Schroeder 1972; Van Evera 1984: 96–101). Unipolarity, on the other hand, is less determinant but, on balance, we argue that it generates entrapment risks falling between unipolar and bipolar systems. Here, and although unipolarity limits a great power's need for allies for balance-of-power reasons, it reifies the need for allies to forestall the emergence of new great powers. In the process, unipolar alliances make moral hazard – the tendency for allies to adopt progressively riskier policies in contravention of the formal or informal terms of an alliance with a stronger actor – particularly likely (Kuperman 2008). Unipolar alliances thus carry real entrapment risks, as a hegemon may need to go to war for allies to sustain its current dominance in the international system. The net result, therefore, is a situation where the United States' large power advantages over allies and prospective rivals may make it especially vulnerable to entrapment.

Together, these dynamics bolster the case for a more restrained US grand strategy and help undercut a key prop used by those advocating for primacist or "deep engagement" strategies. Alliances are not a free lunch for the United States. Although the United States' alliances may be good for many things, helping the United States avoid conflicts is not one of them. Alliances carry greater entrapment risks than often appreciated. Ultimately, even if some crises are deterred or foreclosed, the process of doing so creates new potential conflicts.

The remainder of this chapter develops in five parts. In the next section, we review the debate over the risks and benefits of US security commitments. Second, we lay out the reasons why such security commitments are riskier under unipolarity than they were under bipolarity. Third, we focus on the indirect risks of security commitments under unipolarity, focusing heavily on the particular danger of alliance moral hazard. Fourth, we present some preliminary evidence to support our case drawn from recent developments in East Asia. Finally, we conclude by briefly discussing the implications of the analysis for both international relations theory and US grand strategy.

The debate over engagement

Over the last few years, Russian actions in Ukraine and Chinese assertiveness in the South China Sea have raised the prospect of a return to great power politics, and, with it, a consideration of the role the US should play in those politics (for an overview see Brooks and Wohlforth 2016; Posen 2014). Given the protections offered by both the United States' geography and its massive military capability, US leaders have often thought about grand strategy in terms of the commitments made to others.[1] Since the Cold War, the most important US national interests might be best measured by the alliances it has maintained for most of the last seven decades: those with Western Europe, Japan, South Korea, Israel, and – albeit to a purposefully opaque extent – Taiwan.[2] Indeed, policymakers often speak in these terms, with, for instance, Vice President Joseph Biden announcing in 2009 that "The United States of America remains committed to our alliance with Europe, which we Americans believe, and continue to believe, is the cornerstone of American foreign policy." Conversely, then-candidate Donald J. Trump faced intense criticism for suggesting that American alliances in Europe and Asia were not sacrosanct (Mosk 2009; Lind 2017; Shifrinson 2017). In short, US alliances are widely seen as more or less permanent expressions of the United States' interest in foreign affairs, and the United States' underlying interests in US allies as invariable.

Lost in the discussion, however, is a fundamental question of whether these alliances are "worth it" to the United States. Even at the height of the early Cold War, with the Red Army breathing down the neck of Western Europe, no less a figure than George Kennan questioned whether the United States needed to extend formal alliances to Britain, France, and other states now seen as core American allies (Ireland 1981). After an initial flurry of "Whither NATO?" debates in the wake of the collapse of the U.S.S.R., consideration of the value of these alliances in a post-Cold War world mostly receded (Posen and Ross 1996). To many analysts, at a minimum there seemed to be little cost in maintaining what was already created; at a maximum, US-led alliances were seen as a vehicle for incorporating other countries into the presumably peaceful and democratic West while buttressing the United States' post-Cold War dominance (Joffe 1984). The debate over NATO's future – whether to maintain it or, as was ultimately decided, expand it – turned on precisely these questions, with advocates ultimately carrying the day with arguments about how NATO enlargement would expand the zone of security in Europe (Goldgeier 2010; Asmus 2002).

Today, questions about the value of these security commitments are once again being asked. Proponents of sustaining an assertive US grand strategy, including what has been labeled either "deep engagement" or primacy, see US involvement around the world as critical to the maintenance of peace and security. An active United States, committed to its and others' security, is generally seen as a positive presence in world affairs (Brooks and Wohlforth 2016; Lieber 2012). Advocates of this position are skeptical that such commitments are likely to involve the United States in conflicts that it would otherwise prefer to avoid. Moreover, so the argument goes, the United States can moderate the foreign policy of its allies, lessening the likelihood that they will get involved in conflict in the first place (Pressman 2008). Such commitments entail direct costs in the basing of troops overseas, but those costs are relatively minimal if the benefit is preventing new conflicts that would have adverse consequences for US national and economic security (Brooks, Ikenberry, and Wohlforth 2012; Wright 2015).

In contrast, advocates for a more restrained US grand strategy argue that the United States should pull back from most of its overseas security commitments. They see American commitments as placing the US in harm's way, exposing the United States to conflicts it might prefer to avoid, or even causing conflict (Posen 2013; Layne 2016). Moreover, they argue, US allies are generally the richest and most developed states in their regions, American allies should have the wherewithal to pay for their security on their own. By this logic, winding down the United States' formal and informal alliance network will reduce alliance free-riding while limiting the military and political costs paid by the United States. Because the US' overseas military presence might be causing or exacerbating some conflicts, lowering its risk of entrapment would foster a more stable international system, too (Posen 2014; Gholz, Press, and Sapolsky 1997; Itzkowitz Shifrinson and Lalwani 2014).

Which of these arguments is correct turns heavily on the risk of entrapment. Holding the potential benefits of American alliances – a contentious topic – aside, one way to evaluate the relative merits of these grand strategic approaches is to examine the downsides of American alliances (Drezner 2013; Brooks, Ikenberry, and Wohlforth 2012). Since the direct military costs of foreign commitments are acceptable, the question becomes: what are the diplomatic and political costs of existing American security commitments? After all, if the US can commit overseas with little risk of becoming entrapped in unwanted conflicts, then the costs of maintaining peace are relatively low. On the other hand, if the risks are high, then retrenchment is a better option.

The logic of entrapment

To answer this question, it is worthwhile to first examine and define what we mean by "entrapment." The term emerged in the post-1945 world as the discipline of security studies expanded. Still, statesmen and policymakers since antiquity have understood that alliances require states to risk engaging in crises and fighting wars they would otherwise avoid. Early mention of this phenomenon comes from Thucydides' discussion of the Peloponnesian War – Sparta and Athens came to blows not because of an Athenian attack on Sparta or vice versa, but because Athens challenged a Spartan ally and Sparta, not wishing to risk its allies' confidence, took steps leading to war (Thucydides 1972). In more modern times, scholars have suggested that a series of entrapments caused World War I, while policymakers during the Cold War worried that certain hot spots – especially Germany – could lead to a local crisis that would ensnare the United States and Soviet Union (Sagan 1986; Christensen and Snyder 1990).

As these examples suggest, entrapment has commonly been used to describe a situation where one state, wishing to remain allied to another, exposes itself to political and military conflicts that benefit its ally but that it, left to its own devices, would otherwise not encounter. The source of this dynamic is seemingly simple: as Glenn Snyder argued, states risk entrapment out of fear of abandonment as concerns over losing a valuable ally lead a state to accept increased risks in world affairs and foreign policy (Snyder 1984). This process can lead to a state fighting wars on behalf of its partners – if a state does not want to risk the credibility or durability of an alliance, then it may need to fight on behalf of an ally against another party even if it shares no underlying interest in its ally's conflict in general, or prefers to address the threat to the ally through other means (e.g., through deterrence rather than defense).

This logic implies that the more a state values an alliance, the more likely it is to be entrapped. Especially valuable are alliances that ensure states are able to establish a balance of power against foreign threats (Snyder 1984; Walt 1985). Although the factors that influence whether a balance of power is easy or difficult to obtain vary, states that ultimately lack the will or ability to unilaterally address an external threat tend to need allies – otherwise, a balance will not form and state survival will be imperiled (Walt 1985; Morrow 1993).

In doing so, states risk entrapment. Knowing that its partner *needs* it (or believes it needs it) to maintain a balance of power gives an ally significant leverage over its partners' foreign policy. The ally can compel concessions on a host of issues – diplomatic support, military cooperation, and even war – by threatening to exit the alliance or suggesting the alliance would become unworkable unless it receives assistance. Indeed, this dynamic applies even if all members of an alliance need one another to establish a workable balance since, as long as some members in a security-seeking alliance are more risk-acceptant than others, entrapment remains a possibility.

When and how does entrapment manifest

Still, we should be careful not to think of entrapment as purely an either/or decision whereby one ally that was previously wholly at peace with a third state mobilizes and goes to war out of the blue for the sake of an ally that has a conflict with the third state. To be sure, existing studies of entrapment focus exclusively on the question of whether states are compelled to fight unwanted wars on behalf of allies solely to maintain the alliance. For these studies, entrapment thus occurs if and only if allies end up on the same side in a conflict with one another even if one or more members of that alliance does not share a preference for that conflict (see e.g., Beckley 2015). Such an event would indeed be noteworthy and an obvious case of entrapment, but we should also expect it to be relatively rare. Rational states are not expected to fight wars that are against their national interests, and as skeptics of entrapment have claimed, leaders of those states are more likely to walk away than commit national blood and treasure to a patently unwise war (Waltz 1964). This standard thus sets a theoretically problematic high bar, suggesting that states are sufficiently concerned about their security that they form alliances, yet sufficiently unconcerned about their security that they will roll the iron dice for non-vital interests. It virtually defines away the very phenomenon of interest.

Instead, it is worthwhile relating entrapment to the process by which states tend to end up in crises and war with one another. In the modern world, international events and matters of high politics that may lead to conflict are rarely discrete events. Decisions that lead to war often occur in a series of escalatory steps. In stylized fashion, we can think of this as, first, the emergence of international tensions between two or more states, followed by a response by the threatened states and/or their allies, followed by further escalation on the part of the parties to the dispute, followed by further intra-alliance negotiation, and so on. In the process, states are also likely to put their domestic houses in order by mobilizing public support and sidelining officials who disagree with expanding a confrontation with an opponent or deepening allied support. During and after the Cold War, for instance, the United States and its allies crafted a number of institutional pathways whereby, if and when tensions with the Soviet Union heated up, NATO members would be able to consult, coordinate, and graduate responses to Soviet moves and countermoves; thus, even if states are not entrapped into a war that policymakers decry as against their interests, the conflict itself may still witness entrapment as states are pushed by allies to fight at particular times and places, and for certain objectives, that they would otherwise avoid – entrapment can shape the nature of state participation in conflicts even without causing the underlying source of confrontation. Ultimately, if an ally acts in a way that forces the state to alter its behavior in a costly and meaningful way, then it is reasonable to conclude that the state was entrapped by the actions of its ally.

Accordingly, entrapment is both more likely to occur and more likely to be clearly manifested on finer-grained inter-allied decisions related to the use of force both before and during a conflict. These "entrapment dynamics" reflect the fact that allies, even if they share similar preferences on which other states in the international system need to be opposed – and thus on whether war may be necessary – can still share divergent preferences over the nature of that opposition. More precisely, allies can differ profoundly across three key areas related to the use of force, namely (1) the timing of a war against a common threat, (2) the goals of that conflict, and (3) the relative size and nature of the contributions each state makes in the course of a conflict. Since allied preferences can diverge over these issues even though states value the alliance itself, they create propitious conditions for allies to entrap one another into fighting wars at times, in support of objectives, and with greater contributions over which they disagree with their partners. In short, by breaking war down into these different elements, entrapment becomes evident at different levels aside from the largest question of whether a state was drawn into a war it would otherwise have preferred to avoid. We treat each issue in turn.

Timing entrapment

Timing entrapment refers to a situation where members of an alliance disagree over the optimal moment at which to confront a common opponent. Weaker members of an alliance, for example, may feel proportionally more threatened by an adversary at an earlier date than proportionally stronger members of an alliance, and so be more inclined than stronger members of an alliance to adopt hardline policies that increase the likelihood of war at an earlier date. Likewise, unsettled domestic politics may give some members of an alliance incentive to go to war sooner than its allies prefer if a ruling coalition seeks to resolve an external threat but fears being turned out of office before its allies are prepared for joint action. Under these circumstances, even if Ally A would eventually be willing to fight alongside Ally B against a common opponent, B may initiate the conflict at a time that state A finds unattractive. Put differently, Ally A left to its own devices, might prefer to continue balancing an external threat without resorting to war, feeling it has the capacity to wait or hoping that war can be avoided through deterrence or a negotiated settlement; nevertheless, Ally B may behave in ways that make war more likely in the short term for fear that time is no longer on its side and, even if war came in the future, its ability to obtain desired ends would no longer be feasible.

States seeking to entrap partners into conflict at times when its partners would rather avoid it can do so in a number of ways. Some states, for instance, may spoil negotiations with an opponent designed to settle outstanding disputes so that a diplomatic standoff festers or escalates. More directly, other states may engage in provocative behavior over disputed issues designed to trigger an attack by an opponent that merits a response. And, in extremis, states can simply begin hostilities despite allied opposition, thereby "daring" its partners not to back it up. In all these situations, Ally A is then faced with the choice of either being drawn into an escalating crisis or war, or abandoning B. When A chooses to support, entrapment occurs. To not act, despite the ill-advised timing of B's provocations, would potentially leave B weakened and vulnerable to a defeat in the face of a seemingly pressing threat that, in the end, may be far worse for State A.

As an example of timing entrapment, consider the case of Austro-German relations before 1914. By most accounts, Austria-Hungary wanted to punish Serbia for its role in assassinating Austro-Hungarian Crown Prince Franz Ferdinand, but was unwilling to do so at the risk of war with Russia (Serbia's principal ally) at that particular moment. However, Germany – Austria-Hungary's own powerful patron – saw a closing window of opportunity for a continental war that would help settle European great power relations once and for all; 1914 was the last, best opportunity for Germany to strike and, since Austria-Hungary was relatively weak without German backing, it could not easily afford to ignore German demands. Accordingly, as the July 1914 crisis escalated, Germany pushed Austria-Hungary to reject Serbian-Russian proposals that would settle the growing diplomatic crisis. The resulting negotiating failure – spoiled by Germany – saw Austria-Hungary entrapped into a general European war that few Austrian leaders wanted (Stone 1966; Copeland 2000).

Goal entrapment

The second type of entrapment is goal entrapment. Ally A may be willing to fight alongside Ally B, but the two states may diverge in their preferences for the goals and terms for settling any resulting war. This can occur through two different pathways. First, if Ally A has more modest goals than Ally B, A may become entrapped in the more ambitious goals of its ally once a war begins simply by B's refusal to end a conflict when A desires. In this situation, A's only alternative is to abandon its ally, a risky proposition in the middle of war that raises the possibility of battlefield defeat and political infighting between A and B that would render the entire war effort for naught. Again, entrapment dynamics extend beyond a simple decision about whether to go to war on behalf of an ally or not, to the ways in which the subsequent conflict is resolved.

The US intervention in Vietnam illustrates this type of entrapment. At various stages of the conflict, the US favored a diplomatic resolution and entered into serious negotiations designed to settle the dispute. A negotiated settlement, however, repeatedly proved anathema to the United States' South Vietnamese ally – seeking to minimize the possibility of North Vietnamese and Communist involvement after hostilities ended, South Vietnam repeatedly engaged in diplomatic obfuscation and battlefield aggression to scuttle peace talks. Facing an ally that refused to settle on its terms, the US faced the difficult decision of remaining in Vietnam and fighting, or withdrawing and risking its ally's likely defeat. Ultimately and repeatedly, the United States chose to sustain and expand its support even when its goals and those of its allies no longer agreed.

Second, and closely related, one ally may entrap another by expanding the scope of a conflict. In wartime, it is possible that Ally B might seek postwar gains and so carry a war into new venues or geographic areas. This move risks entrapping Ally A, as failure to back B may result in B's defeat, the loss of crucial resources, and opening up inter-allied political fissures that may dissolve the alliance in the midst of a fight. During World War II, for instance, many US military leaders felt that British calls for an American landing in North Africa – where British forces were already fighting Axis troops – constituted a British effort at entrapping the United States into helping Britain maintain its colonial footholds in Africa and the Middle East.

Means entrapment

Finally, means entrapment describes a situation in which Ally A is maneuvered by Ally B into committing more resources or types of resources to an intervention than it otherwise desires. This is distinct from goal entrapment: even if A and B agree on their strategic objectives, B may still end up entrapping A into a costlier commitment than intended by underproviding the capabilities required and requiring A to make up the difference. This situation can either be intentional – where B withholds available resources from a contest in order to deploy them elsewhere and/or shift the burden onto its partners – or unintentional – where B underestimates the capabilities required to achieve a specified end and, lacking the requisite resources, turns to A. In either case, A is compelled to intervene for fear of harming the alliance's credibility, prestige, and future functions. Metaphorically, and occasionally literally, B calls for A's cavalry to ride over the hill to its assistance.

Although poorly catalogued, means entrapment is likely the most common form of entrapment. States, after all, regularly promise one another the military tools required for joint military action, only to change course and leave their partners high and dry. During the opening days of World War I, for example, Austria-Hungary reneged on agreements to deploy most of its forces against Russia while Germany attacked France, exposing Germany to Russian assault and requiring Germany to shift forces to the Eastern Front earlier than intended. Similarly, Soviet and Chinese officials only agreed to back North Korea in the Korean War when assured by North Korea that the contest would be quickly won and limited in scope; when this assumption proved overly optimistic following the American-backed intervention in June 1950, the U.S.S.R. and China were eventually forced to commit their own forces. More recently, meanwhile, the 2011 allied intervention in Libya illustrates the trend. While the US reluctantly agreed to participate in the intervention, it found that its capabilities were increasingly necessary for success to be possible in the intervention, as allied forces – which were supposed to dominate the fight – rapidly proved wanting. Once committed, the US was either going to be trapped by its allies' inability to succeed with their own capabilities or escape from that trap and accept the likelihood that the intervention in Libya would fail (even sooner than it failed with US participation). As President Obama has admitted, the US went along grudgingly for fear that the alternative was worse.

Entrapment and strategy

Combined, the net effect of these entrapment dynamics is a situation where states are rarely overtly entrapped into conflicts on behalf of their allies, but are often quietly entrapped by their partners on less obvious strategic issues. Indeed, as Snyder's work implies, states that take on allies have to adjust their strategies to accommodate these allies, and it is on this level that allies gain leverage over one's foreign policy. Rich and powerful states like the United States can often accommodate these strategic adjustments without bankrupting the state or risking war to a needlessly large degree, but the adjustment cost is rarely zero – entrapment still occurs and poses problems. As importantly, even rich and powerful states may confront growing dangers from their commitments over time as (1) opponents mobilize and arm to confront one's own alliance, and (2) states take on more security commitments, thereby exposing themselves to more possible situations that can lead to conflict.

Structure and entrapment

In sum, entrapment is more common than often acknowledged. Its frequency does, however, vary in important ways as the international distribution of power waxes and wanes over time: because different distributions of power influence states' need to balance and opportunities for doing so, whether a system has several, two, or only one great power directly affects the risks of entrapment. As we argue in this section, entrapment of all kinds is most common in multipolar worlds, least common in bipolar settings, and fairly common in unipolar settings. As significantly, entrapment is likely to become increasingly prevalent in unipolarity both the longer unipolarity endures and if unipolarity begins to wane (Morgenthau 1954; Waltz 1979).

Multipolarity

Multipolar systems, where there are several great powers of roughly similar strength such that none is dominant, are the most entrapment-prone. In multipolarity, great powers generally cannot deter or defeat one another through internal means alone – they need allies for a workable balance. Indeed, the more each state is of similar size and capability, the larger the need for allies. With several states each seeking friends to offset prospective foes, the risks of entrapment increase.

In multipolar systems, two different pathways can lead to conflict. First, states which feel that their alliance affords them an extra margin of security against potential threats – for instance, if two states ally against a third before the third can find its own partners – may be emboldened and engage in reckless behavior that antagonizes other states. As the risk of war increases, allies thus find themselves on the horns of a dilemma: go to war for an ally over the ally's interests, or fail to support the ally and risk the dissolution of the alliance.

Second, entrapment can occur out of fear of abandonment. If one member of an alliance fears that an ally is soon to defect, it might provoke a foreign conflict to forestall the looming vulnerability. In this type of preventive entrapment, the ally considering defection can have these plans scuttled as the new conflict presents it with an unpalatable choice: to defect under such circumstances risks an ally's defeat and the prospect of facing a newly empowered competitor on its own, while to back the ally requires going to war. To return to the World War I case, for example, German leaders worked during the July 1914 crisis to encourage Austria-Hungary opposition to Serbia (and Russia) out of fear that Austrian leaders would opt for a diplomatic settlement rather than war; in effect, Germany entrapped Austria-Hungary into war out of fear that Austria-Hungary would conciliate Serbia rather than sustain Austro-German collaboration.

Bipolarity

Two features of bipolar systems, where two great powers predominate, make them the least likely to see great power entrapment. First, since the two great powers in bipolarity are both significantly stronger than all other states in the system, allies are, generally, not necessary to maintain a balance of power. Allies still have uses, such as aiding one's geographic reach, defraying military costs, expanding one's influence, and helping great powers establish reputations for resolve. Nevertheless, and as Kenneth Waltz (1979) argued long ago, balancing in bipolarity is principally a matter of great powers' internal efforts, as alliances with relatively small states can do little to meaningfully shape the military balance. Second – and as importantly – the fact that the two great powers themselves constitute the clearest threats to one another's security helps focus policymakers' attention and avoid miscalculations over this basic issue: because the costs of conflict with the other side are clear and there is no confusion over which states are one's opponents, the limited importance of allies to great powers' well-being is singularly transparent.

These two factors combine to lower the risk of entrapment. When an ally threatens to ensnare one of the great powers into a conflict with the other great power, the costs of doing so are unambiguously large. Hence, unless the great power seeks war itself, or policymakers are unable or unwilling to take a hard line with client states, it is unlikely to play along. The latter dynamic was regularly on display in the

Vietnam War as South Vietnam regularly launched diplomatic and military offensives to scuttle peace talks to settle the conflict, forcing the United States – unwilling to coerce South Vietnamese compliance – to continue fighting. Moreover, even when an ally threatens to ensnare a great power into a conflict in which its great power rival is absent, the great power generally cannot act for fear of diverting finite resources to secondary conflicts and leaving the other great power unchecked. Entrapment is likely in bipolarity only if a great power significantly miscalculates the consequences of backing an ally – but here, given the stakes involved, such miscalculation is unlikely. The Korean War illustrates the point. American policymakers entered the fray partly out of concern that the North Korean invasion of South Korea was directed by the U.S.S.R. to test American willingness and resolve to defend its allies. Had the United States known that the conflict was not truly part of a Soviet-led offensive against the West, however, it is debatable whether it would have become involved; after all, faced with the option of escalating the conflict by carrying the war into China and inviting Soviet retaliation, American policymakers demurred, with Army Chief of Staff General Omar Bradley remarking that it would be the "wrong war, at the wrong place, at the wrong time, and with the wrong enemy" (Quoted in Bernstein 1981: 266). Ultimately, bipolarity may encourage a state to act because it thinks its reputation is at stake but, given the stakes involved, these incidents are likely to be fewer and further between than entrapment in other scenarios.

Unipolarity

What of unipolarity, where one power is dominant, as is the case with the United States today? Prima facie, entrapment should be extremely rare in unipolarity. Allies are unlikely to materially affect the unipole's security given the presumed material predominance of a unipolar power; hence, the sole great power around does not need to go to war on its allies' behalf. If pressed, a unipolar power can simply cut the ally off and treat it as any other state.

On further investigation, however, the uniquely advantageous strategic situation that unipoles find themselves in can paradoxically increase the likelihood of entrapment. Because unipolarity is such an advantageous position for a state, a unipolar power has a powerful temptation to roam the system and prevent other great powers from rising and winnowing down its position. Assuming the unipole will not itself engage in preventive wars to stop future competitors, it can either ally with local actors in order to use them as proxies against a future threat, or ally with a prospective challenger itself in order to influence it (Gavin 2015; Ikenberry 2008). Such behavior may be particularly characteristic of waning unipoles that are increasingly wary of the threat posed by other rising great powers.

Both options allow the unipole's allies to gain leverage over its foreign policy, and therefore risk entrapment. In the first case, the unipole may need to back up allies in their disputes with other relatively small states in order to ensure their help against the prospective challenger. In the latter case, the unipole may need to work at the prospective challenger's behest to keep the potential challenger from opposing the unipole's dominance. In either case, shifting power can lead to a unipole's entrapment. On one level, shifting power dynamics can increase an ally's leverage over a unipole's foreign policy. In particular, if a unipole is on the verge of seeing its dominance disappear altogether, allies take on a growing importance in helping slow or stop the rise of new peer competitors. Hence, any given ally can threaten to defect from the unipole's coalition and hinder the unipole's ability to address the looming threat unless the waning unipole fights on behalf of the ally. Put differently, a prospective challenger's threat of defection may undermine a unipole's dominance, making costly sacrifices for an ally more attractive than would otherwise be the case. The more a unipole seeks to prevent the rise of new great powers – something most unipoles want – the greater the risk of entrapment (Monteiro 2014).

Shifting power also increases the risk of moral hazard – a situation in which an actor behaves recklessly, knowing that they have an insurance policy that will cover any losses they incur. In the case of alliance politics, smaller allies may act aggressively if they know that their more powerful ally will come to their aid. Because some allies are uniquely powerful or important to their partners, many security commitments can end up being disproportionate to the threat they address. Though any alliance can face moral hazard problems – witness American concerns over European recklessness during the Cold War – they are likely to be particularly problematic in unipolar settings. Because unipoles are uniquely powerful, the security commitments they hold exist in the absence of a compelling military threat to the unipole itself. However, the same may not apply for the unipole's allies. For them, the international system remains a competitive environment in which other states may challenge their security and other interests. This asymmetry is asking for trouble. For a unipole's allies, the best way to guarantee victory in any conflict is to ensure the unipole enters the contest on their behalf. In this sense, an alliance with a unipole is the best kind of insurance policy, Allies of a unipole have strong incentives to lie, cheat, and steal to convince a unipole to come to their aid. Because the unipole itself may see through the smokescreen, they also have incentives to manipulate events to force a unipole's hand.

In turn, shifts in power increase the unipole's exposure to moral hazard. Because power shifts can also work to the disadvantage of a unipole's allies and – crucially – are likely to affect their security *earlier* than they affect a unipole's security, the risks of an ally seeking to cash in the unipole's insurance policy loom large. That is, since a unipole's allies are unlikely to want to wait for a power shift to occur before the unipole comes to their aid, they have reason both to try to convince the unipole that a rising state endangers international security and to create a situation that buttresses this line of reasoning. The goal of such efforts is to increase the value of the alliance to the unipole and short-circuit the unipole's own calculations regarding the distribution of power. Moral hazard and power shifts can thus create a vicious cycle.

The United States, the unipolar era, and the risk of entrapment

The preceding discussion (summarized in Table 2.1) has large implications for the United States. During the Cold War, bipolarity constrained the importance of allies, limiting the risk of entrapment. Moreover, the prospect of nuclear war discouraged risky behavior by the superpowers and their allies. Today, however, the risk of entrapment born of moral hazard and states' search for security is larger and possibly increasing. As long as the US continues to make commitments overseas and fear the emergence of a peer competitor, American partners will be tempted to act in risky ways, expecting that Washington will feel compelled to come to their rescue should they get into trouble.

Insofar as the United States opposes Chinese or Russian aggression, smaller states will be tempted to provoke China or Russia to garner growing American support. If the United States is opposed to the emergence of great power peer competitors, then it may well opt to come to the aid of smaller states threatened by those potential competitors. This also means that countries that have limited or no explicit security commitments from the United States may try to profit from the insurance policy offered by the United States by provoking conflicts and expecting the United States – whose interests are clear – to ride to their defense.

In the next section, we take a preliminary look at some evidence to test these claims. We focus on events in East and Southeast Asia over the last few years. Some have characterized Chinese aggression in recent years as reactionary. That is, China has felt compelled to respond to perceived provocations from smaller Asian nations such as the Philippines and Vietnam. Even though the US does not have formal security commitments to either country, Washington subsequently feels compelled to signal to these countries that it will stand up to Chinese aggression.

China, Asia, and the risks of entrapment

Recent events in Asia illustrate the logic of our argument. Though China has certainly not been innocent in recent events, US alliance politics helped spur tension in Southeast and East Asia. As Thomas Christensen writes, "Beijing – with a few important exceptions – has been reacting, however abrasively, to unwelcome and unforeseen events that have often been initiated by others" (Christensen

TABLE 2.1 Entrapment in different distributions of power

Multipolarity	*Bipolarity*	*Unipolarity*
Risk of entrapment: large Mechanisms:	Risk of entrapment: small Mechanism:	Risk of entrapment: medium Mechanisms:

– Emboldenment
  – Preventive action
	– Miscalculation	– Forestalling the rise of
		     peer competitors
		  – Moral hazard

2015: 265). Short of this position, one might also see Chinese behavior as part and parcel of a burgeoning insecurity spiral as Chinese actions beget Japanese, Filipino, and Vietnamese reactions, and vice versa. The key here is not who is to blame but how alliance politics factors into the recent escalation of tensions.

Entrapment has contributed to rising tensions between the United States and China. There are two aspects to this dynamic. First, and since the end of the Cold War, the United States has been worried about China's potential power and uncertain long-term intentions. This concern has only grown over time, to the point where many policymakers and some analysts worry China may be emerging as a regional hegemon (Legro 2007). Though American policymakers offered lip service throughout the 1990s to the notion of reassuring all states – including China – in the post-Cold War era, when forced to choose the United States has long prioritized backing other countries against China. For evidence, one need only look at the US decision to retain the US–Japanese alliance after 1991 while quickly forgetting that China itself served as a de facto ally against the U.S.S.R. (Christensen 2006). More importantly, countries like Japan, the Philippines, and Vietnam are aware of the American preference. Towards the end of the 2000s and in the early 2010s, this knowledge afforded East Asian elites a tool with which to pressure the United States to become more involved, both diplomatically and militarily, in East Asia (Bader 2012).

Early in the Obama administration, for example, a meeting of US and Japanese policymakers and analysts saw Japanese delegates voice concerns that the United States was not keeping pace with the rise of China amid broader concerns over "how the US would respond in the event of an attack against Japan." One Japanese commentator went so far as to bluntly warn that "US naval [sic] is losing preponderance in the western Pacific" and allowing China to expand its sphere of influence; another implicitly underlined the United States' own need for Japanese help against China, arguing that "The nature of relations that US has with China and Japan are very different [...] It is important that the US not appear to be conceding too much, or siding with China too deeply, especially in the area of its military buildup" (Glosserman 2009).

South Korean officials voiced similar concerns, arguing that US military commitments elsewhere might diminish the US presence on the Korean Peninsula at a time when there was a real need to "deter Chinese intervention" in the area (Korea Society-Shorenstein Asia-Pacific Research Center 2008). Vietnamese leaders expressed interest in cooperating with the United States at a time when concern with the P.R.C. was growing; Malaysian leaders did the same (Qiang 2015; Manyin 2014; Kuik 2013). The Australian Ministry of Defense noted in its 2009 Defence White Paper that American commitments elsewhere might leave the US ability to project power in Asia "constrained," pushing the United States "to seek active assistance from regional allies and partners," at a time when Australia itself saw its security "best underpinned by the continued presence of the United States" (Australian Government Department of Defense 2009: 33, 43; Dewar undated). Association of Southeast Asian Nations (ASEAN) Secretary General Surin Pitsuwan told then-Secretary of State Hillary Clinton during her first overseas trip that, "Your visit shows the seriousness of the United States to end its diplomatic absenteeism in the region" (Manyin 2014).

Asian policymakers were simply doing what was eminently reasonable from their perspective: seeking firmer US security guarantees as the distribution of power moved against them. The consequence of doing so, however, was to enmesh the United States into simmering regional conflicts. Questions over American credibility in Asia played a major role in spurring what we now know as "the pivot" or "rebalance" to the region, as policymakers reacted to the perception that "a lack of diplomatic focus had not been good for the region" (Quoted in Hemmings 2013; see also Obama 2011; Murphy 2014; Manyin et al. 2012). As Assistant Secretary of State Kurt Campbell explained, the pivot was only partly driven by objective shifts in the distribution of power brought about by China's economic and military rise. More important was the perception that the United States needed to "provide reassurance of its lasting commitment" to East Asia. And here, the "first priority" involved "strengthen[ing] the US alliances that are the foundation of [US] engagement in the region" – in other words, reacting to allied concerns over American credibility in the face of a rising China and a sense of American disengagement (Campbell and Andrews 2013). Then-Secretary of State Hillary Clinton echoed this theme in a prominent 2011 article, noting at a time when states were asking whether the United States could "make – and keep – credible economic and strategic commitments" that the turn to Asia was an unequivocal statement that it could and would (Clinton 2011). President Obama sought to link the pivot to allied concerns, explaining when announcing the policy that while some countries "have wondered about America's commitment" to protecting the status quo in East Asia, the United States was wedded to doing so and would refocus on cooperating with allies to achieve its desired ends (Obama 2011). Allied questions over American credibility, in sum, drove the United States to signal renewed diplomatic and military attention to Asia.

To be sure, the United States has an interest in East Asian stability and may well want to prevent China from dominating Asia. However, these goals themselves can be achieved through a variety of means, not all of which involve buttressing allies. In fact, allies in the late 2000s voiced concerned that the United States would pursue its own interests by directly collaborating with China in a "G-2" condominium that would isolate and ignore traditional American allies (Bush 2011). Instead, the substance, the timing, and the subsequent evolution of the pivot cannot be explained without addressing the role of allied pressures – all of which amounts to American entrapment.

Since its 2010–2011 announcement, the pivot has inserted the United States into a host of Asian political and military disputes with China involving ownership of contested maritime space and islands in the South and East China Seas. Though there may be economic resources beneath the surface around some of these locales, neither the United States nor its allies have an intrinsic interest in ownership of contested areas. Instead, the contested maritime domains are worrisome to US allies for what they suggest about China's territorial ambitions. They are therefore important to the United States for the signal American actions send to allies over American credibility. Thus, the United States has moved to back its allies in their disputes with the P.R.C. by rhetorically portraying China as the principal aggressor, clarifying that US commitments to the allies would cover the maritime areas under dispute, and – above all – has dispatched its own military forces to enforce what the US and its allies define as the "status quo" in contravention of China's own interests (Russell 2014; White House 2014; US Pacific Command 2015; Valencia 2016; LaGrone 2015; Panda 2016). Whatever the legitimacy of these actions, their effect is to create a self-perpetuating cycle: the more the United States stands by its allies in opposing potential Chinese ambitions, the nominally more credible the American resolve to defend its allies, the more the allies are inclined to act aggressively toward China, and the greater the likelihood of a direct US–Chinese confrontation. In other words, treating American support for its allies as a litmus test of the alliances themselves requires the United States to take steps on behalf of its allies that risk conflict with China.

This is entrapment of the purest sort. The United States could readily provide security to its friends in East Asia, maintain Asia's political status quo, or more generally limit the rise of China without involving itself in Asian maritime disputes. To the extent that the United States simply wants to preserve East Asian stability, it could negotiate directly with the P.R.C. to settle conflicts of interest on a bilateral basis. To the extent that the United States wants to prevent China from becoming an Asian hegemon or engaging in military action beyond its borders, it could simply surge forces to the region as crises develop or build up the military forces of its clients (Itzkowitz Shifrinson and Lalwani 2014; Glaser 2015; Mirski 2013). That these options are treated as insufficient suggests entrapment at play. Even if protecting Japan, South Korea, and other regional partners is in the United States' interest, only entrapment explains the timing and form of the American response.[3]

The second driver of entrapment comes from the response by East Asian countries themselves. It will be some time before we have detailed evidence on what was said to whom that convinced the Obama administration to pivot to East Asia. Nevertheless, the East Asian response since 2010–2011 suggests that moral hazard is increasing risks for the United States. One of the most striking trends in East Asia since the pivot is the renewed assertiveness of East Asian states in dealing with China (Johnston 2013; Associated Press 2015). This trend includes independent action by the Japanese, Filipino, Vietnamese, and other military forces to take a forward-leaning stance on maritime disputes that, at minimum, helps to justify a Chinese response. Japan, Korea, and others lobbied for the pivot for the express purpose of having the United States help them manage the rise of China – the implication being that, without an active American role, they would either bandwagon with China or engage in increasingly aggressive policies with a large risk of war.

As things stand, East Asia is already witness to an arms race and militarized interstate disputes: Japan is taking increasing military measures to confront Chinese incursions into the disputed Senkakus, including regularly confronting Chinese aircraft flying over the disputed region (Gady 2015; Reuters 2016a; Kazianis 2016;

Reynolds 2015); Vietnam and the Philippines have grown increasingly willing to confront China in the South China Sea while deepening military ties with other countries challenged by China (Torode 2015; Vietnam Right Now 2015; Bowcott 2015; Reuters 2016b); and even Australia – which has no maritime disputes with China – has taken to militarily challenging Chinese maritime claims (Defense News 2015; News.com.au 2015). Independently, none of these countries (except perhaps Japan) has the wherewithal to defeat China. These actions are almost certainly born of the expectation that the United States will come to their aid if a dispute escalates to war.[4] Thus, unless the pivot has had no effect on allied behavior, then its main influence has been to (1) avoid bandwagoning, but (2) allow the very assertiveness the United States nominally sought to avoid in the first place! To put the issue differently, the claims employed by Asian allies and partners to push what became the pivot strongly suggest that it encouraged their over-assertiveness. This is moral hazard: take away the United States' post-pivot policy, and the East Asian allies would almost certainly not be tilting with China to the same extent. Some smaller allies, in fact, might bandwagon altogether. If so, this suggests the extent to which entrapment dynamics are at play.

In sum, entrapment is alive and well in terms of both the arguments employed and the policies adopted by the United States and its allies since the late 2000s. No war has occurred, but crises are ongoing, and the intensity of American backing for its East Asian clients is growing. This is a recipe for miscalculation. As American forces continue to move into the region, as American diplomacy continues to take an anti-China flavor, and as allies simultaneously spur and build upon these trends, the United States is approaching active involvement in the wrong conflicts, at the wrong time, and in the wrong place. The United States has an interest in maintaining Japan and other major states as independent actors friendly to the United States, noting their particular island disputes with China. Entrapment is alive and well as the United States mistakes the latter for the former. And, importantly, even if the United States decides at some point that conflict with China is necessary to protect its national interests, the US could still be entrapped by its allies into fighting that conflict at an unwelcome time with unattractive goals and using extraordinary means. In short, the US need not be drawn into a wholly unwelcome war for entrapment to nonetheless occur.

Conclusion

Existing studies of entrapment have not appreciated the degree to which the risks of entrapment vary based on the structure of the international system and the threats that states face. They also have failed to recognize that entrapment appears in more forms than simply the question of whether a state gets drawn into an unwanted war. A more comprehensive theory will explain both why the risks of entrapment were relatively low during the bipolar Cold War and why they are now relatively high in the unipolar post-Cold War era. In contrast to those who see little risk in the continuation and expansion of American security commitments around the world, the logic of our argument suggests that the risks of entrapment are considerable at the moment. For the United States, a more restrained grand strategy would reduce the risk of all kinds of entrapment.

Notes

1 Indeed, even at the height of international tensions during and immediately after World War II, American strategy debates turned largely on whether and to what extent the United States should ally with other countries (Stoler 2003; Ireland 1981).

2 Some might contend that only formal treaty commitments constitute an "alliance," while less-formal commitments are part of a more nebulous "alignment" category. This position is patently absurd, as a brief example illustrates: the United States has formal treaty commitments with nearly every state in South and Latin America, yet lacks a formal alliance with Israel. Israel, however, receives billions of dollars in annual military assistance and enjoys among the strongest diplomatic relations of any state with the US government; conversely, not only do a host of South and Latin American states enjoy little American military largesse, but US relations with such "treaty allies" as Bolivia, Cuba, and Venezuela have often been strained (sometimes in the extreme). Clearly, politically meaningful alliances exist irrespective of the formal or informal nature of the interstate cooperation. For US treaty allies, see Department of State (2016).

3 An exchange between Senator Lindsey Graham and PACOM Head Admiral Samuel Locklear captured the extent to which less-assertive policies are constrained by alliance politics:

LOCKLEAR: I think any signal that we send that we're less interested in the Asia-Pacific on the security side than we currently are would be an invitation for change in the region, and that China would be interested in pursuing.

GRAHAM: Do our allies in the region, are they beginning to hedge their bets? What's their view toward our footprint and where we're headed?

LOCKLEAR: Yes. I don't think they're necessarily unsatisfied with our military footprint. I think what they're concerned about most is the growing divide between what they see as the economics in our gravity, which is predominantly Asia or more and more around China, and the securities in our gravity, which is around us. So that creates a conundrum for them as they have to deal with strategic decision-making. You know they want us as a security granter because they believe where we're – I mean, they see us as a benevolent power. And they like how we operate. But they also see us as a diminished economic power in the region that they have to deal with that.

US Pacific Command (2015); see also the exchange between Graham Allison and Senator Richard Blumenthal in United States Senate Committee on Armed Services (2015).

4 The United States has given allies good reason for this. For example, President Obama affirmed in 2014 that the US–Japanese alliance covered disputed territory in the Senkaku Islands, while elsewhere moving to buttress Vietnam via arms sales and military exercises in its disputes with the P.R.C. (see LaGrone 2015; Panda 2014).

References

Asmus, R. 2002. *Opening NATO's Door: How the Alliance Remade Itself for a New Era.* Columbia University Press.

Associated Press. 2015. Japan, Philippines Hail Second Day of Joint Drills in South China Sea. *Japan Times*, June 24. Accessed from www.japantimes.co.jp/news/2015/06/24/national/politics-diplomacy/japan-philippines-hail-second-day-of-joint-drills-in-south-china-sea/#.Vd_G3LxViko.

Australian Government Department of Defence. 2009. *Defence White Paper 2009*.

Bader, J.A. 2012. *Obama and China's Rise: An Insider's Account of America's Asia Strategy*. Brookings Institution Press.

Beckley, M. 2015. The Myth of Entangling Alliances: Reassessing the Security Risks of US Defense Pacts. *International Security*, 39(4), pp.7–48.

Bernstein, B.J. 1981. New Light on the Korean War. *The International History Review*, 3(2), pp.256–277.

Bowcott, O. 2015. UN Tribunal at the Hague to Rule on Rival Claims to South China Sea, Islands. *The Guardian*, November 23. Accessed September 29, 2017, from www.theguardian.com/world/2015/nov/23/south-china-sea-dispute-hague-competing-claims.

Brooks, S. and Wohlforth, W. 2016. *America Abroad: The United States' Global Role in the 21st Century*. Oxford University Press.

Brooks, S.G., Ikenberry, G.J., and Wohlforth, W.C. 2012. Don't Come Home, America: The Case against Retrenchment. *International Security*, 37(3), pp.7–51.

Bush, G.W. 2002. *The National Security Strategy of the United States of America*. The White House.

Bush, G.W. 2006. *The National Security Strategy of the United States of America*. The White House.

Bush, R.C. 2011. The United States and China: A G-2 in the Making? *Gaiko*, July 2011. Accessed March 27, 2017 from www.brookings.edu/research/articles/2011/10/11-china-us-g2-bush.

Campbell, K., and Andrews, B. 2013. Explaining the US "pivot" to Asia. *Americas*, 1.

Christensen, T.J. 2006. Fostering Stability or Creating a Monster? The Rise of China and US Policy toward East Asia. *International Security*, 31(1), pp.81–126.

Christensen, T.J. 2015. *The China Challenge: Shaping the Choices of a Rising Power*. W.W. Norton & Company.

Christensen, T.J., and Snyder, J. 1990. Chain Gangs and Passed Bucks: Predicting Alliance Patterns in Multipolarity. *International Organization*, 44(2), pp.137–168.

Clinton, H.R. 2011. America's Pacific Century. October 11. Accessed March 27, 2017, from http://foreignpolicy.com/2011/10/11/americas-pacific-century/.

Clinton, W.J. 1994. *A National Security Strategy of Engagement and Enlargement*. The White House.

Copeland, D.C. 2000. *The Origins of Major War*. Cornell University Press.

Defense News. 2015. Australian Military Plane Flies Over Disputed South China Sea. December 16. Accessed March 27, 2017, from www.defensenews.com/story/defense/2015/12/16/australian-military-plane-flies-disputed-south-china-sea/77458100/.

Department of State. 2016. US Collective Defense Agreements. Accessed November 2, 2016, from www.state.gov/s/l/treaty/collectivedefense/.

Dewar, S. Undated. *Australia and China and the United States: Responding to Changing Great Power Dynamics*. Australian Centre on China in the World, Australian National University. Accessed March 27, 2017, from http://ciw.anu.edu.au/publications/au_ch_and_us.pdf.

Drezner, D.W. 2013. Military Primacy Doesn't Pay (Nearly As Much As You Think). *International Security*, 38(1), pp.52–79.

Gady, F. 2015. Surprise: Japan Sees China as Its Main National Security Threat. *The Diplomat*, July 21. Accessed March 27, 2017, from http://thediplomat.com/2015/07/surprise-japan-sees-china-as-its-main-national-security-threat/.

Gavin, F.J. 2015. Strategies of Inhibition: US Grand Strategy, the Nuclear Revolution, and Nonproliferation. *International Security*, 40(1), pp.9–46.

Gholz, E., Press, D.G., and Sapolsky, H.M. 1997. Come Home, America: The Strategy of Restraint in the Face of Temptation. *International Security*, 21(4), pp.5–48.

Glaser, C.L. 2015. A US–China Grand Bargain? The Hard Choice between Military Competition and Accommodation. *International Security*, 39(4), pp.49–90.

Glosserman, B. 2009. Japan–US Security Relations: A Testing Time for the Alliance – A Conference Report. *Center for Strategic and International Studies Issues and Insights*, 9(14).

Goldgeier, J.M. 1998. NATO Expansion: The Anatomy of a Decision. *Washington Quarterly*, 21(1), pp.83–102.

Goldgeier, J.M. 2010. *Not Whether but When: The US Decision to Enlarge NATO*. Brookings Institution Press.

Hemmings, J. 2013. China: America Hedges Its Bets. The National Interest, December 6. Accessed March 27, 2017, from http://nationalinterest.org/commentary/china-america-hedges-its-bets-9510.

Ikenberry, G.J. 2008. The Rise of China and the Future of the West: Can the Liberal System Survive? *Foreign Affairs*, January/February, pp.23–37.

Ireland, T.P. 1981. *Creating the Entangling Alliance: The Origins of the North Atlantic Treaty Organization*. Contributions in Political Science No. 50. Greenwood Publishing Group.

Itzkowitz Shifrinson, J.R., and Lalwani, S. 2014. It's a Commons Misunderstanding: The Limited Threat to American Command of the Commons. In Preble, C., and Mueller, J., eds, *A Dangerous World?* Cato, pp.223–244.

Joffe, J. 1984. Europe's American Pacifier. *Foreign Policy*, 54, pp.64–82.

Johnston, A.I. 2013. How New and Assertive is China's New Assertiveness? *International Security*, 37(4), pp.7–48.

Kazianis, H.J. 2016. Japan's Master Plan to Destroy the Chinese Navy in Battle. *The National Interest*, January 1. Accessed March 27, 2017, from http://nationalinterest.org/blog/the-buzz/japans-master-plan-destroy-the-chinese-navy-battle-14779?page=2.

Kim, T. 2011. Why Alliances Entangle but Seldom Entrap States. *Security Studies*, 20(3), pp.350–377.

Korea Society-Shorenstein Asia-Pacific Research Center. 2008. *"New Beginnings" in the US–ROK Alliance: Recommendations to US Policymakers*. Stanford University.

Kuik, C.C. 2013. Malaysia's US Policy under Najib: Structural and Domestic Sources of a Small State's Strategy. *Asian Security*, 9(3), pp.143–164.

Kuperman, A.J. 2008. The Moral Hazard of Humanitarian Intervention: Lessons from the Balkans. *International Studies Quarterly*, 52(1), pp.49–80.

LaGrone, S. 2015. US 7th Fleet Would Support ASEAN South China Sea Patrols. *USNI News*, March 20. Accessed March 27, 2017, from http://news.usni.org/2015/03/20/u-s-7th-fleet-would-support-asean-south-china-sea-patrols.

Layne, C. 2016. Hillary Clinton and Nuclear Weapons: More Dangerous Than Trump? *The National Interest*, October 31. Accessed March 27, 2017, from http://nationalinterest.org/feature/hillary-clinton-nuclear-weapons-more-dangerous-than-trump-18241.

Legro, J.W. 2007. What China Will Want: The Future Intentions of a Rising Power. *Perspectives on Politics*, 5(03), pp.515–534.

Lieber, R.J. 2012. America in Decline? It's a Matter of Choices, Not Fate. *World Affairs*, September/October, pp.88–96.

Lind, J. 2017. The Art of the Bluff: The US–Japan Alliance under the Trump Administration. H-Diplo/ISSF Policy Series 1(5). Accessed September 29, 2017, from https://issforum.org/category/roundtables/policy.

Manyin, M. 2014. Vietnam among the Great Powers: Struggle and Cooperation. *ASAN Forum*, October 17. Accessed March 27, 2017, from www.theasanforum.org/vietnam-among-the-powers-struggle-cooperation/.

Manyin, M.E., Daggett, S., Dolven, B., Lawrence, S.V., Martin, M.F., O'Rourke, R., and Vaughn, B. 2012. *Pivot to the Pacific? The Obama Administration's Rebalancing Toward Asia.* Library of Congress Congressional Research Service.

Mirski, S. 2013. Stranglehold: The Context, Conduct and Consequences of an American Naval Blockade of China. *Journal of Strategic Studies*, 36(3), pp.385–421.

Monteiro, N.P. 2014. *Theory of Unipolar Politics.* Cambridge University Press.

Morgenthau, H.M. 1954. *Politics Among Nations*, 2nd ed. Knopf.

Morrow, J.D. 1993. Arms versus Allies: Trade-offs in the Search for Security. *International Organization*, 47(2), pp.207–233.

Mosk, M. 2009. Biden: US Committed to NATO. *Washington Times*, October 23. Accessed March 27, 2017, from www.washingtontimes.com/news/2009/oct/23/biden-us-committed-to-nato/.

Murphy, K. 2014. US Defence Secretary: "We Are a Pacific Power, We Aren't Going Anywhere." *The Guardian*, August 11.

News.com.au. 2015. Chinese Paper's Threat to RAAF: "It Would Be a Shame if One Day a Plane Fell from the Sky." December 17. Accessed March 27, 2017, from www.news.com.au/technology/innovation/inventions/chinese-papers-threat-to-raaf-it-would-be-a-shame-if-one-day-a-plane-fell-from-the-sky/news-story/1af82a742f134678de32ccc7cda0c15e.

Obama, B. 2011. Remarks by President Obama to the Australian Parliament. November 17. Accessed September 29, 2017, from https://obamawhitehouse.archives.gov/the-press-office/2011/11/17/remarks-president-obama-australian-parliament.

Obama, B. 2015. *The National Security Strategy of the United States of America.* White House.

Panda, A. 2014. Obama: Senkakus Covered Under US–Japan Security Treaty. *The Diplomat*, April 24. Accessed from http://thediplomat.com/2014/04/obama-senkakus-covered-under-us-japan-security-treaty/.

Panda, A. 2016. Return of the FONOP: US Navy Destroyer Asserts Freedom of Navigation in Paracel Islands. *The Diplomat*, January 31. Accessed March 27, 2017, from http://thediplomat.com/2016/01/return-of-the-fonop-us-navy-destroyer-asserts-freedom-of-navigation-in-paracel-islands/.

Posen, B.R. 2013. Pull Back: The Case for a Less Activist Foreign Policy. *Foreign Affairs*, 92(1), pp.116–128.

Posen, B.R. 2014. *Restraint: A New Foundation for US Grand Strategy.* Cornell University Press.

Posen, B.R., and Ross, A.L. 1996. Competing Visions of US Grand Strategy. *International Security*, 21(3), pp.5–53.

Pressman, J. 2008. *Warring Friends.* Cornell University Press.

Qiang, X. 2015. US–Vietnam Security Cooperation: Developments and Prospects. Chinese Institute of International Studies, May 11. Accessed March 27, 2017, from www.ciis.org.cn/english/2015-05/11/content_7894319.htm; www.theasanforum.org/vietnam-among-the-powers-struggle-cooperation/.

Reuters. 2016a. Japan Sends China Warning over Incursions Near Disputed Isles. January 12. Accessed March 27, 2017, from www.reuters.com/article/us-japan-china-senkaku-idUSKCN0UQ06F20160112.

Reuters. 2016b. Vietnam Protests after China Lands Plane on Disputed Spratly Islands. January 3. Accessed March 27, 2017, from www.theguardian.com/world/2016/jan/03/vietnam-protests-after-china-lands-plane-on-disputed-spratly-islands.

Reynolds, I. 2015. Japan Considers Sending Navy to Aid US in South China Sea. *Bloomberg*, November 19. Accessed March 27, 2017, from www.bloomberg.com/news/articles/2015-11-20/japan-considers-sending-navy-to-support-u-s-in-south-china-sea.

Russell, D.R. 2014. Opportunities and Challenges in the US–Japan and US–Republic of Korea Alliances. March 4. Accessed March 27, 2017, from www.state.gov/p/eap/rls/rm/2014/03/222903.htm.

Sagan, S. 1986. 1914 Revisited: Allies, Offense, and Instability. *International Security*, 11(2), pp.151–175.

Schelling, T.C. 2008 [1966]. *Arms and Influence.* Yale University Press.

Schroeder, P. 1972. World War One as Galloping Gertie: A Reply to Joachim Remak. *Journal of Modern History*, 44(3), pp.319–345.

Shifrinson, J.R. 2017. Trump and NATO: Old Wine in Gold Bottles? H-Diplo/ISSF Policy Series 1(5). Accessed September 29, 2017, from https://issforum.org/category/roundtables/policy.

Snyder, G.H. 1984. The Security Dilemma in Alliance Politics. *World Politics*, 36(4), pp.461–495.

Stoler, M.A. 2003. *Allies and Adversaries: The Joint Chiefs of Staff, the Grand Alliance, and US Strategy in World War II*. University of North Carolina Press.

Stone, N. 1966. Moltke–Conrad: Relations between the Austro-Hungarian and German General Staffs, 1909–14. *The Historical Journal*, 9(2), pp.201–228.

Torode, G. 2015. Vietnamese Military Grows to Face China Threat. *Reuters*, December 20. Accessed September 29, 2017, from www.japantimes.co.jp/news/2015/12/20/asia-pacific/vietnamese-military-grows-face-china-threat/#.Vr_r9nQrIy4.

Thucydides. 1972. *History of the Peloponnesian War.* Trans. Rex Warner and M.I. Finley. Penguin.

United States Senate Committee on Armed Services. 2015. Hearing to Receive Testimony on US Defense Policy Issues Pertaining to the Asia-Pacific Theater. April 14. Accessed from www.armed-services.senate.gov/imo/media/doc/15-37%20-%204-14-15.pdf.

US Pacific Command. 2015. TRANSCRIPT: Senate Armed Services Committee Hearing on the US Pacific Command & US Forces Korea. April 17. Accessed September 29, from www.pacom.mil/Media/SpeechesTestimony/tabid/6706/Article/585392/transcript-senate-armed-services-committee-hearing-on-the-us-pacific-command-us.aspx.

Valencia, M.J. 2016. Implications of the US Navy's FONOP Program. *The Japan Times*, January 27. Accessed September 29, 2017, from www.japantimes.co.jp/opinion/2016/01/27/commentary/world-commentary/implications-u-s-navys-fonop-program/#.Vr_Qr3QrIy5.

Van Evera, S. 1984. The Cult of the Offensive and the Origins of the First World War. *International Security*, 9(1), pp.58–107.

Vietnam Right Now. 2015. Vietnam and Philippines to Cooperate Against China. November 18. Accessed March 27, 2017, from http://vietnamrightnow.com/2015/11/vietnam-and-philippines-to-cooperate-against-china/.

Walt, S.M. 1985. Alliance Formation and the Balance of World Power. *International security*, 9(4), pp.3–43.

Waltz, K.N. 1964. The Stability of a Bipolar World. *Daedalus*, 93(3), pp.881–909.

Waltz, K.N. 1979. *Theory of International Politics.* Waveland Press.

White House. 2011. Remarks by President Obama to the Australian Parliament. November 17. Accessed March 27, 2017, from https://obamawhitehouse.archives.gov/the-press-office/2011/11/17/remarks-president-obama-australian-parliament.

White House. 2014. US–Japan Joint Statement: The United States and Japan: Shaping the Future of the Asia-Pacific and Beyond. April 25. Accessed March 27, 2017, from https://obamawhitehouse.archives.gov/the-press-office/2014/04/25/us-japan-joint-statement-united-states-and-japan-shaping-future-asia-pac.

Wright, T. 2015. Should America Power Down? *The American Interest*, August 14. Accessed March 27, 2017, from www.the-american-interest.com/2015/08/14/should-america-power-down/.

3

PRIMACY AND PROLIFERATION

Why security commitments don't prevent the spread of nuclear weapons

Brendan Rittenhouse Green

Halting the spread of nuclear weapons is a goal of American foreign policy that is nearly universally embraced. As historian Francis Gavin (2015: 11) recently put it, "strategies of [nuclear] inhibition have been an independent and driving feature of US national security policy for more than seven decades," and deserve recognition as a major American post-war grand strategic goal, alongside the containment of great power rivals and the promotion of an open international economy. Even analysts who tend to favor greater restraint in American commitments and de-prioritize nuclear threats after the Cold War have been unwilling to dismiss the problem of nuclear proliferation (Posen 2006).

Despite widespread agreement on the importance of stopping further increases in nuclear weapons, there has been little systematic assessment of how American grand strategy affects proliferation. As Frank Gavin notes, there is little evidence that US non-proliferation efforts are the reason why there are far fewer nuclear states than experts generally predicted (Gavin 2015: 39–40). The policymaking community nonetheless developed an implicit consensus: US political and military commitments abroad are an essential tool in preventing proliferation, and bear a large measure of responsibility for the small number of nuclear states in the world.

Lack of evidence aside, the consensus in favor of non-proliferation policy has a clear logic, which, though shared by a number of grand strategies, is articulated most forthrightly by advocates of primacy. The strategy of primacy—which has traveled lately under the gentler sounding name of "deep engagement"—relies on US alliances and military deployments to dampen "the most baleful effects of anarchy" (Preble and Mueller 2014). On one hand, as its advocates Stephen Brooks, John Ikenberry, and William Wohlforth argue, "the United States' overseas presence gives it the leverage to restrain partners from taking provocative action" (Brooks, Ikenberry, and Wohlforth 2012: 34). On the other, "its core alliance commitments also deter states with aspirations to regional hegemony from contemplating expansion," which in turn "make its partners more secure, reducing their incentive to adopt solutions to their problems that threaten others and thus stoke security dilemmas" (Brooks, Ikenberry, and Wohlforth 2012: 39). In short, American political commitments provide security to friends and rivals alike through their deterrent and restraining capabilities. Without these commitments, insecurity is likely to increase, accelerating nuclear proliferation.

The effectiveness of American commitments as anti-proliferation measures follows from three implications of primacy's logic. First, insecurity is the dominant cause of nuclear proliferation. As Brooks et al. note, many fear that in the absence of American protection, "states such as Egypt, Japan, South Korea, Taiwan, and Saudi Arabia all might choose to create nuclear forces." Second, proliferation begets proliferation: "It is unlikely that proliferation decisions by any of these actors would be the end of the game: they would likely generate pressure locally for more proliferation" (Brooks, Ikenberry, and Wohlforth 2012: 37). Third, American commitments give it the leverage to stop proliferation dominoes from falling. Nicholas Miller captures the essence of the claim: "US non-proliferation policy has played a central role in rendering nuclear domino predictions self-defeating," in part because "regional states that depend on the US economically or militarily are likely to be deterred from actively pursuing nuclear weapons by the threat of a rupture in relations with the United States" (Miller 2014b: 34, 72).

Advocates of grand strategic restraint usually make two counterclaims in an attempt to undermine non-proliferation's hold over policymakers. First, they argue that, in some cases, limited nuclear proliferation is good for American security. These arguments build a case for "proliferation optimism," claiming that the nuclear revolution makes serious war between nuclear armed states close to impossible. The threat to use nuclear weapons to stop a conventional invasion is perfectly credible, and therefore no challenger will ever dare to put the survival of their adversary on the line. It may be the case, restraint advocates concede, that the extensive spread of nuclear weapons to states with poor civilian control of the military, or other features suggesting they may not sufficiently approximate a rational unitary actor, is undesirable. But limited proliferation to proto-great powers and advanced industrial democracies like Germany and Japan would stabilize regional politics far better than less credible American promises ever can (Sagan and Waltz 2003; Mearsheimer 2001).

Second, activists for restraint often contend that there would be no return to global security competition if the US distanced itself from its allies and retreated from its forward-deployed positions. These claims are based on defensive realist and liberal claims that the causes of geopolitical competition have receded. In Asia, geography makes conquest difficult; Europe is stabilized by institutions, democracy, and mutually recognized borders; all possible battlefields are characterized by technology that produces defensive advantage; and all potential great powers have discovered that it is more efficient to trade than fight. In short, past historical competitions all occurred when armed conflict was much less costly, but many cross-cutting forces have conspired to raise the expense of war beyond the value of anything states might fight over (Craig et al. 2013).

I believe it is not wise to rest the case for restraint on such arguments, even where I lean toward accepting them. The second half of the Cold War showed how secure nuclear deterrents can be compatible with intense and dangerous security competition; proliferation could therefore be destabilizing. While there are many reasons to believe major war is less likely today than in the past, there are still a number of values over which states might risk its costs. They will certainly continue to prepare for war, and the prospect of a nuclear arms race in Asia or the Middle East is distinctly unappetizing.

In this essay I take a different approach: I challenge primacy's contentions that a world of increased insecurity will result in a sharp increase in nuclear proliferation, and that American political commitments are well suited to preventing such a world. I examine these claims through a survey of the political science literature on nuclear proliferation.

The first section reviews the literature on the motives that drive nuclear proliferation, the so-called "demand side" factors behind nuclear acquisition. I argue that there is an overwhelming scholarly focus on motives *other* than security as the driver of nuclear development activities. The second section reviews the nuclear domino hypothesis. I find that there is a substantial consensus that such dominoes do not fall. In short, if the scholarly center of gravity is correct, then American security commitments are the wrong tools for the job: they are intended to forestall motives that are uncommon and avert problems that do not exist.

However, the academic consensus on these issues is not total. A third section examines recent revisionist work contending that security motives explain most proliferation activities and that nuclear domino theory should be taken seriously. I argue in the fourth section that this work has merit and suggests a more nuanced attitude about the circumstances under which American political and military commitments will be effective anti-proliferation tools. Under some circumstances they may even be counterproductive.

The causes of nuclear proliferation

Primacy's argument for using political and military commitments to tamp down security competition presupposes that proliferation is motivated by security threats. Is this supposition consistent with our knowledge about the causes of nuclear proliferation?

Twenty years ago, the answer was yes. The first wave of literature on proliferation, beginning in the context of the late Cold War, more or less assumed security motives for nuclear acquisition. As Scott Sagan put it, in reviewing the then disjointed literature, scholarly "inattention appears to have been caused by the emergence of a near-consensus that the answer is obvious …. States will seek to develop nuclear weapons when they face a significant military threat to their security that cannot be met through alternative means; if they do not face such threats, they will willingly remain non-nuclear states" (Sagan 1996: 54). Or as Bradley Thayer summarized, "security is the only necessary and sufficient cause of nuclear proliferation" (Thayer 1995: 486).

However, as the systematic study of nuclear proliferation grew, the field turned away from its emphasis on security. Three major empirical patterns drove the shift. First, it would appear that security explanations vastly over-predicted the number of nuclear weapons states. According to Jacques Hymans, any theory of nuclear proliferation should start with "the basic fact of the history of nuclear proliferation: the large and fast-growing number of nuclear-weapons capable states, contrasted with the small and slow-growing number of actual nuclear weapons states" (Hymans 2006: 1). Many states face security threats, but comparatively few have achieved a nuclear arsenal.

Second, because the instances of nuclear proliferation are few, and the process of acquiring nuclear weapons long, scholars have tended to subdivide the dependent variable and ask theories of proliferation to explain this greater range of variation in decisions and non-decisions. For instance, one popular distinction is between different phases of nuclear programs: technological "exploration"; military "pursuit"; and weapons "acquisition" (Bleek 2010). With more observations to explain, the dominance of security concerns in a few prominent cases was naturally going to carry less weight.

Third, historical cases revealed observations that were anomalous from the security point of view—behavior that security motives struggled to explain. That is, if the theory is correct, and security concerns drive nuclear proliferation, these actions should not occur. States like Taiwan and South Korea, for example, pursued nuclear options but abandoned their programs short of acquisition without the disappearance of their major security threat. Similarly, states like Sweden and Iraq, situated in dangerous environments, never got very far with their nuclear programs. Finally, archival evidence produced at least a case that some "classic" instances of proliferation previously considered security-motivated are open to other interpretations: France, India, and South Africa (Sagan 1996: 65–71, 76–80).

As a result, recent proliferation literature focuses on different causal forces (Hymans 2011: 154). These include: sectoral economic preferences of ruling coalitions; the social identity of top leaders; the structure and competence of nuclear bureaucracies; and the diffusion of non-proliferation norms stemming from the Non-Proliferation Treaty (NPT).

Etel Solingen argues that the political economy of domestic coalitions drives nuclear ambition and abnegation. Internationalist coalitions, composed of export-intensive sectors, capital, skilled labor, professionals, and others, who benefit from economic openness, tend to oppose nuclearization because of its international costs. Pursuing nuclear capabilities increases regional security competition and creates unstable conditions unfavorable for business abroad. It also draws the ire of international actors who govern access to markets and capital. The opposite is true for nationalist coalitions, comprised of import-competing sectors, military-industrial complexes, state-subsidized interests, and ethno-religious nationalist groups. Nuclearization benefits such coalitions because it allows them to build large autonomous bureaucracies that suck up resources while also providing fodder for nationalist mobilization around security issues (Solingen 2007: 40–43). Solingen uses this model to explain the very different proliferation dynamics in East Asia and the Middle East.

Jacques Hymans offers an alternate model of nuclear proliferation rooted in political psychology. He argues, "To go nuclear is to take a leap in the dark" (Hymans 2006: 11). It is a classic example of a decision made under extreme uncertainty; one not amenable to the normal standards of cost–benefit analysis; one where the risks are incalculable. When faced with such momentous choices, decision-makers fall back on their own identities and worldviews. Most are cautious.

Hymans discovers one identity type as a driver of decisions to proliferate, which he calls "oppositional nationalism." Oppositional nationalists see the world in "us vs. them" terms, and view their own state as the equal or superior of the primary reference group. Threat perceptions of the other increase a felt need to act decisively, while pride increases a sense of relative power, control over events, and the desire to act autonomously (Hymans 2006: 25–40).

Hymans provides two other theories of nuclear proliferation that focus on the structure and competence of nuclear bureaucracies, as mediators and obstacles to states acting on security incentives. One stresses the institutional environment in which decisions to proliferate or abandon nuclear programs are made (Abraham 1998). Hymans argues that states with dedicated nuclear bureaucracies are more likely to have nuclear programs turned toward military ends. By contrast, institutional landscapes that divide nuclear decision-making across multiple organizations, subject them to checks and balances, and feature prominent roles for private economic actors and political interests groups are less likely to develop nuclear weapons (Hymans 2011).

Hymans also investigates how the technical and managerial acumen of nuclear bureaucracies impacts the probability of proliferation, whatever its motives. He notes that nuclear programs depend on effective management more than on raw skill or knowledge; highly skilled workers must be motivated and coordinated to produce cutting-edge results to tough timescales according to the highest technical standards (Hymans 2012: 22–29). Hymans uses his theory of nuclear weapons project efficiency to explain a number of cases, in particular shedding new and surprising light on the Iraqi and Chinese nuclear programs (Hymans 2012: 83, 126).

Finally, several scholars have stressed the importance of the norms and incentives resulting from NPT as a critical source of drying-up demand for nuclear proliferation. Maria Rublee argues that the NPT spawned international non-proliferation norms that encouraged actors to comply, due to either social pressure or habit (Rublee 2009: 16–20). In democracies—like Japan, Germany, and Sweden—this meant that those who favored the bomb faced domestic opposition and attacks on the legitimacy of their preferences, which in time helped transform them. In autocracies, like Libya and Egypt, compliance was more grudging, and required outside pressure, but was ultimately adopted in part because of its international normative benefits.

Andrew Coe and Jane Vaynman argue that the NPT reduces the demand for nuclear weapons. Most states will forgo nuclear weapons provided others will, they argue, if they can be sure the treaty will be enforced against occasional spoilers. Meanwhile, great powers have an interest in colluding to prevent nuclear proliferation, but only if the enforcement costs are not too high and if other great powers do not undermine the cartel (Coe and Vaynman 2015).

In sum, the literature is surprisingly clear: primacy presumes a security motive for proliferation that is not nearly as prevalent as its proponents expect. Such security concerns as they do exist are mediated by a number of forces that place serious obstacles in the path of a potential proliferator. To the extent that this research is correct, primacy's claims that US alliances tamp down on proliferation by eliminating the security fears that cause it are made more dubious.

Nuclear tipping points

Primacy's argument for political and military commitments also relies on the notion that a little proliferation goes a long way. That is, nuclear acquisition is a reactive phenomenon prone to cascades and tipping points, such that once a state develops nuclear weapons the probability of other regional states responding in kind abruptly rises. How does this proposition accord with the state of our knowledge?

The tipping-point hypothesis has long enjoyed widespread currency among policymakers. As Sagan summarizes, "Every time one state develops nuclear weapons to balance against its main rival, it also creates a nuclear threat to another state in the region, which then has to initiate its own nuclear weapons program to maintain its national security" (Sagan 1996: 57–58). However, as Nick Miller points out, nuclear dominoes are compatible with a variety of motives for proliferation, including "by strengthening the hand of domestic and bureaucratic forces that were already pushing a nuclear weapons program, tipping the balance in their favor, or … by creating a new demand for prestige" (Miller 2014b: 36; Hymans 2006: 208–216).

The cascade argument also possesses a certain empirical plausibility. The history of proliferation does look a bit like a "nuclear chain reaction." The United States won a race among the great powers to the bomb during World War II, where all the participants feared its acquisition by their competitors. The Soviet Union followed a mere four years later after Stalin instituted a crash program driven by the need to compete with the Americans. The Russian bomb in turn triggered British and French acquisition, while clashes with a nuclear United States in the 1950s and the Sino-Soviet split inspired China's test in 1964. This test deeply unsettled Asian politics, and resulted in an accelerated Indian nuclear program. After India's peaceful nuclear explosion in 1974, Pakistan was sure to follow (Sagan 1996: 58–59).

During the nuclear era, government intelligence analyses routinely forecast a rapidly growing nuclear club that would number dozens in the long term. These were driven in substantial part by predictions of reactive proliferation. The famous Gilpatric Committee report commissioned by President Lyndon Johnson warned that:

> The Chinese communist nuclear weapons program has brought particular pressure on India and Japan …. An Indian or Japanese decision to build nuclear weapons would probably produce a chain reaction of similar decisions by other countries, such as Pakistan, Israel, and the UAR. In these circumstances, it is unrealistic to hope that Germany and other European countries would not decide to develop their own nuclear weapons.
>
> *Committee on Nuclear Proliferation 1965: 174*

Despite the popularity of the nuclear domino theory among policymakers, the academic literature has turned against it. The reason is obvious: several decades of pessimistic proliferation forecasts based on falling dominoes were proved embarrassingly wrong by history. Moeed Yusuf notes that if all the "first tier" suspects for nuclear acquisition identified in such reports had become weapons states there would be nineteen nuclear powers today (Yusuf 2009: 61). Instead, as noted above, the number of technically capable nuclear states has grown, while the number of weapons states has remained small. Moreover, there was relatively little variation in the number of states in the "exploration" or "pursuit" phases of nuclear programs during the Cold War, despite instances of proliferation that ought to have caused domino behavior. After the Cold War, there has been a striking decline in nuclear interest, as more states abandon their programs and fewer states initiate new ones (Miller 2014a: 10–11).

The judgment of scholars has been scathing. Yusuf concludes that "an evident shortcoming of historical predictions was their inability to accurately estimate the pace of developments … the majority of [potential nuclear dominoes] never even came close to crossing the threshold. In fact, most did not even initiate a weapons program" (Yusuf 2009: 61). John Mueller suggests that projections of falling nuclear dominoes "have shown a want of prescience that approaches the monumental—even the pathological … [fear of a nuclear tipping point] continues to flourish despite the fact that it has thus far proven to be almost entirely wrong" (Mueller 2009: 89). Francis Gavin finds no "compelling evidence that a nuclear proliferation chain reaction will ever occur" (Gavin 2009: 18). A two-volume study led by William Potter and Gaukhar Mukhatzhanova cites a "consensus among the case study authors … that nuclear weapons spread is neither imminent nor likely to involve a process in which one country's pursuit of nuclear weapons leads to a 'chain reaction' involving other states" (Potter and Mukhatzhanova 2010: 337–338).

Research also suggests that even where security concerns matter for proliferation, their influence is more diffuse and complex than is generally believed. Thus, even where proliferation causes security fears, it may not beget more proliferation. Phillip Bleek's statistical analysis suggests that nuclear acquisition by regional competitors has only a modest effect on state exploration of nuclear programs and no impact on whether they pursue or acquire an arsenal. In contrast, a state's history of conventional military disputes with its rivals strongly impacts all three phases of nuclear development (Bleek 2010: 177). Bleek interprets these results to mean, in part, that states seek nuclear weapons for a particular sort of security—deterring attack, not because of security competition in general. That conclusion is consistent with other recent studies (Sechser and Fuhrmann 2013: 173–195). Thus, Bleek concludes that his "findings strongly contradict the conventional 'reactive proliferation' wisdom that underpins widespread predictions … of proliferation cascades, dominoes, tipping points, and the like" (Bleek 2010: 179).

The causes of nuclear weapons proliferation reviewed above offer a reason to reject nuclear dominoes and tipping points. As Potter and Mukhatzhanova summarize, "a fixation on security drivers … is apt to result in the neglect of important domestic economic and political constraints and to exaggerate the propensity of states to proliferate," even given proliferation elsewhere (Potter and Mukhatzhanova 2010: 338). Hymans' focus on individual psychology, for instance, implies that:

> Leaders' preferences are actually not highly contingent on what other states decide. Therefore, proliferation tomorrow will probably remain as rare as proliferation today, with no single instance of proliferation causing a cascade of new nuclear weapons states.
>
> *Hymans 2006: 225–226*

Likewise, Solingen's "emphasis on political economic factors" suggests that one state's nuclear decisions will not directly drive another's. In the same vein, Hymans' other work implies major bureaucratic constraints on reactive proliferation. States are not likely to shuck off multiple nuclear veto players with ease, even if their international environment seems more dangerous. Finally, if NPT scholarship is correct, the treaty is likely to provide at least a modest barrier to reactive proliferation. States that absorb its norms, à la Rublee, will be less inclined to proliferate or at least more constrained in their decision-making. States that perceive the treaty as a grand bargain, as posited by Coe and Vaynman, are likely to stick to the agreement so long as the great powers appear to be sanctioning the rule-breaking states.

Overall, the political science literature undermines primacy's claims about nuclear dominoes, and the probability that a little insecurity will spawn spirals of proliferation. American alliance commitments, in so far as this research is correct, are correspondingly diminished in their usefulness as an anti-proliferation measure.

Against the grain: new work on security motives and tipping points

Scholarship on nuclear proliferation is not uniformly hostile to the assumptions of primacy, however. Dissenters to the research just described have emerged in recent years.

A strategic theory of nuclear proliferation

Nuno Monteiro and Alexandre Debs (2014) have recently proposed a theory of nuclear proliferation rooted in a state's security environment. Their innovation shifts the locus of analysis to the security environment that a state faces in the period before it obtains nuclear weapons. They envision nuclear proliferation as a lengthy process that is contingent upon interaction between the proliferating state, its adversaries, and its allies.

Monteiro and Debs' argument has many moving parts, but its basic logic is fairly straightforward. The major impulse that creates a willingness to proliferate is the degree to which states perceive that they will gain a "security benefit" from nuclear acquisition—that is, how much will proliferation change the balance of power? If the security benefits exceed the material costs of a nuclear weapons program, states are willing to proliferate. The major constraint on proliferation is whether other states can credibly threaten them with preventive war before they do so. If the costs of preventive war are lower to an adversary than accepting a state's proliferation, then that state lacks the opportunity to proliferate: it will either be deterred from doing so by explicit or implicit threats of preventive war, or it will (foolishly) try to proliferate in a clandestine fashion.

Thus, for Monteiro and Debs, there is a sweet spot for potential proliferators in the balance of power: if nuclear weapons only modestly improve a state's position, they are not worth the trouble of a program lasting a decade or more and costing billions of dollars; if they improve a state's position too much (relative to the costs of preventive war), the incentive for rivals to quash them with military force is large enough to deter investment, or at least prevent success. The major theoretical question is: what factors determine the security benefit of proliferation and the cost of preventive war? Monteiro and Debs identify three variables: the level of security threat facing a potential proliferator; its relative power vis-à-vis its adversaries; and the level and reliability of any outside security guarantees its allies provide.

Monteiro and Debs' theory is powerful because it promises to remedy many of the flaws in the original wave of security-focused literature on nuclear proliferation. Their framework no longer faces the problem of "over-predicting" proliferation, since the simple existence of security threats is not sufficient to generate a nuclear program. Similarly, the problem of anomalous observations—states abandoning programs before a threat disappears or refusing to start them despite living in dangerous neighborhoods—appears less strange when the full suite of alliance and adversarial relationships is considered. Finally, though Monteiro and Debs aim to explain only the outcome of nuclear acquisition or restraint, their variables could theoretically explain why states advance greater or lesser distances down the nuclear path. That is, they could explain a state's decisions to explore, pursue, or abandon programs as well, exploring the same rich set of observations as its domestic political competitors.

Tipping points as self-defeating prophecy

Nicholas Miller argues that the consensus against nuclear tipping points is much too strong. Nuclear dominoes do not fall because they provoke outside response. US non-proliferation efforts hide the best evidence of nuclear tipping points.

Miller documents that nuclear testing—in particular, the 1964 Chinese nuclear test—can lead to reactive nuclear behavior in the form of nuclear weapons exploration and pursuit by a number of countries. After the Chinese test, India, Taiwan, Australia, Japan, and Indonesia all began nuclear programs or intensified existing ones. Similarly, in the Middle East, "Egypt, Iran, Iraq, Syria, and Saudi Arabia all considered or pursued nuclear weapons to varying degrees during this time period, and all were at least partially motivated by the Israeli nuclear capability or the efforts of other regional states to match Israel's capability" (Miller 2014b: 69)

This behavior remains obscured because the United States took numerous steps to prevent it from spiraling into a proliferation cascade. Miller claims that the Chinese nuclear test set off a burst of non-proliferation activity in the US government from 1964 to 1968, culminating in the signing of the NPT. During this period, Washington used international law, promises of security guarantees, and economic carrots and sticks to slow down the reactive proliferation caused by the Chinese test (Miller 2014b).

These policies stopped the fall of nuclear dominoes and concealed the existence of potential nuclear tipping points, Miller argues. Using statistical analysis of sanctions, Miller shows that US policy explains the decline in new nuclear programs. States understand that positive security and economic relationships with Washington require good nuclear behavior, reducing willingness to start nuclear programs. The success of non-proliferation policies is hidden because of a selection effect: sanctions are only applied to states that do not value good relations with America and are not dependent on it for economic and security goods, making sanctions ineffective tools (Miller 2014c).

Miller and Or Rabinowitz also argue that US policy has prevented nuclear dominoes from falling even after states have crossed the nuclear threshold. They argue that three US non-proliferation failures—Israel, South Africa, and Pakistan—are more successful than they appear. Even after these states obtained nuclear weapons, the US brokered deals "to prevent them from conducting nuclear tests, publically declaring their capabilities, engaging in weaponization, transferring nuclear materials to other states, or some combination thereof." The success of these post-proliferation efforts helped to tamp down reactive proliferation in other states (Rabinowitz and Miller 2015: 47).

Implications for primacy as a non-proliferation measure

The new work on the security causes of nuclear proliferation and the validity of the nuclear domino theory is more favorable for primacy's recommendations concerning American alliances and military guarantees as instruments of non-proliferation policy. But the implications are more nuanced than they might appear at first blush.

If Monteiro and Debs are correct, then security is a central concern of potential proliferators. We have simply been looking in the wrong place for evidence of this concern, focusing too heavily on the difference between a state's security environment before and after it proliferates, and not enough on the strategic interaction between proliferators, adversaries, and allies in the long run-up to the nuclear threshold. Furthermore, their theory suggests a strong role for US alliance commitments and military guarantees as tools of non-proliferation. They argue that US security commitments can be used as carrots rewarding strong partners willing to forgo nuclear weapons and as sticks to coerce weak allies who would flounder against rivals absent US protection. Likewise, if Miller is right, then proliferation is more likely to cause a domino effect than the current literature expects. The implication is clear: American alliance and security commitments are useful instruments of non-proliferation.

This picture needs to be qualified: the research just discussed does indeed cast American commitments in a more favorable light, but it also highlights previously under-emphasized drawbacks and limitations of Washington's alliances. For instance, while Monteiro and Debs identify a sweet spot where American alliances can be used to coerce its protégés, they also show how alliance relationships can facilitate nuclear proliferation. This occurs when the protégé is not confident enough in an ally's guarantee to abandon its nuclear programs, but its adversaries are confident enough in that guarantee to preclude launching a preventive war. Such situations may occur frequently: the common wisdom in the defense community during the Cold War was that it took 5% uncertainty about the probability of American retaliation to deter the Soviet Union from invading Europe, but 95% certainty about American retaliation to reassure NATO allies about Washington's commitment. American commitments may often be strong enough to drag the US into war, but too weak to credibly restrain allies.

Weak allies, like Taiwan and South Korea, present opportunities for restraint as well as for primacy under Monteiro and Debs' theory. If they are correct, then the threat of abandonment can be used to coerce weak allies to abandon their nuclear programs. But why stop with the threat? Actual abandonment will leave them at the mercy of their adversary's preventive war threats, which should restrain nuclearization.

In other words, we do not need to retain American alliances to gain the coercive benefits posited by Debs and Monteiro. Each alliance with weak states can be evaluated on its own merits—the proliferation leverage is a bonus accompanying any alliance decision. It may even make sense to abandon an ally or two simply to encourage others; even strong allies might think twice about nuclearization if they see that the United States is serious about cutting off those who defy its wishes on such important issues. If Seoul and Taipei will adopt Washington's preferred policies while under its protection, they will nevertheless be hesitant to proliferate in the face of a Chinese threat. And such an example would be instructive to US partners in Europe and the Middle East, the next time they defy American requests.

At the same time, the strategic approach to proliferation highlights the dangers that strong allies pose: they can extort endless streams of concessions from the United States. The only way to stop them from acquiring nuclear weapons is to assure them that American guarantees cover every foreseeable circumstance. This is a recipe for a never-ending cycle of hand-wringing and special pleading for goodies—which, not coincidentally, is how many characterize American alliance relationships (Posen 2014). Even an ally who is reasonably satisfied with Washington's promises will be able to credibly engage in this type of behavior. An ally with sincere concerns will be near impossible to satisfy. Its concerns will probably be based on genuine differences of national interest.

Miller's work does imply that reactive proliferation may be more worrisome than most scholars have imagined, but it leaves open the questions of exactly how worrisome, and precisely how useful American alliance and military commitments are for combating it. It is not clear from Miller's research whether there are any cases for which his counterfactual expectation absent American non-proliferation policy is nuclear acquisition.

How far do nuclear dominoes tilt before they fall? Evidently pretty far, if four states can obtain nuclear weapons whose existence is common knowledge internationally, but refrain from incentivizing a nuclear cascade by virtue of the fact that they don't acknowledge their nuclear status or test a weapon. In the Middle East, treated only briefly by Miller, lots of reactive behavior apparently just petered out after a while, without the kind of dedicated efforts from Washington that we observe in other cases. The Israelis may declare, in the surrealist fashion of Rene Magritte, *Ceci n'est pas une nuke*, but who believes them? Nuclear dominoes in the Middle East appear as Weebles that wobble but don't fall down. It may be that proliferation does naturally trigger exploratory behavior, as Bleek's work cited above argues, but that the cycle stops there.

Along the same lines, it seems evident that not all nuclear dominoes are created equal. The Chinese nuclear test clearly triggered a fair bit of reactive behavior, as did more opaque Israeli nuclear proliferation. But both of India's nuclear tests appear to have been limited in their domino effects on Pakistan, which is hardly surprising. Moreover, the Vela Incident of 1979, where Israel (and possibly South Africa) tested an atomic weapon in the South Atlantic, does not look to have triggered any falling nuclear dominoes, despite an obvious US government cover-up denying the event was a nuclear test.

The importance of American security commitments in Miller's research also needs to be caveated somewhat. First, it is clear that in several cases, all Washington's best efforts were insufficient to keep several states from crossing the nuclear threshold. It may be, as Miller argues, that subsequent US bargaining succeeded in ensuring nuclear opacity in these states. But what, if anything, the US gained from its efforts to promote this opacity is unclear, since it is uncertain whether we should expect a high degree of reactive proliferation if acquisition occurred openly.

Second, in some cases, the US was unwilling to prioritize non-proliferation highly enough to achieve its goals: it would not pay the costs of making a credible security guarantee to India, Israel, or Pakistan. If it would not pay the costs in these cases, one wonders how decision-makers will assess similar cases in the future. Would the US really be willing to make iron-clad promises to Taiwan, for instance, if they were necessary to prevent a nuclear program? Third, Miller defines sanctions broadly, and identifies a range of powerful tools in arguing that the US has tamped down reactive behavior. Most of these tools would still be available even absent American alliances.

In sum, new dissenting work on the security causes of nuclear proliferation and the incidence of nuclear tipping points does cast primacy's preferred policies in a more favorable light. However, Monteiro and Debs' insights also underscore additional dangers for proliferation evident in alliances, as well as opportunities for leaders who favor restraint. Miller convincingly argues that reactive proliferation is more common than advertised, but the scale of the problem, and the degree to which alliance and military commitments are the solution, have yet to be demonstrated.

Conclusions

It is difficult to imagine an interest more important to American national security policy than preventing a nuclear detonation on the homeland. Even a nuclear exchange that took place elsewhere in the world would be sure to produce such horrendous outcomes, and so radically reshape international politics, that the consequences for the United States cannot be lightly dismissed. The grinding logic of statistical probability means that these dangers can only rise as the number of nuclear states increases. The more actors with nuclear weapons, the more potential dyads exist for nuclear war; the more opportunity there is for those weapons to fall into the hands of terrorists; the more likely it is that organizational pathologies will result in irrationally risky nuclear decision-making; the more likely it is that some variable outside the austere logic of mutual deterrence will end up determining outcomes. Even if these risks are small, nuclear proliferation multiplies them, and the consequences are massive. In principle, therefore, it is worth paying something to prevent the spread of nuclear weapons in the right circumstances.

That logic is why policymakers display such unanimous support for nuclear inhibition as a goal of American foreign policy. In a world where genuine dangers to American security are few and far between, the potential negative consequences of nuclear proliferation stand out. They serve as something of a trump card in the grand strategic debate between primacy and restraint. In one recent exchange, primacy advocates Brooks, Ikenberry, and Wohlforth retreated from a number of security-based justifications for American political and military commitments, substituting instead the threat that increased international competition might pose to the international economic and institutional order. But they retain their emphasis on the potential consequences of nuclear use (Craig et al. 2013). Primacy's simple syllogism—retrenchment increases insecurity; insecurity causes proliferation; proliferation begets more proliferation; while military and political engagement reduce all of the preceding variables—is a powerful weapon against efforts to restrain American commitments.

But according to the large mass of literature in political science, primacy's syllogism is flawed. At its heart is the strong intuition that security concerns represent the core reason for acquiring nuclear weapons—an intuition many of the realist champions of restraint share. Yet if we are to take the mainstream of research on "demand side" drivers of proliferation seriously, then this motive is far less powerful than either the policymaking world or the grand strategy debate generally acknowledge. Author after author emphasizes instead the multiple and wide-ranging set of constraints that confront would-be proliferators. Even if US withdrawal were to increase regional insecurity, security concerns have high hills to climb in order to push states toward the fateful step of nuclear acquisition. Proliferation has been a historically slow and haphazard process, and is likely to remain so.

Primacy's arguments receive their strongest support from relatively recent, dissenting research. But this research—impressive as it is—cuts in multiple directions. If Monteiro and Debs are correct, then US commitments will incentivize nuclear proliferation as often as they deter it. The weak states that Washington's mentorship are most likely to influence are also the least likely to proliferate if its protection is withdrawn. If Miller is correct, dominoes may indeed be more likely to fall than the literature suspects, but it is unclear how much more likely. If Hymans or Solingen is right, then there are strong internal impediments to proliferation even in the face of a regional state's nuclear acquisition. Moreover, a number of sanctions will remain available for influencing the calculations of would-be proliferators.

Looking to the future, what can be said about the odds of proliferation in a world with greatly weakened alliance commitments? East Asia, where the chance of major war with a regional power is greatest, would appear to have a number of factors pushing against further proliferation after American withdrawal. Regional allies are dominated by internationalist, trade-oriented coalitions unlikely to risk the consequences of American economic coercion. While their legal-rational Weberian bureaucracies would likely make them more technically adept at weaponization, these same bureaucracies provide a number of veto points for any decision to do so. In any case, there are not so many oppositional nationalists in these democratic polities who might be willing to take the fateful leap. Finally, South Korea and Taiwan are weak, making them exposed to Chinese coercion without American protection. Beijing is not likely to look kindly on either state proliferating.

The trajectory of proliferation in the Middle East, absent continued American efforts to manage its politics, is more uncertain. Nuclear bureaucracies in the region are more likely to suffer from neo-patrimonial management practices, which will make nuclear acquisition difficult. Still, the Iranian nuclear program has obtained a reasonable level of sophistication, even if it took thirty years. Saudi Arabia, Egypt, Turkey, and other regional actors have increasingly professional military bureaucracies, suggesting that if properly motivated they might produce a technically competent program. If the nuclear deal between Tehran and the P5+1 were to collapse, and Iran to return to its previous enrichment activities, such motivation might exist in ample supply.

Moreover, other restraining forces are less prevalent in the Middle East. The concentration of political power in the hands of autocrats suggests there would be few veto points to obstruct a leader's decision to pursue the bomb. The domestic politics of these societies suggest that oppositional nationalism is not uncommon, so the right kind of leader might be available. The region is permeated by trade restrictions and politically dominated by inward-facing coalitions resistant to US economic pressure. With Israeli threats of preventive war against Iran proven hollow, the only systemic constraint on proliferation is the threat of US preventive attack. Fears of dominoes will be better founded if there are several ongoing nuclear programs in the region, rather than one dubiously disguised nuclear arsenal.

These speculations have three implications. First, contrary to the common wisdom, the likelihood of nuclear proliferation in East Asia may not rise very much following US retrenchment; such a withdrawal is thus far less dangerous for nuclear reasons than usually imagined. Second, the fulfillment (and eventual extension) of the P5+1's deal with Iran should remain a top non-proliferation priority, since the abrogation of this agreement is likely a condition for nuclear competition in the Middle East. Third, the United States will probably not be able to do without the threat of force if it wishes to manage proliferation in the region. Monteiro and Debs' and Coe and Vaynman's research suggests that credible threats of counter-proliferation actions against rogue states remain essential for dealing with proliferators not numbered among American friends.

In short, the political science literature is not all good news for advocates of restraint. Nevertheless, on our current evidence, primacy's core propositions about nuclear proliferation are probably mistaken, or at least greatly overstated. Restraint is therefore significantly more viable, even adopting the traditional assumptions that have motivated policy debate. Policymakers should be told as much.

References

Abraham, I. 1998. *The Making of the Indian Atomic Bomb: Science, Secrecy and the Postcolonial State*. Zed Books.

Bleek, P.C. 2010. Why Do States Proliferate? Quantitative Analysis of the Exploration, Pursuit, and Acquisition of Nuclear Weapons. In Potter, W.C., and Mukhatzhanova, G., eds, *Forecasting Nuclear Proliferation in the 21st Century: The Role of Theory, Volume 1*. Stanford University Press, pp.159–192.

Brooks, S.G., Ikenberry, G.J., and Wohlforth, W.C. 2012. Don't Come Home, America: The Case against Retrenchment. *International Security*, 37(3), pp.7–51.

Coe, A.J., and Vaynman, J. 2015. Collusion and the Nuclear Nonproliferation Regime. *The Journal of Politics*, 77(4), pp.983–997.

Committee on Nuclear Proliferation. 1965, January 21. In Foreign Relations of the United States (FRUS), 1964–1968, Vol. 11, p.174.

Craig, C., Friedman, B.H., Green, B.R., Logan, J., Brooks, S.G., Ikenberry, G.J., and Wohlforth, W.C. 2013. Debating American Engagement: The Future of US Grand Strategy. *International Security*, 38(2), pp.181–199.

Gavin, F.J. 2009. Same as It Ever Was: Nuclear Alarmism, Proliferation, and the Cold War. *International Security*, 34(3), pp.7–37.

Gavin, F.J. 2015. Strategies of Inhibition: US Grand Strategy, the Nuclear Revolution, and Nonproliferation. *International Security*, 40(1), pp.9–46.

Hymans, J.E. 2006. *The Psychology of Nuclear Proliferation: Identity, Emotions and Foreign Policy.* Cambridge University Press.

Hymans, J.E. 2011. Veto Players, Nuclear Energy, and Nonproliferation: Domestic Institutional Barriers to a Japanese Bomb. *International Security*, 36(2), pp.154–189.

Hymans, J.E. 2012. *Achieving Nuclear Ambitions: Scientists, Politicians, and Proliferation.* Cambridge University Press.

Mearsheimer, J.J. 2001. The Future of the American Pacifier. *Foreign Affairs*, September/October, pp.46–61.

Miller, N.L. 2014a. Hegemony and Nuclear Proliferation. Doctoral dissertation, Massachusetts Institute of Technology.

Miller, N.L. 2014b. Nuclear Dominoes: A Self-Defeating Prophecy? *Security Studies*, 23(1), pp.33–73.

Miller, N.L. 2014c. The Secret Success of Nonproliferation Sanctions. *International Organization*, 68(4), pp.913–944.

Monteiro, N.P., and Debs, A. 2014. The Strategic Logic of Nuclear Proliferation. *International Security*, 39(2), pp.7–51.

Mueller, J. 2009. *Atomic Obsession: Nuclear Alarmism from Hiroshima to al-Qaeda.* Oxford University Press.

Posen, B.R. 2006. *Nuclear-Armed Iran: A Difficult But Not Impossible Policy Problem.* Century Foundation.

Posen, B.R. 2014. *Restraint: A New Foundation for US Grand Strategy.* Cornell University Press.

Potter, W.C., and Mukhatzhanova, G., eds, 2010. *Forecasting Nuclear Proliferation in the 21st Century*, Vol. 2. Stanford University Press.

Preble, C.A., and Mueller, J., eds, 2014. *A Dangerous World? Threat Perception and US National Security.* Cato Institute.

Rabinowitz, O., and Miller, N.L. 2015. Keeping the Bombs in the Basement: US Nonproliferation Policy toward Israel, South Africa, and Pakistan. *International Security*, 40(1), pp.47–86.

Rublee, M.R. 2009. *Nonproliferation Norms: Why States Choose Nuclear Restraint.* University of Georgia Press.

Sagan, S.D. 1996. Why Do States Build Nuclear Weapons? Three Models in Search of a Bomb. *International Security*, 21(3), pp.54–86.

Sagan, S.D., and Waltz, K. 2003. Why Do States Build Nuclear Weapons? Three Models in search of a Bomb. In Waltz, K., and Sagan, S.D., eds, *The Spread of Nuclear Weapons: A Debate Renewed.* W.W Norton & Company.

Sechser, T.S., and Fuhrmann, M. 2013. Crisis Bargaining and Nuclear Blackmail. *International Organization*, 67(1), pp.173–195.

Solingen, E. 2007. *Nuclear Logics: Contrasting Paths in East Asia and the Middle East.* Princeton University Press.

Thayer, B.A. 1995. The Causes of Nuclear Proliferation and the Utility of the Nuclear Non-Proliferation Regime. *Security Studies*, 4(3), pp.463–519.

Yusuf, M. 2009. *Predicting Proliferation: The History of the Future of Nuclear Weapons.* Brookings Institution.

4

RESTRAINT AND OIL SECURITY

Eugene Gholz

Oil underpins transportation, some important industrial processes, and modern military power. Consequently, political disruptions in oil-producing regions that have the potential to interfere with oil markets, interrupt supplies, and elevate short-term prices might impose significant costs on major oil-consuming countries like the United States. Thus prosperity and security, two of the key goals of US grand strategy, rest on access to reliable oil supply. Because different strategic choices may affect reliable supply, debates about oil security (or, more broadly, energy security, although in most cases the real focus is on oil) have long played a major role in grand strategy debates. Alleged threats to reliable oil supply and efforts to reduce political-military shocks to the oil market have justified both military interventions and peacetime military alliances, the headline grand strategy choices.

The current US grand strategy, often referred to as "deep engagement," ranks the Persian Gulf as one of the three key regions of the world in which the United States has strategic interests, specifically including the protection of oil transportation from the region to global markets (Brooks and Wohlforth 2016: 118–120, 187–189).[1] The United States maintains military forces at bases in Bahrain, Kuwait, Oman, Qatar, and the United Arab Emirates and has close diplomatic relations (a tacit if not a formal military alliance) with Saudi Arabia and the other members of the Gulf Cooperation Council. At times, the United States has intervened with military force to promote political development in oil-rich regions, trying to encourage stability and solve "above-ground problems" that limit oil production; though such democracy-promoting interventions may not be deemed necessary in all versions of deep engagement, they are an ever-present temptation under the current strategy, which justifies them on security grounds at least as much as on humanitarian grounds (Yergin 2006; Barnes, Jaffe, and Morse 2004; Yetiv 2015). Conceptually, the argument for deep engagement rests on the idea that US hegemonic leadership tamps down local conflicts and provides a public good by protecting oil supply and transportation that benefits all oil consumers linked to the unified global oil market (Brooks and Wohlforth 2016: 156–161; Rovner and Talmadge 2014).

The grand strategy of restraint seeks the same goals of security and prosperity (and liberty), but it offers different estimates of the threat and of the effectiveness of various means of addressing international security challenges. It does not rest on arguments that oil is unimportant to the United States, that the United States should seek autarky, or that balance between US domestic oil supply and demand would insulate the United States from fluctuations in global oil markets. It recognizes that Persian Gulf oil supplies make an important contribution to the global oil supply and that the security situation in the Persian Gulf bears monitoring by US strategic intelligence assets. However, restraint holds that the threats to US security and prosperity connected to Persian Gulf oil supply are now quite limited, and unless long-term intelligence suggests that those threats are changing dramatically, neither US military presence nor attempts to actively shape the security environment in the Persian Gulf can constructively add to US security and prosperity.

Under a strategy of restraint, the United States military would continue to patrol the blue-water maritime commons, but it would stay away from the relatively small contested zones where local land-based military forces could threaten the American assets (Posen 2003). In those contested zones, the provision of oil supply creates private benefits for oil producers, not public goods; the public-goods aspects of the oil market come in the economic policies of demand management or perhaps in the blue-water commons that would still be protected under the strategy of restraint. The argument for US global leadership specifically through military commitments to the Persian Gulf is very weak. Conceptually, restraint rests on the resilience of the oil market that limits the threat and impact of severe political-military disruptions, on the inability of US forward military presence to tamp down regional conflicts in the Persian Gulf, and on the lack of need for an outside power acting as a regional hegemon to protect oil supplies. This chapter develops the theory and provides empirical evidence to support the US grand strategy of restraint with respect to the global oil market.

Oil market resilience: no need for deep engagement[2]

The fear that motivates deep engagement advocates to propose US alliances, forward military presence, and even military interventions to protect oil access is that supply disruptions will translate into sudden spikes in the price of oil. Because the price elasticity of demand for oil is quite low – that is, large changes in price lead to only very small changes in the amount of oil consumed in the short run – such supply-driven price surges can dramatically reduce consumers' buying power and, through several economic mechanisms, lead to recessions (Vincent 2016). Grand strategy may make reasonable investments in the use of military power to protect US (or even global) prosperity. However, if the oil market itself adjusts to supply disruptions relatively quickly, the costs of political-military shocks will be relatively low, reducing the costs that the United States should be willing to bear to try to prevent the political-military shocks (Glaser and Kelanic 2016). Because of oil market resilience, deep engagement is unnecessary.

Supply, demand, and the price of oil

Supply depends on the difficulty (and hence cost) of oil exploration and production and on companies' economic decisions about how much money to spend looking for new oil fields, developing pumping capacity from the fields they find, and filling pipelines with oil, day-in and day-out. Prices and expectations about future prices drive fluctuations in oil supply. Oil companies, some of which are owned by the governments of countries with large reserves, decide how much to invest in exploration, new extraction technologies, refining, and transportation infrastructure, and whether to pay large upfront costs to tap difficult-to-reach fields. These major decisions – more than geological constraints – determine how much oil can be produced in the coming decades.[3] In the shorter term, the amount of oil that companies supply varies because they change the effort they put into enhanced oil recovery and other techniques to encourage oil flow (e.g., pumping more oil out of a field by heating it underground to increase its flow rate or by pumping water into the field to displace the oil, forcing it to the surface). Companies also manage the amount of inventory they hold above ground: even if oil flows out of a field at a nearly steady rate, the company that owns that oil does not necessarily sell it at that same rate. When they judge prices to be high, they sell more; price troughs encourage them to hold or expand their inventories, reducing supply in the short term.

Oil prices do not merely affect oil supply – they also play a key role in determining global demand. In the short term, demand does not change much in response to price fluctuations. People need to drive to work and heat their houses even if oil prices soar, so they tend to cut expenses elsewhere rather than go without oil. Knowing that short-term demand is relatively inelastic, some industrial consumers and oil market brokers hold inventories of oil to protect themselves against supply fluctuations, or invest in futures contracts that hedge against the risk of price spikes. Consumers' inventory management also contributes to the short-term supply–demand balance that sets the market price of oil. Day-to-day prices may bounce around quite a bit as consumption, extraction, and inventory strategies adjust, but that volatility is centered on a price level determined by real supply and demand (Adelman 2002; Verleger 2006).

These arguments do *not* rest on the (unreasonable) assumption that companies and countries always act rationally, or that profit motives always determine foreign policy choices. The overarching message is simply that market forces (rather than military deployments) are the key factors that affect oil supply and prices. The United States does not need to be militarily active – or confrontational – to allow the oil market to function.

Political risk and cartels

Market forces shape oil prices, but they do not act alone. More than in most other industries, political risk tempers companies' enthusiasm for making expensive investments because many oil-producing regions are politically volatile. Will local governments nationalize companies' investments or raise taxes and fees for future extraction? Will terrorists destroy key equipment, or will a war disrupt the flow of oil to markets? In essence, companies explore and drill less intensively in unstable regions than they would otherwise because the expected costs from the political risks must be added to the purely economic costs. Companies must expect oil prices to rise by an extra margin before they are willing to invest in volatile regions.

Oil companies understand political risk; they have made their profits by dealing with it (Yergin 1991; Nowell 1994). The big corporations each manage a portfolio of investments in different parts of the world, increasing the likelihood that at least one of their investments will be affected by political events at any given time but reducing the probability that a substantial fraction of their oil revenue will be disrupted all at once. Because oil companies' investments account for a baseline level of political risk, that baseline is built into the overall level of today's available oil supply (Hill 2004). In times when little goes wrong politically, an unexpectedly high level of oil will be available on world markets, and oil prices may fall; conversely, in especially unlucky times, oil prices may temporarily rise.

In this framework, changes in risk affect the future supply of oil. The risk of nationalization or *ex post* renegotiation of fees and taxes depresses investment by international oil firms, and an increase in the estimated level of that risk can have a significant effect on investment and future supply (Bohn and Deacon 2000). Similarly, any increase in the expected frequency of physical disruptions at oil facilities – such as from terrorist attacks or wars – depresses investment levels (Frynas and Mellahi 2003). In sum, political risk affects the overall level and geographic location of investments in the oil industry, but it does not change the fundamental supply dynamic: the quantity of oil available today depends on the investment decisions made in the past.

Political risk is not the only necessary adjustment to the basic supply–demand framework in oil markets. The world's major oil exporters have formed a cartel – the Organization of Petroleum Exporting Countries (OPEC) – to try to affect prices by controlling supply. The cartel members negotiate agreements to mute the normal, competitive market pressure to produce up to the point where price equals marginal cost.[4]

While the logic is simple, making a cartel work is difficult. First, even monopolists are uncertain about the actual strength of demand for their product, and OPEC members often disagree about how much to restrict supply (Gately 1984: 1109; Stevens 1995: 867–868; Moran 1987: 602). They also often disagree about how much production to expect from countries that are not members of the cartel (Stevens 1995: 863–864). Second, even if the members can agree about the ideal level of production, they have to allocate market shares among themselves. Huge sums of money are at stake in this zero-sum negotiation; not surprisingly, agreements are often hard to reach (Adelman 2002; Griffin and Neilson 1994: 544–558). Finally, even when OPEC members completely agree about total production and the allocation of production quotas, each has a short-term interest in cheating, because each producer can increase *its own* profit by exceeding its quota. The decline in oil prices in the early 1980s, for example, is generally explained as a result of widespread cheating among OPEC producers. The Saudis tried to compensate for this cheating by cutting back their own production until 1986, when they gave up and opened the taps (Evenett, Levenstein, and Suslow 2001: 1223; Adelman 1995: 4–5, 30; Griffin and Neilson 1994: 545, 557–558).

These challenges to cartel management lead some analysts to conclude that all of OPEC's public maneuvering is just political theater with no real effect on actual market dynamics (e.g. Colgan 2014). It is almost certainly true that OPEC has more influence at some times than at others, because OPEC's difficulty managing oil supply varies depending on political, technical, and market conditions; member countries change their investment and production strategies depending on their short-term political needs.[5] If investment and production patterns or political events change the number of key players in the OPEC negotiations, the cartel management task will change, too. Agreements are easier to reach and cheating is easier to detect and punish if fewer players are involved (Spar 1994: 5; Evenett, Levenstein, and Suslow 2001: 1223). Moreover, cartels work better when the members are willing to sacrifice some of today's profits for the long-term benefits of a strong cartel, and the political and market conditions in the OPEC member states determine how much each country will sacrifice for future gains (Spar 1994: 20–23; Griffin and Xiong 1997: 302–308). Each time the global oil supply-and-demand situation changes, OPEC members have to adjust their cartel agreement, providing another opportunity for a breakdown in cartel cohesion and an opportunity for the amount of oil flowing onto world markets to increase compared with the level that OPEC had preferred to offer in the past (Bohi and Quandt 1984: 18).

Overall, like political risk, cartel behavior does not change the underlying importance of supply and demand in determining the market price for oil. It simply modifies the supply–demand balance, implying that an unusually large amount of spare production capacity will often be available and concentrating the likely response to supply disruptions in a few key countries that participate actively in cartel management, at least in those times when the cartel is working. On other occasions, when cartel cohesion happens to be weak, the oil market functions more like a normal, competitive market in which a large number of price-takers each adjust their investments in line with shifts in political risk and adjust the quantity that they sell in line with shifts in market price (Gholz and Press 2001).

The market response to political-military shocks

Left to their own devices, buyers and sellers of oil have strong incentives to adapt to oil shocks, bringing new oil into the market to compensate for oil taken out by disruptions. This compensation mitigates economic damage and undermines the argument that military effort, as part of a grand strategy of deep engagement, is required to prevent unbearable economic harm.

Political-military disruptions that reduce oil production or inhibit the transit of oil through key chokepoints do not directly translate into reduced oil access for consumers in a global market: non-disrupted producers or other activities by consumers can add oil to the market to replace barrels lost in the disruption. The market itself is like "one great pool" or a "global bathtub" into which suppliers pump oil and from which consumers drain oil; economically, the market mixes different sources of oil together, allowing various producers to substitute for each other in sending oil to a particular consumer and making specific producer–consumer relationships essentially irrelevant (Griffin 2015). In a competitive market, an unexpected contraction in the amount supplied by one producer puts upward pressure on price, signaling other producers to increase their output, thereby restoring the pre-disruption equilibrium. This logic applies to OPEC members in times when the cartel's political control is weak, and it always applies to non-OPEC oil producers, although their capacity to respond rapidly to disruptions with large output increases is generally limited.

In a market dominated by fewer suppliers (e.g., at times when the OPEC cartel is relatively cohesive), non-disrupted producers do not require the price signal to notice an opportunity to increase their output: they can watch specific other members of the oligopoly and respond directly to their changing output levels. They see another member's under-production as an opportunity to increase their own output without over-supplying the entire market and disturbing the established oligopoly price. In studying oligopoly, economists describe the effect of reduced production by one supplier on the amount of output offered by other producers as the "reaction function." That function intercedes between the disruption and the effect of the price elasticity of demand: as long as other oil supply compensates for the disruption, the price of oil will not rise, and even price-inelastic consumers will not have to suffer the cost of a price spike.

Separately from the incentive for non-disrupted suppliers to replace the "missing barrels" that drop out of the market in a political-military shock, a shock may also undermine cartel cohesion, leading to more replacement barrels being offered over time than the disruption removed from the market. Some shocks to the oil market result from conflict among oil suppliers themselves, and open warfare, proxy warfare, or "cold war" conditions within the potential cartel surely complicate the bargaining that is necessary for the cartel to decide on its preferred total oil production and to allocate quotas within the cartel, driving the equilibrium back towards the competitive market level based on greater total supply. But even in disruptions that do not politically split the oligopoly of leading oil producers, every non-disrupted producer would like to be the one that takes the opportunity to make up for the disrupted output – that is, each producer has an incentive to increase its production, and temporary quota modifications will have to be allocated (and followed) within the cartel, creating an opportunity for cartel bargaining to break down. Instability can have the direct effect of removing some oil production from the market, but at the same time it can also create conditions for more production overall.

In addition to the supply-side reaction to shocks, consumers can take advantage of a substantial cushion on the demand side to respond to supply disruptions (Gholz and Press 2008). Privately held inventories routinely absorb variations in oil supply of hundreds of thousands of barrels a day of production. They give the market, including non-disrupted producers, time to adjust, and since the total quantity of oil available to consumers will not drop, the rigidity implied by well-known price-elasticity estimates – those that suggest that even small supply disruptions might cause large price changes – need not kick in.

Beyond the private stocks, government-owned strategic reserves provide an additional resource. For years the world's major consumers have bought extra oil to fill their emergency petroleum reserves – hundreds of millions of barrels that could compensate for any plausibly sized supply disruption, barrel-for-barrel, for months at a time. Even though the International Energy Agency agreement specifies that member countries should set the size of their oil stocks based on their total oil imports, in actual practice the reserves only need to supply enough to make up for the missing barrels, a much easier task. The biggest disruptions in history have taken several million barrels of oil per day off the market, and draws from consumer-country strategic supplies can readily match that rate. The most terrible scare scenario discussed in strategy debates, complete closure of the Strait of Hormuz to tanker traffic, would bottle up some 17 million barrels per day, if there were (implausibly) no shift at all to alternative transportation routes and no compensation from oil producers outside the Strait. In that very worst case and accounting for the limits on the rates at which consumer governments can pump oil from their strategic reserves, the government stockpiles in the United States, other IEA countries, and non-IEA consumers like China could make up a significant fraction of the disruption for months – though not enough to prevent a real price spike.

Whereas the world's reserve supply once sat in relatively inaccessible pools, much of it now sits in easily accessible salt caverns and storage tanks where consumers control the spigots. Even if consumer governments manage their reserves imperfectly, not releasing at the economically optimal time, the combination of producers' excess capacity, private inventories, and strategic stocks significantly reduces the need for activist energy security policies. Moreover, politicians' real-world hesitancy to tap strategic stockpiles actually serves to protect the oil market: if governments were too aggressive about managing price variation, they would suppress private investors' efforts, limiting the energy security value of the private inventories. But even politicians will take action in the largest, clearest disruption scenarios (e.g., civil unrest in Saudi Arabia) – precisely the scenarios in which the government stockpiles are needed to backstop the normal market response.

The empirical record of political-military oil supply disruptions

Empirically, in the six major oil supply shocks caused by political disruptions in the past forty years, market dynamics quickly mitigated the costs borne by consumers (Gholz and Press 2010b). Figure 4.1 tracks the decline and recovery of world oil production in the six cases: (1) Iranian oil industry strikes in 1978; (2) the collapse of the Iranian oil industry in 1979; (3) the start of the Iran–Iraq war; (4) the 1990 Iraqi invasion of Kuwait; (5) the 2002–2003 strikes in the Venezuelan oil fields; and (6) the 2011 Libyan civil war.[6]

The cases reveal five key findings. First, in five of the six cases (the exception is the 1979 Iran disruption) major reductions in any country's oil production quickly triggered compensating increases elsewhere (along with efforts to restore output in the disrupted country).[7] For example, in 1978 strikes in the Iranian oil industry deprived global markets of nearly 5 million barrels per day, which was then more than 4 percent of world production. But the world responded quickly, and global

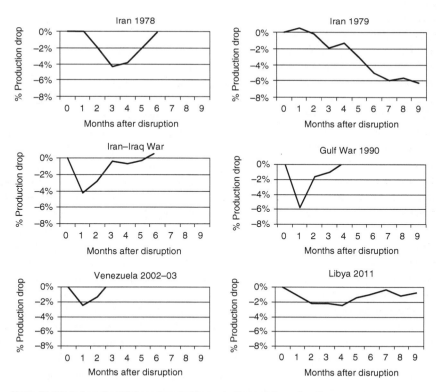

Note: All data is from the US Department of Energy's Energy Information Agency.

FIGURE 4.1 World oil production after major disruptions

production had fully recovered in six months. The outbreak of the Iran–Iraq war removed 3.4 million barrels per day of Iranian and Iraqi oil from global markets (5.8 percent of global production), but total global supply did not fall by that full amount. Other producers increased their output within the same month, so net global supply only dropped by 4.2 percent. As adjustment efforts continued, the losses to the world market were nearly replaced in three months and fully replaced in five.

In the most serious disruption of all – stemming from Iraq's 1990 invasion of Kuwait – United Nations sanctions eliminated 5.3 million barrels per day of Iraqi and Kuwaiti oil from world markets, a loss of 8.8 percent of world production. Again, total world supply did not drop that far, because other producers quickly ramped up their output. One month after the Iraqi invasion, net world production was down by 5.9 percent, but a month later it was only short by 1.7 percent, and two months after that, total global production had fully recovered.

In the Venezuelan case, it only took three months in 2003 to replace the 2.3 million barrels per day of production disrupted by strikes. Finally, during the 2011 Libyan civil war, Saudi Arabia quickly calmed markets by promising to ramp up production, and other countries, primarily OPEC members, also increased their exports (Hasselbach and Goebel 2011; EIA Today in Energy 2011).

Second, in five of six cases (with the same exception) oil prices either remained nearly constant or quickly returned to pre-disruption levels. Figure 4.2 shows the increase in oil prices after each of these disruptions and their recovery over time. The 1978 Iranian oil strikes did not have a significant effect on prices, but the later 1979 disruption is the exceptional case of a sustained increase.[8] The outbreak of the Iran–Iraq War triggered a jump in oil prices, but they returned to pre-war levels in about eighteen months. (Furthermore, during the Iran–Iraq war, the repeated attacks on shipping during the Tanker War phase, which intensified in 1984 and continued until July 1988, had no discernible effect on global prices.) Even after the Iraqi invasion of Kuwait and the subsequent UN embargo, oil prices nearly dropped to pre-war levels in eight months, and the Venezuelan oil strikes caused only a brief spike in oil prices that passed within five months. Finally, prices dropped considerably within seven months of the onset of the Libyan civil war in 2011, although other factors led to a further price increase that prevented the price from dropping all the way to its pre-war level for another year thereafter, even though substantial Libyan production had returned to the market.

Third, international oil markets appear to have become increasingly efficient at replacing disrupted oil supplies, thereby reducing the duration of price spikes. Figures 4.1 and 4.2 show that more recent disruptions generally required less time for markets to adapt. The invention of new international financial and investment tools since the 1970s has enabled sophisticated spot and futures markets for oil, facilitating quick market adjustments and allowing producers, wholesalers, refiners, and major consumers to smooth risks (Bohi and Toman 1996: 37, 81–87).

Fourth, the Iran–Iraq War demonstrates the intra-cartel bargaining problems that price spikes trigger. Five months after the war's sudden beginning, worldwide oil

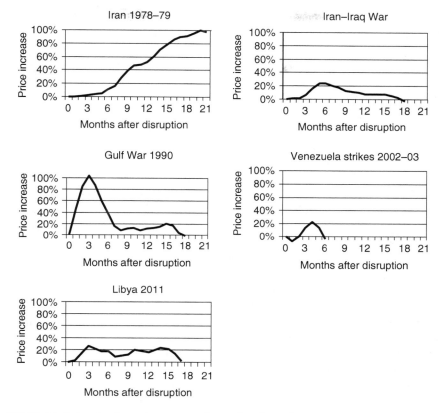

FIGURE 4.2 Price shocks and recovery after major disruptions

Note: Data on prices are from the US Department of Energy's Energy Information Administration. Prices reflect the refiner acquisition cost of oil, adjusted into constant dollars.

production matched prewar levels and then immediately exceeded them; OPEC proved unable to reverse the sustained price decline that followed. From 1981 to 1985, Saudi Arabia tried in vain to re-establish cartel discipline. But as war raged in the Gulf, the belligerents pumped oil as quickly as possible, and the other OPEC members chose sides. Finding OPEC agreements that the cartel members would keep became impossible. The West enjoyed the benefits of these disputes in the form of several years of cheap oil (Yergin 1991: 748).

Finally, governments have used their strategic stockpiles to aid adjustment to oil supply shocks. The releases have not been perfectly smooth, either technically or politically, and there is always debate about their timing and market effects (Victor and Eskreis-Winkler 2008). But the International Energy Agency coordinated sales from its member countries' reserves in response to the Gulf War in 1991 and to the disruption caused by the Libyan civil war in 2011. In the former case, the sales of stockpiled oil came during the war to liberate Kuwait and several months after the UN sanctions had removed Iraqi and Kuwaiti oil from world markets. Because the supply from the war zone was already shut off by the sanctions, it was by then unlikely that the war would remove additional barrels of supply. Nevertheless, the planned release may well have contributed to the markets' lack of a risk premium bump in early 1991. More meaningfully, the release in the summer of 2011 helped compensate for the increased seasonal demand for oil in the summer driving season while Libyan production was offline, keeping supply and demand in balance without an upward trend in prices (Clayton 2012). Even if the operations of reserves do not reach their ideal potential, they in practice contribute to adjustment that mitigates the economic impact of supply shocks.

Critics might reply that these examples all draw from a time when oil producers had slack production capacity – that is, when past investment in exploration and oil field development enabled them to pump more oil than consumers demanded at the pre-shock price level. Some analysts fear that the cost of carrying spare capacity has increased to the point where no producers will do so in the future (McNally and Levi 2011; Levi 2013). However, these analysts mistook temporary situations of low spare capacity, such as during the pre-2008 bubble economy and during the period immediately after other producers responded to the Libya disruption, for a permanent condition. Spare capacity should be expected to vary over time, as producers respond to market conditions, but the producers have a continuing, systematic incentive to rebuild spare capacity at times when it is low. In fact, the circumstances of relatively low spare capacity after temporary market disruptions reflect the action of exactly the mechanism of market resilience that protects consumers from sustained effects of political-military shocks (Gholz and Press 2013: 139–147).

Overall, given the logic that governs supply, demand, and investment decisions in the oil industry, concerns about political-military disruptions are exaggerated. As the historical cases suggest, market responses limit the costs that the United States should pay to try to control instability in oil-producing regions using military force.

Does market response rely on US grand strategy?

The resilience of the oil market seems to limit the need for grand strategy to prevent political-military disruptions to oil supply, but it is possible that the direction of causality runs the other way – that US forward military presence and alliance commitments enable oil market response to supply disruptions.[9] Superficially, the history of post-1973 supply disruptions (and market response) generally overlaps with the timeframe of explicit US commitment to defend Persian Gulf oil. Prior to 1973, the United States was able to provide stability in the global energy market because excess oil production capacity in the United States gave the United States substantial power to balance market disruptions and coerce US allies into coordinating their energy policies. It was only when US oil fields matured and US spare production capacity dissipated that the international oil market dynamics started to follow the cartel logic explained in the previous section (Kapstein 1990). After the first major oil crisis of the OPEC era, President Carter proclaimed the

US commitment to defend access to Persian Gulf oil, and market response to post-1979 crises functioned relatively smoothly.

The timing of the expanded US commitment to defend the Persian Gulf was not coincidental: though the Carter Doctrine primarily aimed at the Soviet Union, responding to fears that the 1979 Soviet invasion of Afghanistan increased the threat of Soviet conquest of the Gulf, the context of the oil crisis induced by the Iranian revolution surely contributed to President Carter's declaration. But the fact that US policymakers interpreted the 1979 crisis as showing the need for a military commitment to protect the oil market does not mean that their analysis was correct. In fact, the concurrency between the US military commitment and oil market resilience is a case of correlation rather than causation.

Hegemonic stability theory and the oil market

Hegemonic stability theory provides the logic that allegedly links oil market response to US grand strategy. The core idea is that normal function of the global economy relies on certain public goods – goods that are non-excludable and non-rival such that all consumers benefit from them, whether or not they contribute to their provision. According to the familiar logic of collective action, consumers of public goods hope to "free-ride" on others' efforts, so public goods are generally underprovided through voluntary transactions. Instead, their provision requires either coercion or a large consumer who enjoys enough benefit from the public good that s/he has an incentive to provide it regardless of others' free-riding (Olson 1965). In the domestic policy context, government regulation or government spending money collected through taxes can provide public goods via coercion, but in international relations, there is no world government to provide public goods. According to hegemonic stability theory, the next best alternative is for a very powerful country, the hegemon, to provide public goods itself, to coerce other countries to contribute, or to create international institutions that provide the public goods (Keohane 1984).

Hegemonic stability theory requires action by the hegemon – that is, a particular choice of grand strategy. Most of the action concerns international economic policy (e.g., acting as a lender of last resort to support global financial markets), but some concerns foreign military policy. Recent discussion of deep engagement alleges that US alliances, military spending, and forward military presence dampen security competition and restrain arms races around the world, securing trade flows and reducing instability and uncertainty that would otherwise limit foreign investment (Brooks and Wohlforth 2016). That argument extends beyond the global oil market, but hegemonic stability theorists and advocates of deep engagement both take oil as a key case where hegemonic action is especially important. Oil was one of the main case studies in Robert Keohane's (1984) foundational work on the theory. Ethan Kapstein's (1990) book on the international political economy of oil crises explicitly rests on hegemonic stability theory. And Joshua Rovner and Caitlin Talmadge's (2014: 551) recent study of US force posture in the Persian Gulf claims that "the historical evidence shows that hegemonic stability is a very real phenomenon in the Gulf."

However, none of these authors carefully identifies the public good connected to oil that US hegemony allegedly needs to provide. Oil itself is clearly a private good: one consumer's use of a particular barrel of oil burns it or otherwise changes it chemically, preventing another consumer from using that same oil, and the benefit of using the oil is localized and allows its owner to exclude others, e.g., from transport in a privately owned car. The value that the current owner would gain from consuming the oil or the amount that another potential user would be willing to pay to use the oil – that is, oil's market price – provides the incentive for producers to locate and pump oil from its natural reservoirs, just as value (along with cost of production) determines price and provides incentives for other normal goods.

Rovner and Talmadge suggest that the global nature of the oil market provides the public-goods logic that requires hegemonic action. They write, "Oil is traded in a global market, so the hegemon cannot easily provide it for some states and not others," and they cite the "one great pool" argument to support their claim of non-excludability (Rovner and Talmadge 2014: 555–556). They are of course right that supply from any producer affects the equilibrium market price paid by all consumers, just as in any normal market. In this way, oil is like wheat or soap or salt, and the oil market does not require any more hegemonic action than the markets for other goods. This global price effect of changing supply (or demand) is sometimes called a "pecuniary externality" (Holcombe and Sobel 2001). It is precisely the market mechanism in action, not an example of a market failure that might be used to justify government intervention.[10] Political leaders' inability to distinguish between pecuniary externalities and technological externalities, and their consequent attempts to "correct" pecuniary externalities, are a fairly common source of market distortions that undermine market efficiency (Holcombe and Sobel 2001). Rovner and Talmadge have fallen into the same analytical error, so they have not found a public good that might make hegemonic stability theory apply to the oil market.

The broader debate about hegemonic stability theory included the analysis of the global system of free trade promoted in the post-World War II era by the United States through the GATT/WTO negotiations, which might suggest a related mechanism for oil trade. Analysts of hegemonic stability initially included free trade as one of its economic requirements, reacting to the negative experience of "beggar thy neighbor" trade policies during the Great Depression, but others pointed out that countries very often apply different tariffs to different goods and even to the same goods exchanged with different trade partners. Economic discrimination is relatively easy in trade policy: the benefits of free trade are excludable; hence there is no public good for the hegemon to supply (Oye 1992). But trade agreements that provide for tariff reductions are enforced via the threat of economic sanctions that are costly to impose, meaning that signatories to a trade agreement prefer that some other country punish shirkers – that is, members of the global trade regime may underprovide enforcement according to the logic of collective action, so scholars have argued that in practice free trade requires a component of hegemonic effort (Gowa 1994: 20–21, 25–30). Analysts discussing "secure access to oil" may have a similar idea in mind, because the defense spending and troop deployments necessary to physically protect oil shipments are costly.

The circumstances in trade policy and oil markets differ, however. In trade policy, while economic logic gives all states a unilateral incentive to lower their trade barriers, regardless of what other countries do, a familiar political logic points out that concentrated, and hence politically powerful, producer interests benefit from protectionism, while diffuse and politically weak consumer interests benefit from free trade (Alt and Gilligan 1994). While reciprocity in tariff reductions may draw concentrated export interests into the domestic politics of trade policy, offsetting the normal protectionist bias, each country's resolve in sticking with a free trade agreement faces a steady challenge, so free trade interests may benefit from an external power's threat to punish backsliding (Milner 1988). In the oil market, on the other hand, each producing country has a natural incentive to get its product to market and does not need a reminder from an external enforcer. Producers' domestic economic and political incentives align, because export-oriented oil firms are politically powerful, concentrated interests that profit by supplying the global market in response to their competitors' inability to deliver oil; that many oil producers are state-owned national champions gives them even easier access to the levers of power, helping them act on their incentive to participate in the global oil market, even if it requires defense spending or military action. Again, despite seeming similarities to the public goods cited in the literature on hegemonic stability theory, the oil market lacks public goods that would be underprovided without forceful action by the hegemon.

Finally, it might seem as if oil is a valuable enough commodity that militarily powerful countries might have an interest in simply taking it by force rather than purchasing it from producing countries – a struggle for control over normal, private goods rather than a public good, but a struggle that might raise the cost of producing a good that is important to everyone. The hegemon might provide a crucial underpinning to the global oil market by promising to defend oil producers from external threats, as President Carter promised in the wake of the Soviet invasion of Afghanistan. According to economic logic, an oil producer's conqueror would have the same incentive to sell oil that the previous owner had, but uniting several oil producers under a single political system would simplify cartel bargaining, likely raising the price of oil to consumers. If the cartel premium were large enough and the cost of preventing conquest of oil-producing regions were small enough, the difference might provide an economic justification for the hegemon's military intervention to prevent oil wars. But given the military balance in the Persian Gulf region today and likely for some time to come – weak, militarily flawed countries with forces poorly adapted for conventional offensives – there is no threat of conquest that would unify political control of the oil fields (Gholz and Press 2010b; Rovner 2016).

Furthermore, occupying and operating oil fields as a conqueror would prove extremely challenging in the face of local nationalist resistance and sabotage, diminishing countries' interest in launching an effort at conquest. Even the mighty United States struggled to protect the flow of oil during its occupation of Iraq, and other great powers would face the same challenges (Gholz and Press 2010a). The grinding civil and sectarian wars in the region give little reason to believe that Iran, Iraq, Saudi Arabia, or any other local power could hold foreign territory and dominate oil supply. Overall, the economic and military challenges to profiting from oil wars have made them extremely rare in history, whether or not a hegemon exerted power to deter or defend against such conquest (Meierding 2016).

It is plausible to think that net oil producers would want to attack each other's productive capacity even if they could not hope to seize it and operate it themselves, simply to inhibit a competitor's ability to bring product to market or to help enforce cartel restraints on output, but this scenario is unlikely. Potential external attackers are inhibited by the limited effectiveness of stand-off attacks on oil facilities and transportation equipment, which are difficult to hit and seriously damage and are relatively easy to repair (Itzkowitz Shifrinson and Priebe 2011; Gholz et al. 2009). The threat of retaliation and the costs of a major war surely also deter such aggression, especially because international wars in the Persian Gulf region might spill over into civil wars that pose a much greater threat to the oil industry and, more importantly, might threaten petro-states' authoritarian leaders. Instability within major oil producers always poses a threat of disruption to the global oil supply, but neither principle nor practice of hegemonic stability theory has suggested that the hegemon should take on the role of protecting other countries against internal security threats. The hegemon, as suggested by recent US military experience in Iraq, would likely not be very good at providing such domestic security, and the presence of foreign security forces might even exacerbate internal security threats (Gholz and Press 2010b).

Given the challenge of finding a public-goods logic to connect oil supply to hegemonic stability theory – that is, a public-goods aspect to events in major producing countries overseas that could be affected by the hegemon's military statecraft – it is unsurprising that classic studies of the international relations of the oil market emphasize the demand side of the market. For example, investment in fuel-switching technology, which allows energy consumers to change to other fuels like natural gas, biofuels, or electricity when oil prices rise, has more public-good characteristics than the supply-side military policy issues. Increasing one country's elasticity of demand for oil inherently affects the elasticity of the entire market's demand, creating a non-excludable benefit that gives all net consuming countries an incentive to free-ride. Similarly, all net oil consumers hope that *other* consumers will release strategic oil reserves during crises.[11] Thus a hegemon might play a productive role in international coordination of economic policies to promote energy security among major oil consumers.[12] But as Robert Keohane pointed out decades ago, the emphasis on demand-side coordination of economic policies mostly takes military strategy off the table in discussions of oil security (Keohane 1984: 40–41, 203–204).[13]

A US grand strategy of restraint, which would change US military alliances, force posture, and military interventions, is in principle consistent with oil-related international economic policy coordination, if such coordination is necessary or desirable. But the logic of hegemonic stability theory does not suggest that the United States should use foreign military policy to try to protect or shape the oil market.

The US military in the Persian Gulf

Despite the weakness of the theoretical claims linking hegemonic stability theory to a need for US military presence in the Persian Gulf, Rovner and Talmadge claim to have established empirically that the United States has used its military – often successfully, though with some side effects – to stabilize the region and provide oil security. They do not attempt to directly show a connection between the military missions and oil market outcomes, which are influenced by many factors other than Persian Gulf stability, but they conclude that "hegemonic behavior explains variation in oil security in the Gulf since 1945 and has implications for US posture today" (Rovner and Talmadge 2014: 558). However, their conclusion does not follow from their evidence. In fact, variation in US military activity in the Persian Gulf does not correlate well with variation in the level of oil exports from the Persian Gulf, let alone with overall market supply of oil to major consumers like the United States. Persian Gulf supply disruptions often stemmed from domestic rather than international dynamics to which US military presence might have been addressed; robust oil exports continued despite the main international disruption, the Iran–Iraq War; and as discussed earlier, market responses rather than US military action generally ameliorated the effects of disruptions on consumers. Hegemonic behavior does not, in fact, explain variation in oil security. Instead, market behavior does – and it would continue to provide oil security under a US grand strategy of restraint.

Rovner and Talmadge provide the most robust attempt to connect empirical evidence to hegemonic stability theory and specifically to oil security, so it is appropriate to review their arguments in detail. Some of their evidence is unpersuasive because they do not consider alternative explanations. Specifically, they recount the history of British responsibility for providing "hegemonic stability" in the Persian Gulf before the UK's withdrawal from East of Suez, but at that time the United States was also a dominant actor in oil markets, with substantial spare production capacity that was used to moderate supply shocks. It is difficult to disentangle the effects of British troop deployments from the effects of US oil market dominance, and Rovner and Talmadge do not try. Previous studies of the period, principally Ethan Kapstein's book, attribute oil security then to US leadership on the supply side of the oil market (Kapstein 1990). But just as it is fair to criticize Rovner and Talmadge for not considering the alternative hypothesis of US market power, it is fair to criticize Kapstein for not considering the alternative hypothesis of British military activity. The decisive tests of the hegemonic stability hypothesis must come from a later period, when the hypothesis that US producers provided oil security is no longer plausible.

The 1970s and 1980s are the key decades here. Rovner and Talmadge argue that the 1970s saw an absence of hegemonic military power in the Persian Gulf and also a lack of oil security. For comparison, they suggest that the US military engaged with the "light footprint" of the Rapid Deployment Joint Task Force in the 1980s and that simultaneously oil security was provided (Rovner and Talmadge 2014: 558). They acknowledge that the main oil market disruptions in the 1970s – the 1973 OPEC embargo and the 1979 Iranian revolution – could not have been prevented by hegemonic military action (Rovner and Talmadge 2014: 564, 567). But they avoid the logical conclusion that hegemonic stability theory is not the best explanation for variations in oil security. Instead, they cite the arms race and growing potential for conflict between Iran and Iraq as a lack of oil security that could have been prevented with a more robust hegemonic military presence. The biggest difficulty with that claim is their admission in their 1980s section that the Iran–Iraq War "settled into a stalemate" and did not interrupt the general flow of Persian Gulf oil to the global market, even if it hampered Iraqi and Iranian exports (Rovner and Talmadge 2014: 558, 568–569). If the conflict, when it came, did not cut off oil supplies, then there is no reason to code the *threat* of that conflict in the 1970s as a "failure" to provide oil security – and no reason to note a correlation between absence of hegemonic military forces and lack of oil security as evidence in favor of hegemonic stability theory. Considering the 1973 and 1979 disruptions, too, there does not seem to be an important causal relationship between lack of hegemonic military activity and lack of oil security in the 1970s.

Furthermore, Rovner and Talmadge's analysis of the 1980s is suspect. They point out that the United States intervened in 1987 to protect Kuwaiti oil tankers from Iranian attacks, but they do not dwell on the fact that the overwhelming majority of attacks on oil tankers during the "tanker war" phase of the Iran–Iraq War were launched by Iraq over the three years before the US convoy operation started (Rovner and Talmadge 2014: 569; see also Gholz and Press 2010b; Gholz et al. 2009). Neither the cumulative effect of attacks nor a growing Iranian military capability to attack tankers forced the United States to intervene. Rather, it was clever Kuwaiti diplomacy: asking the Soviet Union to convoy the tankers as a mechanism to pressure the United States. The key fact about attempts to disrupt oil shipping during the Iran–Iraq War is that they failed to substantially dent exports even as the hegemon stood by and did nothing. The most reasonable interpretation of the 1980s history is that lack of hegemonic military intervention to protect oil did not cause serious difficulty for the global oil market.

The 1990s and 2000s saw substantially more forceful US intervention in the Persian Gulf. Rovner and Talmadge code the results as contributing to oil security but with nasty side effects, and they argue that the United States could better provide oil security with a 1980s-style light footprint rather than such large-scale military action.[14] But the evidence that hegemonic military action contributed at all to oil security in this period is thin: the observed US military interventions mainly aimed at the political goals of regime change in Iraq and hunting down al Qaeda and ISIS terrorists. Furthermore, the market response theory and the hegemonic stability theory both predict oil security, so the history of the 1990s and 2000s cannot offer a decisive test. But it is also worth noting that although some advocates applaud the robust hegemonic military activity at this time, the critics' view is at least as plausible – that the US military intervention was a major cause of regional instability and potential oil market disruption.

Overall, like the theoretical arguments about public goods and oil security, the empirical analysis purporting to connect US military effort to oil security is weak. Scholars on both sides of the debate acknowledge that the US military could not have prevented the biggest oil market disruptions, and the most direct evidence on oil supply during a period in the 1970s and 1980s without hegemonic military engagement – and during a period of regional war that specifically targeted oil exports – shows that oil supply is resilient. Market response to supply disruptions does not depend on activist US grand strategy.

Conclusion

The case for restraint and oil security is mostly a negative one. Rather than arguing that restraint provides more oil security than the alternative grand strategy of deep engagement, restraint points out that US military activism is not necessary for oil security. The theoretical case for deep engagement is weak, because its logic is built on the presence of public goods that would be underprovided in the absence of hegemonic activism, but the relevant goods in the oil market are private, normal goods – that is, there is no market failure in oil supply for US overseas military action to correct. The empirical case for deep engagement is weak, too, because specific historical evidence shows that oil supplies continue to flow without hegemonic protection, even in the face of military threats and attacks. Furthermore, the biggest historical oil crises did not follow the causal pathways that hegemonic military action could plausibly interrupt. *Any* side effects of oil security-related military activity – and everyone acknowledges that there are some side effects – are too grievous, given that the military activity is largely irrelevant to its purported goal.

Restraint instead leaves the oil market to function. It is resilient to disruptions. The logic of its resilience makes sense in theory, and modern history shows that resilience in action. Suppliers' desire to make money motivates them to increase their sales during disruptions, and consumers' desire to limit the effects of price spikes induces them to tap reserve inventories. No one needs superhuman foresight or insight, and no one needs to be coerced – by the hegemon or anyone else. Restraint can support US efforts to achieve security, prosperity, and liberty, including with respect to oil security.

Notes

1 This is the term that Brooks and Wohlforth prefer; elsewhere in this volume authors refer to this grand strategy as primacy. Another synonym is liberal hegemony.

2 This section updates and adapts the text in Eugene Gholz and Daryl G. Press (2007).

3 Economic decisions about past production rates also affect current production capacities. Pumping oil too rapidly from a field can reduce the future flow rate (or raise production costs tomorrow) and can even cut down a field's long-term total output (using current technology). For an accessible discussion of some of the technical background on investment and production, see Norman J. Hyne (2012).

4 Cartels increase profits for producers by cooperatively reducing production below the level predicted by competitive behavior – thus driving price up above the marginal cost of production. Producing an additional unit would be profitable on a one-off basis, but the increase in output would drive down the price of *all* units sold, so combined profits of all cartel members would drop if a member used its excess production capacity.

5 For example, as oil prices plunged in 2014 in the wake of the US tight oil production boom, and OPEC leaders opted not to curtail their own production to prop up prices, many pundits declared OPEC "dead," but not too long thereafter, OPEC started to cooperate on production restraint again, and oil prices responded as one would expect, by trending upward (Zhdannikov and Gamal 2016; Habboush, Mahdi, Wilkin, and Alloway 2017).

6 To varying degrees, each event described here surprised world markets, so the disruption and adjustment can be observed using aggregate data on oil production and price. In contrast, the 2003 US invasion of Iraq was widely anticipated, so oil markets gradually adjusted prior to the attack, and the precise effects of the invasion on oil markets are therefore harder to tease out.

7 The surprise in the 1979 case was that Saudi Arabia responded to the Iranian output cutback by cutting Saudi production rather than increasing output. One plausible hypothesis is that the Gulf monarchs were stunned by the Iranian revolution, and increased concern about their own domestic stability made them – particularly the Saudis – susceptible to pressure from Islamic fundamentalists or Palestinian groups to punish the West by raising oil prices. See Quandt 1981, pp. 130–132 and Yergin 1991, p. 704.

8 The 1979 collapse of the Iranian oil industry closely followed the 1978 strikes, so those two incidents are combined into a single panel of Figure 4.2.

9 This hypothesis would parallel Robert Gilpin's classic argument that multinational corporations thrived as a result of "the international political order created by dominant powers primarily in their security interests" (Gilpin 1975: 19).

10 Externalities used to justify government intervention in markets are often defined as effects on third parties that *are not included in the price*.

11 However the strategic interaction among reserve holders should be less subject to freeriding than the strategic interaction in the fuel-switching investments case, since each country with reserves has an individual incentive not to hold its reserves longer but rather to profit by selling at the crisis-heightened price.

12 In the classic studies, Robert Keohane is more optimistic than Ethan Kapstein on this score, at least with respect to the United States' ability to fulfill this role.

13 Granted, Keohane was writing in the context of the Cold War, when the other major oilconsuming countries were US military allies, and the alliances constrained the United States from using military leverage to gain cooperation on things like use of strategic petroleum reserves. In principle, under a grand strategy of restraint, when the other major net consumers would not be permanent military allies of the United States, the

United States could use military policy to try to influence other consumers' oil security policies. It is hard to imagine that it would be worth the costs of military threats to gain oil security cooperation, and it is also hard to imagine that it would be worth maintaining a military alliance solely to gain economic policy cooperation given that the alliance was not very effective at gaining such cooperation even when the allies faced the mutual threat of the Soviet Union. For details on the history of alliance dynamics and oil security policy, see Kapstein 1990.

14 Other advocates of the grand strategy of deep engagement view the costs as so high that they take great pains to explain that deep engagement, properly implemented, would not require intervention like the Iraq War (e.g. Brooks and Wohlforth 2016).

References

Adelman, M.A. 1995. *The Genie Out of the Bottle: World Oil since 1970.* MIT Press.

Adelman, M.A. 2002. World Oil Production & Prices 1947–2000. *The Quarterly Review of Economics and Finance*, 42(2), pp.169–191.

Alt, J.E., and Gilligan, M. 1994. The Political Economy of Trading States: Factor Specificity, Collective Action Problems and Domestic Political Institutions. *Journal of Political Philosophy*, 2(2), pp.165–192.

Barnes, J., Jaffe, A., and Morse, E.L. 2004. The New Geopolitics of Oil. *National Interest*, December 17, pp.7–15.

Bohi, D.R., and Quandt, W.B. 1984. *Energy Security in the 1980s: Economic and Political Perspectives.* Brookings Institution.

Bohi, D.R., and Toman, M.A. 1996. *The Economics of Energy Security.* Springer Science & Business Media.

Bohn, H., and Deacon, R.T. 2000. Ownership Risk, Investment, and the Use of Natural Resources. *American Economic Review*, 90(3), pp.526–549.

Brooks, S., and Wohlforth, W. 2016. *America Abroad: The United States' Global Role in the 21st Century.* Oxford University Press.

Clayton, B. 2012. *Lessons Learned from the 2011 Strategic Petroleum Reserve Release.* Council on Foreign Relations.

Colgan, J.D. 2014. The Emperor Has No Clothes: The Limits of OPEC in the Global Oil Market. *International Organization*, 68(3), pp.599–632.

EIA Today in Energy. 2011. Libyan Supply Disruption May Have Both Direct and Indirect Effects. March 7.

Evenett, S.J., Levenstein, M.C., and Suslow, V.Y. 2001. International Cartel Enforcement: Lessons from the 1990s. *The World Economy*, 24(9), pp.1221–1245.

Frynas, J.G., and Mellahi, K. 2003. Political Risks as Firm-Specific (Dis)advantages: Evidence on Transnational Oil Firms in Nigeria. *Thunderbird International Business Review*, 45(5), pp.541–565.

Gately, D. 1984. A Ten-Year Retrospective: OPEC and the World Oil Market. *Journal of Economic Literature*, 22(3), pp.1100–1114.

Gholz, E., and Press, D.G. 2001. The Effects of Wars on Neutral Countries: Why It Doesn't Pay to Preserve the Peace. *Security Studies*, 10(4), pp.1–57.

Gholz, E., and Press, D.G. 2007. Energy Alarmism: The Myths that Make Americans Worry about Oil. Cato Institute Policy Analysis #589, April.

Gholz, E., and Press, D.G. 2008. All the Oil We Need. *New York Times*, August 20, p.A23.

Gholz, E., and Press, D. 2010a. Footprints in the Sand. *American Interest*, 5(4), pp.59–67.

Gholz, E., and Press, D.G. 2010b. Protecting "the Prize": Oil and the US National Interest. *Security Studies*, 19(3), pp.453–485.

Gholz, E., and Press, D.G. 2013. Enduring Resilience: How Oil Markets Handle Disruptions. *Security Studies*, 22(1), pp.139–147.

Gholz, E., et al. 2009. Threats to Oil Flows through the Strait of Hormuz. Strauss Center Working Paper, The University of Texas at Austin, December.

Gilpin, R. 1975. *US Power and the Multinational Corporation: The Political Economy of Foreign Direct Investment*. Basic Books.

Glaser, C.L., and Kelanic, R.A. 2016. Should the United States Stay in the Gulf? In Glaser, C.L., and Kelanic, R.A. eds., *Crude Strategy: Rethinking the US Military Commitment to Defend Persian Gulf Oil*. Georgetown University Press, pp.233–250.

Gowa, J. 1994. *Allies, Adversaries, and International Trade*. Princeton University Press.

Griffin, J.M. 2015. Petro-Nationalism: The Futile Search for Oil Security. *The Energy Journal*, 36.

Griffin, J.M., and Neilson, W.S. 1994. The 1985–86 Oil Price Collapse and Afterwards: What Does Game Theory Add? *Economic Inquiry*, 32(4), pp.543–561.

Griffin, J.M., and Xiong, W. 1997. The Incentive to Cheat: An Empirical Analysis of OPEC. *The Journal of Law and Economics*, 40(2), pp.289–316.

Habboush, M., Mahdi, W., Wilkin, S., and Alloway, T. 2017. OPEC Chief Sees Oil Producers Closer to Re-Balancing Market. *Bloomberg.com*, April 19.

Hasselbach, C., and Goebel, N. 2011. Disruption to Libyan Oil Supply Highlights Need for EU Energy Diversification. *Deutsche Welle*, March 1.

Hill, F. 2004. Pipelines in the Caspian: Catalyst or Cure-all? *Georgetown Journal of International Affairs*, 5(1), pp.17–25.

Holcombe, R.G., and Sobel, R.S. 2001. Public Policy toward Pecuniary Externalities. *Public Finance Review*, 29(4), pp.304–325.

Hyne, N.J. 2012. *Nontechnical Guide to Petroleum Geology, Exploration, Drilling, and Production*. PennWell Books.

Itzkowitz Shifrinson, J.R., and Priebe, M. 2011. A Crude Threat: The Limits of an Iranian Missile Campaign against Saudi Arabian Oil. *International Security*, 36(1), pp.167–201.

Kapstein, E.B. 1990. *The Insecure Alliance. Energy Crises and Western Politics since 1944*. Oxford University Press.

Keohane, R.O. 1984. *After Hegemony: Cooperation and Discord in the World Political Economy*. Princeton University Press.

Levi, M. 2013. The Enduring Vulnerabilities of Oil Markets. *Security Studies*, 22(1), pp.132–138.

McNally, R., and Levi, M. 2011. A Crude Predicament: The Era of Volatile Oil Prices. *Foreign Affairs*, July/August, pp.100–111.

Meierding, E. 2016. Dismantling the Oil Wars Myth. *Security Studies*, 25(2), pp.258–288.

Milner, H.V. 1988. *Resisting Protectionism: Global Industries and the Politics of International Trade*. Princeton University Press.

Moran, T.H. 1987. Managing an Oligopoly of Would-Be Sovereigns: The Dynamics of Joint Control and Self-Control in the International Oil Industry Past, Present, and Future. *International Organization*, 41(4), pp.575–607.

Nowell, G.P. 1994. *Mercantile States and the World Oil Cartel, 1900–1939*. Cornell University Press.

Olson, M. 1965. *The Logic of Collective Action*. Harvard University Press.

Oye, K.A. 1992. *Economic Discrimination and Political Exchange: World Political Economy in the 1930s and 1980s*. Princeton University Press.

Posen, B.R. 2003. Command of the Commons: The Military Foundation of US Hegemony. *International Security*, 28(1), pp.5–46.

Quandt, W.B. 1981. *Saudi Arabia in the 1980s: Foreign Policy, Security, and Oil*. Brookings Institution Press.

Rovner, J. 2016. After America: The Flow of Persian Gulf Oil in the Absence of US Military Force. In Glaser, C.L., and Kelanic, R.A. eds., *Crude Strategy: Rethinking the US Military Commitment to Defend Persian Gulf Oil.* Georgetown University Press, pp.233–250.

Rovner, J., and Talmadge, C. 2014. Hegemony, Force Posture, and the Provision of Public Goods: The Once and Future Role of Outside Powers in Securing Persian Gulf Oil. *Security Studies*, 23(3), pp.548–581.

Spar, D.L. 1994. *The Cooperative Edge: The Internal Politics of International Cartels.* Cornell University Press.

Stevens, P. 1995. The Determination of Oil Prices 1945–1995: A Diagrammatic Interpretation. *Energy Policy*, 23(10), pp.861–870.

Verleger, P.K. 2006. Explaining the Unexplainable: Crude Oil Prices – A Review of Theoretical Hypotheses, 1950–2006, and Empirical Evidence. *Petroleum Economics Monthly*, November.

Victor, D.G., and Eskreis-Winkler, S. 2008. In the Tank: Making the Most of Strategic Oil Reserves. *Foreign Affairs*, July/August, pp.70–83.

Vincent, K.R. 2016. The Economic Costs of Persian Gulf Oil Supply Disruptions. In Glaser, C.L., and Kelanic, R.A. eds., *Crude Strategy: Rethinking the US Military Commitment to Defend Persian Gulf Oil.* Georgetown University Press.

Yergin, D. 1991. *The Prize: The Epic Quest for Oil, Money and Power.* Simon & Schuster.

Yergin, D. 2006. Ensuring Energy Security. *Foreign Affairs*, March/April, pp.69–82.

Yetiv, S.A. 2015. *Myths of the Oil Boom: American National Security in a Global Energy Market.* Oxford University Press.

Zhdannikov, D., and Gamal, R. 2016. Exclusive: Shift in Saudi Oil Thinking Deepens OPEC Split. *Reuters.com*, May 5.

5

DOES SPREADING DEMOCRACY BY FORCE HAVE A PLACE IN US GRAND STRATEGY?

A skeptical view

Alexander B. Downes and Jonathan Monten

Is foreign-imposed regime change by the United States and other democratic states an effective means of spreading democracy? The answer to this question is of great importance to US foreign policy because regime change operations can be costly. The United States, by some estimates, has expended $3 trillion to bring democracy to Iraq after US policymakers promised before the invasion that removing Saddam Hussein and democratizing the country could be done at minimal cost (Stiglitz and Bilmes 2008). US military forces suffered nearly 37,000 casualties (4,500 dead) in Iraq from 2003 to 2011 and more than 20,000 casualties (2,400 dead) in Afghanistan through August 2016.[1] Despite these substantial investments of blood and treasure, neither country has yet made a transition to democracy.[2] The effectiveness of foreign-imposed regime change (FIRC) for spreading democracy also matters greatly to citizens of countries targeted for transformative interventions. The removal of the Baathist and Taliban regimes triggered civil war and terrorism that took almost 120,000 civilian lives in Iraq from the US invasion in March 2003 until its withdrawal in December 2011; as many as 31,000 Afghan civilians have been killed since October 2001 (Iraq Body Count 2012; Crawford 2016).

Although democratic states have frequently attempted to spread democracy "at the point of bayonets" over the past century, scholars remain divided over whether sustainable democratic institutions can be imposed through military intervention. Optimists point to successful cases, such as the transformation of West Germany and Japan into consolidated democracies after World War II, as evidence that democracy can be engineered by outsiders through military intervention (Krauthammer 2004; Rice 2005; Bermeo 2010). Pessimists interpret these successes as outliers from a broader pattern of failure typified by cases such as Iraq and Afghanistan. Empirical studies have yielded little support for the view that targets of democratic interventions experience much democratization, concluding that intervention has either no effect or even a negative effect on a state's subsequent democratic trajectory (Bueno de Mesquita and Downs 2006; Pickering and Peceny 2006; Berger, Corvalan, Easterly, and Satyanath 2013). Still others take a conditional view: these scholars agree that, in general, democratic military intervention has little liberalizing effect in target states, but contend that democracies can induce democratization when they explicitly pursue this objective and invest substantial effort and resources (Peceny 1999; Hermann and Kegley 1998; Meernik 1996; Dobbins 2003).

Previous attempts to determine the effect of military intervention on democratization have been undermined by three problems. First, earlier studies have struggled to identify an appropriate universe of cases. Some tend to define intervention too broadly, including many cases that did not result in armed hostilities, an incursion by one state into the territory of another, a dispute over the composition of the respective governments, or the actual removal of foreign leaders (Bueno de Mesquita and Downs 2006). Other studies focus on the most encompassing forms of intervention—nation building or military occupation—but omit other instances in which democracies used less radical means of intervention to impose new leaders or regimes (Dobbins 2003).

Second, almost all existing studies fail to consider the possibility that states that are targeted for democratization differ systematically from states that are not targeted (an exception is Berger, Corvalan, Easterly, and Satyanath, 2013). For example, states may resort to regime change only after less drastic attempts at democratization have failed, and therefore intervene in states where the prospects for democracy are poor. This tendency would cause studies to underestimate the effect of intervention on subsequent democratic change. Interveners might also choose only those cases where prospects for democratization are good, causing studies to overestimate the effect of intervention on democratization.

Third, the literature remains divided over why intervention causes democratic change. Most analyses emphasize the motives, efforts, and choices of the intervening state—such as undertaking pro-democratic reforms or committing substantial material resources—in explaining democratization outcomes (Meernik 1996; Peceny 1999; Dobbins 2003).[3] By focusing on the intervening state, however, these arguments neglect the importance of favorable conditions for democracy—such as economic development and ethnically or religiously homogeneous populations—in targeted states (for overviews of the comparative politics literature that emphasize these and other domestic variables, see Teorell 2010; Geddes 1999). A key question is therefore whether democratization outcomes after intervention are the product of deliberate policy choices by interveners or a function of how hospitable local conditions are to democratic change. Answering this question will enable policymakers to better understand and assess the risks and future likelihood of success when contemplating regime change.

In this chapter, we conduct a new analysis of military intervention and democratization that seeks to improve on these shortcomings.[4] First, we introduce a new dataset of foreign-imposed regime change that identifies the universe of interventions that actually change the effective leader or governing institutions of a targeted state. We examine the democratizing effect of FIRC by democracies in the twentieth century, differentiating between cases where interveners change only leaders and those where they change leaders but also help undertake democratic reform. Second, to adjust for the possibility that states may select the easiest (or most difficult) cases for intervention, we use an empirical strategy that identifies pairs of states that did and did not experience FIRC, but were otherwise highly similar, to isolate the effects of FIRC on democratization. Finally, we argue that, in addition to the intentions or incentives of external actors, analysts must take into account domestic conditions in targets of FIRC to explain variation in democratization success and failure.

Our empirical findings support our theoretical expectations. First, we find that states that experience FIRC initiated by democracies on average gain no significant democratic benefit compared with similar states where democracies did not intervene. Second, successful democratization following FIRC depends on both the strategy adopted by the intervener and whether domestic conditions in the target state are favorable to democracy. When intervening democracies target individual leaders for removal but leave the underlying political institutions of a regime intact, democratization is unlikely to occur, even if conditions favorable to democracy are present. Interventions that implement concrete, pro-democratic institutional reforms, such as sponsoring elections, can succeed when conditions in the target state are favorable to democracy. When domestic preconditions for democracy are lacking, however, the democratizing efforts of the intervener are largely for naught: states that are economically underdeveloped or ethnically heterogeneous, or lack prior experience with representative government, face serious obstacles to democratization, and even outsiders with good intentions are typically unable to surmount these barriers no matter how hard they try.

These conclusions suggest that policymakers contemplating intervention and regime change as a potential path to democracy in foreign states face a paradox. Decapitating a regime by removing its leader may appear to be a quick and low-cost means to initiate democratic change, but decapitation alone is unlikely to succeed. FIRCs that aim to reform the institutions of a regime, however, can be effective if favorable internal preconditions are present. These conditions, unfortunately, are rare in countries where the costs of intervention are low. Germany and Japan in the 1930s had favorable preconditions for democracy, but overthrowing their governments involved enormous costs. The same might be said of powerful autocracies today, such as China and Russia. Countries that lack favorable preconditions tend to be weak, and thus the immediate costs of toppling their regimes are low, making them tempting targets. But democracy is unlikely to take hold in these states, and the costs of intervention can grow exponentially in the wake of regime change because the conditions that hinder democratization are also those that increase the likelihood of civil war. The United States has experienced this paradox first-hand in its recent interventions in Afghanistan, Iraq, and Libya. Conceived as quick and easy fixes to pressing problems, regime change instead triggered chaos and violence, and drew the United States ever deeper into costly quagmires.

The chapter proceeds as follows. First, we lay out and critique the current literature on intervention and democracy. Second, we offer our theory and hypotheses
for the conditions under which FIRC by democracies leads to democratization.
Third, we discuss our research design. Fourth, we present the statistical results. Fifth,
we briefly discuss recent US FIRCs, arguing that the outcomes in these cases are
consistent with our broader results. We conclude by discussing the policy implications of our findings.

The debate about intervention and the spread of democracy

Scholars who debate whether countries can be forcibly democratized from the outside in can be divided into three groups: optimists, pessimists, and conditionalists.
This section describes and critiques the main positions in this debate.

Scholars and policymakers alike have at times evinced optimism about the usefulness of military force for spreading democracy. Of recent US presidents, George
W. Bush was the most upbeat in this regard.[5] Although Bush came into office as an
opponent of nation building, after the attacks of September 11, 2001, he embraced
forceful democratization as a means to combat the terrorist threat he perceived as
emanating from authoritarian states in the Middle East (Bush 2002). A principal
justification put forward by the Bush administration for invading Iraq and toppling
Saddam Hussein was that democratizing Iraq would initiate a wave of liberalization
in surrounding countries, removing repressive regimes that sponsored international
terrorism (Bush 2003).

The view that outsiders can democratize other countries through military force
has found some support in the scholarly literature (Bermeo 2010; Mansfield and
Snyder 2010; Whitehead 1996). Democratization scholars have identified several
ways that foreign intervention can promote democratic change. One argument
suggests that intervention is necessary to dismantle and remove abusive political
and military institutions that have become entrenched against popular pressure
(Bermeo 2003; Stepan 1986). Others contend that military defeat can discredit
ruling elites or foster new elite bargains that favor democracy (Dogan and Higley
1998; Higley and Burton 1989). Intervention and occupation by a democracy can
make it costly for the armed forces or other potential antidemocratic spoilers to use
violence to challenge a new regime, which can establish and ensure civilian control
over the military (Bermeo 2010: 73). Democratic regimes established in this way
may also have advantages that contribute to their future durability and reduce the
likelihood of breakdown, including access to international resources and links with
democratic actors abroad (Bermeo 2010: 91–93).

Pessimists variously argue that regime-changing interventions are likely to provoke a nationalist backlash against political institutions imposed from the outside
(Mearsheimer 2005); weaken domestic institutions by cultivating dependency on
external support (Fukuyama 2004: 37–39); or founder on a lack of knowledge or
influence over local politics and actors (Fukuyama 2004: 37).

One rigorous attempt to examine this question is Bruce Bueno de Mesquita and George Downs's study of military intervention and democracy. This study compares the democratic trajectories of states that did and did not experience military intervention by a democracy from 1946 to 2001. The results are striking: whether the intervener is the United States or some other democracy, targets of intervention experience no meaningful degree of democratization afterward (Bueno de Mesquita and Downs 2006: 647). Bueno de Mesquita and Downs contend that intervention by democracies fails to spur democratization because democratic interveners have no incentive to build true democracy in states where they intervene. Democratic leaders care most about their own political survival, and institutionalizing a democratic system in another state does not serve this goal. From the perspective of a democratic leader in an intervening state, democracy induces uncertainty because "there is no guarantee that a candidate sympathetic to the policy goals of the intervener will even be running much less be victorious." It is thus "safer and less costly" to empower a dictator because autocratic leaders do not have to cater to the whims of their population; they can undertake policies that benefit the intervener. Democratic interventions thus fail to spread democracy by design (Bueno de Mesquita and Downs 2006: 631–632; see also Bueno de Mesquita, Smith, Siverson, and Morrow 2003).

Bueno de Mesquita and Downs's argument may be unusual in insisting that democracies purposefully refrain from propagating democracy abroad, but their empirical result is common: many studies find that although democratic intervention may have a small positive effect on target democratization, it does not instigate transitions to consolidated democracy (Pickering and Peceny 2006: 549–555; Hermann and Kegley 1998: 97; Goldsmith 2008).

Conditionalists eschew categorical judgments in favor of identifying factors associated with better or worse democratic outcomes among countries that experience intervention. One explanation for variation in the success or failure of interventions concerns the level of effort put forward by the intervener(s). A study led by James Dobbins, for example, argues that although many factors contribute to nation-building success, the single most important variable "is the level of effort the United States and the international community put into their democratic transformations …. This higher level of input accounts in significant measure for the higher level of output measured in the development of democratic institutions and economic growth" (Dobbins 2003: xix).

A second conditional argument highlights the pro-democracy intentions or actions of interveners. Several studies maintain that US military interventions exert a positive effect on democratization only when the objective of these interventions is explicitly to liberalize the target state. In an examination of US interventions from 1950 to 1990, James Meernik found that intervention alone had little discernible impact on subsequent levels of democracy in target states. When "the US president declared democracy was a goal of the intervention," however, these operations resulted in positive democratic change (Meernik 1996: 399).

A final set of arguments identifies conditions in the target state—not interveners' efforts or actions—as the key variables influencing the success or failure of military interventions in producing democratic change. This view draws on the comparative politics literature on democratization, which identifies factors associated with democratic transition, consolidation, and breakdown, such as a state's level of wealth, the extent of ethnic or social divisions in a society, whether a state has any prior experience with democracy, or a state's level of external and internal security threat (Teorell 2010; Geddes 1999; Lipset 1959; Przeworski, Alvarez, Cheibub, and Limongi 2000). Several scholars argue that these factors also strongly influence the likelihood that foreign intervention will result in sustainable democratic change (Brownlee 2007; Bellin 2004/05; Pei and Kasper 2003). Andrew Enterline and Michael Greig, for example, find that the level of wealth in "imposed democracies" and the degree of ethnic or religious fractionalization affect the survival of these regimes: only 40 percent of imposed democracies with high levels of ethnic fractionalization survive their first decade, and just one-quarter of the poorest such states last for twenty years (Enterline and Greig 2008: 335–339).

Critical evaluation

The evidence behind each of the views discussed above has important weaknesses. The difficulty with the democratization optimists' argument is the historical rarity of successes. Aside from West Germany and Japan after World War II, there are few positive outcomes to point to, and hardly any in less-developed countries (Pei and Kasper 2003). The failure thus far of Afghanistan and Iraq to join the ranks of consolidated democracies conforms to this trend.

Democratization pessimists, such as Bueno de Mesquita and Downs, initially appear to be on firmer ground, yet these studies have theoretical and methodological problems that undermine their persuasiveness. First, Bueno de Mesquita and Downs argue that democratic leaders have no incentives to promote democracy abroad when in fact there are many instances where democracies have done just that. Examples include Nicaragua and the Dominican Republic in the early twentieth century; West Germany and Japan after World War II; Grenada, Panama, and Bosnia in the 1980s and 1990s; and Afghanistan, Iraq, and Libya in the early twenty-first century. Although the jury is still out on these recent democratic transformations, the actions of US policymakers in these cases defy Bueno de Mesquita and Downs's logic.

Second, owing to the loose way in which they operationalize intervention, pessimistic studies include few cases of regime change. Bueno de Mesquita and Downs, for example, in addition to using data on UN peacekeeping and intervention in civil wars, code as interveners "any state with a Militarized Interstate Dispute (MID) hostility level score above 1; that is, any state that actively participated in a militarized dispute provided it is not coded as the initiator in the MIDs data" (Bueno de Mesquita and Downs 2006: 637). No effort is made to determine whether interveners in these cases actually changed leaders or governing institutions. Pickering and Peceny use a more appropriate measure of intervention consisting of the "movement of regular troops or forces (airborne, seaborne, shelling, etc.) of one country inside another, in the context of some political issue or dispute" (Pickering and Peceny 2006: 546). Although these data track the direction of intervention—supportive of, or in opposition to, a target government—they do not indicate whether interveners actually overturned—or otherwise tried to change—leaders or governing institutions in the target state. The results of these studies are thus based largely on cases that have nothing to do with regime change.

Studies that make conditional arguments regarding post-intervention democratization also provide grounds for skepticism. Evidence for the expenditure-of-effort argument, for example, is far from clear-cut (Dobbins 2003). Japan—one of the few unqualified successes—is actually an anomaly for the argument, as it was garrisoned by low levels of troops and received a small amount of aid relative to the size of its population. Even Germany—the other major success—obtained far less aid per capita than did Bosnia and Kosovo, and only marginally more than Haiti, a failure (Dobbins 2003: 150–158). According to a 2006 report by the Congressional Research Service, Iraq has received comparable levels of aid to Germany and twice the amount of aid that Japan received from 1946 to 1952, and it was the largest recipient of US official development assistance from 2004 to 2008 (Serafino, Tarnoff, and Nanto 2006).

Proponents of the view that targets democratize when democratic interveners specifically undertake democratic reforms have produced little systematic evidence to support their argument. Meernik's study, for example, is limited to a small sample of twenty-seven US interventions and tracks democratic change for only three years afterward (Meernik 1996). Other work includes more interventions and covers a longer time period, but is confined to US interventions and measures democratization decades after US intervention ended, which increases the likelihood that factors other than intervention are responsible for any positive democratic change (Peceny 1999: 202–207). Finally, most studies find only that pro-democratic intervention made targets more democratic, not that they became consolidated democracies (Hermann and Kegley 1998; Meernik 1996).

Finally, studies that highlight the importance of domestic conditions in explaining democratization success following intervention have been dominated by qualitative studies focusing on single cases, such as Iraq (Byman 2003; Bellin 2004/05), or by studies that use a different universe of cases than ours (Enterline and Greig 2008; Pei and Kasper 2003). Almost 90 percent of the imposed democracies in Enterline and Greig's work, for example, consist of states where a democratic government was put in place at the time of decolonization. Only five of the forty-three cases in their study were independent states where a nondemocratic government was forcibly replaced with a democratic one (Enterline and Greig 2008: 326). Existing empirical evidence for the importance of domestic conditions as the key factor driving democratization success after intervention thus rests largely on the experience of postcolonial states rather than states that have experienced FIRC.

A theory of foreign-imposed regime change and democratization

In this section, we offer a two-step theory of the conditions under which FIRC fosters democratization. No single factor determines whether FIRC promotes democracy. Interveners, we argue, must undertake concrete democratic reforms, but these steps will falter where important preconditions for democracy are absent.

Conditions favorable to democracy

First, many democratization scholars posit a strong relationship between a state's level of economic development and democratic institutions (Inglehart and Welzel 2009; Teorell 2010; Boix and Stokes 2003; Przeworski, Alvarez, Cheibub, and Limongi 2000). Although the link between development and democracy is complex, economic growth is associated with several social and political changes that appear to favor democracy, including rising personal incomes, greater access to education, an expanding middle class, and a stronger civil society and independent media. States that are more advanced economically may also have more developed bureaucratic institutions, another factor associated with a greater potential to democratize. As a result, wealthier autocracies may be more likely to transition to democracy, and they may be less at risk of backsliding once they make the transition.

Second, democracy may be more difficult to sustain in countries with greater ethnic, linguistic, and religious diversity (Teorell 2010; Horowitz 1993; Lijphart 1977; but see Fish and Brooks 2004). Social and ethnic diversity can impede the development of democratic institutions in several ways. Political parties are more likely to organize predominantly around ethnic cleavages, encouraging politicians to "outbid" one another by appealing to their respective in-groups and making consensus and compromise more difficult (Horowitz 1985: 291–332). Heterogeneous societies also run a greater risk of sectarian violence, further hardening communal boundaries and inhibiting the functioning of democracy (Sambanis 2001). Minority groups may fear insecurity or a loss of power from open electoral competition, particularly in the absence of strong state institutions or constitutional limits on the exercise of power by the majority (Posen 1993).

A third important precondition for democracy identified by many analysts is past experience with representative government (Moon 2009; Bellin 2004/05: 599–600). Previous democratic regimes possibly laid an institutional foundation that leaders can make use of, rather than having to build entirely new institutions. Populations that have had some experience with democracy may be more likely both to demand greater political participation and to overthrow despotic rulers who deny them popular sovereignty. Political elites likely were previously socialized into a political system characterized by norms of compromise and the nonviolent resolution of political disputes. States that have had some experience with democratic institutions in the past therefore may be more likely to sustain them in the future.

Finally, the act of intervention—by itself or in combination with some of the preconditions just discussed—may increase the likelihood of civil war, which could in turn hinder democratization. Recent studies have linked foreign-imposed regime change to an increased risk of civil conflict afterward in target states. One study finds that this effect is more pronounced when interveners change the target's political institutions in addition to its leadership (Peic and Reiter 2011). Another study shows that FIRCs that change target state institutions increase the likelihood of civil war in countries where the preconditions for democracy are absent: poor and heterogeneous societies (Downes 2016). Foreign-imposed regime change in countries like these touches off struggles for power among contending groups or results in status reversals for groups displaced from power, which fight to regain their previous position. This is what happened in Iraq and Afghanistan—both highly heterogeneous countries—and the resulting insurgencies have slowed democratic transitions in those countries to a crawl. Democratization after FIRC is thus hindered by the fact that FIRC sometimes causes democracy-inhibiting civil wars.

Intervener strategy

Preconditions for democracy are important in creating fertile grounds for FIRC to bring about positive democratic change, but by themselves they cannot ensure democratization unless the external intervener takes the initiative and enacts democratic reforms. A second key factor is therefore whether the intervener removes a state's primary leader, but leaves the main political institutions and selection procedures that make up the regime intact (leadership FIRC), or whether the intervener overthrows and replaces a state's political institutions as well (institutional FIRC).

There are several reasons to expect that leadership FIRC is unlikely to be a catalyst for democratic change. Institutions—such as elections, parliaments, and constitutions—are not generated spontaneously; they require effort to design and construct. If foreign interveners install a new leader but make no effort to build democratic institutions, the onus falls on the leader they empower, who may be more interested in securing and extending his rule than in building democracy. Leaders who continue to rely on the support of foreign interveners to remain in power may also fail to cultivate a broad domestic base of support, making them more reluctant to risk their rule to open democratic elections. Moreover, external interveners sometimes take steps to inhibit democratic change, such as putting a dictator in office and strengthening the state's repressive apparatus, as when the United States returned the Shah to power in Iran in 1953. Similarly, the Soviet Union clearly had no interest in instilling democracy in the eastern European countries it occupied at the end of World War II. Many of these countries were promising candidates for democratization (some, such as Czechoslovakia, had previously been democracies), but without external assistance in jump-starting the process by helping to create democratic institutions, positive preconditions for democracy cannot be translated into actual democratic change.

Summary and hypotheses

In sum, we expect FIRC by democracies to make targets more democratic and increase the likelihood of a transition to consolidated democracy when interveners take concrete steps to implement democratic reforms and targets possess the preconditions for democracy. This argument implies the following three hypotheses.

H1: The effect of institutional FIRC on democratization increases as targets' level of economic development increases.

H2: The effect of institutional FIRC on democratization increases as targets' level of ethnic homogeneity increases.

H3: The effect of institutional FIRC on democratization is greater if targets have previous experience with democracy.

By contrast, democratization is unlikely to occur when either of these two factors—preconditions for democracy or intervener actions to facilitate reform—is absent.

H4: Institutional FIRC has no effect on democratization in the absence of preconditions for democracy.

H5: Leadership FIRC has no effect on democratization.

Research design

This section presents the research design we employ to estimate the effect of FIRC on democratization. We begin by defining these two variables. We then briefly discuss the matching method we use to account for the reality that interventions are not randomly assigned.[6]

Coding democratization

There is no perfect way to measure democracy or democratization. Scholars disagree not only about what democracy consists of, but also whether it is a dichotomous or continuous phenomenon (Collier and Adcock 1999; Munck and Verkuilen 2002). Although we cannot resolve this debate, we employ the leading dataset of democracy used by scholars of international relations and comparative politics, the Polity index (Marshall and Jaggers 2010). The Polity index is a widely used measure of the level of democracy in a political system. The index comprises several components that take into account how political leaders are recruited, whether there are institutionalized constraints on executive power, and the degree of political competition. The Polity2 variable ranks states on a 21-point scale by subtracting each state's autocracy score from its democracy score; the resulting variable ranges from -10 (most autocratic) to $+10$ (most democratic), with states scoring $+6$ or higher considered to be consolidated democracies. For ease of interpretation, we transform the index to make it strictly positive by adding eleven; the resulting variable ranges from 1 to 21, with the threshold for consolidated democracy set at 17.

We use the Polity index to create two dependent variables that capture both change in a state's level of democracy and whether a state crosses the threshold of consolidated democracy. The first dependent variable measures the change in a state's Polity2 score from one year to the next. For example, the dependent variable for Uganda in 1985 is the difference between its Polity score in 1985 and its Polity score in 1984. The resulting variable ranges from −20 to +20, although in our dataset the largest one-year change in either direction is 19. The second dependent variable codes whether a state experienced a democratic transition in a particular year. In other words, a country must shift from less than 17 on the Polity index to 17 or above (on defining democratic transitions and consolidations, see Schedler 1998; Linz and Stepan 2011). After a state experiences a democratic transition, we code the variable as missing because it is no longer possible for that country to transition to democracy. If the country reverts to autocracy, however, it is then eligible to experience another democratic transition and is coded 0 unless or until it undergoes another democratic transition.

Defining and coding foreign-imposed regime change

We define foreign-imposed regime change as the forcible or coerced removal of the effective leader of one state—which remains formally sovereign afterward—by the government of another state. Three conditions must be met for a case to be coded as FIRC. First, targets of FIRC must be independent, sovereign states. We do not consider the imposition of regimes on newly independent states by departing colonial powers, for example, to constitute FIRC. Second, targets of FIRC must retain at least nominal sovereignty after regime change occurs. Targets of intervention that are formally annexed by an intervener—such as Nazi Germany's incorporation of Austria, Czechoslovakia, and much of Poland (1938–39)—are excluded from the universe of FIRC, as are states that are absorbed into empires, such as Britain's conquest of Sind (1843) and Punjab (1846). Interveners may temporarily occupy and govern a state whose leader they have overthrown—as in the US occupations of Haiti (1915–34) and the Dominican Republic (1916–24)—as long as the assumption of power is not intended to be permanent (on the distinction between occupation and colonialism see Edelstein 2008: 3).

Third, an external actor must be primarily responsible for deposing the leader. Most commonly, interveners use their own military forces to remove a leader, such as the United States did in late 1989 to apprehend Panamanian President Manuel Noriega. Less frequently, the threat of force is enough to prompt a leader to relinquish power, as when Haitian junta leader Gen. Raoul Cedras agreed to step down with the US 82d Airborne Division poised to come ashore in October 1994.[7] External actors may also work behind the scenes to overthrow the targeted regime using their intelligence agencies or covert military force, or by providing critical aid to domestic actors (O'Rourke 2013). We code these cases as FIRC if (1) the foreign government officially (although not necessarily publicly) made removing the target regime its objective; (2) agents of the foreign government were present in the target country and working toward regime change; and (3) the extent of the aid provided by foreign forces was of such a magnitude that regime change would have been unlikely to succeed absent that support.

According to these criteria, there were 109 cases of FIRC from 1816 to 2008.[8] Because there was only one FIRC by a democracy in the nineteenth century—France's FIRC against the Roman Republic in 1849 that restored the Pope—we limit the time span of our analysis to the twentieth century. Some states had multiple leaders removed in a single year (e.g., Guatemala 1954); because our unit of analysis is the country-year, these additional FIRCs are not included in the analysis. Several other countries experienced FIRC shortly before exiting the international system (e.g., Estonia, Latvia, and Lithuania 1940). These cases are omitted from the analysis because it is impossible to measure the dependent variable. Afghanistan (2001) and Iraq (2003) are also omitted because they occurred outside of the time-frame of our study. These omissions—and missing data for a few cases—leave the number of FIRCs in the analysis at 70.

FIRC BY DEMOCRACIES. We differentiate FIRCs undertaken by democratic interveners from those carried out by nondemocracies. Interveners that rank 17 or higher on the Polity index are assigned a value of 1 on a dummy variable for intervener democracy. Interveners with Polity scores less than 17 are coded as autocratic interveners. Of the 70 FIRCs in our analysis, democracies carried out 37 (53 percent) compared with 33 by nondemocracies (47 percent).

Because transitions to democracy may unfold over time, however, the key independent variable in our analysis is whether a country experienced a FIRC by a democracy within the last ten years. This ten-year window enables us to measure the effect of FIRC on democratic change over an extended period of time.[9] A ten-year window allows sufficient time for democratic reforms to be implemented and to take hold, but remains short enough that democratization can still be attributed to FIRC (Bueno de Mesquita and Downs 2006: 638).

LEADERSHIP AND INSTITUTIONAL FIRC. To differentiate the effects of FIRCs by democracies that change only leaders from those that also change institutions, we code two dummy variables denoting whether the intervening democracy replaced one leader with another, or instead took action to democratize the target state's political institutions after deposing a leader. We code a FIRC as "institutional" if an intervener either assisted local authorities in organizing or conducting elections, or made holding elections a condition for recognizing a successor government.[10] For example, the US intervention in Nicaragua 1926 is coded as an institutional FIRC because after the United States coerced the removal of Emiliano Chamorro, US soldiers supervised Nicaraguan elections in 1928, 1930, and 1932 (Gobat 2005: 208).

To qualify as an institutional FIRC, elections need to be "free and fair" in the sense that voters are not coerced to cast their ballots for one candidate or another. It is not necessary for suffrage to be universal, however. Several US interventions took place at a time when the political participation of women, black people, or both in the United States was restricted if not banned. The United States still undertook good-faith efforts to promote democracy as it was understood at the time; these mainly involved holding elections in which more than one candidate and political party was allowed to run.

To code institutional FIRCs, we began with Peceny's coding of whether or not US leaders adopted "proliberalization" intervention policies. Peceny defines proliberalization policies as "the combination of active support for free-and-fair elections with active promotion of at least one of the following: centrist political parties, reformist interest groups, reductions in human rights abuses, and/or formal subordination of the military to civilian authority" (Peceny 1999: 15). Our definition is thus broader than Peceny's, although in practice these other reforms often go hand-in-hand with promoting elections, and almost all of our US cases are also coded by Peceny as instances of proliberalization interventions (Peceny 1999: 20–21). We did additional research using material from the *Foreign Relations of the United States* collection and the secondary literature for each US FIRC that appeared on Peceny's list of cases as well as for those (by the United States but also other democracies) that did not. Ten institutional FIRCs are included in the analysis (constituting 27 percent of FIRCs by democracies), compared to 27 leadership FIRCs (73 percent).[11] The United States participated in 28 of the 37 FIRCs by democracies in our analysis (76 percent); democracies other than the United States participated in 20 (54 percent).[12]

Control variables

We include seven variables to capture the effects of factors previously shown to be correlated with democracy: level of economic development (proxied by the log of a state's energy consumption), state age (how long a state has been independent), previous experience with democracy, whether a state was a British colony, ethnic heterogeneity (proxied by the ethnolinguistic fractionalization index), and whether a state was involved in an interstate or a civil war.[13] To assess whether the effects of FIRCs by democracies are contingent on the target state's level of economic development, ethnic heterogeneity, or previous experience with democracy, we generate interaction terms by multiplying our measures of these factors by dummy variables for institutional and leadership FIRCs.

Accounting for selection effects with matching

All studies designed to measure the effect of an intervention—whether it be FIRC or a new cancer drug—must confront the problem of selection bias. Medical trials deal with this problem via randomization, which ensures that the group that receives the drug (the "treated" group) does not differ appreciably from the group that receives the placebo (the "control" group). Researchers can thus confidently attribute any difference in outcome between the two groups to the treatment. The problem with estimating the effect of FIRC on democratization is that states do not randomly select targets for intervention. The danger thus arises that differences in democratization outcomes may stem not from FIRC but from differences between the two groups in some other factor, such as economic development or ethnic homogeneity.

To address the issue of non-random selection, we use a technique known as genetic matching that pairs cases of FIRC with cases that did not experience FIRC, but which were extremely similar to those that did. This procedure minimizes the risk that our estimate of the effect of FIRC on democratization is biased by systematic differences in where democratic states choose to intervene (to implement matching, we used the MatchIt program. See Ho, Imai, King, and Stuart 2007). Using this method, we constructed six datasets—one for each type of FIRC we examine: FIRCs by democracies and nondemocracies; leadership and institutional FIRCs by democracies; and FIRCs by the United States and other democracies.[14] Variables used to match cases of FIRC to similar non-FIRC cases include all seven control variables plus Polity score (before FIRC), population, and region of the world. This procedure yielded datasets in which the mean values for all variables did not differ appreciably across cases that did and did not experience FIRC. In every case, matching greatly reduced the difference in the mean values of all variables between the FIRC and non-FIRC groups (between 85 and 99 percent depending on the type of FIRC). We evaluate the effects of FIRC using these "most similar" sets of cases.

Analysis and results

We tackle our five hypotheses in reverse order, first examining the effects of leadership and institutional FIRC on democratization individually and then analyzing their effects conditional on domestic factors in targets. For ease of interpretation, we rely primarily on graphs to demonstrate the effects of different types of FIRC on our measures of democratization.

FIRC and democratization: a matched analysis

To test the unconditional effect of each type of FIRC on democratization, we perform t-tests to compare the mean values of our dependent variables for states that experienced each type of FIRC to states that did not. Figure 5.1, for example, shows the results of t-tests for our first dependent variable, the average change in targets' Polity scores over the ten years following FIRC. The capped lines inside each bar indicate 95 percent confidence intervals. Figure 5.2 repeats this exercise for our second dependent variable, the probability that targets experience a transition to consolidated democracy. The first two sets of columns in each figure show the effect on target democratization of experiencing a FIRC by a nondemocracy and a democracy, respectively, compared to similar states that did not undergo regime

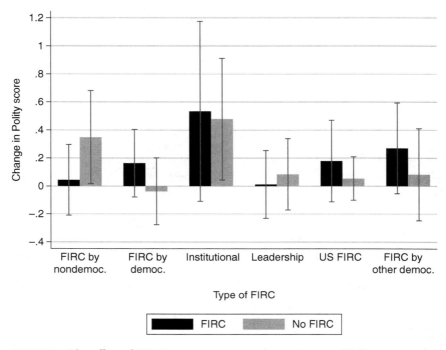

FIGURE 5.1 The effect of FIRC over ten years on change in targets' Polity score

change. For change in Polity score, as shown in Figure 5.1, FIRCs by nondemocracies reduce targets' Polity scores by about three-tenths of a point, a difference that is marginally statistically significant (p < 0.10). Experiencing a FIRC by a democracy, by contrast, increases targets' Polity scores by two-tenths of a point compared to no FIRC (slightly less than 1 percent on the 21-point Polity scale), but—as indicated by the broad and overlapping confidence intervals—this difference is not significant. The pattern is similar in Figure 5.2: FIRCs carried out by nondemocracies reduce the chance that targets will experience a democratic transition by about two-thirds, whereas FIRCs by democracies increase the chance of transition by nearly 80 percent. Neither of these results is statistically significant, however. Thus, although there is some weak evidence that undergoing a FIRC by a nondemocracy has negative repercussions for target democratization, there is no support for the argument that experiencing a FIRC by a democracy has positive implications for democratization.

The two pairs of columns in the middle of each figure—which show the effect on target democratization of experiencing an institutional or a leadership FIRC—test H4 and H5. Recall that we argued that neither of these types of FIRCs by democracies should enhance the prospects for democratization in targets—leadership FIRC because it does nothing to promote democratic change, and institutional FIRC because the success of efforts to implement democracy are contingent on factors internal to the target. The results support both hypotheses.

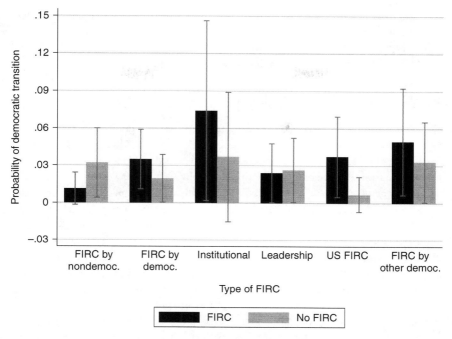

FIGURE 5.2 The effect of FIRC over ten years on the probability that targets experience a transition to consolidated democracy

Leadership FIRC, for example, has barely any effect on target democratization: it decreases targets' Polity scores by 0.07 points on the 21-point index (three-tenths of 1 percent) and their chances of experiencing a democratic transition by 9 percent. Institutional FIRC similarly has a barely perceptible effect on target Polity scores, nudging them up by 0.06 points. Institutional FIRC has a much larger effect on the probability that targets undergo democratic transitions, however, doubling the chance that targets cross the democratic threshold compared to states that did not experience institutional FIRC. As indicated by the very broad confidence intervals surrounding these estimates, however, this effect is not statistically significant.

Finally, because the United States has been the world's most prolific regime changer since 1900, we compared the democratizing effect of US FIRCs to that of FIRCs implemented by other democracies. As the right-most columns in Figures 5.1 and 5.2 show, both types of FIRC have a positive effect on targets' levels of democracy, but the size of these effects is tiny (0.12 and 0.19 Polity points, respectively, each of which is less than a 1 percent increase) and statistically insignificant. US FIRCs, however, appear to have a large effect on the chances that targets undergo a democratic transition, increasing that probability more than five-fold. This effect is only marginally significant, though, and disappears in a multivariate analysis (Downes and Monten 2013: 120). FIRCs by other democracies, by contrast, increase the prospect of a democratic transition only 50 percent, an effect that fails to attain significance.

In short, the evidence from our matched datasets indicates that all types of FIRCs implemented by democracies fail to promote target democratization.

The conditional effect of institutional FIRC on democratization

Table 5.1 lists the twelve cases of institutional FIRC carried out by democracies. The table suggests initial plausibility for some of our conditional hypotheses: countries that have made sizable democratic gains or successful democratic transitions—with a few exceptions—appear to be relatively wealthy and homogeneous, and to have had some prior experience with democratic rule. For example, the United States attempted to democratize the Dominican Republic and Nicaragua in the early part of the twentieth century, perpetrating a total of five institutional FIRCs in those countries. In no case did these FIRCs have the desired effect. The United States overthrew three Dominican governments in succession in 1912, 1914, and 1916, and occupied the country from 1916 to 1924 (Calder 1984: 5–19). Not only did the Dominican Republic make no headway in its level of democracy, the government the Americans left in place was overthrown six years later by the leader of the Guardia Nacional, an institution created by the US occupiers (Calder 1984: 239). The country's Polity score plummeted to 2 under Rafael Trujillo's dictatorial rule. Similarly,

TABLE 5.1 Democratization in targets of institutional FIRC

Country	Year	Increase in polity score over ensuing ten years	Successful democratic transition over ensuing ten years
Nicaragua	1910	0	no
Dominican Republic	1912	0	no
Dominican Republic	1914	0	no
Dominican Republic	1916	0	no
Costa Rica	1919	0	no†
Nicaragua	1926	−5	no
Japan	1945	+9	yes
Federal Republic of Germany	1955	+19	yes
Panama	1990	+17	yes
Haiti	1994	+14	yes‡
Afghanistan	2001	n/a	n/a
Iraq	2003	n/a	n/a

† Costa Rica is coded as a democracy before and after the removal of Federico Tinoco and is thus not coded as experiencing a democratic transition.
‡ With the election of Jean-Bertrand Aristide in 1990, Haiti experienced a transition to democracy that was interrupted by a coup the following year. US intervention in 1994 restored democracy to a previously democratic state rather than creating democracy anew. Haiti was unable to maintain its democratic momentum, however, slipping from the ranks of consolidated democracies in 1999.

Nicaragua gained little democratic benefit from US institutional FIRCs in 1910—
which ousted Liberal leader José Madriz and empowered Nicaragua's Conservative
Party—and in 1926—which removed Emiliano Chamorro in favor of Adolfo Diaz
(Kerevel 2006; Gobat 2005: 137–149, 205–216). In both cases, the United States was
forced into further military intervention to save its newly empowered protégé. In
an eerie replay of events a few years earlier in the Dominican Republic, Anastasio
Somoza—the head of the Guardia Nacional created by the American occupiers—
overthrew the government in 1936 and established a dictatorship.

The only real success stories for institutional FIRCs are West Germany and
Japan following World War II, and Panama after the removal of Manuel Noriega
(Grenada would constitute a fourth success, but it is not included in the Polity dataset owing to its small population). These three states were characterized by relatively
high levels of income (GDP per capita between $3,000 and $6,000 in the year prior
to intervention, in 1996 dollars) and low levels of ethnic diversity (ethnolinguistic
fractionalization scores between 0.01 and 0.21).[15] Germany and Japan were also
highly developed bureaucratic states with industrial economies. Germany was a
democracy for a decade in the Weimar period, but all three states had experience
with constitutional rule (if not complete democracy) in the past.

Figures 5.3 to 5.6 and Table 5.2 present the results of several interaction models
estimated on the complete dataset to buttress these claims.[16] The solid lines in the
figures indicate the marginal effect of FIRC; the dotted lines graph the 95 percent

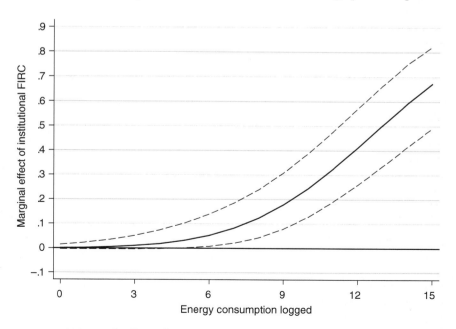

FIGURE 5.3 Marginal effect of institutional FIRC over ten years on probability of
transition to consolidated democracy as target's level of economic development (log of
energy consumption) increases

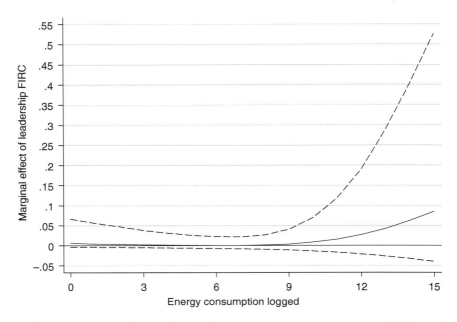

FIGURE 5.4 Marginal effect of leadership FIRC over ten years on probability of transition to consolidated democracy as target's level of economic development (log of energy consumption) increases

confidence interval. The effect is significant when these dotted lines are each above (or below) zero.

Figures 5.3 and 5.4 test H1 by graphing the marginal effect of institutional and leadership FIRCs on the probability of targets experiencing a democratic transition as these states become more economically developed.[17] If the hypothesis that FIRCs that reform target state institutions lead to better democratization outcomes in more developed states were correct, the line in Figure 5.3 should be upward-sloping. As is evident from the figure, this is indeed the case. States that are the least developed economically, such as the Dominican Republic, receive no significant democratic benefit from institutional FIRCs. The effect quickly becomes significant as states grow wealthier, however, and by the time a country reaches Japan's level of industrialization in the 1940s, its chance of democratizing increases by 24 to 32 percent after an institutional FIRC. At West Germany's level of development in the 1950s, the probability of democratization increases by 41 to 50 percent. Compare these sizable effects to those in Figure 5.4 for targets of leadership FIRC, which register essentially no improvement in the likelihood of becoming a consolidated democracy: the marginal effect of leadership FIRC is 0 for most of the range of economic development, and the confidence interval straddles 0 throughout, meaning that the effect is also insignificant. These graphs lend support to H1, that institutional FIRCs improve targets' prospects for democratization only when these states are economically developed.

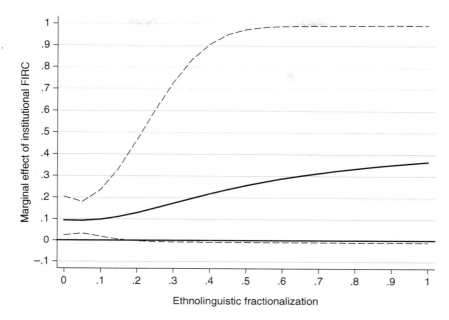

FIGURE 5.5 Marginal effect of institutional FIRC over ten years on probability of transition to consolidated democracy as target's level of ethnic heterogeneity increases

Figures 5.5 and 5.6 evaluate H2 by graphing the marginal effect of institutional and leadership FIRC on democratic change as targets become increasingly ethnically heterogeneous. Figure 5.5 shows that only the most homogeneous states receive a significant boost in their chances of transitioning to consolidated democracy. States at or below 0.15 on the ethnolinguistic fractionalization index are about 10 percent more likely to democratize after an institutional FIRC. By the time the index reaches 0.2, the effect is already insignificant, and remains so even as the point estimate increases. The small number of cases causes the confidence interval to balloon, meaning we should not put any confidence in the estimated effect of institutional FIRC at high levels of heterogeneity. Leadership FIRCs, by contrast, have no significant effect on the probability of democratization at any level of diversity. The estimated effect decreases as targets become more heterogeneous but is never significant. These two figures provide solid evidence for H2: democratization outcomes are better when target state populations are homogeneous and democratic interveners make efforts to reform institutions.

Table 5.2 provides evidence on H3, which holds that democratization outcomes are superior after FIRC if interveners promote institutional change and the target was a democracy at some point in the past. The table shows the probability of democratization after institutional and leadership FIRCs when the target was and was not previously democratic. As is evident from the upper-left corner of each two-by-two, both types of FIRC significantly increase the likelihood of a democratic transition when the target was a democracy in the past. The absolute

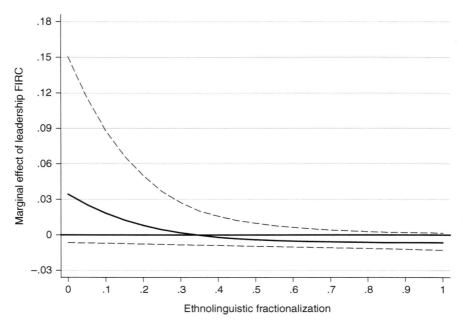

FIGURE 5.6 Marginal effect of leadership FIRC over ten years on probability of transition to consolidated democracy as target's level of ethnic heterogeneity increases

TABLE 5.2 The effect of previous democracy and type of FIRC on the probability of transitions to democracy, 1900–2000

		Previous Democracy	
		Yes	No
Institutional FIRC	yes	0.200	0.043
	no	0.039	0.010
Leadership FIRC	yes	0.111	0.007
	no	0.038	0.011

probability of a transition, however, is nearly twice as large after an institutional FIRC than following a leadership FIRC. When states were previously democratic but did not experience FIRC, the probability of democratic transition in a given year was 4 percent. When previously democratic states experienced a leadership FIRC, the probability of a transition increased to 11 percent, but it increased to 20 percent after an institutional FIRC. Regime changes that alter governing institutions thus result in a higher probability of democratic transitions when targets have previous experience with democracy, and a higher probability than leadership FIRCs under the same circumstances.

In short, the evidence supports H1, H2, and H3 that it is the combination of intervener actions to promote institutional change and fertile preconditions for democracy that increase target-state levels of democracy and the prospect for transitions to consolidated democracy. FIRC is unable to effect positive democratic change—even when the intervener specifically takes actions to bring about elections—when domestic conditions in the target are not amenable to democracy. Similarly, positive preconditions do not translate into democratization absent intervener efforts to change institutions.

Foreign-imposed regime change under the Obama administration

The record of US interventions during the last decade is largely consistent with the argument that externally imposed regime change is unlikely to lead to democratization without favorable domestic preconditions. The Obama administration came into office in 2008 promising to focus on "nation-building right here at home" (Dueck 2015: 4). Yet, while reducing US military commitments to Iraq and Afghanistan, the Obama administration embraced regime change as a policy goal in the conflicts in Libya and Syria. The outcomes of US interventions in these four cases further support our analysis of the historical record. Prior to US-led regime change, Afghanistan, Iraq, and Libya were comparatively poor, ethnically diverse states that had experienced decades of autocratic rule. The outcomes in each of these cases suggest that even when democratic interveners pursue an institutional regime change strategy, foreign military intervention is an unlikely path to democratization without favorable domestic conditions in place.

In Afghanistan and Iraq, US interventions triggered protracted civil conflicts that prevented either country from consolidating any democratic gains. In Iraq, the US invested billions of dollars in economic and military assistance and supervised the drafting of a new constitution and national elections, resulting in a Shia-majority government. Yet, more than a decade later, Iraq continues to be designated as "Not Free" according to Freedom House's ranking of civil and political rights.[18] Similarly, following the overthrow of the Taliban regime in Afghanistan, the US and United Nations oversaw a "Transitional Administration" resulting in national elections in 2004 and 2005. Yet, the democratic legitimacy of the Afghan state has been undermined by electoral fraud, endemic corruption, and the inability to secure large areas of the country from insurgent violence (Freedom House 2011).

The international intervention in Libya in 2011 resulted in a similar pattern. In March 2011, the UN Security Council authorized intervention in Libya to protect civilians from a violent government crackdown. Following UNSC Resolution 1973, NATO established a no-fly zone and used air support to aid domestic rebel groups in overthrowing the Qaddafi regime. Although Libya held a democratic election in July 2012, it quickly returned to civil conflict characterized by collapse of central state authority, widespread human rights abuses, and ethnic violence.

According to Alan Kuperman, "Libya has not only failed to evolve into a democracy; it has devolved into a failed state" (Kuperman 2015: 67).

Finally, Syria is an unlikely candidate for democratization led by external regime change. The Obama administration pursued a mixed strategy towards the Assad regime since the outbreak of the Syrian civil conflict in 2011. In August 2011, Obama stated that "the time has come for President Assad to step aside," and in March 2013 that "Assad must go" (McGreal and Chulov 2011; Obama 2013). The Obama administration also initiated a limited program to train and aid moderate opposition forces in Syria, while resisting proposals for military strikes directed at the Assad regime (Landler 2016). Yet, any US attempt to directly install a new regime in Syria would likely encounter the same obstacles as other recent cases. In Daniel Byman's assessment, a US policy of imposing a new regime in Syria would "require decades and prove costly in lives and money" (Byman 2015: 178).

Conclusion

Policymakers in democracies tend to be optimistic about the possibility of spreading democracy, but their optimism is not supported by the conclusions of most scholarly studies of forceful democracy promotion. These studies, however, use inexact proxies of intervention and focus on the motives and efforts of interveners. We therefore examined the effect of interventions that actually changed the composition of foreign governments and emphasized preconditions for democracy in target states in addition to intervener actions.

Accounting for non-random selection using matching, we found that neither leadership FIRC nor institutional FIRC had a significant effect on post-FIRC democratization. Moreover, the effect of institutional FIRC is contingent on preconditions for democracy in target states. Our analysis of these conditional effects showed that democratization was more likely to occur after institutional FIRC in places with high levels of wealth, ethnic homogeneity, and previous experience with democracy. By contrast, the effect of leadership FIRC was not contingent on domestic preconditions. Thus, our findings put us squarely in the conditional camp.

This analysis suggests several lessons for scholarly and policy debates over regime change and democratization. First, simply overthrowing foreign leaders is unlikely to enhance democracy, and may actually contribute to chaos and even civil war in target states (Peic and Reiter 2011; Downes 2016; Downes and O'Rourke 2016; Zachary, Deloughery, and Downes 2017). This is an important lesson given the rise of precision airpower and remotely piloted drone aircraft. Just as some analysts of airpower have argued against the effectiveness of decapitation as a military strategy for winning wars (Pape 1996), our findings indicate that democratization via decapitation is unlikely to work. Moreover, it is especially unlikely to work in places where it is most likely to be employed: weak states such as Syria with little experience with democracy and significant societal divisions. In fact, leadership FIRC in these types of countries may help trigger civil war. US leaders should thus resist the temptation to use airpower to effect a quick and easy regime change in the hope that democracy will somehow emerge in the aftermath.

A second lesson is that intervention to restore democracy in recently democratic countries that have reverted to autocracy—either through a coup or foreign occupation—can succeed. Foreign-imposed regime change may thus be better at getting countries that have managed to make democratic transitions back on track than at fostering democracy in the first place. FIRC may have a role to play in safeguarding democracy instead of promoting it.

Finally, if democracies hope to promote their institutions abroad, they must not only take concrete actions—such as facilitating elections—but realize that these actions are not enough. Domestic context matters: some countries are better candidates for democratization than others, and external efforts to bring about democratic change are more likely to work where those preconditions are present than where they are absent.

Regime change may appear to be a low-cost option for powerful democracies such as the United States in the twenty-first century because potential targets are weak states, but looks can be deceiving. Democracy is unlikely to take root in these places, and the United States may find itself drawn into protracted quagmires such as Afghanistan and Iraq. Democracies may be better off employing nonforceful means—such as foreign aid, development assistance, and attempts to build civil society—to bring about a more democratic world.

Notes

1 See Iraq Coalition Casualty Count, www.icasualties.org.
2 According to Freedom House, an independent organization that monitors democracy worldwide, Afghanistan and Iraq were both considered "not free" in 2016. See Freedom House (2016: 20–21).
3 Some studies of US failure in Iraq and Afghanistan reflect this view. See, for example, Diamond (2005).
4 This chapter draws on material from Alexander B. Downes and Jonathan Monten, "Forced to Be Free? Why Foreign-Imposed Regime Change Rarely Leads to Democratization" (2013), published in *International Security*, copyright 2013 by the President and Fellows of Harvard College and the Massachusetts Institute of Technology. Reprinted with permission.
5 International democracy promotion has historically been a central aspect of US foreign policy. See, for example, Smith (1994: 311–345).
6 For a more detailed discussion of the data and research design, interested readers are directed to Downes and Monten (2013: 107–116), and that article's online appendix, available at https://dataverse.harvard.edu/dataverse/downes.
7 In this case, we require that the intervener formally demand that the targeted leader step aside, and that this demand be accompanied by an implicit or explicit threat to use force in case of noncompliance. On these criteria, see Sechser (2011).
8 The complete list of cases is available in the online appendix of Downes and Monten (2013).

9 In cases where a second FIRC occurred before the initial ten-year period elapsed, we code the period of the initial FIRC as ending in the year before the new FIRC. We then code a new ten-year period as beginning in the year of the second FIRC, and a dummy variable is coded with the regime type of the second intervener.

10 Interveners may also help draft constitutions, design governing institutions, set up financial institutions, or assist with any manner of additional reforms, but at a minimum they must facilitate free and fair elections in some material way that goes beyond mere rhetoric.

11 There are actually thirteen institutional FIRCs, but Grenada (1983), Afghanistan (2001), and Iraq (2003) are omitted.

12 The United States was the sole intervener in twenty cases; other democracies intervened alone in twelve cases.

13 Detailed information on the sources and coding of these variables is available in the online appendix for Downes and Monten (2013).

14 Country-years of FIRC (e.g., Guatemala 1954) were matched with country-years of non-FIRC (e.g., Uruguay 1904). The following ten years were then added to the dataset for each country, allowing us to adjudicate the effect of FIRC on democratization over equal amounts of time.

15 The exception to the rule is Haiti—a poor if ethnically homogeneous country—but this case consists of the United States restoring a previously democratic government to power rather than constructing democracy from scratch. Haiti thus provides limited evidence for the democratizing force of institutional FIRC. Moreover, in 1999 Haiti slipped from the ranks of consolidated democracies. Panama also has a restoration aspect to it since the US invasion in late 1989 reinstated Guillermo Endara, who won the elections in May of that year but was prevented from taking office by Manuel Noriega.

16 It is not possible to estimate conditional effects using the matched datasets because matching removes most of the variation in the variables of interest. Models with change in Polity score as the dependent variable are analyzed using ordinary least squares regression; the Prais-Winsten method is used to correct for autocorrelation. Models that estimate the probability of a transition to consolidated democracy use probit. All models include the control variables discussed above. For complete regression results, see Downes and Monten (2013: 118–120), and that article's online appendix.

17 Graphs using change in Polity score as the dependent variable look remarkably similar and are posted in the online appendix of Downes and Monten (2013).

18 According to Freedom House's 7-point scale, with 7 being the least free, in 2015 Iraq was assigned a score of 5 on political rights and 6 on civil liberties (Freedom House 2016: 21). Polity was unable to code Iraq's regime type through 2009; from 2010 to 2013, it was coded as 3 (on the −10 to +10 scale), and in 2014 it increased to 6. Polity thus now codes Iraq as a democracy. The difference between the Freedom House and Polity coding likely stems from their different emphases: the former privileges political rights and freedoms, whereas the latter focuses on procedures and institutions.

References

Bellin, E. 2004/05. The Iraqi Intervention and Democracy in Comparative Historical Perspective. *Political Science Quarterly*, 119(4), pp.595–608.

Berger, D., Corvalan, A., Easterly, W., and Satyanath, S. 2013. Do Superpower Interventions Have Short and Long Term Consequences for Democracy? *Journal of Comparative Economics*, 41(1), pp.22–34.

Bermeo, N. 2003. What the Democratization Literature Says – or Doesn't Say – about Postwar Democratization. *Global Governance*, 9(2), pp.159–177.

Bermeo, N. 2010. Armed Conflict and the Durability of Electoral Democracy. In Kier, E., and Krebs, R.R. (eds.), *In War's Wake: International Conflict and the Fate of Liberal Democracy*. Cambridge University Press, pp.67–94.

Boix, C., and Stokes, S.C. 2003. Endogenous Democratization. *World Politics*, 55(4), pp.517–549.

Brownlee, J. 2007. Can America Nation-Build? *World Politics*, 59(2), pp.314–340.

Bueno de Mesquita, B., and Downs, G.W. 2006. Intervention and Democracy. *International Organization*, 60(3), pp.627–649.

Bueno de Mesquita, B., Smith, A., Siverson, R.M., and Morrow, J.D. 2003. *The Logic of Political Survival*. MIT Press.

Bush, G.W. 2002. *The National Security Strategy of the United States of America*. The White House.

Bush G.W. 2003. President Discusses the Future of Iraq. Speech given to the American Enterprise Institute, Washington, D.C., February 26. Accessed at http://georgewbush-whitehouse.archives.gov/news/releases/2003/02/20030226-11.html.

Byman, D. 2003. Constructing a Democratic Iraq: Challenges and Opportunities. *International Security*, 28(1), pp.47–78.

Byman, D. 2015. Six Bad Options for Syria. *The Washington Quarterly*, 38(4), pp.171–186.

Calder, B. 1984. *The Impact of Intervention: The Dominican Republic during the US Occupation of 1916–1924*. University of Texas Press.

Collier, D., and Adcock, R. 1999. Democracy and Dichotomies: A Pragmatic Approach to Choices about Concepts. *Annual Review of Political Science*, 2, pp.537–565.

Crawford, N.C. 2016. *Update on the Human Costs of War for Afghanistan and Pakistan, 2001 to Mid-2016*. Watson Institute for International and Public Affairs, Brown University, August. Accessed at http://watson.brown.edu/costsofwar/costs/human/civilians/afghan.

Diamond, L. 2005. *Squandered Victory: The American Occupation and the Bungled Effort to Bring Democracy to Iraq*. Macmillan.

Dobbins, J.F., McGinn, J.G., Crane, K., Jones, S.G., Lal, R., Rathmell, A., Swanger, R.M., and Timilsina, A.R. 2003. *America's Role in Nation-Building: From Germany to Iraq*. RAND Corporation.

Dogan, M., and Higley, J. 1998. Elites, Crises, and Regimes in Comparative Analysis. In Dogan, M., and Higley, J. (eds.), *Elites, Crises, and the Origins of Regimes*. Rowman & Littlefield, pp.3–28.

Downes, A.B. 2016. Catastrophic Success: Foreign-Imposed Regime Change and Civil War. Unpublished paper, George Washington University.

Downes, A.B., and Monten, J. 2013. Forced To Be Free? Why Foreign-Imposed Regime Change Rarely Leads to Democratization. *International Security*, 37(4), pp.90–131.

Downes, A.B., and O'Rourke, L.A. 2016. You Can't Always Get What You Want: Why Foreign-Imposed Regime Change Seldom Improves Interstate Relations. *International Security*, 41(2), pp.43–89.

Dueck, C. 2015. *The Obama Doctrine: American Grand Strategy Today*. Oxford University Press.

Edelstein, D.M. 2008. *Occupational Hazards: Success and Failure in Military Occupation*. Cornell University Press.

Enterline, A.J., and Michael Greig, J. 2008. The History of Imposed Democracy and the Future of Iraq and Afghanistan. *Foreign Policy Analysis*, 4(4), pp.321–347.

Fish, M.S., and Brooks, R.S. 2004. Does Diversity Hurt Democracy? *Journal of Democracy*, 15(1), pp.154–166.

Freedom House. 2011. Afghanistan: Country Report 2011. Accessed at https://freedomhouse.org/report/freedom-world/2011/afghanistan.

Freedom House. 2016. *Freedom in the World 2016: Anxious Dictators, Wavering Democracies: Global Freedom under Pressure*. Freedom House. Accessed at https://freedomhouse.org/sites/default/files/FH_FITW_Report_2016.pdf.

Fukuyama, F. 2004. *State-Building: Governance and World Order in the 21st Century*. Cornell University Press.

Geddes, B. 1999. What Do We Know about Democratization after Twenty Years? *Annual Review of Political Science*, 2, pp.115–144.

Gobat, M. 2005. *Confronting the American Dream: Nicaragua under US Imperial Rule*. Duke University Press.

Goldsmith, A.A. 2008. Making the World Safe for Partial Democracy? Questioning the Premises of Democracy Promotion. *International Security*, 33(2), pp.120–147.

Hermann, M.G., and Kegley Jr., C.W. 1998. The US Use of Military Intervention to Promote Democracy: Evaluating the Record. *International Interactions*, 24(2), pp.91–114.

Higley, J., and Burton, M.G. 1989. The Elite Variable in Democratic Transitions and Breakdowns. *American Sociological Review*, 54(1), pp.17–32.

Ho, D.E., Imai, K., King, G., and Stuart, E.A. 2007. Matching as Nonparametric Preprocessing for Reducing Model Dependence in Parametric Causal Inference. *Political Analysis*, 15(3), pp.199–236.

Horowitz, D.L. 1985. *Ethnic Groups in Conflict*. University of California Press.

Horowitz, D.L. 1993. Democracy in Divided Societies. *Journal of Democracy*, 4(4), pp.18–38.

Inglehart, R., and Welzel, C. 2009. How Development Leads to Democracy: What We Know about Modernization. *Foreign Affairs*, 88(2), pp.33–48.

Iraq Body Count. 2012. Iraqi Deaths from Violence, 2003–2011. Accessed at www.iraqbodycount.org/analysis/numbers/2011/.

Kerevel, Y.P. 2006. Re-examining the Politics of US Intervention in Early 20th Century Nicaragua: José Madriz and the Conservative Restoration. *LAII Research Paper Series*, 43.

Krauthammer, C. 2004. *Democratic Realism: An American Foreign Policy for a Unipolar World*. AEI Press.

Kuperman, A.J. 2015. Obama's Libya Debacle: How a Well-Meaning Intervention Ended in Failure. *Foreign Affairs*, 94(2), pp.66–77.

Landler, L. 2016. 51 Diplomats, in Dissent, Urge Strikes on Assad. *New York Times*, June 17, p.A1.

Lijphart, A. 1977. *Democracy in Plural Societies: A Comparative Exploration*. Yale University Press.

Linz, J.J., and Stepan, A. 2011. *Problems of Democratic Transition and Consolidation: Southern Europe, South America, and Post-Communist Europe*. Johns Hopkins University Press.

Lipset, S.M. 1959. Some Social Requisites of Democracy: Economic Development and Political Legitimacy. *American Political Science Review*, 53(1), pp.69–105.

Mansfield. E., and Snyder, J. 2010. Does War Influence Democratization? In Kier, E., and Krebs, R.R. (eds.), *In War's Wake: International Conflict and the Fate of Liberal Democracy*. Cambridge University Press, pp.23–49.

Marshall, M.G., and Jaggers, K. 2010. *Polity IV Project: Political Regime Characteristics and Transitions, 1800–2010*. Accessed at www.systemicpeace.org/polity/polity4.htm.

McGreal, C., and Chulov, M. 2011. Syria: Assad Must Resign, says Obama. *The Guardian*, August 18.

Mearsheimer, J.J. 2005. *Hans Morgenthau and the Iraq War: Realism versus Neo-Conservatism*. OpenDemocracy. Accessed at www.opendemocracy.net/democracy-american power/morgenthau_2522.jsp.

Meernik, J. 1996. United States Military Intervention and the Promotion of Democracy. *Journal of Peace Research*, 33(4), pp.391–402.

Moon, B.E. 2009. Long Time Coming: Prospects for Democracy in Iraq. *International Security*, 33(4), pp.115–148.

Munck, G.L., and Verkuilen, J. 2002. Conceptualizing and Measuring Democracy: Evaluating Alternative Indices. *Comparative Political Studies*, 35(1), pp.5–34.

Obama, B. 2013. Remarks by President Obama and Prime Minister Netanyahu of Israel in Joint Press Conference. The White House, Office of the Press Secretary, March 20.

O'Rourke, L.A. 2013. *Secrecy and Security: US-Orchestrated Regime Change during the Cold War*. Ph.D. dissertation, University of Chicago, Department of Political Science.

Pape, R.A. 1996. *Bombing to Win: Air Power and Coercion in War*. Cornell University Press.

Peceny, M. 1999. *Democracy at the Point of Bayonets*. Pennsylvania State University Press.

Pei, M., and Kasper, S. 2003. *Lessons from the Past: The American Record on Nation Building*. Policy Brief No. 24. Carnegie Endowment for International Peace.

Peic, G., and Reiter, D. 2011. Foreign-Imposed Regime Change, State Power and Civil War Onset, 1920–2004. *British Journal of Political Science*, 41(3), pp.453–475.

Pickering, J., and Peceny, M. 2006. Forging Democracy at Gunpoint. *International Studies Quarterly*, 50(3), pp.539–560.

Posen, B.R. 1993. The Security Dilemma and Ethnic Conflict. *Survival*, 35(1), pp.27–47.

Przeworski, A., Alvarez, M., Cheibub, J.A., and Limongi, F. 2000. *Democracy and Development: Political Institutions and Well-Being in the World, 1950–1990*. Cambridge University Press.

Rice, C. 2005. The Promise of Democratic Peace. *Washington Post*, December 11, p.B07.

Sambanis, N. 2001. Do Ethnic and Nonethnic Civil Wars Have the Same Causes? A Theoretical and Empirical Inquiry (Part 1). *Journal of Conflict Resolution*, 45(3), pp.259–282.

Schedler, A. 1998. What is Democratic Consolidation? *Journal of Democracy*, 9(2), pp.91–107.

Sechser, T.S. 2011. Militarized Compellent Threats, 1918–2001. *Conflict Management and Peace Science*, 28(4), pp.377–401.

Serafino, N., Tarnoff, C., and Nanto, D.K. 2006. US Occupation Assistance: Iraq, Germany and Japan Compared. Library of Congress Congressional Research Service.

Smith, T. 1994. *America's Mission: The United States and the Worldwide Struggle for Democracy*. Princeton University Press.

Stepan, A. 1986. Paths toward Redemocratization: Theoretical and Comparative Considerations. In O'Donnell, G., Schmitter, P.C., and Whitehead, L. (eds.), *Transitions from Authoritarian Rule: Comparative Perspectives*. Johns Hopkins University Press, pp.64–84.

Stiglitz, J., and Bilmes, L. 2008. *The Three Trillion Dollar War: The True Cost of the Iraq War*. W.W. Norton.

Teorell, J. 2010. *Determinants of Democratization: Explaining Regime Change in the World, 1972–2006*. Cambridge University Press.

Whitehead, L. 1996. Three International Dimensions of Democratization. In Whitehead, L. (ed.), *The International Dimensions of Democratization: Europe and the Americas*. Oxford University Press, pp.3–25.

Zachary, P., Deloughery, K., and Downes, A.B. 2017. No Business Like FIRC Business: Foreign-Imposed Regime Change and Bilateral Trade. *British Journal of Political Science*, 47(4), pp.749–782.

6

THE TYRANNIES OF DISTANCE

Maritime Asia and the barriers to conquest

Patrick Porter

Rumours of the death of distance have been exaggerated. In this chapter, I argue that distance continues to exert itself as a strategic force.[1] Technology may shrink physical space, the miles that separate people or things. It does not, however, necessarily shrink strategic space – the ability to project power affordably, against resistance, across the earth. Here I demonstrate this argument in the context of Asia's maritime peripheries, where rivalries between China and the US and its allies still carry the greatest weight of international politics. A convergence of military-strategic developments, especially access denial technologies and the coming of 'multipolarity', means that neither China nor the US can easily dominate East Asia.

This matters, because the fear of the shrinking world, where technology compresses and collapses distance, is one foundation of America's pursuit of 'leadership', or primacy. In the words of NSC 68, the signature document of America's Cold War, 'it is not an adequate objective merely to seek to check the Kremlin design, for in a shrinking world the absence of order among nations is becoming less and less tolerable', requiring 'world leadership' (Nitze 1950). In other words, American preponderance, globally applied and sustained, is vital because the smallness of the world makes disorder anywhere intolerable. This is what we might call the doctrine of 'globalism'. That the world is a shrinking and more dangerous place, and that the shrinking world therefore needs uncontested American primacy to keep the peace, is a recurrent claim in every codified National Security Strategy, and underpinned most presidential 'doctrines' from Truman to Obama.[2]

The ability of China, the US and even smaller third parties to raise the costs on expansion, especially expansion over bodies of water, makes it all the more prudent to accept co-existence as a political reality. While distance, created by space and technology, imposes constraints on American power, it can be a source of security as well as a tyranny. Put simply, a shift not only in the material power balance, but in the range and lethality of weapons, means that the emerging world order is one where no single power is likely to be able to dominate. This insight could be used to argue for a withdrawal from the region. Here, however, I will argue that it can also be the basis for pragmatic power sharing.

The chapter proceeds in three parts. I first introduce the concept of distance as a strategic force, and how perceptions of distance shape American security fears. I then examine the issue in the context of East and South Asia, demonstrating through an estimate of one important case that technology, skilfully deployed, does as much to enlarge as to shrink the world strategically, so that offensive power does not efface the force of distance in armed conflict. Finally, I argue that the demonstrable power of distance as a strategic creation suggests that America is less powerful, but more secure, than 'globalists' think.

1 The shrinking world

Distance, or the intervening space between points, has long generated a mix of opportunities and problems for American statecraft. Until the mid-twentieth century, most American strategic minds assumed that distance was a source of security. Being 'far' from the world's power centres in Eurasia, with ocean moats and powerful air-maritime forces to patrol the ocean approaches, afforded Americans the benefits of space and time. This acted as a buffer against potential threats. Once threats appeared, distance generated the ability to mobilise resources and power that could be employed once conflict was underway, and to apply it with a level of discretion denied to states closer to violent turmoil. At the same time, 'farness' created difficulties. Successfully projecting power took great effort, especially after 1941 when the Atlantic and Pacific Oceans were strongly contested by Axis powers. Even after overcoming the barriers of geography, it remained the case that America could choose to withdraw. This created obvious problems of credibility and commitment, not least for America's extended deterrence: when it came down to it, could European allies really trust that Washington would trade New York for Paris in a nuclear exchange? Equally, the same quality of applying power 'from a remove' made America a more attractive ally or partner than ambitious major states who had nowhere to withdraw to (Levy and Thompson 2010; Shifrinson 2014).

Two contradictory fears haunted American policymakers, and continue to do so. Technology might destroy the power of distance, creating a shrinking world that is closing in. Such fears – that offensive violence could be waged quickly and easily by faraway predators – took on new life in the wake of surprise attacks such as Pearl Harbor or 9/11. New long-range capabilities, from naval aviation to long-range airpower, combined with predatory ideologies such as fascism or militant Islamism, meant that American security could no longer be based on continental or hemispheric insulation. For the majority, assault by transoceanic predators, in the form of Imperial Japan or Al Qaeda, demonstrated 'that the rise of hostile states anywhere in the world could endanger our security' (Gaddis 2004: 69). Yet in this same world, for America to project power would take investment and political will. President Franklin Roosevelt combined both fears in his wartime articulation of America's position. Roosevelt, who cast himself as America's geography teacher, warned that Americans could no longer measure security in terms of miles on a map. Thanks to the strategic bomber and the aircraft carrier, the world was dangerously closing in, putting every adversary within striking distance. Yet, he also warned, unless America acquired a far-flung network of bases and preponderant power, it could not impose itself abroad, and could be evicted from East Asia, the Gulf or Western Europe (Roosevelt 1941). The possibility that distance imposes constraints on both the US and its adversaries deserves greater attention: if it would be difficult for the US to fight its way back into the Pacific across contested waters, might not the same constraints impose themselves on China?

Alongside these anxieties, there is a similar notion that each generation since 1941 has reinvented. This is the claim that globalisation, or the circulation of ideas, materials, capital, people and weapons, collapses distance so thoroughly that the US is both more insecure, and yet for the same reasons more powerful, than ever before. Pondering the assault on America's financial and military nerve centres, the 9/11 Commission reprised Roosevelt's claim that there was no longer 'home' and 'away'. In the age of the mobile phone, cheap travel and digital finance, 'the American homeland is the planet' (National Commission on Terrorist Attacks 2004: 362). The attacks of 9/11, they inferred, demonstrated both that geography no longer functioned as a shield, and that America's ambition must be to extend its security domain to the whole planet. President George W. Bush saw that day as a lesson in the irrelevance of traditional security barriers. 'It used to be that oceans would protect us, that we saw a threat, we didn't have to worry about it because there were two vast oceans. And we could pick and choose as to how we deal with the threat. That changed on September 11th' (Bush 2004: 606). His administration optimistically assumed that, given the ascendancy of American technological power and ideological appeal over traditional geographical barriers, it was within their gift to transform the greater Middle East in their way, to their timetable. Security elites also widely share this impression. The world is 'more dangerous than it has ever been', claimed General Martin Dempsey, Chairman of the Joint Chiefs of Staff (Dempsey 2013: 22). His logic is that the West's very success creates a 'security paradox'. The worldwide commercial peace that it designed is making destructive technology 'available to a wider and more disparate pool of adversaries' (Dempsey 2012) so that a single person with a computer can disrupt a city or a nation. As these statements suggest, the apprehension of a dangerously shrinking world lends itself to 'threat inflation' and the loosening of restraint.

The ideology of 'globalism' has long attracted strategic minds, impressed by the capacity of technological revolution to destroy the tyrannies of distance. Political scientist Robert Keohane argued that 'Geographical space, which has been seen as a natural *barrier* and a locus for human barriers, now must be seen as a *carrier* as well'. Globalisation means 'threats of violence to our homeland can occur from anywhere. The barrier conception of geographical space, already anachronistic with respect to thermonuclear war and called into question by earlier acts of globalized informal violence, was finally shown to be thoroughly obsolete on September 11'

(Keohane 2002: 29–43, 32–33). Decades earlier during America's war in Vietnam, Robert Wohlstetter went as far as to claim that new technologies undermined the classical theory of the 'distance decay effect', whereby power weakens the further it is extended. Long-haul transport of materiel was surprisingly cheap, and ever more powerful transport and communications would reduce it further. America's ability to supply and sustain campaigns in Asia suggested the same conclusion as the range and instantaneity of modern weapons, that distance as a strategic concept was now an 'illusion' (Wohlstetter 1968: 242–255; Wohlstetter 1959).

Notice the structure of these arguments. Keohane conflates physical space – and the apparent ease of physical travel in particular historical moments – with strategic space, the ability to project power affordably across the earth. Al Qaeda was able to strike American soil on 9/11 in ways that have become much harder since, because the long supply chain and forward operating bases it relied upon were quickly disrupted, because vulnerabilities in America's homeland defenses were addressed, and because it aroused the attention of a superpower that made the spaces in which the terrorist network operated more dangerous and obstructed, forcing it into a networking organisation just to survive. Geography itself did not provide a 'shield', but it never has: distance in human conflict is not intrinsic to space but a product of human exploitation of it. While it is true that land borders or bodies of water *in themselves* do not obstruct actors with sufficient capability to cross them, water or land has never functioned this way. If we consider 'distancing' as a verb, not just 'distance' as a noun – an act that separates strategically – then human agency can turn spaces into what Alan Henrikson calls 'distancing units' (2002: 454). We are not talking merely about traversing space as though it were a politically uncontested thoroughfare of climate and terrain. We are considering space as the medium into which other humans intrude, space through which (and for which) violent political struggle takes place. This explains the puzzle that some relatively short physical spaces, such as the English Channel in 1940, represent more of a barrier than some larger ones, such as the Atlantic Ocean, which did not work as a 'moat' against the Spanish Conquistadores. Distance is a real thing, but not a 'given'. To become a defensive asset, it must be created and exploited.

The temporary ease of travel also underpins Wohlstetter's observations about America's ability to project power into Asia. In the late 1960s, this observation was when Americans could naturally assume the ease of transoceanic travel, based on unchallenged Western dominion over space between its heartland and theatres of war, when the US dominated the Pacific and Indian Oceans as its lakes, and when carrier and expeditionary strike groups could sail with impunity through maritime backyards of Asian states. As Asian states acquire means of force projection and access denial, this is increasingly redundant, and American forward bases are potentially more vulnerable as targets themselves. As Paul Bracken anticipated at the close of the twentieth century, the coming of disruptive technologies, from the ballistic missile to WMD to tracking and reconnaissance grids to sea mines, would transform East Asia into a zone of exclusion (Bracken 1999: 48–52). Whereas in the past decades, the US as a maritime heavyweight could operate with relative ease,

Asian states with weapons of increasing range and lethality would deny America the freedom to mass its forces and fight from its advanced bases by threatening those very bases. They would threaten America's ability to move its forces into the region. In short, they would turn the free thoroughfare into an obstructive battlespace, turn owned space into contested space, raising the stakes of any intervention. If Asia was entering a 'crisis of room' as technology compressed time and space, from the outlook of Washington the region strategically was getting further away. Both American intervention and Chinese expansion would be constrained by crowded South Asian waters. One potential staging ground for this debate as a flashpoint where the weaker side can present, and possibly is presenting, a viable defence is over the Taiwan Strait.

2 Access denied

Is East Asia getting smaller or larger? An important site of the debate lies along Asia's maritime peripheries. I argue that new weapons and instruments have widened, rather than shrunk, Asia-Pacific space. The defining change within the maritime sphere is the coming of an age of 'sea denial' and the increasing difficulty of 'sea control'. In other words, given the increased ability to find and sink surface ships through sensor technologies and standoff precision munitions, it will be easier to disrupt approaching naval forces and raise costs on interlopers, and harder to secure control of maritime approaches in order to enter an adversary's region to wage an offensive campaign. This complicates greatly some traditional core tasks of surface fleets and expeditionary forces, such as opposed landings and offshore support for expeditionary land operations. Surveillance assets in the hands of watchful defenders make it harder to inflict a sudden surprise long-range attack like Pearl Harbor. Tools of 'access denial' – such as long-range anti-ship missiles – make it easier for states to fend off enemy fleets and raise the costs of aggression. This makes it harder for America to intervene in a war with China – but harder also for China to expand. Conquest against armed opposition has become an expensive rarity. Such are the material demands of modern navies for resupply and maintenance that forward bases are now more important, not less. Paradoxically, modern tools of access denial place those bases in the crosshairs. As Toshi Yoshihara argues, the sophistication of modern military technology that puts such a high premium on bases, with their storage tanks, ammunition depots or repair facilities, also renders bases at Yokosuka or Okinawa increasingly vulnerable. China's stocks of long-range ballistic missiles such as the DF-15 and the DF-21 missiles threaten to disable American naval and air bases in the 'first island chain' of the western Pacific, in Japan and Okinawa, forcing the US to operate from thousands of miles further eastward, thereby depleting its forces' staying power.

An estimate of the prospects of Taiwan in the event of a Chinese invasion suggests that amphibious assaults, projecting ground forces from sea to land, against a determined adversary making prudent doctrinal and technological choices remain complex and demanding. There are numerous sources available for this case. These include campaign analyses of Richard E. Bush and Michael O'Hanlon (2007), the RAND Corporation (Shlapak et al. 2009), estimates by the Center for Strategic and International Studies (Cordesman, Hess, and Yarosh 2012), and the United States–Taiwan Business Council (2010), all supplemented by US Secretary of Defense appraisal in 2013 and by doctrine produced in open source by both the People's Republic of China and the Republic of China. As well as official strategic documents, we can identify patterns suggested by the choices of weapons, training and preparation Beijing and Taipei have made. Given the secrecy of defence plans and capabilities, a precise estimate is impossible. But this case is offered as an investigation of broader patterns in the offence/defence balance. To test the claim that a globalised world is an 'offence dominant' world, we can design a plausible 'worse-case' scenario that favours the offence where we assume that areas of doubt 'break' for the benefit of the invader.

What proposition exactly are we testing here? To specify: historically an amphibious invasion usually requires three steps to succeed. The assailant must achieve air supremacy, or such a dominant amount of air superiority that it can operate at will. It must capture a defensible beachhead that it can securely insert its ground forces onto from sea to land and that it must be able to sustain and resupply. And it must then turn its foothold into a 'breakout' before the defender can focus its defences on the point of entry and cut it off. For globalism to offer a robust account of what might happen, the invader should be able to neutralise and overcome the barriers created by terrain and human agency to the extent that the clash would unfold on a 'level playing field', where the outcome would be determined by the material balance between the two sides and where the exploitation of terrain would hardly matter. Using its formidable first-strike advantages, China would successfully 'jump the gun' with a bombing campaign that would suppress Taiwan's air defences, interdict Taiwan's lines of communications and supply, gain strong advantage or even air and maritime supremacy, be able to supply and sustain combat operations, and, after seizing a secure foothold on the island, break out and march on Taipei. With its strengthening access and area denial capabilities that might seriously complicate any US intervention, Beijing could plausibly threaten to fight a localised war against an isolated and overmatched island.

For the sake of argument, the scenario presented here works in favour of the assailant to make it an 'easy test' where globalist theory ought to perform well. We give the invading China optimum diplomatic circumstances, namely a purely localised war in which third parties do not intervene. For the defender, regional security arrangements and strategic ties to the United States come to nil. In a purely dyadic or two-sided contest, this takes off the table Taiwan's preferred strategy of holding the invader off until the US navy enters the conflict as a relief force. Where expert observers suggest China lacks sufficient transport equipment, namely sealift and landing platform dockships to get troops ashore, or aerial refueling and logistics, we grant it these things, optimised in line with its short- and medium-term plans (Taylor Fravel 2010: 509, 523). As we are weighing up the interaction of technology, geography and doctrine, we need to 'control' for other variables such as shortfalls in the invader's military capabilities. There is a fluidity about constantly evolving defences in competitive rearmament, but for the purpose of analysis we grant China the platforms it would desire while restricting Taiwan to the equipment it currently has. We also exempt China from the rule of thumb where the attacker's army needs to outnumber the defender's forces 3:1 (United States Army 2002). For China's forces to prevail, a 1:1 ratio of forces is the necessary condition of minimal numerical parity (though not a sufficient condition) to seize and establish a beachhead. I assume that China refrains from nuclear strikes. Its primary aim is not to destroy or punish but to conquer, to apply enough force to overwhelm Taiwan's defences. I assume that both sides would be willing to fight. A supposed norm against conquest would not apply to China, while closer ties to the mainland and the emergence of a more reluctant younger generation would not lead Taiwan to capitulate without a struggle. Where in doubt, we give the benefit of the doubt to China.

So this is a case where, in an 'offence dominance' world, the stronger party should find the balance shifting decisively in its favour. China cares as much, or almost as much, about the outcome as the defender (China regards the disputed territories as its sovereign possession) and has the 'first-strike' advantage. Neither side has an appreciable advantage in recent military experience; both powers are relatively inexperienced at real armed conflict. Here in this scenario I control for shortfalls in China's current inventory of equipment and for the outside intervention of a stronger party. In real life there are unknowns: we do not know the exact pain thresholds or cost intolerance of either side, precisely how many casualties and resource losses China would be willing to suffer, and whether Taiwan would be willing to fight to the death. So for the purpose of this analysis, we presume that once hostilities commence, the motivation for both sides is roughly equal (on this issue see Cole 2012b).

There is little doubt that in a war that the US stayed out of, China would probably eventually prevail, at least as far as neutralising Taiwan's air force and navy, if not simply sending repeated waves of ground troops if it could keep enough sea and airlift capability. Until the past five years or so, assessments were more doubtful of China's ability to suppress Taiwan's air defences before storming the beaches to the extent that it would seize supremacy rather than just the edge (Bush and O'Hanlon 2007: 189; Edmonds and Tsai 2004). But as both countries modernise their militaries, reducing the overall numbers of aircraft and replacing them with more powerful advanced aircraft, the gap in the 'air and missile balance' may be widening in China's favour. According to later studies, China's present capability to neutralise Taiwan's air defences, seize command of the skies over Taiwan and exploit that command to disrupt Taiwan's other defences is considerable, and it is ramping up that capability further.[3]

But even if Taiwan was forcibly stripped of its surface-to-air missiles (SAMs) and China could command the skies at low cost, in a wider context China faces a dilemma, a tradeoff between surprise and preparation. Whether it struck in 2009, 2014 or 2019, surprise and deception would come at the expense of preparedness and speed of engagement with large-scale forces, and vice versa. To inflict a surprise first strike that successfully suppressed Taiwan's air defences to the extent that it achieved air dominance, China would need to do so from a standing start, and to avoid giving the game away would have to forgo the prior preparation of a large-scale invasion force into a cross-strait armada, to cross the 100 nautical miles (nm) from its bases closest to the most plausible point of assault, the small number of locations on the north-west beaches of Taiwan. It could hardly amass this force invisibly if a watchful Taiwan was minimally alert and used its surveillance technology efficiently. The interval between the first strike and then preparation for the attempted invasion would afford a vital window of time for Taiwan to recover and prepare for the next phase, including the roughly seven hours it would take for a fleet travelling at 15 knots to make the one-way crossing. Conversely, to prepare adequately with a buildup of force would sacrifice surprise, giving Taiwan days at least to disperse its forces, ensure the survival of large parts of its air force and get its planes off the airfields. Taiwan's topography is such that there are only a few landing-friendly points along its 500-mile coastline where a massed invasion could take place and where the defender could concentrate its forces. Consider the contrast with the Allied invasion of Normandy, where an amphibious assault could have taken place along a coastline 1,200 miles long and without the surveillance assets of today. Since the invasion fleet would have to be a sizable one of 100 assault ships loading vehicles, troops and supplies, and since a fully loaded invasion fleet would take about seven hours going at 15 knots in a one-way crossing of 100 nautical miles at the closest point, it is inconceivable that Taiwan would not see the buildup or see them coming.

Given China's greater strength of numbers and firepower and the problem that Taiwan would simply be unable to out-match it in crude material terms, a vital part of Taiwan's defence is the degree to which it has chosen prudent 'doctrine', and how realistically it defines victory. Doctrine simply means ideas of force employment. It scarcely determines outcomes, and relies on execution, but is needed to link technological means with strategic ends. Taiwan may not be able to out-gun China materially, but as history suggests, well-prepared weaker defending sides can return fire by optimising what they have to create an imposing defensive system. Taiwanese and international observers have intensively debated what it should do with its lesser resources in the face of an adversary whose relative material strength is growing alarmingly. Several competing doctrinal options have been on the table. None of these are mutually exclusive but there are tradeoffs involved, as each would draw resources from the others. They can be organised around two ideal-typical 'poles', 'classical defence' and 'porcupine defence'.

The 'classical defence' grows out of Taiwan's traditional doctrine of defence against an invader. When it had the greater qualitative military edge, Taiwan defined victory in offensive terms, to win in a direct clash for control of the seas and skies, overpowering China's larger but less advanced forces. It also planned on interdicting China's approaching forces far from Taiwan's coast. Designed for a symmetrical, toe-to-toe clash, this approach was capital-intense and involved hi-tech conventional forces at the cutting edge. It sought to thwart Chinese invading forces out at sea and in air space well beyond its islands, which would also be defended by a mass citizen army. Budgetary constraints, China's military modernisation fuelled by economic growth, disenchantment with conscription and a shift to an all-volunteer army have made this approach problematic. Today the model is reinvented in the argument that Taiwan should compete with China's modernisation programme with its own, lobbying hard for state-of-the-art aircraft such as the F 16 C/D or the Joint Strike Fighter, as well as developing the ability to engage in a conflict via bombing the Chinese mainland with surface-to-surface missiles with extended range, which would also form a pre-emptive strike capability. In a struggle that would entail a clash of advanced machines, Taiwan would not give up its effort to compete in the same technological contest and match its quality with China's.

By contrast, the 'porcupine defence' is more deliberately asymmetrical in the sense that it seeks to exploit the differences between invader and defender – differences of strategic objective as well as differences in the type of forces being used (Murray 2008). Instead of an expensive modernisation programme that attempts to match the quality if not the quantity of China's forces, it looks more to a 'passive defence' that would ensure that enough of Taiwan's forces could survive the initial onslaught. The porcupine approach invests more in the survivability of forces, their dispersal and concealment, the hardening of command and control systems, the repair of damaged assets such as runways, and resilience against electromagnetic and cyber attacks. It is a more army-centric doctrine that places more investment in fortifying ground-based infrastructure and training personnel for a land war. It emphasises the exploitation of terrain. It is less reliant on American largesse and technology transfer. In an alternative version, a low-tech porcupine strategy could also extend out to sea, with guerrilla warfare in nearby waters waged by 'swarms of light combatants' (Holmes 2013a).

What we know of Taiwan's actual strategy mixes features from both models. The evidence that we have suggests that Taiwan is making prudent choices about how it allocates its resources and is redefining its objectives realistically. It draws from the porcupine logic the shift from ambitious to achievable strategic goals. Rather than seeking to defeat Chinese forces outright in a decisive Mahanian naval clash, its objective is to deny China an affordable conquest by raising costs on invader to defend *de facto* independence. When it had the greater qualitative military edge, Taiwan defined victory in offensive terms – to win in a direct clash for control of seas and skies, overpowering and destroying China's larger but less advanced forces. It designed its defences accordingly, around capital ships and advanced planes and matching its adversaries' investments. Judging by its own published doctrine, the *National Defense Report* of 2011, Taiwan recognises that victory in these terms is no longer realistic and it is switching accordingly (Cole 2013a). Taiwan now defines victory as ensuring the survival of enough forces and preventing land forces establishing a foothold on Taiwan (Republic of China 2011: 131–132).[4] Its *Quadrennial Defense Review* of 2013 also suggests a doctrinal shift, emphasising the preservation of critical infrastructure to prevent being paralysed by 'sudden and high-intensity assaults' and the exploitation of Taiwan's advantages in space and time (Republic of China 2013: 38–40, 41). The same logic that enables China with today's tools to raise the costs of US intervention into its maritime space to unpalatable levels enables Taiwan to do the same at a price more suited to its limited GDP expenditure on defence (Blumenthal 2011; Holmes 2013b). To turn the nautical approaches to the island into contested zones, it exploits 'swarming' methods by preparing small-attack craft armed with anti-ship cruise missiles as light guerrillas at sea.

There is evidence that Taiwan is putting these doctrinal decisions into practice (Minnick 2010; Cole 2012a; Cole 2013b; Cole 2013c; United States–Taiwan Business Council 2010). Taiwan has built a hidden underground sanctuary inside a mountain near its Hualien air base on its east coast, a bomb shelter large enough to shelter 200 fighters linked to the above-ground base by a 7,500 foot taxiway. At least since 2010, it has been hardening airfield facilities, has introduced a major hardened aircraft storage facility at Taitung in south-eastern Taiwan, and is now addressing one of the weaknesses identified by RAND in 2009 by strengthening its Rapid Runway Repair crews to improve the survivability of runways at several air bases. It invests in mobile launchers for missiles and has acquired and now fields road-mobile missile launchers that can be dispersed and camouflaged, armed with rockets capable of firing at ships (such as the HF-3 supersonic anti-ship cruise missile) and Ray Ting 2000s with an artillery range of up to 45 km into China's mainland. To turn the point of amphibious landing into a shooting gallery, it is digging in with entrenched anti-ship and anti-air missile sites. To make both the sea approach and the beachhead more perilous, it prepares sea and land mines, the former of which could be scattered by artillery tubes. And it prepares to wage a 'war of the flea' out at sea with small, fast and low-signature missile-armed ships (31 Kuang Hua VI class boats) that are harder to locate and sink than heavier frigates and destroyers. They would be assisted by 12 maritime patrol aircraft. These lighter ships are armed with cruise and surface-to-surface missiles, thereby mixing the asymmetric logic of the porcupine strategy with the active extended defence desired by the classical approach. There is some uncertainty about how effectively these could operate in a full-scale war scenario, given their reliance on off-board radar and datalinks for targeting, which are located on vulnerable radar sites within range of China's missiles. Regardless, Taiwan has also diversified and expanded its number of smaller ships, increasing the number of its coastal patrol craft from 51 to 61 – a 20% increase as of 2012 (Cordesman, Hess, and Yarosh 2012: 198) – and armed seven patrol boats and a radar-evasive fast attack corvette with Hsiung Feng III (HF-3) ramjet-powered supersonic anti-ship missiles to increase the probability of having a surviving naval defence off its coastline. This prudently trades off Taiwan's ability to fight a high-seas naval battle for the ability to mount a defence closer to its littoral. Taipei has also developed the ability to push the defence line further out from its coast through the alternative means of long-range missiles that enable the interdiction of enemy forces out at sea. If the 'swarming' orchestration of smaller assets against larger forces is potentially a potent way for weaker states like Taiwan to threaten surface fleets with their large, expensively acquired capital ships, on the evidence we have, a *prima facie* overview suggests that Taiwan has developed both the doctrine and the tools to carry it off (Holmes and Yoshihara 2012). Since RAND produced its estimate in

2009, Taiwan's increasing investment in and attention to building a passive defence by increasing the probability that its capabilities will be dispersed, concealed and survivable is possibly the most significant development in Taiwan's preparation to counter the growing 'missile' imbalance across the straits.

Even though there remains uncertainty about the success of any of these measures in a conflict, each of them adds a 'layer' of defence that increases the probability that China will not be able to clear the seas and skies sufficiently to create a safe corridor for its invading forces to approach, and that Taiwan can punch back and inflict significant damage after the first barrage. Just as importantly, each extra layer of potential surviving defence adds uncertainty to China's calculations about the costs of invasion.[5] Through passive defensive measures, Taiwan would aim to keep its forces survivable: through mobility, redundancy, and the hardening and camouflage of its assets, as well as the stockpiling of food and fuel. These would not prevent large-scale damage to Taiwan's military and civilian property but could preserve enough combat power to keep material costs on following-on invading force high. This doctrine, properly applied, would help it raise costs on amphibious force as it approached and as it reached the shore in the following phases.

The 'bottom line' in an amphibious campaign is the ability to transport enough troops to the point of invasion, and securely enough to land and supply them. Let us assume that China now possesses the 100 transport ships it aims to acquire. Going on a rough 1:1 personnel ratio, RAND estimated in 2009 that China would need to get at least two group armies, or roughly 60,000 troops, ashore, and that this would require 194 successful naval trips or sorties.[6] The difficulty for China is that unless its initial effort to suppress Taiwan's defences and deflect its air and naval attacks succeeds almost perfectly, its ability to get enough ships across safely will be in jeopardy. Unless China could successfully neutralise Taiwan's ability to 'thin the herd' by taking out its air bases, its fixed and mobile land-based missile launchers (such as RBS-17 coastal-defence missiles mounted on trucks), its missile-armed Apache helicopters and its swarming fast-attack ships, its invasion will be in trouble.

To take one layer of defence alone: RAND estimates that if Taiwan's 31 Kuang Hua VI class fast missile boats, armed with four Hsiung Feng II ASCMs each, launch half of their payload, that would put 60 in the air, enough to inflict a disabling 'mission kill' on perhaps 12 Chinese transport ships. Going on RAND's estimate that, distributed evenly, each ship represents 310 troops and six vehicles, 12 ships sunk or turned back would see off 3,700 troops and 72 vehicles, and prevent those ships from participating in the three extra sorties needed for the entire transport fleet to get 60,000 troops and their equipment across within a reasonable span of five days. If China would want each ship to attempt four sorties, 12 ships taken out of action before completing their first sortie would mean a total of 48 sorties denied of the 194 out of 400 needed to succeed.

In this first phase, the weight of forces would favour China, but the conditions of space and time would favour Taiwan. On the more optimistic end of the spectrum, Taiwan's early-warning system would succeed, giving it vital minutes to protect its forces from incoming strikes and preserving enough planes to contest the skies.

But taking a worse-case scenario would also leave it with warning of another kind. The Chinese air force, with saturation missile attacks and then fixed-wing attacks, lands a knockout punch against Taiwan's air bases, following the failure of its early-warning system, Taiwan would be forced to use degraded air bases with a degraded capacity to generate air sorties. But, to ensure deception and surprise, China would have to refrain from large-scale preparatory buildup of amphibious forces. The air attack plus the time it would take to build up invasion forces would place Taiwan on notice to mobilise forces for defending ground. If Taiwan had time and depending on levels of preparation, it could adopt a 'layered' forward defence, looking to 'thin the herd' of China's amphibious forces at sea before defending at the water's edge. It would take aim primarily at its transport ships.

Let us suppose that despite the many problems the task would entail, China has seized the ability to cross the distance of 100 nautical miles from the bases closest to north-west Taiwan, neutralised Taiwan's sea and air defences, and reached the coast bearing platforms to operate from, such as several Type 071 Landing Platform Dock ships with hangers and landing and vehicle decks, loaded with marines, vehicles and helicopters, and over a dozen landing ships. The next task would be to forcibly enter terrain in the face of reinforced defences while vulnerable, establish a beach-head, and continuously supply a very large military force across the ocean despite adversary actions.

In a worst-case scenario for Taiwan, where China successfully destroyed its air bases and runways, the defender would probably still be able to mount a robust defence that inflicted serious costs by creating a lethal zone at the point of 'run-in' where the approaching forces must operate in plain sight, unmasked by electronic sensors (see Shlapak et al. 2009: 114–115). Taiwan's coastline means that it could anticipate the approximate point of invasion. China's transport ships would enter a kill zone in which Taiwan would have roughly a 20-minute window to fire Hellfire missiles at transports, or five minutes to fire at faster air-cushion landing craft. Then with a minimal surviving blend of Apache helicopters, dug-in and mobile artillery, and missile forces and mines, Taiwan could be expected to turn the point of disembarkation into a shooting gallery and a chaotic traffic jam, even if it lacked control of the skies over the beach and even if its aircraft were pinned in shelters or immobilised by destroyed runways. If it would take two 1,000 lb bombs, such as Joint Direct Attack Munitions, to destroy a warship, 100 fired by a B-1B plane could disable 50 ships, or failing that, helicopters, ground launchers, infantry and tanks could deliver Hellfire missiles over a short range of five miles. In this respect, RAND's estimate of 2009 still holds, only Taiwan has taken greater steps to ensure that its arsenal would survive the preliminary bombardment.

This is not the place for a precise forecast that ignores the play of chance and the effect of 'unknowns', not least China's relative ability to mount cyber attacks against Taiwan's increasing preparations of cyber defence, an aspect of the conflict too secretive and untraceable to measure precisely in advance. But on this analysis, the scenario is more difficult for the invader than the attacker, to the extent that the stars must align more or less perfectly for the attacker. The defender, Taiwan, would merely have to ride out the first bombardment well enough to be able to make an attempted invasion expensive. As I argue, a Chinese invasion would be costly, protracted and geopolitically dangerous. There is no certain way to measure the political will of either side in a neat cost–benefit calculs. Taiwan represents something bigger politically than just an island with resources, to both its inhabitants and the larger state that covets it, and the history of the issue is drenched with emotion. We can estimate, however, what an attempted conquest would entail and the kinds of costs and risks that the invader would be wise to consider. The longer the struggle continued, the greater would be the fear of it escalating and drawing in other powers. Taiwan's objective would be to pose the question to China of just how large a sacrifice it was prepared to make to achieve its objectives. Despite the eroding defence advantages and closing gap between China and Taiwan's forces, Taiwan could still inflict grave, possibly prohibitive costs on the invader. China's increasing airpower 'edge' and strengthening cross-strait strike and invasion capabilities would not be enough to negate the possibility of exploiting geography to the defender's decisive advantage. Taiwan's objective, within reach of its capabilities, would not be to sink/destroy China's navy and air force, but to make adventurism very expensive, to the point where successful conquest would set China's military back years if not decades. This confirms the recent warning of RAND that 'forced entry' via large-scale, over-the-shore amphibious assault against resistance is obsolete for many environments (Davis and Wilson 2011: 13–14). The same logic that enables China with today's tools to raise the costs of US intervention into its maritime space to unpalatable levels enables Taiwan to do the same at a price more suited to its limited GDP expenditure on defence. For America, these developments both generate security and constrain its power at the same time. As Christopher Layne argues, 'Far from shrinking the world grand strategically, for the United States, modern weaponry – naval and strategic airpower, intercontinental delivery systems, and nuclear weapons – has *widened* it' (Layne 2006: 278).

3 No-one's world: negotiating power in an unconquerable Asia

If we really do inhabit a globalising world where distance loses its force, that process should make conquest easier. This should be so to the extent that the outcomes of conflicts are generated by the balance of material forces, mediated far less by the effects of exploiting terrain than they would have been historically. But as this chapter argues, our era is different. Across bodies of water, it is one of fire without conquest. New weapons with their range and lethality have the capacity to increase distance and erect new barriers to interlopers. Space, therefore, is better conceived as an interplay of political will, capabilities and geography. As I have demonstrated here, the history of the continual shifting balance between sword and shield, and the tendency of states to measure the stakes involved according to the 'nearness' or 'farness' of the war, casts doubt on strategic visions where technology erases the dilemmas of distance or creates unambiguous 'offence dominance'. We are seeing the emergence of a period of access denial. These issues are pressing in maritime

East Asia, where the strategic implications of new weapons shape the rivalries and mutual fears of rising powers. An illustrative case where offensive technology would meet the exploitation of time, space and terrain for defensive purposes is the cross-strait military balance and the prospects for a Chinese invasion of Taiwan.

The estimate here suggests that amphibious assaults, projecting ground forces from sea to land, against a determined adversary making prudent doctrinal and technological choices, remain complex and demanding. There is little doubt that in a war that the US stayed out of, China would probably eventually prevail at least as far as neutralising Taiwan's air force and navy, if not simply sending repeated waves of ground troops if it could keep enough sea and airlift capability. But it would be costly, protracted and geopolitically dangerous. This problem is reflected also in the projections of future campaigns by the US Marine Corps, the world's premier amphibious force. Its 'Expeditionary Force 21' concept predicts that ever longer range capabilities, such as precision guided missiles, along with widely available and cheap sensors like nautical radar, 'will force the fleet to stay at least 65 nautical miles offshore, a dozen times the distance that existing Marine amphibious vehicles are designed to swim' (Freedberg 2014)

Of course, this is about more than capabilities. There is no certain way to measure the political will of either side in a neat cost–benefit calculus. To itself and its hostile larger neighbour, Taiwan represents something bigger politically than just an island with resources, and the history of the issue is drenched with emotion. We can estimate, however, what an attempted conquest would entail and the kinds of costs and risks that the invader would be wise to consider. The longer the struggle continued, the greater fear of it escalating and drawing in other powers. Taiwan's objective would be to pose the question to China of just how large a sacrifice it was prepared to make to achieve its objectives. Despite the eroding defence advantages and closing gap between China and Taiwan's forces, Taiwan could still inflict grave, possibly prohibitive costs on the invader. China's increasing airpower 'edge' and strengthening cross-strait strike and invasion capabilities would not be enough to negate the possibility of exploiting geography to the defender's decisive advantage. Taiwan's objective, within reach of its capabilities, would not be to sink/destroy China's navy and air force, but to make adventurism very expensive, to the point where successful conquest would set its military back years if not decades. This confirms the recent warning of RAND that 'forced entry' via large-scale, over-the-shore amphibious assault against resistance, is obsolete for many environments (Davis and Wilson 2011: 13–14).

What does all this mean in the bigger picture? It should both caution and reassure US policymakers. Taiwan can present an ominous defence against an invader without America going to the trouble of ramping up its security assistance and arms trade with Taiwan, and the deterioration of relations with China that this may create. Taiwan's vulnerability is easily exaggerated. In terms of its ability to conquer, a rising China is not as strategically threatening as sometimes assumed. This is also important for the wider security environment. Contrary to the views of some observers, it is not clear that Beijing has an appetite for limitless expansion, or that China's strategy of 'peaceful rise' is comparable to that of the Third Reich. But even if China does increase its appetite and make a bid for region-wide supremacy, now or in the future, conditions are not promising for a would-be conqueror. East Asia is not a power vacuum open to the predations of a single aggressor like Nazi Germany or Imperial Japan, but a region crowded with states developing their own formidable defensive maritime-air capabilities to deter and respond to one power's adventurism.

The other side of that coin is that American military power is more greatly constrained than before. If it is true that the home defender enjoys advantage against the cross-sea invader, so too does China's geographic and strategic position make life increasingly difficult for America as an Asia-Pacific power. China's greater proximity to Taiwan in West Pacific or East Asian waters combined with its growing capacity for access and area denial threatens America's ability to intervene at acceptable cost, and more broadly therefore to maintain its credibility as a security guarantor. It is harder for America to function as the guardian of the Pacific region if its ability to operate there is strained and it can no longer act as though the sea lanes were its uncontested lake. This poses difficulties to America's 'air-sea battle' concept. Washington's 'pivot' towards Asia is 'a foreign-policy enterprise by which US joint forces concentrate for action in remote theaters. The military must mass strategically significant quantities of soldiers and armaments in a contested theatre like the Far East, surmounting both transoceanic distances and regional antagonists' attempts to veto intervention' (Holmes 2013a). The increasing range and lethality of weapons systems coupled with the determination of states to defend themselves means that, paradoxically, the growing capacity of states to strike over range has also empowered defenders to an unusual degree.

We are left with a paradox. On the one hand, today's war-making tools with their reach seem to have collapsed distance in a physical sense. On the other hand, as this chapter demonstrates, it seems *prima facie* that the conquest of territory against defenders with a minimal level of will and capability mostly no longer pays. The greater reach and lethality of weapons today empowers defenders as well as attackers, and, at least in the case of attempted territorial expansion across bodies of water, there remains an overall imbalance that favours defenders if they are willing and competent enough to resist. The likely costs of conquest most of the time make it prohibitively difficult. Measured in these terms, for would-be conquerors and for those who would ride to the rescue of the conquered, the world has never been so large.

Undeniably, with modern weapons systems some states have unprecedented capacity to inflict devastation or annihilation from afar. That is a meaningful thing if destruction is the aim in itself. But short of such absolute and rare ambitions, the co-evolution of defensive power (weapons systems combined with doctrines of access denial) is making the use of the military instrument as a tool of expansion more difficult, not less. Today's condition is a paradoxical one of 'fire without conquest', where the rising costs of expansion caused by increased firepower disrupt the linkages between military force and territorial expansion. The same tools that are physically shrinking the world may be strategically expanding it. For America, this both generates security and constrains its power at the same time. That same logic that assists US territorial security when playing on defence also constrains American power on offence, and the capacity of even powerful air/maritime states to apply force across space or even to operate.

What of the claim that swords used in a 'first strike' overpower shields? This is not necessarily the case. States may threaten each other's astral and cyber-dependent command and control systems with instant knockout blows. But in response to the offensive capabilities of the space age, states like China are bringing their defences back down to earth. Since 1995, China has constructed an underground 'great wall'. Turning to the 'passive defences' of antiquity in updated form, it is moving some of its defences into a complex of hardened subterranean facilities, hundreds of miles long, to increase their survivability, along with around forty 'super-hardened' underground air bases that may be difficult to destroy (Minnick 2013; Holmes 2011). The Second Artillery Corps reports that it has dug an underground tunnel 3,107 miles long in Hebei Province of northern China to give China's nuclear weapons survivability, and through which missiles, equipment and personnel can be transported unseen (Hsiao 2009). Grounding defences in the earth in this way would have both direct and subtle benefits. We can never know for certain the offence–defence balance in this regard, given the secrecy that surrounds the covert development of 'passive defence'. But that secrecy in itself can create doubts about the feasibility of a first strike, lest the attacker miscalculate and overestimate the defender's vulnerability and invite retaliation. If attacks on Chinese satellites proved insufficient to blind its command and control system, a persistent adversary wanting to land a decisive hit would need to inflict attacks on Chinese soil itself. A strike on the country's territory, as opposed to a celestial one, would raise the stakes considerably. And as we will see, the doubts and difficulties around first strikes that help China in these ways could also hinder it when it is the overdog. Against adversaries that can project offensive power across all domains, their adversaries reinvent low-tech fortifications and 'passive defense'. This is evidence against the claim that there is a de-territorialisation underway that empties terrain of weight and creates a liquid world. This misperception is encouraged by the misleading 'TV/video game effect', accentuated in the pyrotechnic displays of long-range firepower in the Gulf Wars of 1991 and 2003, that offers seductive images of instant war (Elden 2009: xxvii).

Just as it builds a great wall below the earth, China is also creating blue-water ramparts. Maritime East Asia today presents increasingly formidable barriers to expansion or even incursion. China's 'Assassin's Mace' defence system, marrying submarines, anti-ship missiles and information technology, is designed to expand its maritime periphery and raise costs on any force encroaching on its environment (Cliff et al. 2007: 17–44; Krepinevich, Watts, and Work 2003: ii, 3). The military modernisation programmes underway in East Asia, through ballistic and cruise missiles, submarines, sea mines and surveillance systems, are creating formidable exclusion zones. The range of China's preventive strikes against air bases is growing. China's buildup of access denial and area denial defence has extended its defensive perimeter out to a range of roughly 1,500 km (900 miles), the range of missiles and combat radius of fighters and naval strike aircraft (Cliff 2011). According to the Pentagon, the entire South China Sea and Malacca Strait will fall within the range of the PLA's anti-ship ballistic missiles, making it able to lock on to moving warships from hundreds of miles away (United States Office of the Secretary of Defense 2010: 32). Modern ships rely on electronics as much as armour, so can be disabled or taken off the board through damage to radar aerials or missile launchers. This is both a constraint and a shield. The same maritime barriers between China and neighbouring states that make it a 'dragon in a bathtub' (Glaser 2011; Rehman 2013) also give it the ability to stretch the strategic distance of the Pacific Ocean against interlopers. The costs China could impose, with its growing ability to sink American ships and strike its bases, mean that an American president today would probably think twice before dispatching aircraft carrier battlegroups to the Taiwan Strait, as President Clinton did in 1996, to coerce China from conducting missile tests to intimidate Taiwanese voters. The risk such escalation would pose to US surface ships would now be greater. Throwing one's weight around in this way is now a more risky and complicated affair. Uncontested command of the seas, especially 100–200 miles from China's coast, is probably a thing of the past.

This is a debate about space and time, and the calculations about space and time based on information and secrecy. Changes in surveillance, intelligence, reconnaissance and warning technology, therefore, are crucial to the issue. The improved ability to identify, track and pinpoint enemy forces makes surprise attacks more difficult, provided the defender is paying attention to the oncoming military offensive. Satellite reconnaissance, sharp visual sensors and rapid data-crunching provide the wary observer with more warning time, making a large-scale offensive out of the blue, such as Pearl Harbor or the German assault through the Ardennes in May 1940, more difficult. Importantly, these new hi-tech 'eyes' do not make failures of imagination impossible: analysts can still misinterpret the movement of forces preparing to strike, whether at the borders of the Soviet Union in 1941 or the multiple warnings of Al Qaeda's activity in 2001. And concealment is still possible for defenders staying under cover. But for forces coming out of cover to strike, the hi-tech 'eyes' available to their opponents mean that deception is harder to achieve and they are more likely to be ready. The pursuit of a Hannibalic feat of deception and shock annihilation, a 'Cannae', has long obsessed militaries, but may be more out of reach than ever (Knorr and Morgan 1982: 250; Hanson 2010: 80–86; O'Connell 2010: 266).

The paradoxical effects flowing from new weapons make themselves felt in the task of supplying war over land at sea. Ever more complex and powerful weapons systems make forward bases even more important. All combat operations rely upon a system of delivery, and more sophisticated technology demands more physical support. Jet fighters, tanks and helicopters need constant maintenance and logistical backup. To wage war against Iraq in 1991, the US amassed a gigantic quantity of supplies in Saudi Arabia. US sealift and airlift moved 9.7 million short tons, including 2 million gallons of drinking water and 22,000 vehicles (Webb 2007: 297). For the US to project power into Asia, it would need forward bases to project power and sustain military operations. Without those bases, it would have to exert far greater effort to fight its way into the region than China. Contrary to claims that the US could simply abandon all forward-leaning bases and rely on the reach of its weapons, Toshi Yoshihara (2012: 6) reminds us that:

> Naval bases, then, are mundane yet indispensable. Nearly a century ago, Rear Adm. Bradley Fiske likened their purpose to 'supplying and replenishing the stored-up energy required for naval operations.' To stay with his physics simile, the fleet swiftly discharges its potential energy at sea. Smaller warships such as destroyers and frigates, which defend aircraft carriers and other 'high-value units' against air, surface, and undersea attack, refuel underway every three to four days lest they exhaust their bunkers. A virtually inexhaustible fuel source drives nuclear-powered flattops through the water. Thirsty air wings nonetheless demand jet fuel to stay aloft, sustaining sortie rates typical of aerial combat. By no means does nuclear power liberate carriers from their bases. Submarines boast the greatest at-sea endurance in modern navies. During the Cold War, US ballistic-missile submarines routinely undertook seventy-day patrols. Even so, their crews still need food—and they must put into harbor periodically to load it.

Yet as Yoshihara also recognises, the sophistication of modern military technology that puts such a high premium on bases with their storage tanks, ammunition depots or repair facilities also renders those bases increasingly vulnerable. China's increasing stocks of long-range ballistic missiles such as the DF-15 and the DF-21 missiles threaten to disable American naval and air bases in the 'first island chain' of the western Pacific, in Japan and Okinawa, forcing the US to operate from thousands of miles further eastward, thereby depleting its forces' staying power (Yoshihara 2012). Making America's forward bases more vulnerable and extending China's defensive perimeter would stretch time and space, especially considering the time it still takes to sail a Carrier Battle Group from America's Pacific Coast, not to mention the heavy sustainment of food, fuel and ammunition that carrier groups require. For America to project power without prohibitive costs into those regions, it would be forced to rebuild its military to strike from far over the horizon. This could place in jeopardy the operating assumption that has held for generations, that America's forward presence and its bases are sanctuaries from which it can impose its will.

Once again, similar dynamics would constrain China from the ability to dominate other Asian states. It is not clear that Beijing has an appetite for limitless expansion. Even if it does, now or in the future, conditions are not promising for a would-be conqueror. East Asia is not a power vacuum open to the predations of a single aggressor like Nazi Germany or Imperial Japan. It is a region crowded with increasingly wealthy states developing their own formidable defensive maritime-air capabilities to deter and respond to any one power's adventurism. Even smaller states have the capacity to inflict damaging stings. Though Vietnam could be expected to lose heavily in a capital- and technologically intensive war with China, it also bears the capacity to punish Chinese adventurism on the way down, with an access denial system made up of an impressive air defence network, anti-ship cruise missiles and Kilo-class submarines (Farley 2014).

How should these observations guide America's choices? At present, East Asia is a place of escalating rivalries, of rearmament, territorial disputes, tense standoffs and competing claims to leadership. It is also a place, as I have demonstrated, where primacy is beyond the affordable grasp of any major power. One response could be that, given the difficulty of China imposing its will on smaller states, and the constraints on power projection, America can conclude that it is essentially secure. It can simply abandon the region, liquidate its commitments and become an offshore balancer from its own continental perch, intervening only as a last resort and focusing on defending its heartland and cyber domain.

There are two difficulties with this temptation, however. Firstly, America may not have an existential stake in the fate of East Asia, whether through the direct threat of a transoceanic aggressor or through the disruption caused by a war between other states such as Japan and China (Gholz and Press 2001; Gholz 2014). It does, however, have non-trivial security interests in the region. America has direct stakes in a wide range of things, from the freedom of navigation and the security of the flow of trade and goods through maritime choke points, to the combating of organised crime and the suppression of Islamist terrorism. It also has an interest in preventing a conflict between two major antagonists, Japan and China. It would be unwise to delegate the task of protecting these interests entirely to third parties: the better focus should lie on how best to design the regional order to secure these interests at acceptable cost. Even if this were not true, the blunt political reality is that it will be difficult for any American president to order a withdrawal, even in these populist times. America has been an Asian power for longer even than it has been a European power, and any relevant advice must assume a continued role in the region.

That Asia is strategically an enlarged place can be the basis for an alternative choice, between leaving or trying to dominate, namely staying and sharing power. We can draw upon a strain of classical realist thought, recently revived, which counsels states in such moments of change in the distribution of power to accommodate one another in a set of informal bargains, and more broadly, to renegotiate their universe to an agreed order, or set of principles (Glaser 2015; White 2012; Goldstein 2015; Kissinger 2015). Given the pressures of an anarchic world where changes in relative power often beget insecurity, this is far from easy. As Jonathan Kirshner argues, 'the classical realist, however inherently wary and sceptical (very, always), seeks to accommodate rising power' (Kirshner 2012: 54). What we might call 'world order realism' looks to the possibility of mutual self-restraint, at least for a time, through compromises that are unsatisfactory but durable. To make this work, it would also take two to tango. In contrast to appeasement, the asymmetric offering of concessions to satiate the ambitions and anxieties of another, this would require mutual concessions. Concrete steps could include the easing of tensions over the South China Sea through joint development and the forging of a maritime strategic preserve (Valencia and Nong 2013: 102–109); through the agreement of a stable nuclear deterrence relationship; and through reciprocal arms control measures, based on verification rather than trust, such as limitations on Prompt Global Strike and space weaponisation. It would also entail a distancing, to some extent, of America from the issue of China's claims over Taiwan, abstaining from a position on Taiwan's status but possibly selling arms to maintain its ability to defend itself.

Conclusion

Globalisation is not like the weather. It is something states make and unmake. Historically, global orders, with their trading protocols and monetary regimes, sea lanes, commercial routes, and control of raw materials, are designed and imposed by the strong. At the core of the 'small world' argument is this myth, that technology mechanically transforms the world independent of human politics and the struggle for power. Thanks to the interplay of politics and technology, projecting power affordably over space is now more difficult, not less. This constrains the superpower and its adversaries. It makes us all less powerful, but more secure, than we think.

Notes

1 This chapter draws on material from Patrick Porter, *The Global Village Myth: Distance, War, and the Limits of Power*, pp.148–193. Copyright 2015 Georgetown University Press. Reprinted with permission. www.press.georgetown.edu.

2 I lay out a biography of this idea, and a more extensive critique of it, in *The Global Village Myth* (Porter 2015).

3 The United States–Taiwan Business Council (2010: iv) warned that the situation then was 'both widening the quantitative gap in the cross-Strait power balance, and narrowing TAF's qualitative edge in aircraft performance and pilot training/experience'. It should be borne in mind that the Council, through this document, was agitating for the US to sell F-16C/D to Taiwan, so it should be treated cautiously. Since then the quantitative gap (at least) with regard to fighters has shifted back in Taiwan's favour, as reported by Cordesman, Hess, and Yarosh (2012: 205).

4 Republic of China (2011: 131–132): 'In the past, "victory" was perceived as overcoming the enemy on the battlefield. However, considering the military strength of the two sides of the Taiwan Strait, we must use a practical attitude to reconsider the definition of "victory" if we are to achieve "resolute defense and credible deterrence." After studying and analyzing the current situation of the Taiwan Strait, the definition of "victory" was adjusted from "defeating the enemy in a full confrontation" to "striking the enemy half way across the Taiwan Strait and preventing the enemy from landing and establishing lodgment"; the force structure of the Armed Forces was planned with a focus on gaining a relative advantage in this critical period of war. This will not only allow a "small but superb, strong and smart" force to achieve "resolute defense," but also avoid engaging in an "armaments race" with the PRC, which might affect the nation's overall competitiveness.'

5 In the words of one Taiwanese analyst, the objective is 'to complicate Chinese strategic calculations by raising the strategic uncertainty of military action against the island,

to disrupt the tempo of People's Liberation Army operations, thereby mitigating their intended effects and affording Taiwan more time to seek outside assistance/intervention' (Minnick and Kallender-Umezu 2013).

6 At the time of writing, Taiwan's active duty army forces numbers have reduced to approximately 235,000, but the figure of roughly 60,000 comes from RAND's assessment that its approximately 100-ship armada could transport a maximum of 31,000 troops at a time, and that conducted over a matter of days in a time-sensitive campaign, we can reasonably assume two crossings. It is still to China's benefit in this scenario that, along with RAND, I assume that this would be enough to constitute a sufficient 1:1 personnel ratio.

References

Blumenthal, D. 2011. Rethinking Taiwan's Defense. *Wall Street Journal*, September 29. Accessed April 4, 2017, from www.wsj.com/articles/SB10001424052970204831304576596212311323194.

Bracken, P. 1999. *Fire in the East: The Rise of Asian Military Power and the Second Nuclear Age.* Harper Collins.

Bush, G.W. 2004. President Bush's Remarks on Freedom for the People of Afghanistan. White House.

Bush, R.C., and O'Hanlon, M.E. 2007. *A War Like No Other: The Truth about China's Challenge to America.* John Wiley & Sons.

Cliff, R. 2011. Anti-Access Measures in Chinese Defense Strategy. *Testimony before the US–China Economic and Security Review Commission.*

Cliff, R., Burles, M., Chase, M.S., Eaton, D., and Pollpeter, K.L. 2007. *Entering the Dragon's Lair: Chinese Antiaccess Strategies and Their Implications for the United States.* RAND Corporation.

Cole, J.M. 2012a. ROC Navy Eyes "War of the Flea" Option. *Strategic Vision* 1(5), pp.20–23.

Cole, J.M. 2012b. Would Taiwan Fight? *The Diplomat*, September 24. Accessed April 4, 2017, from http://thediplomat.com/2012/09/would-taiwan-fight/.

Cole, J.M. 2013a. A New Definition of Military Success. *Taipai Times*, February 22. Accessed April 4, 2017, from www.taipeitimes.com/News/editorials/archives/2013/02/22/2003555383.

Cole, J.M. 2013b. Taiwan's New Rocket Launchers? *The Diplomat*, July 11. Accessed April 4, 2017, from http://thediplomat.com/2013/06/taiwans-new-rocket-launchers/.

Cole, J.M. 2013c. Taiwan Unveils Road-Mobile "Carrier Killer" Launcher. *The Diplomat*, August 16. Accessed April 4, 2017, from http://thediplomat.com/2013/08/taiwan-unveils-road-mobile-carrier-killer-launcher/.

Cordesman, A.H., Hess, A., and Yarosh, N.S. 2012. *Chinese Military Modernization and Force Development: A Western Perspective.* Rowman & Littlefield.

Davis, P.K., and Wilson, P.A. 2011. *Looming Discontinuities in US Military Strategy and Defense Planning: Colliding RMAs Necessitate a New Strategy.* RAND Corporation.

Dempsey, M.E. 2012. Nation Faces Security Paradox. *American Forces Press Service*, April 13. Accessed April 4, 2017, from www.defense.gov/News/NewsArticle.aspx?ID=67921.

Dempsey, M.E. 2013. Testimony to the Senate Armed Service Committee. *Hearing to Receive Testimony on the Impacts of Sequestration and/or a Full Year Continuing Resolution On the Department of Defense*, February, 12, 2013.

Edmonds, M., and Tsai, M., eds. 2004. *Taiwan's Security and Air Power: Taiwan's Defense Against the Air Threat from Mainland China.* Routledge.

Elden, S. 2009. *Terror and Territory: The Spatial Extent of Sovereignty.* University of Minnesota Press.

Farley, R. 2014. If Vietnam and China Went to War: Five Weapons Beijing Should Fear. *The National Interest*, July 12. Accessed April 4, 2017, from http://nationalinterest.org/feature/if-vietnam-china-went-war-five-weapons-beijing-should-fear-10861.

Freedberg, S.J. 2014. Marines Seek New Tech to Get Ashore against Missiles; Reinventing Amphib Assault. *Breaking Defense*, April 16. Accessed April 4, 2017, from http://breaking-defense.com/2014/04/marines-seek-new-tech-to-get-ashore-vs-missiles-reinventing-amphib-assault/.

Gaddis, J.L. 2004. *Surprise, Security, and the American Experience* (Vol. 1). Harvard University Press.

Gholz, E. 2014. Assessing the "Threat" of International Tension to the US Economy. In Preble, C.A., and Mueller, J.E., eds. *A Dangerous World? Threat Perception and US National Security*. Cato Institute, pp.209–221.

Gholz, E., and Press, D.G. 2001. The Effects of Wars on Neutral Countries: Why It Doesn't Pay to Preserve the Peace. *Security Studies*, 10(4), pp.1–57.

Glaser, C. 2011. Will China's Rise Lead to War? Why Realism Does Not Mean Pessimism. *Foreign Affairs*, March/April, pp.80–91.

Glaser, C.L. 2015. A US–China Grand Bargain? The Hard Choice between Military Competition and Accommodation. *International Security*, 39(4), pp.49–90.

Goldstein, L.J. 2015. *Meeting China Halfway: How to Defuse the Emerging US–China Rivalry*. Georgetown University Press.

Hanson, V.D. 2010. Tomorrow's Wars. *City Journal*, 10(1), pp.80–86

Henrikson, A.K. 2002. Distance and Foreign Policy: A Political Geography Approach. *International Political Science Review*, 23(4), pp.437–466.

Holmes, J.R. 2011. China's Underground Great Wall. *The Diplomat*, August 20. Accessed April 4, 2017, from http://thediplomat.com/2011/08/chinas-underground-great-wall/.

Holmes, J.R. 2013a. Partner in the Pivot? In Goto, S., ed. *Taiwan and the US Pivot to Asia: New Realities in the Region?* Woodrow Wilson Center, pp.25–32.

Holmes, J.R. 2013b. Partner in the Pivot? *The Diplomat*, April 23. Accessed April 4, 2017, from http://thediplomat.com/the-naval-diplomat/2013/04/23/partner-in-the-pivot/.

Holmes, J.R., and Yoshihara, T. 2012. *Defending the Strait: Taiwan's Naval Strategy in the 21st Century*. Jamestown.

Hsiao, R. 2009. China's "Underground Great Wall" and Nuclear Deterrence. *China Brief*, 9(25), pp.1–2.

Keohane, R.O. 2002. The Globalization of Informal Violence, Theories of World Politics, and the "Liberalism of Fear". *Dialogue IO*, 1(01), pp.29–43.

Kirshner, J. 2012. The Tragedy of Offensive Realism: Classical Realism and the Rise of China. *European Journal of International Relations*, 18(1), pp.53–75.

Kissinger, H. 2015. *World Order*. Penguin Books.

Knorr, K.E., and Morgan, P.M., eds. 1982. *Strategic Military Surprise: Initiatives and Opportunities*. Transaction.

Krepinevich, A.F., Watts, B.D., and Work, R.O. 2003. *Meeting the Anti-Access and Area Denial Challenge*. Center for Strategic and Budgetary Assessments.

Layne, C. 2006. *The Peace of Illusions: American Grand Strategy from 1940 to the Present*. Cornell University Press.

Levy, J.S., and Thompson, W.R. 2010. Balancing on Land and at Sea: Do States Ally against the Leading Global Power? *International Security*, 35(1), pp.7–43.

Minnick, W. 2010. Taiwan's Hidden Base Will Safeguard Aircraft. *Defense News*, May 3. Accessed April 4, 2017, from http://minnickarticles.blogspot.com/2010/05/taiwans-hidden-base-will-safeguard.html.

Minnick, W. 2013. China Pursues Systems to Keep US Forces at Bay. *Defense News*, September 17. Accessed April 4, 2017, from https://engineeringevil.com/2013/09/17/china-pursues-systems-to-keep-us-forces-at-bay/.

Minnick, W., and Kallender-Umezu, P. 2013. Japan, Taiwan Upgrade Strike Capability. *RP Defense*, May 7. Accessed April 4, 2017, from http://rpdefense.over-blog.com/japan-taiwan-upgrade-strike-capability.

Murray, W.S. 2008. Revisiting Taiwan's Defense Strategy. *Naval War College Review*, 61(3), pp.14–31.

National Commission on Terrorist Attacks. 2004. Final Report of the National Commission on Terrorist Attacks upon the United States. W.W. Norton.

Nitze, P. 1950. NSC 68: United States Objectives and Programs for National Security. *American Cold War Strategy: Interpreting NSC*, 68.

O'Connell, R.L. 2010. *The Ghosts of Cannae: Hannibal and the Darkest Hour of the Roman Republic*. Random House.

Porter, P. 2015. *The Global Village Myth: Distance, War, and the Limits of Power*. Georgetown University Press.

Rehman, I. 2013. Dragon in a Bathtub: Chinese Nuclear Submarines and the South China Sea. *BBC Vietnam*, March 9. Accessed April 4, 2017, from http://carnegieendowment.org/2013/03/09/dragon-in-bathtub-chinese-nuclear-submarines-and-south-china-sea-pub-51163.

Republic of China, 2011. *National Defense Report*.

Republic of China, 2013. *Quadrennial Defense Review*.

Roosevelt, F.D. 1941. Fireside Chat, December 9. *Public Papers and Addresses of Franklin D. Roosevelt* (New York, 1938–1950), vol. 10, pp.528–529.

Shifrinson, J. 2014. The Other Shield of the Republic: Geography and American National Security. Paper presented at the International Studies Association.

Shlapak, D.A., Orletsky, D.T., Reid, T.I., Tanner, M.S., and Wilson, B. 2009. *A Question of Balance: Political Context and Military Aspects of the China-Taiwan Dispute*. RAND Corporation.

Taylor Fravel, M. 2010. International Relations Theory and China's Rise: Assessing China's Potential for Territorial Expansion. *International Studies Review*, 12(4), pp.505–532.

United States Army, 2002. Field Manual 3–34.2, *Combined Arms-Breaching Operations*. Headquarters, Department of the Army.

United States Office of the Secretary of Defense. 2010. *Annual Report to Congress: Military and Security Developments involving the People's Republic of China*.

United States–Taiwan Business Council. 2010. *The Balance of Air Power in the Taiwan Strait*.

Valencia, M., and Nong, H. 2013. Joint Development Possibilities: What, Where, Who, and How? *Global Asia*, June 20. Accessed April 4, 2017, from https://www.globalasia.org/about13.php?alpha_idx=22.

Webb, K. 2007. The Continued Importance of Geographic Distance and Boulding's Loss of Strength Gradient. *Comparative Strategy*, 26(4), pp.295–310.

White, H. 2012. *The China Choice: Why America Should Share Power*. Black Inc.

Wohlstetter, A. 1959. The Delicate Balance of Terror. *Foreign Affairs*, 37, p.211.

Wohlstetter, A. 1968. Illusions of Distance. *Foreign Affairs*, 46, p.242.

Yoshihara, T. 2012. How Vulnerable Are US Bases in the Pacific Now? *Global Public Square*, December 7. Accessed April 4, 2017, from http://globalpublicsquare.blogs.cnn.com/2012/12/07/u-s-bases-in-japan-sitting-ducks/.

PART II

The politics and policy of restraint

7

NOT SO DANGEROUS NATION

US foreign policy from the founding to the Spanish–American War

William Ruger[1]

In the post-Cold War era, the United States has been, for good or for bad, a "dangerous nation" (Kagan 2006: 3).[2] It has toppled – directly or indirectly – regimes in Afghanistan, Iraq, and Libya; fought two wars in the Balkans that helped reshape the boundaries and politics of that region; and intervened in places such as Somalia and Haiti. The US has also expanded the US-dominated NATO alliance into Russia's front yard and up to its doorstep, promoted social movements and insurgencies in some places while supporting repression of the same in others, and frequently sent military forces and soft power assets around the globe trying to shape events to its liking.

The United States' approach to the world in this period has not only posed a danger to others; it has often been dangerous to itself. The nation has spent trillions of dollars and nearly 7,000 lives in Afghanistan and Iraq alone, with limited or even negative impacts on American interests. Even bracketing war costs, the US defense budget has eaten up hundreds of billions of dollars each year, contributing to the nation's fiscal woes. And thanks to treaty obligations, the US is now on the hook to defend 68 other countries whose own contribution to American safety is marginal at best (Taylor 2015). These commitments are financially costly; more importantly, they risk unnecessarily provoking security fears in other countries while threatening to "chain-gang" the US into wars not of its choosing.

An increasing number of people, including important political elites, are questioning whether this active approach is working to secure our national interests. They look at the last 15–25 years of grand strategy (alternately referred to as "primacy," "liberal hegemony," or "deep engagement") and see little or even a negative return on investment. President Donald Trump, for example, argued in his February 24, 2017, CPAC speech that:

> We've spent trillions of dollars overseas, while allowing our own infrastructure to fall into total disrepair and decay. In the Middle East, we've spent as

of four weeks ago, $6 trillion. Think of it. And by the way, the Middle East is in – I mean, it's not even close, it's in much worse shape than it was 15 years ago. If our presidents would have gone to the beach for 15 years, we would be in much better shape than we are right now, that I can tell you.

Borchers 2017

Senators Rand Paul and Mike Lee, on one end of the political spectrum, and Senator Ron Wyden and Representative Tulsi Gabbard, on the other end, are just a few prominent examples of elites expressing some unease with US foreign policy today.

A significant segment of the public is also dissatisfied with the status quo approach. In three polls conducted by the Charles Koch Institute and the Center for the National Interest in October 2016, December 2016, and January 2017, a majority of Americans expressed the view that US foreign policy over the last 15 years has made us less safe, and relatively few thought it had made us safer (CKI/CTNI 2016a, 2016b, 2017). Nonetheless, people may legitimately ask whether there is really any well-grounded and realistic alternative to what the US is currently doing, especially since this approach is still the consensus view of the bi-partisan foreign policy establishment in Washington.

Furthermore, despite the establishment consensus, there is serious debate among academics and even in a few think tanks in Washington – the places where future approaches germinate. Within this largely academic discussion, some would suggest that we just need to do primacy "smarter" – or continue to lead and engage, but just a bit more selectively. Others would argue for something more orthogonal to the status quo. This includes the more thoroughgoing critics of post-Cold War US foreign policy, who would suggest greater realism or what is often called "restraint."

Restraint is as much a mindset or family of similar approaches as a specific plan. Indeed, it is defined as much by what restrainers want to avoid as what they want to do. This family includes off-shore balancers (Mearsheimer and Walt 2016), with their emphasis on preventing the emergence of regional hegemons in the major power centers of the world and otherwise doing a lot less (given their very strict conception of national interests and when to engage militarily). The restraint family also encompasses more serious challengers to the status quo, including those who first coined the term "restraint" (Gholz, Press, and Sapolsky 1997; Posen 2014). This variant is not isolationism (despite what its critics say), but it is more sanguine about America's security environment and the effects of the nuclear revolution than the off-shore balancers – and thus less supportive of more active efforts to promote balancing (such as peacetime alliances in Asia to promote balancing of China). Regardless of differences, most factions within the restraint family favor a more realist-inspired foreign policy focused on securing vital interests rather than altruistic or idealistic ends, on using military power with greater discrimination, and on limiting US commitments abroad.

Unfortunately for non-experts who may be unsatisfied with the status quo and wonder if another strategy would serve our nation better, they have little frame of reference for alternatives. Primacy is all they know, given the US has been pursuing this approach for at least the last 25 years (if not since 1949). This chapter will show that a more restrained approach – rather than being something foreign, exotic, idealistic, or untested – is in fact a very American approach to foreign policy and one that has deep, deep roots in American ideals and history. Whether it is a wise strategy is another question altogether. But as this chapter will make clear, the critics of restraint certainly cannot claim it would be unprecedented, unrealistic, or un-American.

Specifically, this chapter will describe and explain the Founders' approach to US foreign policy, with particular emphasis on grand strategy. While tension has always existed in American thinking on foreign policy (the liberal interventionists have always been among us), the chapter will argue that the Founders generally held a particular vision about foreign policy very similar to modern-day conceptions of restraint. This vision dominated US foreign policy thinking and behavior from Washington's administration until at least the Spanish-American War in 1898, in what we might call the Washingtonian era in US foreign policy.

The Founders' vision

So how did the Founders envision the way in which the United States ought to approach foreign policy?

According to the consensus view of scholars of the history of US foreign policy, the Founders (and those who followed them) conceived of and pursued a foreign policy with two key pillars: (1) strategic independence (i.e., neutrality or non-entanglement) and (2) military non-interventionism abroad. This traditional vision guided American foreign policy for more than a century. In fact, conventional historical treatments hold that it lasted from Washington's administration through at least the Spanish-American War in 1898 (Nordlinger 1995: 49).[3]

Many have called this approach "isolationism" – though, in truth, few adherents have ever actually called for US isolation from the world. Historian Selig Adler carefully warned that "American isolationism has never meant total social, cultural, and economic self-sufficiency. Such a concept has had few rational advocates and the very idea is nullified by the history of the United States" (Adler 1957: 28). Likewise, historian Manfred Jonas noted that "No American isolationist made a principle out of cutting off all foreign trade nor seriously advocated trying to attain economic self-sufficiency. None sought to close this country's doors to immigrants or foreign travelers" (Jonas 1990: 5). Nor did it mean that the US would never go to war when the country's safety demanded it. Yet, despite its lack of accuracy, the term "isolationism" has largely stuck as a descriptor of American foreign policy in this era. The label stuck partly because of its slanderous connotation rather than its descriptive accuracy: those with an expansive view of the proper extent of US involvement in the world in their own time (whether in the period before World War II, the Cold War era, or more recently) have used it to besmirch their more restrained critics.[4] To be fair, though, some have attempted to use the term as a value-neutral description or even attempted to use it positively (Jonas 1990; Tucker 1972; Nordlinger 1995).

The strategic independence pillar encompassed a firm commitment to avoiding political connections, particularly "entangling alliances." Although it was Thomas Jefferson who coined that phrase, George Washington's paean to non-entanglement and neutrality in his famous Farewell Address provided the touchstone for American leaders throughout this period. But the Founding vision was not one of mere unilateralism and a desire for a free and independent hand in international politics. If that were the case, then the Founders' approach would be compatible with that of some modern neo-conservatives, since they are often attracted to going it alone or tend to see multilateral institutions and their member states as barriers to American interests (when they don't see those actors as auxiliaries to the accomplishment of US goals). But the Founders weren't merely worried about alliances. They also wanted to stay out of Old World fights. As Adler noted in his study of isolationism, "One can probe anywhere into the writings of the Founding Fathers and be certain to come upon the suggestion that the United States, alliance or no alliance, should stay out of Europe's wars." Indeed, Selig went on, "it is safe to say the Father of our Country made neutrality and non-intervention national fixations" (Adler 1957: 10–11).

Thus the second pillar of the Washingtonian approach was non-interventionism focused on avoiding overseas wars and remaining aloof from the power politics of the Old World (Jonas 1990: 15).[5] Therefore, the US did not do very much outside the western hemisphere other than trade. And when the US did go abroad militarily, as in the fights with the Barbary pirates, it was mostly about protecting American trade and did not involve fighting long land wars in places far from our shores. The comparison with the post-1898 period in terms of overseas fighting is striking, as will be discussed below. Of course, the US did fight some foreign wars close to home during this period, most prominently the War of 1812, the Mexican War, and the sad conflicts with Native American nations. But even these North American fights were more limited in number and scale when compared to the history of other great powers.

The four ur-texts of the Washingtonian (or Great Rule) era

Four key documents from the Founding period provide the intellectual and rhetorical cornerstones of the Washingtonian era in American foreign policy. They are Thomas Paine's *Common Sense*, Washington's Farewell Address (and its assist in Jefferson's First Inaugural), John Quincy Adams' July 4, 1821, address, and the Monroe Doctrine.[6] Although there are other aligned documents, these are the most important exemplars of this approach. Moreover, the ideas they contained informed American perspectives throughout the century. This is especially the case for Washington's Farewell Address and its Great Rule.

Many would turn first to Washington, Alexander Hamilton, John Adams, James Madison, or Jefferson to begin to flesh out the Founders' vision of US foreign policy. However, it would be a major error not to begin instead with Thomas Paine. Paine was important for laying some of the key intellectual foundations upon which the others would build. This is explicated at length in historian Felix Gilbert's well-respected work on early American thought. To Gilbert, Paine was a critical source of future American thinking about the relationship between America and the Old World. Indeed, Gilbert goes so far as to conclude that "for a long time, every utterance on foreign policy starts from Paine's words and echoes his thoughts" (Gilbert 1961: 43). Paine was also important for conveying to the New World a strain of British thought about Britain's own relationship with Europe. In particular, Paine, according to Gilbert, explicitly paralleled and applied the arguments of "the English radicals who had attacked England's 'Continental connections' and had emphasized the peculiarity of the English geographical situation and her special interests as a trading nation" (Gilbert 1961: 43). These ideas were to hold great sway among the Founding generation.

Paine's *Common Sense* contains his most important contributions to the early American mindset about its place in the world. Published in 1776, it stressed several key themes related to foreign policy that would arise repeatedly in the late 18th and the 19th centuries. The first of these concerned the benefits of being disconnected from both British and Continental political affairs. Paine argued that "not a single advantage is derived" from connection with Britain. Indeed, he thought that:

> the injuries and disadvantages we sustain by that connection, are without number; and our duty to mankind at large, as well as to ourselves, instruct us to renounce the alliance: Because, any submission to, or dependance [sic] on Great Britain, tends directly to involve this continent in European wars and quarrels; and sets us at variance with nations, who would otherwise seek our friendship, and against whom, we have neither anger nor complaint.
>
> *Paine 1955 [1776]: 24*

It was not just connection with Britain that was problematic to Paine: it was any political connection whatsoever to the Old World:

> As Europe is our market for trade, we ought to form no partial connection with any part of it. It is the true interest of America to steer clear of European contentions, which she never can do, while by her dependence [sic] on Britain, she is made the make-weight in the scale of British politics.
>
> *Paine 1955 [1776]: 24–25*

Another key theme laid out by Paine was the importance of America's geographic advantages (and the notion that this separation might be possible by divine plan) and the sanctuary that distance allowed:

> Even the distance at which the Almighty hath placed England and America, is a strong and natural proof, that the authority of the one, over the other,

was never the design of Heaven. The time likewise at which the continent was discovered, adds weight to the argument, and the manner in which it was peopled encreases [sic] the force of it. The reformation was preceded by the discovery of America, as if the Almighty graciously meant to open a sanctuary to the persecuted in future years, when home should afford neither friendship nor safety.

Paine 1955 [1776]: 25

And:

O ye that love mankind! Ye that dare oppose, not only the tyranny, but the tyrant, stand forth! Every spot of the old world is overrun with oppression. Freedom hath been hunted round the globe. Asia, and Africa, have long expelled her. – Europe regards her like a stranger, and England hath given her warning to depart. O! receive the fugitive, and prepare in time an asylum for mankind.

Paine 1955 [1776]: 25

Paine was also cognizant of the difficulty of projecting power across vast oceans – what John Mearsheimer (2001) in our own time has called the "stopping power of water." He also appreciated the advantages of not having an overseas empire that would divert defensive resources from the periphery (another argument utilized today by latter-day Paines). Paine explains the advantage we derived from distance and what this meant to the balance of naval forces, noting:

for if America had only a twentieth part of the naval force of Britain, she would be by far an over match for her; because, as we neither have, nor claim any foreign dominion, our whole force would be employed on our own coast, where we should, in the long run, have two to one the advantage of those who had three or four thousand miles to sail over, before they could attack us, and the same distance to return in order to refit and recruit.

Paine 1955 [1776]: 40

And lastly, Paine stressed the importance of trade not just to prosperity but to America's security. On this point, he noted that "Our plan is commerce, and that, well attended to, will secure us the peace and friendship of all Europe; because, it is the interest of all Europe to have America a free port. Her trade will always be a protection, and her barrenness of gold and silver secure her from invaders" (Paine 1955 [1776]: 24).

Of course, Paine's wishes could not be immediately satisfied. Despite the colonists' desire to avoid typical alliances, the exigencies of the Revolutionary War forced the colonies to conclude just such a commitment with France in 1778. Thus the "isolationist" phase in American history was not its first but followed on the heels of the colonies' uneasy but absolutely necessary and ultimately successful immersion in European great power politics. Indeed, the colonists were able to use the great power political struggles between the British and the French to their advantage by getting the French to enter the conflict and provide the crucial weight in the balance of the Revolutionary War. While enjoying the benefits of that particular entanglement during the war, the newly independent American government soon faced the problems inherent in such relations, namely the question of what to do when your interests and your commitments diverge. This began the crucial debate in the United States' young life concerning its treaty obligations during the War of the First Coalition between most of Europe and the US's ally, France.

This seminal foreign policy moment arose at the beginning of Washington's second term as president and dominated political attention in America for much of the rest of that period. It involved the more idealistic pro-French wing and the realist Hamiltonian wing of the administration. And the struggle between these two factions helped bring about the American party system. Ultimately, in his Proclamation of Neutrality and more importantly, his Farewell Address, Washington sided with Hamilton and laid the foundation of what became America's distinct tradition in foreign policy.

Washington, in the portion of his address dedicated to foreign policy, counseled future Americans to beware emotional and political ties with foreign powers. In terms of the former, he argued that "Excessive partiality for one nation and excessive dislike of another, cause those whom they actuate to see danger on only one side, and serve to veil and even second the arts of influence on the other side"[7] (something he saw in his own administration and that Americans were to see repeatedly in its history, including in the 20th century, perhaps most clearly during Woodrow Wilson's administration). Washington went on to announce his "Great Rule," which was to be the north star of our foreign policy for generations. He exclaimed that the "The Great rule of conduct for us, in regard to foreign Nations is in extending our commercial relations to have with them as little *political* connection as possible." Ever the realist, he (and Hamilton, a key intellectual force behind his vision and co-drafter of the address) understood that this position flowed from America's particular interests and geopolitical position, arguing that:

> Europe has a set of primary interests, which to us have none, or a very remote relation. – Hence she must be engaged in frequent controversies, the causes of which are essentially foreign to our concerns. – Hence therefore it must be unwise in us to implicate ourselves, by artificial ties, in the ordinary vicissitudes of her politics, or the ordinary combinations and collisions of her friendships, or enmities:- Our detached and distant situation invites and enables us to pursue a different course.

Washington well understood, concerning such connections, "that 'tis folly in one nation to look for disinterested favors from another – that it must pay with a portion of its independence for whatever it may accept under that character." The President appreciated that the interests of the United States and the interests of foreign powers would not be the same and that foreign conflicts might be unrelated to our needs – and thus the country ought to stay away from political connections that could embroil us in those conflicts.

Washington, later seconded more thoroughly by John Quincy Adams, also counseled against the dangerous adventurism characterized by intervention in the affairs of others. He argued:

> Why forego the advantages of so peculiar a situation? – Why quit our own to stand upon foreign ground? – Why, by interweaving our destiny with that of any part of Europe, entangle our peace and prosperity in the toils of European ambition, Rivalship, Interest, Humor, or Caprice?

The answer he gave was that "'Tis our true policy to steer clear of permanent alliances, with any portion of the foreign world." Yet he also knew that this general counsel against political connection must in rare circumstance, in extreme necessity, be temporarily abandoned. Therefore, the departing president argued that "we may safely trust to temporary alliances for extraordinary circumstances."

One might speculate, when looking at Washington's first draft, that he was even more firm about the ideal of non-entanglement than indicated by the strong statement in the final version. The first draft, which Hamilton revised in a nod to realism's caution (as Gilbert suggests) rather than an evisceration of the ideal itself, held that "we may avoid connecting ourselves with the Politics of any Nation, farther than shall be found necessary to regulate our own trade" (Gilbert 1961: 130, 138).

It is difficult to overstate the importance of Washington's address. He made political connections the third rail of 19th-century American politics, much like Social Security is today. As political scientist Eric Nordlinger argued:

> Washington's counsels closely guided the United States for a century. They were considered on a par with the Constitution and the Declaration of Independence in their political wisdom. The "great rule" of political-military detachment serves as the "country's most fundamental theory of foreign policy." Not a single administration throughout the nineteenth century had reason to diverge from it, and were the temptation present, none dared to act upon it.
>
> *Nordlinger 1995: 51*

Indeed, it was so much a part of the fabric of America's political culture that, as historian Walter McDougall points out, "the Senate, beginning in 1862 and then annually since 1893, recited the Farewell Address in liturgical fashion at the start of each session" (McDougall 2016: 49). Even as the country was on the verge of fighting Spain and gaining an overseas empire in the Spanish-American War, Washington's words echoed in American politics. Republican representative David Henderson of Iowa blasted the idea that the US should be "the regulator of the wrongs of the earth" and argued that "So long as that question is before us, I follow the advice of Washington, recommending that we mind strictly our own business" (Kinzer 2017: 36).

Both presidents who followed Washington stayed true to his dictums. John Adams, though engaged in what was called the Quasi-War with France, wanted to stay out of Europe's wars and remain neutral. He ultimately arranged for an end to hostilities (and the formal end of the alliance) with the Treaty of Mortefontaine in 1800. Thomas Jefferson, in his first Inaugural, also showed that he would continue with Washington's Great Rule. Always able to coin a phrase, Jefferson famously proclaimed that one of the "essential principles" of our government that would guide his presidency would be "peace, commerce, and honest friendship with all nations, entangling alliances with none" (Jefferson 1801). And he too held to this approach in office. Indeed, historian Walter McDougall claims that Jefferson so thoroughly adopted Washington's civil religion, which included the foreign policy catechism, that he became "a magnificent high priest, subtle in theology and skilled in evangelism" (McDougall 2016: 54). And while later in life (in a letter to President James Monroe) Jefferson flirted with the idea of a temporary alliance with Britain against the Holy Alliance, he nonetheless held firm that "Our first and fundamental maxim should be, never to entangle ourselves in the broils of Europe. Our second, never to suffer Europe to meddle with cis–Atlantic affairs" (Jonas 1990: 11).

Moving forward more than 20 years from Washington's address, during which time the US had experienced conflict with France in the Quasi-War (under Adams) and the British in the less-than-successful War of 1812 (under Madison), John Quincy Adams provided the most intense statement of the Washingtonian approach. In response to growing American sympathy towards the Greek independence movement, then Secretary of State Adams vociferously challenged the call for intervention in a July 4, 1821, public address in the Capitol.

In this oft-quoted speech, Adams made the case that America should only fight for its national interests, narrowly defined, and that to do otherwise would jeopardize those interests and American values. Arguing the former point, he said of the United States:

> Wherever the standard of freedom and Independence has been or shall be unfurled, there will her heart, her benedictions, and her prayers be. But she goes not abroad in search of monsters to destroy. She is the well-wisher to the freedom and independence of all. She is the champion and vindicator only of her own.
>
> *Adams 1821*

While sympathetic to the good causes of others, Adams feared the consequences of intervention for American interests, this time broadly defined to include its ideals, even if the cause was just. He thought that:

> By enlisting under other banners than her own, were they even the banners of foreign independence, she would involve herself beyond the power of

extrication, in all the wars of interest and intrigue, of individual avarice, envy, and ambition, which assume the colors and usurp the standard of freedom. The fundamental maxims of her policy would insensibly change from *liberty* to *force* … She might become the dictatress of the world. She would be no longer the ruler of her own spirit … [America's] glory is not *dominion*, but *liberty*.

Adams 1821

With these words, Adams firmly embraced and explicated the second pillar of Washingtonian-era foreign policy: military non-interventionism.

The fourth major document in the Founding foreign policy canon is the Monroe Doctrine. It warned the Old World powers to stay out of the New World and reiterated the Washingtonian vision. This doctrine was boldly worded but difficult to defend (without the British Navy defending the moat, that is) and was delivered in response to growing concern about the potential for European intervention in regard to the independence movements in Latin America. Monroe issued it in his annual message to Congress in 1823, and it contained several points that were consistent with the tenor of this era. It enjoined the Europeans from future colonizing in the Americas and insisted that the Europeans essentially keep out and not try to extend their system to the western hemisphere. As Monroe wrote, "as a principle in which the rights and interests of the United States are involved that the American continents, by the free and independent conditions which they have assumed and maintain, are henceforth not to be considered as subjects for future colonization by any European powers" (Monroe 1823). Moreover, as the President continued:

we should consider any attempt on their part to extend their system to any portion of this hemisphere as dangerous to our peace and safety. With the existing colonies or dependencies of any European power we have not interfered and shall not interfere. But with the Governments who have declared their independence and maintain it, and whose independence we have, on great consideration and on just principles, acknowledged, we could not view any interposition for the purpose of oppressing them, or controlling in any other manner their destiny, by any European power in any other light than as the manifestation of an unfriendly disposition toward the United States.

Lastly, Monroe forcefully expressed the US's policy of non-interference and non-intervention consistent with that of his predecessors:

In the wars of the European powers in matters relating to themselves we have never taken any part, nor does it comport with our policy to do so. It is only when our rights are invaded or seriously menaced that we resent injuries or make preparation for our defense.

And:

> Our policy in regard to Europe, which was adopted at an early stage of the wars which have so long agitated that quarter of the globe, nevertheless remains the same, which is, not to interfere in the internal concerns of any of its powers; to consider the government de facto as the legitimate government for us; to cultivate friendly relations with it, and to preserve those relations by a frank, firm, and manly policy, meeting in all instances the just claims of every power, submitting to injuries from none.

The Monroe Doctrine was simpatico with the three other ur-texts of the period as well as Hamilton's argument in the Federalist Papers about the dangers of Old World balance-of-power politics in the New World. But it remains to be shown whether those who followed this founding generation of thinkers held true to these words throughout the rest of the 19th century.

The historical record: did the US practice what the Founders preached?

The historical record from the 19th century supports the claim that the US did in fact practice what its Founders preached. The United States stayed true to the cause of neutrality and conducted a relatively non-interventionist policy with respect to the overseas use of military force. It was no "dangerous nation" in deed, even if its liberal example and its rise to power represented a future threat to the Old World. Of course, a bias towards abstaining from European conflicts did not mean the US never stood up for its territorial integrity and sovereign rights. The War of 1812 was an instance in which it attempted to do so, though without greatest success, as was its more successful fight with the Barbary states. But the historical record clearly shows a studied avoidance of land wars outside the western hemisphere and a hostility toward peacetime alliances. This is in marked contrast with the country's more well-known 20th- and 21st-century experiences.

According to the Congressional Research Service, from 1798 to the Spanish-American War in 1898, the United States deployed force abroad notably (meaning when it has "used military forces abroad in situations of military conflict or potential conflict to protect US citizens or promote US interests," but not including covert actions or foreign stationings) fewer than 100 times (Torreon 2016). Of these, the majority were short, minor uses or displays of force to punish pirates, plunderers, and those molesting seaman/explorers/surveyors; and to protect life and property during political disturbances in Asia and Latin America. Other incidences related to home defense and America's expansion west and south. Only a few involved the great powers, including major uses during the undeclared naval war with the French in the late 18th century and the War of 1812 with the British. Other important uses involved the protection or opening up of trade routes, the securing of coaling stations, and punishing or threatening Latin American governments. A host of others were odd minor uses or displays (Torreon 2016). It is worth noting, especially in light of Robert Kagan's "dangerous nation" argument, that expansion on the continent did not violate the Founders' vision or prove the thesis that there was continuity in the vision and path of US foreign policy since the beginning (as opposed to a rupture starting in 1898). This is because, as Nordlinger explains, Washington was primarily worried about overseas involvement and the negative consequences the Founders believed would come of it (Nordlinger 1995: 51). What is remarkable is actually how seldom the US used force outside of the hemisphere and how few foreign wars it fought despite rising to great power status by the end of the 19th century. Indeed, the US even avoided crises that could have brought it into conflict with other powers. Certainly there were the minor Barbary wars, the War of 1812, and the Mexican War from 1846 to 1848. And the US faced the risk of war with the French during its Intervention in Mexico in the 1860s, with Spain in the Virginius Affair of 1873, with Chile in the Baltimore Crisis in 1891, and with the British during the Venezuela Boundary Crisis in 1895–1896. But again, the relative number, location, and stakes involved were generally a lot lower compared with the period from 1898 to the present. And these uses of force did not require dangerous alliance commitments. By comparison, during the period following the Spanish-American War in 1898 to today, the United States used force abroad nearly 300 times, including major foreign wars in Europe and Asia such as World War I, World War II, the Korean War, the Vietnam War, the Persian Gulf War, the Iraq War, and the War in Afghanistan. Even the minor uses were more serious in this period than the prior ones and threatened to involve the US in the political machinations of faraway places. For example, US intervention in Lebanon in 1982–1983 and in Somalia during 1992–1993 drew the country into the kinds of conflicts that Adams had warned about.

In terms of entanglements, the United States did not enter a permanent peacetime alliance from the demise of the treaty with France due to Washington's Neutrality Proclamation in 1793 (though it was not officially ended until 1800) until the creation of NATO in 1949.[8] In fact, American leaders were suspicious of any connections other than commercial ones that might violate its precious non-entanglement (though this, like other Founding concerns, diminished the closer the country got to the 20th century). After examining the historical record, it is quite easy to conclude that the US followed Adams' advice not to enlist under banners other than her (sic) own.

This is not a radical conclusion. It is the consensus of key historians of this time period. Manfred Jonas, for example, concluded from the record that, "Since the foreign policy of Washington and Jefferson proved serviceable, it was followed consistently until the end of the nineteenth century" (Jonas 1978: 498). Gilbert (1961) agreed, noting that, "The 'Great Rule' which Washington had set down in the Farewell Address served as a guide to American foreign policy for over a century; of all the Political Testaments of the eighteenth century, the Farewell Address alone succeeded in achieving practical political significance." This comes through strongly in examination of both the revealed preferences of US leaders and their rhetoric.

The pre-Civil War period witnessed numerous instances in which the Washingtonian approach was hailed by the Chief Executive. For example, President Martin Van Buren noted in his 1837 Inaugural Address:

> Our course of foreign policy has been so uniform and intelligible as to constitute a rule of Executive conduct which leaves little to my discretion, unless, indeed, I were willing to run counter to the lights of experience and the known opinions of my constituents. We sedulously cultivate the friendship of all nations as the conditions most compatible with our welfare and the principles of our Government. We decline alliances as adverse to our peace. We desire commercial relations on equal terms, being ever willing to give a fair equivalent for advantages received. We endeavor to conduct our intercourse with openness and sincerity, promptly avowing our objects and seeking to establish that mutual frankness which is as beneficial in the dealings of nations as of men. We have no disposition and we disclaim all right to meddle in disputes, whether internal or foreign, that may molest other countries, regarding them in their actual state as social communities, and preserving a strict neutrality in all their controversies.
>
> *Van Buren 1837*

Likewise, President James Polk in his 1845 Inaugural reminded the country about the dangers of alliances in a way that would have made Adams proud, explaining that, "All alliances having a tendency to jeopardize the welfare and honor of our country or sacrifice any one of the national interests will be studiously avoided" (Polk 1845). President Zachary Taylor repeated many of the Washingtonian-era themes in his 1849 Inaugural, stating that:

> As American freemen we can not but sympathize in all efforts to extend the blessings of civil and political liberty, but at the same time we are warned by the admonitions of history and the voice of our own beloved Washington to abstain from entangling alliances with foreign nations. In all disputes between conflicting governments it is our interest not less than our duty to remain strictly neutral, while our geographical position, the genius of our institutions and our people, the advancing spirit of civilization, and, above all, the dictates of religion direct us to the cultivation of peaceful and friendly relations with all other powers. It is to be hoped that no international question can now arise which a government confident in its own strength and resolved to protect its own just rights may not settle by wise negotiation; and it eminently becomes a government like our own, founded on the morality and intelligence of its citizens and upheld by their affections, to exhaust every resort of honorable diplomacy before appealing to arms. In the conduct of our foreign relations I shall conform to these views, as I believe them essential to the best interests and the true honor of the country.
>
> *Taylor 1849*

Millard Fillmore, in his 1850 Annual Address, dug deep into Founding era themes and provided one of the best examples of the non-interference and non-intervention claim – and in a way that connected with the old disdain for Old World balance-of-power politics:

> Among the acknowledged rights of nations is that which each possesses of establishing that form of government which it may deem most conducive to the happiness and prosperity of its own citizens, of changing that form as circumstances may require, and of managing its internal affairs according to its own will. The people of the United States claim this right for themselves, and they readily concede it to others. Hence it becomes an imperative duty not to interfere in the government or internal policy of other nations; and although we may sympathize with the unfortunate or the oppressed everywhere in their struggles for freedom, our principles forbid us from taking any part in such foreign contests. We make no wars to promote or to prevent successions to thrones, to maintain any theory of a balance of power, or to suppress the actual government which any country chooses to establish for itself. We instigate no revolutions, nor suffer any hostile military expeditions to be fitted out in the United States to invade the territory or provinces of a friendly nation. The great law of morality ought to have a national as well as a personal and individual application. We should act toward other nations as we wish them to act toward us, and justice and conscience should form the rule of conduct between governments, instead of mere power, self interest, or the desire of aggrandizement. To maintain a strict neutrality in foreign wars, to cultivate friendly relations, to reciprocate every noble and generous act, and to perform punctually and scrupulously every treaty obligation – these are the duties which we owe to other states, and by the performance of which we best entitle ourselves to like treatment from them; or, if that, in any case, be refused, we can enforce our own rights with justice and a clear conscience.
> *Fillmore 1850*

And despite his terrible management of domestic politics, President James Buchanan did his best to imitate Washington on the international front with a more religious flavor. In his 1857 Inaugural, he noted:

> We ought to cultivate peace, commerce, and friendship with all nations, and this not merely as the best means of promoting our own material interests, but in a spirit of Christian benevolence toward our fellow-men, wherever their lot may be cast. Our diplomacy should be direct and frank, neither seeking to obtain more nor accepting less than is our due. We ought to cherish a sacred regard for the independence of all nations, and never attempt to interfere in the domestic concerns of any unless this shall be imperatively required by the great law of self-preservation. To avoid entangling alliances has been a maxim of our policy ever since the days of Washington, and its wisdom's [sic]

no one will attempt to dispute. In short, we ought to do justice in a kindly spirit to all nations and require justice from them in return.

Buchanan 1857

Of course, with domestic troubles on the horizon, this approach would have been consistent not only with Founding ideals but also with cold realism.

The period between the Civil War and the Spanish-American saw continued adherence to the Founders' vision. Indeed, according to Adler, the traditional policy reached its heights during this time: "Pristine isolationism reached its heyday in the decades that followed the Civil War. Ironically, the tradition was in full glory just as its foundations began to crumble" (Adler 1957: 18). There was simply little foreign controversy of note between the demise of the French intervention in Mexico in the 1860s and the Spanish-American War.[9] However, it is interesting that there was a decline in the number and strength of Washingtonian themes in inaugural addresses and annual messages, which may have been due as much to the lesser importance of foreign policy during this time of internal recovery and dynamism than a radical decline in sympathy with them (until at least the 1890s). But there were exemplars. President Grover Cleveland offered, in his 1885 Inaugural, what Adler called "fully matured isolationist dogma," which will be discussed in more depth below. And four years later, President Benjamin Harrison, in his 1889 Inaugural Address, noted that "We have happily maintained a policy of avoiding all interference with European affairs" (Harrison 1889). Yet it was with his administration that elites more enthusiastic about a shift in approaches really started to stir. Indeed, *Harper's Weekly* chastised Harrison's administration in 1893 for its "entangling alliances and intrigues … [and] its series of departures of the gravest nature from the old and fixed traditions of the Government" (Grenville and Young 1966: 86). But it is also worth noting that even the Naval Policy Board in 1890 remarked, according to Stephen Kinzer, that "We fear no encroachments on our territory, nor are we tempted at present to encroach on that of others." It went on, claiming that "We have no colonies, nor any desire to acquire them" (Kinzer 2017: 22). Moreover, Cleveland's second administration provided a (temporary) snapback.

Given what Adler remarked about President Cleveland, the best example of the Washingtonian era − outside of the Founding period itself − may have been Cleveland's first stint in the White House. Therefore, it is worth discussing this case in more depth. As noted above, in his 1885 Inaugural, Cleveland provided "fully matured isolationist dogma" (Adler 1957: 18). Indeed, his words hew quite closely to the Founders' vision and provide evidence for just how deeply embedded that vision was within the American political culture:

> The genius of our institutions, the needs of our people in their home life, and the attention which is demanded for the settlement and development of the resources of our vast territory dictate the scrupulous avoidance of any departure from that foreign policy commended by the history, the traditions, and the prosperity of our Republic. It is the policy of independence, favored

by our position and defended by our known love of justice and by our power. It is the policy of peace suitable to our interests. It is the policy of neutrality, rejecting any share in foreign broils and ambitions upon other continents and repelling their intrusion here. It is the policy of Monroe and of Washington and Jefferson – "Peace, commerce, and honest friendship with all nations; entangling alliance with none."

Cleveland 1885

More importantly for our purposes here, Cleveland did not simply repeat the Founders' approach but walked the walk during his two non-consecutive terms. The US encountered very few problems during his first term from 1885 to 1889, and Cleveland did not go abroad to find any. His administration did work on immigration and fisheries issues, but there would be nothing momentous on his first watch (though there were tensions with the Germans over Samoa at the end of his term, but nature – in the form of a hurricane that destroyed ships on both sides – ended the tempest early in the next administration). Historians John Grenville and George Young note that Cleveland "gave little thought to America's role in world affairs and instead interpreted the advice of the founding fathers simply and literally: he sought to avoid foreign complications, to settle existing disputes amicably, and to limit American responsibilities as far as possible. He could see no serious danger from abroad, and he was content to leave the conduct of foreign policy to his Secretary of State" (Grenville and Young 1966: 41).

Foreign policy played a more important role during Cleveland's second term from 1893 to 1897, owing especially to the Venezuela Boundary Crisis of 1895–1896. But his behavior throughout his second term was still generally consistent with the Founders' vision despite the rise of overseas expansionists in the body politic. Right off the bat in 1893, at the opening of his second term, Cleveland prevented the annexation of Hawaii. This aborted move had been engineered by the expansionists in the Republican party towards the tail end of Harrison's presidency. But Cleveland was able to snuff it out. Historian Robert Beisner claims that Cleveland's response to the Republicans' Hawaii gambit "epitomizes his approach to foreign policy." He explained that Cleveland "was an unbending foe of annexing new territory, partly because he feared that imperialism would lead to an overbearing federal government" (Beisner 1986: 114). This shows continuity with the Founders, since fear of what our foreign policy would do to our domestic liberty was front and center for both. It also shows that disdain for overseas activity was not merely rooted in American weakness, since the US was a potential great power at this point.

The Venezuela Boundary Crisis between the US and the British was the most serious foreign policy event of Cleveland's presidency. This short dispute over British territorial claims threatened to lead to war. Fortunately, the British swerved and the dispute ended peacefully. But for a moment events looked ominous, especially following Cleveland's special message to Congress in which he indirectly threatened war if the British did not cooperate in setting the boundary between

British Guiana and Venezuela. In particular, Cleveland noted that "it will in my opinion be the duty of the United States to resist by every means in its power as a willful aggression upon its rights and interests the appropriation by Great Britain of any lands or the exercise of governmental jurisdiction over any territory which after investigation we have determined of right belongs to Venezuela" (Cleveland 1895). Although Cleveland risked war with Britain, he did not violate the Founders' vision since he was only asserting a strong interpretation of the Monroe Doctrine and defending against, as Beisner notes "British policy there [that] directly threatened American interests" (Beisner 1986: 114). It is also worth noting that Cleveland supported modernization of the Navy. Although this would play into the hands of the imperialists who would follow him, he did so in keeping with the traditional approach. A strong Navy allowed the US to defend itself, keep the Old World out of the New World through enforcement of the Monroe Doctrine, and to do so while adhering to the principle of non-entanglement (Beisner 1986). There is nothing inconsistent between having a strong national defense and restraint in foreign policy.

Unfortunately for his cause, Cleveland was followed by William McKinley and Theodore Roosevelt – who were buoyed by the ideas of folks like Alfred Thayer Mahan and Albert Beveridge, not to mention the interests of those who would benefit from an American empire – and the Founders' approach was on the wane.

But the "Great Rule" did not evaporate without a fight – and there was a resurgence of the traditional approach at various points between 1898 and the 1940s, when the US embraced a global role and, ultimately, primacy. Of particular note were the prominent members of the Anti-Imperialist League who fought in the 1890s and early 1900s to preserve the traditional view. But the Spanish-American War (and what followed in the Philippines), World War I, World War II, and ultimately the rejection of non-entanglement at the beginning of the Cold War ended the Washingtonian age.

At this point, it might be useful to say a few more words about the ideas and experiences behind the Founders' views on foreign policy. (For a more comprehensive account of the sources of Founding thinking, especially the Farewell Address, that this section builds upon, see Gilbert 1961.) As we saw in Paine's rhetoric, one of the key drivers of their vision was the notion of separateness and difference from the Old World and its sins. Of course, this notion has even earlier origin as seen in Winthrop's vision of a "city upon a hill." But later, Jefferson exemplified this idea when he noted (in the previously referenced letter to Monroe in 1823) that "America, North and South, has a set of interests distinct from those of Europe, and peculiarly her own. She should therefore have a system of her own, separate and apart from that of Europe. While the last is laboring to become the domicile of despotism, our endeavors should surely be, to make our hemisphere that of freedom" (Jonas 1966: 11). And nearly four-score years after Jefferson, when Cleveland railed against the prospect of imperialism, his predecessors echoed: "Our government was formed with the express purpose of creating in a new world a new nation that foundation of which should be man's self-government, whose safety and prosperity should be secured in its absolute freedom from Old World complications and in its renunciation of all schemes of foreign conquest" (Kinzer 2017: 61).

Chief among the sins of the Old World was monarchical power politics and war – with all of their attendant negative consequences. Although he later went to war (after both he and Jefferson before him had tried to avoid it), Madison (1795) well exemplified this when he wrote:

> Of all the enemies to public liberty war is, perhaps, the most to be dreaded, because it comprises and develops the germ of every other. War is the parent of armies; from these proceed debts and taxes; and armies, and debts, and taxes are the known instruments for bringing the many under the domination of the few. In war, too, the discretionary power of the Executive is extended; its influence in dealing out offices, honors, and emoluments is multiplied; and all the means of seducing the minds, are added to those of subduing the force, of the people. The same malignant aspect in republicanism may be traced in the inequality of fortunes, and the opportunities of fraud, growing out of a state of war, and in the degeneracy of manners and of morals, engendered by both. No nation could preserve its freedom in the midst of continual warfare.

This followed his earlier thoughts in 1792, when he wrote that, "War contains so much folly, as well as wickedness." Likewise, John Adams embraced this in his Draft Treaty in 1776 and then again in 1783 when he expressed the desire to stay detached and out of war:

> We should calculate all our measures and foreign negotiations in such a manner, as to avoid a too great dependence upon any one power of Europe – to avoid all obligations and temptations to take any part in future European wars; that the business of America with Europe was commerce, not politics or war.
>
> *Quoted in Gilbert 1961: 45*

A fear of standing armies was also part of the Founders' mindset. This was written directly into the Constitution, both in the body of the text and in the Third Amendment. The Founders knew first-hand through quartering and occupation by red coats – not to mention the English experience and the Whig interpretation – about the dangers of militaries. In particular, as Adler notes, "They resented a system that forced young men into military service and disrupted the even tenor of family life" (Adler 1957: 17). Much of this anti-power politics, anti-war, and anti-military sentiment owed to American experience. As Gilbert notes, "the entire colonial experience made foreign policy particularly alien and repulsive to Americans. This is one reason why Americans wanted to create a new system, a Novus Ordo Seclorum" (Gilbert 1961: 17, Ch. 3).

Americans were also hopeful about the power of commerce to provide for peace and prosperity. Hence they spoke frequently about the power of commerce, did not worry about commercial connections as they so earnestly sought to avoid political and military ones, and spent much of their early foreign relations focused on securing commercial treaties with other states (including their once and future enemy, the British). The focus on the power of trade in helping the cause of peace was similar to that shared by 19th-century classical liberals in Britain and their intellectual followers around the world today. However, realists would argue that the pacifying effect of trade is overstated, and the political issues with mere commercial connections under-appreciated, even if liberal trade can be a powerful force for building economic power.

The Founding generation, like restrainers since, also understood how geography worked in their favor. Washington appreciated very clearly this geographic reality and the wisdom of taking advantage of it, writing in 1788 and 1785, respectively, that "Separated as we are, by a world of water, from other nations, if we are wise, we shall surely avoid being drawn into the labyrinth of their politics, and involved in their destructive wars" and that "America may think herself happy, in having the Atlantic for a barrier" (Quoted in Schroeder 1854: 105). Likewise, in 1793, John Quincy Adams expressed this well, noting:

> As men, we must undoubtedly lament the effusion of human blood, and the mass of misery and distress which is preparing for the great part of the civilized world; but as the citizens of a nation at a vast distance from the continent of Europe; of a nation whose happiness consists in a real independence, disconnected from all European interests and European politics, it is our duty to remain, the peaceable and silent, though sorrowful spectators of the sanguinary scene.

Adams 1793

Even Hamilton, a hero today to many with a less restrained vision of American foreign policy, appreciated the importance of our geographic advantage and what it meant for our foreign policy. Indeed, he thought this distance allowed us to avoid standing armies, "the same engines of despotism which have been the scourge of the old world" (Cited in Carey and McClellan 2001: 34). In Federalist #8, Hamilton wrote:

> If we are wise enough to preserve the union, we may for ages enjoy an advantage similar to that of an insulated situation. Europe is at a great distance from us. Her colonies in our vicinity will be likely to continue too much disproportioned in strength, to be able to give us any dangerous annoyance. Extensive military establishments cannot, in this position, be necessary to our security.

Cited in Carey and McClellan 2001: 36

Lincoln, too, understood the geographic reality, arguing two decades before becoming president that:

> Shall we expect some transatlantic military giant, to step the Ocean, and crush us at a blow? Never! – All the armies of Europe, Asia and Africa combined, with all the treasure of the earth (our own excepted) in their military chest; with a Buonaparte for a commander, could not by force, take a drink from the Ohio, or make a track on the Blue Ridge, in a trial of a thousand years. At what point then is the approach of danger to be expected? I answer, if it ever reach us, it must spring up amongst us. It cannot come from abroad.
>
> *Lincoln 1838*

Two vast oceans and weak neighbors made this desire for detachment even easier. Thus it is no exaggeration to note, as French diplomat Jean Jules Jusserand did (as paraphrased by Ferrell) that "America was geographically the most fortunate of nations, with weak neighbors to north and south, and on east and west nothing but fish" (Ferrell 1975: 9).

The Founders also mixed their idealism and liberalism with a heavy dose of realism about their situation and their power. As the late Eric Nordlinger argued, our policy in this period was the product of a "studied appreciation of the fit between American interests and international realities." That being said, the US also had idealistic reasons for pursuing non-interventionism and non-entanglement: war and political connection would harm our experiment in liberty and democracy. Therefore, the US's overall approach was guided by the view that non-interventionism was consistent with our security requirements and our commitment to liberalism. As Adler noted:

> In retrospect, the original policy was both necessary and wise. There was no other sensible attitude to have taken toward Europe in the early days of the republic. We were weak, our population was small, and distrustful monarchs snarled at us from across the Atlantic. For many years after 1815 it would have been foolish to have disturbed the existing balance of power. We needed a "seek-time" to absorb our immigrants, to settle our domestic schism, and to subdue our thorny wasteland.
>
> *Adler 1957*

But it would be wrong to suggest that these were aggressive hawks merely biding their time until they had the power to pursue something like primacy today – though Washington did note in his Farewell Address that in the future, America would be in a better position to "defy material injury from external annoyance," have our neutrality "scrupulously respected," and enjoy the fact that "belligerent nations ... will not lightly hazard giving us provocation," allowing America to "choose peace or war, as our interest guided by justice shall counsel" (Adler

1957: 145). This was merely a statement of confidence and power that would further US security, neutrality, and its experiment in liberty. To think otherwise would ignore the other aspects of thinking, particularly their pessimistic view of war and intervention, that also contributed to their restraint-oriented approach.

As this chapter has demonstrated, the idea of restraint has a long record in the annals of US foreign policy. The Founding Fathers preached a consistent message of non-entanglement and non-interventionism, believing these principles to be in the best interests of the nation. They were even remarkably prophetic about the potential destructive effects, on both the nation and liberty, should the United States ever depart from these guidelines. Restraint is grounded in some of our nation's sacred texts and rooted in the very American desire to conceptualize government and relate to the rest of the world in a completely new and different way.

Thus, the idea of restraint is not new, nor is it un-American, nor is it untested in the course of our political experiment. This approach, embodied in Washington's "Great Rule," was first adopted in our nation's infancy, and American leaders adhered to it for more than 100 years. During that time, the United States was far from being a "dangerous nation," engaged in continual warfare throughout the globe and drumming up feelings of insecurity in its citizens. Rather, during the Washingtonian era, the US used military force sparingly and steadfastly avoided being drawn into faraway conflicts on the basis of alliance or ideology. This approach to foreign policy, for the most part, kept the US out of major wars and unentangled in the squabbles of other countries for a century. Again, whether a more restrained approach would work in the current era is a separate question. However, restraint cannot be categorically rejected as outlandish or untried. It is, quite simply, a part of our history.

Notes

1 The author would like to thank Trevor Thrall and Christopher Preble for their comments on an earlier draft, as well as Michelle Newby, Julie Thompson, and Hugo Kirk for their research support.

2 The term "dangerous nation" is a paraphrase by Robert Kagan (2006: 3) of a description used by John Quincy Adams in his 1817 discussion of European sentiment about the US in a report to William Plumer. In it, Adams noted that Europeans thought the US would "if united, become a very dangerous member of the society of nations." It is also the misleading title of his revisionist book on early American foreign policy that attempts to challenge some of the common historical views on this time period.

3 The real disagreement is over when exactly the traditional approach breaks down and a new era begins. Of course, there are also a few radical dissenters who don't agree with what Robert Kagan (2006) calls the "widely believed" view. He finds more continuity between early American history and the current age than is often thought, and thinks "Non-entanglement was a selective tactic, not a grand strategy" (Kagan 2006: 3, 125). This belies the history of the 19th century as well as the key defining speeches and actions (or more importantly, non-actions). Indeed, Kagan seems to confuse the outlier data points for the best line of fit!

4 Republican Wendell Willkie frequently called out "isolationists" who weren't eager to get enmeshed in the war in Europe, noting in one of many examples, "The isolationists originally opposed the expansion of our navy. They opposed the expansion of our army. They opposed the passage of the Lease-Lend bills. They opposed the passage of the Selective Service Act. If the policy which they advocated had been adopted, the United States today would be facing a victorious Nazism in a world-wide conflict in which we might ultimately be destroyed." See Wendell Willkie, "Wendell Willkie Lashes Out at Isolationists," www.youtube.com/watch?v=kjWQ1xatF8Y. Dean Acheson delivered a Cold War example in *Foreign Affairs*, writing in 1958: "May I conclude by repeating that the new isolationism which we have been discussing, and the reception it has received, is gravely disturbing, not only because it is utterly fallacious, but because the harder course which it calls on us to forego has been so successful" (Acheson 1958). A more recent example (that includes a bonus charge against realism) comes from senators Joseph Lieberman and Jon Kyl (2013), when they argued that "The case for American retrenchment has gained new traction in Washington. Much as in the past, economic problems and public war-weariness have spurred calls from Democrats and Republicans alike for neo-isolationist policies – demands for retreat from the world clothed in the language of fiscal prudence and disinterested realism."

5 Jonas disagrees that non-interventionism – or more squarely, avoiding foreign war – was a pillar of our 19th-century foreign policy and argues that the isolationists of the 1930s added this to the traditional desire for strategic independence. However, this understates the reluctance of 19th-century Americans to fight in foreign wars, especially those outside of the Western Hemisphere (and even within, as we saw in the opponents of the Mexican War and the Spanish-American War – not to mention the numerous times when the US chose not to go to war during a crisis, to stand aloof from conflicts, and to pursue as a nation other paths to greatness).

6 Though we should be careful about reading too much into the Monroe Doctrine's importance at the time. It was certainly another significant touchstone of this era, but, as Ferrell (1975: 169) notes, more in retrospect given how it was used later in the 19th century and into the 20th than at its time.

7 References to the Farewell Address are to Appendix D in Gilbert's *To the Farewell Address* (1961), where the section on foreign policy can be found.

8 According to the website of the US State Department's Office of the Historian, "NATO was the first peacetime military alliance the United States entered into outside of the Western Hemisphere." https://history.state.gov/milestones/1945–1952/nato

9 Two notable exceptions were the crises known as the Virginius Affairs in 1873 between the US and Spain and the Baltimore Crisis of 1891 between the US and Chile.

References

Acheson, D. 1958. The Illusion of Disengagement. *Foreign Affairs*, 36(3), pp.371–382.

Adams, J.Q. [Marcellus II]. 1793. *Columbian Centinel*, May 4, 1793.

Adams, J.Q. 1821. Warning against the Search for Monsters to Destroy. July 4, p.1821. Available from http://teachingamericanhistory.org/library/document/speech-on-independence-day/.

Adler, S. 1957. *The Isolationist Impulse: Its Twentieth Century Reaction*. Abelard-Schuman.

Beisner, R.L. 1986. *From the Old Diplomacy to the New, 1865–1900*, 2nd edition. Harlan Davidson.

Borchers, C. 2017. Donald Trump's CPAC Speech Proves It: He's Totally Obsessed with the Media. *Washington Post*, February 24. Available from www.washingtonpost.com/news/the-fix/wp/2017/02/24/trumps-media-obsessed-cpac-speech-annotated/?utm_term=.9896fee9a09d.

Buchanan, J. 1857. Inaugural Address. March 4, 1857. Available from www.bartleby.com/124/pres30.html.

Carey, G.W., and McClellan, J. 2001. *The Federalist: The Gideon Edition.* Liberty Fund.

CKI/CTNI 2016a. Poll 1 (October 27, 2016): NEW POLL: Majority Believe US Foreign Policy Has Made Americans Less Safe Over Last 15 Years.

CKI/CTNI 2016b. Poll 2 (December 22, 2016): NEW POLL: This Holiday, Americans Wish for a More Peaceful Approach to Foreign Policy.

CKI/CTNI 2017. Poll 3 (February 7, 2017): New Poll: Americans Crystal Clear: Foreign Policy Status Quo Not Working.

Cleveland, G. 1885. Inaugural Address. March 4, 1885. Available from http://avalon.law.yale.edu/19th_century/cleve1.asp.

Cleveland, G. 1895. Message of the President, December 17, 1895, in *FRUS* 1895, 545.

Ferrell, R.H. 1975. *American Diplomacy: A History.* W.W. Norton.

Fillmore, M. 1850. First Annual Address. December 2, 1850. Available from www.presidency.ucsb.edu/ws/index.php?pid=29491.

Gholz, E., Press, D.G., and Sapolsky, H.M. 1997. Come Home, America: The Strategy of Restraint in the Face of Temptation. *International Security,* 21(4), pp.5–48.

Gilbert, F. 1961. *To the Farewell Address: Ideas of Early American Foreign Policy.* Princeton University Press.

Grenville, J.A.S., and Young, G.B. 1966. *Politics, Strategy, and American Diplomacy: Studies in Foreign Policy, 1873–1917.* Yale University Press.

Harrison, B. 1889. Inaugural Address. March 4, 1889. Available from http://avalon.law.yale.edu/19th_century/harris.asp.

Jefferson, T. 1801. First Inaugural Address. March 4, 1801. Available at http://avalon.law.yale.edu/19th_century/jefinau1.asp.

Jonas, M. 1966. *Isolationism in America, 1935–1941.* Cornell University Press.

Jonas, M. 1990. *Isolationism in America, 1935–1941. Second Edition.* Imprint Publications.

Jonas, M. 1978. Isolationism. In Chatfield, C., and DeConde, A., eds, *Encyclopedia of American Foreign Policy.* Scribner's Sons.

Kagan, R. 2006. *Dangerous Nation: America's Foreign Policy from Its Earliest Days to the Dawn of the Twentieth Century.* Vintage.

Kinzer, S. 2017. *The True Flag: Theodore Roosevelt, Mark Twain, and the Birth of American Empire.* Macmillan.

Lieberman, J.I., and Kyl, J. 2013. The Danger of Repeating the Cycle of American Isolationism. *Washington Post*, April 25. Available from https://www.washingtonpost.com/opinions/the-danger-of-repeating-the-cycle-of-american-isolationism/2013/04/25/16da45f8-a90c-11e2-a8e2-5b98cb59187f_story.html?utm_term=.9b0dffc69df5.

Lincoln, A. 1838. The Perpetuation of Our Political Institutions. Address Before the Young Men's Lyceum of Springfield, Illinois, January 27. Available from www.abrahamlincolnonline.org/lincoln/speeches/lyceum.htm.

Madison, J. 1792. Political Observations. April 20. Available from https://founders.archives.gov/documents/Madison/01-15-02-0423.

Madison, J. 1795. Universal Peace. For the *National Gazette*, January 31. Available from https://founders.archives.gov/documents/Madison/01-14-02-0185.

McDougall, W.A. 2016. *The Tragedy of US Foreign Policy: How America's Civil Religion Betrayed the National Interest.* Yale University Press.

Mearsheimer, J.J. 2001. *The Tragedy of Great Power Politics.* W.W. Norton.

Mearsheimer, J.J., and Walt, S.M. 2016. The Case for Offshore Balancing: A Superior US Grand Strategy. *Foreign Affairs*, 95, pp.70–83.

Monroe, J. 1823. Seventh Annual Message to Congress, December 2, 1823. In *A Century of Lawmaking for a New Nation: US Congressional Documents and Debates, 1774–1875.* Available from http://avalon.law.yale.edu/19th_century/monroe.asp.

Nordlinger, E.A. 1995. *Isolationism Reconfigured: American Foreign Policy for a New Century.* Princeton University Press.

Paine, T. 1955 [1776]. *Common Sense.* In Paine, T., *Collected Writings.* Library of America.

Polk, J.K. 1845. Inaugural Address, March 4, 1845. Available from http://avalon.law.yale.edu/19th_century/polk.asp.

Posen, B.R. 2014. *Restraint: A New Foundation for US Grand Strategy.* Cornell University Press.

Schroeder, J.F., ed. 1854. *Maxims of Washington: Political, Social, Moral and Religious.* Appleton and Company.

Taylor, A. 2015. Map: The US Is Bound By Treaties to Defend a Quarter of Humanity. *Washington Post*, May 30. Available from www.washingtonpost.com/blogs/worldviews/wp/2015/05/30/map-the-u-s-is-bound-by-treaties-to-defend-a-quarter-of-humanity/.

Taylor, Z. 1849. Inaugural Address, March 5, 1849. Available from http://avalon.law.yale.edu/19th_century/taylor.asp.

Torreon, B.S. 2016. Instances of Use of United States Armed Forces Abroad, 1798–2016. Congressional Research Service, October 7, 2016.

Tucker, R.W. 1972. *A New Isolationism: Threat or Promise?* Universe Books.

Van Buren, M. 1837. Inaugural Address, March 4, 1837. In *Inaugural Addresses of the Presidents of the United States from George Washington 1789 to George Bush 1989*, 69: 69–78. Available from www.presidency.ucsb.edu/ws/?pid=25812.

8

THE SEARCH FOR MONSTERS TO DESTROY

Theodore Roosevelt, Republican *virtu,* and the challenges of liberal democracy in an industrial society

Edward Rhodes

> *[America] has, in the lapse of nearly half a century, without a single exception, respected the independence of other nations, while asserting and maintaining her own. She has abstained from interference in the concerns of others, even when the conflict has been for principles to which she clings, as to the last vital drop that visits the heart ... Wherever the standard of freedom and independence has been or shall be unfurled, there will her heart, her benedictions and her prayers be. But she goes not abroad in search of monsters to destroy ... She well knows that by once enlisting under other banners than her own, were they even the banners of foreign independence, she would involve herself, beyond the power of extrication, in all the wars of interest and intrigue, of individual avarice, envy, and ambition, which assume the colors and usurp the standard of freedom. The fundamental maxim of her policy would insensibly change from liberty to force. The frontlet on her brows would no longer beam with the ineffable splendor of freedom and independence; but in its stead would soon be substituted an imperial diadem, flashing in false and tarnished luster the murky radiance of dominion and power. She might become the dictatress of the world; she would be no longer the ruler of her own spirit.*
> John Quincy Adams, July 4, 1821 (Adams 1821: 31–32)

> *We of this generation do not have to face a task such as that our fathers faced, but we have our tasks, and woe to us if we fail to perform them! We can not, if we would, play the part of China, and be content to rot by inches in ignoble ease within our borders, taking no interest in what goes on beyond them, sunk in a scrambling commercialism; heedless of the higher life, the life of aspiration, of toil and risk, busying ourselves only with the wants of our bodies for the day, until suddenly we should find, beyond a shadow of question, what China has already found, that in this world the nation that has trained itself to a career of unwarlike and isolated ease is bound, in the end, to go down before other nations which have not lost the manly and adventurous qualities. If we are to be a really great people, we must strive in good faith to play a great part in the world*

> ... *The timid man, the lazy man, the man who distrusts his country, the overcivilized man, who has lost the great fighting, masterful virtues, the ignorant man, and the man of dull mind, whose soul is incapable of feeling the mighty lift that thrills "stern men with empires in their brains" – all these, of course, shrink from seeing us build a navy and an army adequate to our needs; shrink from seeing us do our share of the world's work, by bringing order out of chaos in the great, fair tropic islands from which the valor of our soldiers and sailors has driven the Spanish flag. These are the men who fear the strenuous life, who fear the only national life which is really worth leading.*
> Theodore Roosevelt, April 10, 1899 (Roosevelt 1899: 7–8)

It is hard to imagine a more striking contrast of visions. For John Quincy Adams – the great philosopher of America's early foreign policy – overseas intervention would destroy the very essence of a liberal republic. For Theodore Roosevelt – the great Progressive leader whose face joins those of George Washington, Thomas Jefferson, and Abraham Lincoln on Mt. Rushmore as a carven idol of Americanism – overseas intervention was essential if America's experiment in republicanism were to survive. For neither man was foreign policy a matter of idle choice, momentary exigency, party advantage, class favoritism, or special interest pleading. For both Adams and Roosevelt American foreign policy was intimately and necessarily linked to the fundamental nature, the very essence, of a liberal republic. Both conceived of the American political system as one of the great achievements of the ages – the creation of a true *novus ordo seclorum*. They understood, too, that as a fundamentally new type of polity, the United States was indeed "exceptional" and would need to pursue an "exceptional" foreign policy, one dictated by the peculiar character of a liberal republic.

The differences between the policies they advocated – Adams's restrained, archetypically liberal non-entanglement and Roosevelt's progressive, republican imperialism – can in part be explained in terms of the different socio-political challenges their eras presented to a liberal republic. But to understand why Roosevelt's path departed from Adams's and why the United States became an involved player in the world's politico-military politics, it is necessary to examine the competing demands of America's liberalism and its republicanism (See, for example, Shalhope 1990). It is not sufficient simply to observe that the world and America's position in it changed over the course of the nineteenth century, or to dismiss Adams and Roosevelt as men of their times. If we are to make sense of our past and of our present choices, it is necessary to understand the Scylla that terrified Adams and the Charybdis that dominated Roosevelt's nightmares, and to recognize the complex pathway between the two that the American liberal republic has always needed, and presumably will always need, to thread.

The arguments presented elsewhere in this volume make a strong case that the costs of a foreign policy seeking American primacy or liberal hegemony, or indeed of any foreign policy deeply entangling the United States in global politico-military affairs, greatly outweigh the geopolitical and economic benefits. As Will Ruger points out in his contribution to this project, the fact that even in pure realist terms

America was better served by non-intervention than by intervention was obvious to early American foreign policymakers. The goal of the present chapter is to try to explain why, despite these calculations and despite the recognition of the benefits of politico-military non-engagement, beginning in the late 1800s American decision-makers turned away from restraint.

The liberal pursuit of "the ineffable splendor of freedom and independence"

For the founders of the American republic, it was quickly apparent that the preservation of a liberal republic necessarily dictated politico-military separation from the Old World. Politico-military participation in a European, balance-of-power world system would – for the United States just as for the European powers – demand the maintenance of a substantial military establishment, the disproportionate growth of executive power, onerous taxation or the development of a permanent public debt and the emergence of the class system associated with it, a secretive and publicly unaccountable foreign policy, and an increasingly regulated economy and society.

Although the pithy adage that "war made the state, and the state made war" would not be coined for nearly 200 years (Tilly 1975: 42), the reality of this mutually constitutive relationship between war and the Leviathan states that emerged in the seventeenth and eighteenth centuries was clear to the founders of the American republic. Membership in a balance-of-power international system; war; and the empowerment of the state were three faces of the same political order. To reject any one of them – and the American founders were resolved to reject the tyranny of an overweening government – meant the rejection of all three.

Interestingly, as American statesmen quickly discovered, the peculiar character of a Madisonian republic also made the avoidance of entanglement in the European balance-of-power system essential for a second reason. It was by creating a republic so large, so diverse, and so heterogeneous that no interest group could count on maintaining permanent control over the levers of government that Madison hoped to solve the problem of "the tyranny of the majority" and to create a government that *every* interest group preferred to keep weak (Madison 1787). But the necessary diversity and heterogeneity came at a price: it meant that there would be no consensus within the republic over which of the world's nations were natural friends and which were natural enemies. As the vicious struggles between the pro-French party and the pro-British party quickly revealed, foreign policy had the potential to be the rock on which a federal American republic would split apart. Only by agreeing to eschew either alliance as a matter of principle could the polity avoid ripping itself in two.

From nearly the beginning, then, it was clear that a liberal polity would need to pursue a foreign policy with two distinct strands. Not only liberal theory but America's economy demanded that America remain deeply enmeshed – indeed, become increasingly enmeshed – in the global economy. Tariff barriers might be established to protect certain industries. But given its agricultural and mineral wealth, American prosperity required European markets, and ideally ones in Latin America and Asia, too. Liberalism's assumptions about private ownership and about the philosophical as well as practical desirability of market solutions reinforced this presumption in favor of expanded international trade. But at the same time, the survival of a liberal polity required avoidance of politico-military entanglement. As Washington explained in his Farewell Address:

> The great rule of conduct for us in regard to foreign nations is in extending our commercial relations, to have with them as little political connection as possible. So far as we have already formed engagements, let them be fulfilled with perfect good faith. Here let us stop … It is our true policy to steer clear of permanent alliances with any portion of the foreign world … Taking care always to keep ourselves by suitable establishments on a respectable defensive posture, we may safely trust to temporary alliances for extraordinary emergencies.
>
> *Washington 1796*

The genius of American foreign policy in its first century was that American policymakers were able to simultaneously pursue this politico-military non-involvement and this economic integration in world affairs. Genius was indeed required because, like most brilliantly clear commandments, those of the Farewell Address were far easier stated than executed. As the republic's early statesmen recognized, avoiding politico-military entanglement in the European-dominated, increasingly global system required an active, foresighted, and sometimes aggressive foreign policy. The goal of non-entanglement could not be successfully achieved simply through non-activity. If not forestalled by American diplomatic or military action, European states could and would force the United States to become enmeshed in Europe's political struggles.

The Monroe Doctrine of 1823 formalized and codified the logic of separating the New World's political system from that of the Old. Faced with the perceived threat of a French or Franco-Spanish empire in Latin America, understanding the danger that this would pose to the preservation of a liberal republican political system, and recognizing the Faustian bargain that would be involved in entering into an alliance with Britain to prevent such a development, Adams convinced President James Monroe to reject British foreign minister George Canning's demarche. The United States, Monroe told the European great powers, would "consider any attempt on their part to extend their system to any portion of this hemisphere as dangerous to our peace and safety" (Canning 1823; Jefferson 1823; Adams 1823).

Adams's logic clearly extended beyond the immediate problem and beyond simple colonization. If the danger were that the European *system* – that is, the balance-of-power system – would spread to encompass parts of the western hemisphere, then equally threatening would be the emergence of independent republics on America's borders that depended on Britain or France for their security or that might potentially ally together to try to balance against the United States.

This concern helped force President John Tyler's not-unwilling hand to annex Texas, lest the sovereign Republic of Texas degenerate into a *de facto* British puppet state.[1] The same logic drove Tyler's successor in the White House, James Polk, to provoke a war with Mexico in order to gain control of San Francisco and as much of California as possible before a British- or French-dominated "Bear Flag Republic" wrested its own liberty from a failing Mexican empire. Polk's corollary to the Monroe Doctrine made explicit the reasoning:

> The American system of government is entirely different from that of Europe. Jealousy among the different sovereigns of Europe, lest any one of them might become too powerful for the rest, has caused them anxiously to desire the establishment of what they term the "balance of power." It can not be permitted to have any application on the North American continent, and especially to the United States.
>
> *Polk 1845*

But just as the Monroe Doctrine and its Polk Corollary dictated a willingness to intervene pre-emptively in the western hemisphere to block the great powers, there were other corollaries that dictated politico-military restraint in all other circumstances. In the same way that European involvement in the western hemisphere would force the United States to become a "normal" great power – that is, lose its essential liberal character – so too would *voluntary* US politico-military engagement outside its borders. As Adams recognized, it did not matter *why* the United States intervened abroad – it did not matter that America's motives were pure and the principles at stake were ones like liberalism and republicanism, "to which she clings, as to the last vital drop that visits her heart." What mattered were the means that would inevitably be required. Politico-military intervention abroad, like the balance-of-power system into which such intervention would tend to drag America, would demand a substantial standing army and would lead down the path to an imperial presidency, taxes, debt, secrecy, and economic and social regulation.

For roughly seventy years, therefore, Adams's injunction that America go "not abroad in search of monsters to destroy," like his Monroe Doctrine and Washington's Farewell Address, was a bedrock principle of American foreign policy. Defense of the Monroe Doctrine might demand territorial expansion, sharp-elbowed diplomacy, and preventive war. But however aggressive or violent the means employed, American foreign policy was clearly and explicitly limited both in its objectives and, more importantly, by its underlying assumptions about the mortal dangers to a liberal polity that were associated with becoming a "normal" balance-of-power state or with attempts to export American values through politico-military intervention. Imposing American values abroad could be accomplished only at the cost of destroying them at home, and joining the European powers in the struggle for colonies or domination would, in the end, reduce America to the same fallen nature as the European powers. Only by pursuing a foreign policy that avoided politico-military entanglement could the United States preserve a Madisonian republic and an American "empire of liberty."[2]

Ensuring "the worth of a civilization": the *virtu* of the citizen

And then, in the 1890s, American foreign policy departed from Adams's bedrock principle.

The individual most closely associated with this departure was Theodore Roosevelt. It was Roosevelt who most clearly explained the logic that led him, his fellow Progressives, and ultimately the American nation to embrace what historians have described as "Progressive Imperialism" and who as a writer, public figure, and political leader most effectively mobilized support for it (McDougall 1997: 101–121).

Two immediate observations about Progressive Imperialism need to be made. The first is that it cannot be explained as a logical, much less an inevitable, consequence of America's growing power. While Hamilton, Washington, John Quincy Adams, and the other makers of early US foreign policy all looked forward to a day when the United States would be more populous, more wealthy, and territorially more extensive, and all believed that the American people would be safer and the Madisonian liberal republic more secure when that day was reached, none of them believed their policy recommendation would be any less correct or the arguments underlying them any less valid when America had reached its full growth.[3] It was not America's power relative to the European empires that they saw dictating US politico-military disengagement from Old World politics and US avoidance of ideologically motivated interventions. What drove their thinking was what they saw as the corrupting nature of balance of power, war, and empire. They eschewed playing on the world's politico-military stage not out of *realpolitik* necessity, but by choice.

The second observation is that Progressive Imperialism was *part* of US foreign policy, not the entirety of it. Despite their abandonment of Adams's injunction against seeking to "become dictatress of the world," Roosevelt and his fellow Progressive Imperialists did *not* abandon the logic and calculations of the earlier republic. Washington, Hamilton, and John Quincy Adams were heroes to Roosevelt, not villains, and though Roosevelt saw military service as a means of strengthening the republic's foundations rather than a threat to them, he remained firmly committed to the core elements of the traditional, liberal foreign policy master plan: expansion of international trade, avoidance of entangling alliances, and unwavering support for the Monroe Doctrine.

But Roosevelt and his Progressive colleagues faced what they saw as a fundamental internal crisis in American society. If in the new industrial age America's great experiment in liberal republicanism was to continue to succeed – if the effort to build the *novus ordo seclorum* was not to be abandoned – then in their view there would need to be a Progressive overhaul of foreign policy as well as of domestic policy and the state itself. For Roosevelt, the new foreign policy, like the Progressive domestic program, was aimed not at external dangers but at internal ones.

America's embrace of Progressive Imperialism must thus be understood as part of a deliberate strategy to respond to the social transformation taking place in America. As the nineteenth century moved into its final decade, the American social fabric was ripping apart. It was not simply that blood was flowing in the streets, though this was certainly the case. It was that the very roots of republicanism – the socio-cultural values that nourished it – were perceived to be eroding as urbanization, industrialization, immigration, and the reincorporation of the South transformed the nature of American life. For Theodore Roosevelt and the Progressives, the core problem confronting this new, "modern" America was not simply to create a republican political order that could bridge the chasms of class, ethnicity, religion, language, culture, geography, and urban–rural separation that were tearing apart the republic's bonds, but to somehow create or preserve republican *virtu*.

America's crisis, in Roosevelt's appraisal, was caused not by any weakness of liberalism but rather by the excesses of liberalism not balanced by healthy republicanism. The resulting personal and societal moral decadence, in all classes and stations, undermined capacity for republican self-government and for the higher personal fulfillment offered by republican life. Restoring America's republican *virtu*, Roosevelt argued, required not only a reformation of domestic institutions but a foreign policy that would inculcate the manly qualities and demand the moral regeneration offered by a "strenuous life." If it failed to seize the opportunities for service and moral growth presented by the wider world, American society would continue its slide into decay. Only by going "abroad in search monsters to destroy" could Americans regain their capacity for action, heroism, and sacrifice – and their fitness for republican life.

The key to understanding how both Roosevelt's Progressive Imperialism and Adams's pursuit of "the ineffable splendor of freedom and independence" were logical corollaries of America's philosophical endowment thus starts with recognizing that American political thought is rooted in *both* classical liberalism *and* classical republicanism. What was always apparent was that there are inherent tensions between the two. Concerns about preserving republicanism may yield policies that risk liberal values and rights; unrestrained liberal policies may result in a decline in republican *virtu*. With this tension in mind, one can begin to understand the analysis which led the Progressives to conclude that to preserve the American liberal republic in the modern conditions of an industrial society it would be necessary to rein in liberalism – to increase the power of the state, limit certain American property rights, and employ or expand the state's powers to teach or inculcate *virtu*.

The liberal bases of the American political system are perhaps too obvious to deserve discussion. In the Declaration of Independence, Jefferson explicitly laid out the essential elements. The individual's rights – the right to life; the right to do *whatever* one chose to do with one's life without external constraints except those that one willingly chose to accept; and the right to keep *all* the fruits of one's labor except those that one willingly chose to give up – were *not* granted by government. They preceded any government. They were the logical corollary of each individual's ownership of himself or herself, a grant of ownership coming directly from God or nature rather than the gift of any human institution, secular or religious. Government existed solely because individuals willingly contracted with each other to form a political community. In liberal thinking, the only legitimate political contract was one whose sole purpose was to *protect* its members' ability to enjoy their natural rights against possible infringement by others inside or outside that community. As a human rather than divine creation, government – any government – inevitably suffered from the flaws inherent in human nature, including a desire to exert arbitrary power (that is, tyranny) over others. The challenge in building a liberal state was to design one in which the natural tendencies of the state to become tyrannical were held in check, while still ensuring that the state possessed the capacity to protect its subjects' natural rights. The roots of this American liberalism are not difficult to identify: they lie in the emerging bourgeois, market-oriented, proto-industrial society of seventeenth-century Protestant northern Europe, particularly Britain and the Netherlands, and in the intellectual tradition associated with writers such as Thomas Hobbes and John Locke.

America's republicanism, by contrast, had entirely different roots. Its heroes can be found not in Manchester, Edinburgh, or Amsterdam but in Greece and especially Rome. The starting point of its logic is not with the idea that each individual owns himself or herself and willingly parts with some of this self-ownership (sovereignty) only to protect her or his effective ownership of what remains. Rather, the starting point for republicanism is the recognition that human beings are not simply physical and social creatures but also political ones, and that it is the political nature of human beings that sets them apart from and above animals. Yes, human beings require water, food, and shelter to survive. Yes, a human being denied the social interaction provided by family or friends is simply a hollow shell, alive physically but empty inside, devoid of real humanity. But to be fully human, to be a complete human, it is necessary not only to be alive in body and in soul but also to participate fully and in some sense equally in the making of the rules that shape the communal existence. Only by sharing in communal governance can an individual acquire the moral qualities necessary to be a complete human. Only through participation in public life can human beings fully develop the *virtu*, the fundamental qualities of self-control and responsibility, which sets man above the animals. Individuals excluded from this political life are less than complete humans – slaves, perhaps, or children, or incompetents, but not fully achieved human beings.

The difficulty, as the ancients as well as the founders of the American republic realized, was that while *virtu* was developed through participation in republican life, successful republican life itself required *virtu*. Only if individuals were able to subjugate their animal passions (anger, fear, greed, lust) to their power of human reason; only if they were able to sacrifice the short-term for the long-term, to consider what would be good for their grandchildren's grandchildren yet unborn just as they considered what was best for today; and, most importantly, only if they could put aside their self-interest and that of family and friends, and to propose, embrace, and carry out decisions that were good for the community as a whole even if these meant their own death, impoverishment, or enslavement; only if members of the republic had this kind of *virtu* could a republic survive. This degree of *virtu* is, however, a historical rarity, and the ancient republics all failed.

The genius of Madison, of course, was to design a new type of republic, one that could operate with a minimum of *virtu*, relying on counterbalancing self-interest within the society and within the machinery of government to make up for the lack of self-control, far-sightedness, and willingness for self-sacrifice shown by normal human beings. Through deliberate constitutional arrangements and by ensuring a heterogeneous citizenry, the natural tendency of government to become tyrannical would be held in check by the self-interest of *all* citizens and of *all* government institutions in seeing to it that the government as a whole remained weak. *Virtu* was still required, of course, but the Madisonian republic was a less delicate plant than the ancient republics. This would be a republic, the Founders hoped, that could also accommodate and protect the individualistic, self-interested essence of liberalism.

"The sinews of virtue"[4]

In agrarian America, with its open frontier, its strong Calvinist tradition in religious and moral life, and (at least in some parts of the country) its history of township-based community self-rule, developing the minimum *virtu* required to operate a Madisonian republic had been a manageable challenge. But if the Civil War represented a zenith of republicanism (as it certainly did in Roosevelt's imagination), the social and economic developments of the last third of the nineteenth century combined both to stimulate exuberant liberalism and to erode the sources of the *virtu* – and by doing so, in Roosevelt's estimation, destroy the capacity of the American liberal republic to survive.

In 1902 and 1903, during his first term in office, Roosevelt toured the United States, delivering speech after speech, repeating the themes, and occasionally some of the texts, that he had preached to the American people during the preceding decade. Roosevelt's message in August 1902 to an audience in Bangor, Maine, was entirely typical:

> During the century that has closed, the growth of industrialism has necessarily meant that cities and towns have increased in population more rapidly than the country districts. And yet, it remains true now as it always has been, that in the last resort the country districts are those in which we are surest to find the old American spirit, the old American habits of thought and ways of living. Conditions have changed in the country far less than they have changed in the cities, and in consequence there has been little breaking away from the methods of life which have produced the great majority of the leaders of the Republic in the past …
>
> [T]he countryman – the man on the farm, more than any other of our citizens to-day, is called upon continually to exercise the qualities which we like to think of as typical of the United States throughout its history – the

qualities of rugged independence, masterful resolution, and individual energy and resourcefulness. He works hard (for which no man is to be pitied), and often he lives hard (which may not be pleasant); but his life is passed in healthy surroundings, surroundings which tend to develop a fine type of citizenship. In the country, moreover, the conditions are fortunately such as to allow a closer touch between man and man, than, too often, we find to be the case in the city. Men feel more vividly the underlying sense of brotherhood, of community of interest.

Roosevelt 1902

While on first blush it would be possible to see Roosevelt as a reactionary, looking back to some sort of idealized agrarian, indeed Arcadian, past, he is not. As he goes on to argue:

All this does not mean condemnation of progress. It is mere folly to try to dig up the dead past, and scant is the good that comes from asceticism and retirement from the world. But let us make sure that our progress is in the essentials as well as in the incidentals. Material prosperity without the moral lift toward righteousness means a diminished capacity for happiness and a debased character. The worth of a civilization is the worth of the man at its centre. When this man lacks moral rectitude, material progress only makes bad worse, and social problems still darker and more complex.

Roosevelt 1902

Reflecting on the conquest of the west that followed on the Louisiana Purchase, Roosevelt mused on what pioneer *virtu* consisted of and observed that:

[t]he old days were great because the men who lived in them had mighty qualities; and we must make the new days great by showing these same qualities. We must insist upon courage and resolution, upon hardihood, tenacity, and fertility in resource; we must insist upon the strong, virile virtues; and we must insist no less upon the virtues of self-restraint, self-mastery, regard for the rights of others; we must show our abhorrence of cruelty, brutality, and corruption, in public and in private life alike. If we come short in any of these qualities we shall measurably fail; and if, as I believe we surely shall, we develop these qualities in the future to an even greater degree than in the past, then in the century now beginning we shall make of this Republic the freest and most orderly, the most just and most mighty, nation which has ever come forth from the womb of time.

Roosevelt 1903a

The essential question for Roosevelt, then, was how Americans and the American nation could develop these qualities. Though with an author as prolific as Roosevelt it is always possible to find counter-examples, Roosevelt's social Darwinism emphasized culture rather than biology. The great races, the great peoples, the great nations were great not because of their biological or genetic superiority over their rivals. They were great because of their cultural superiority – because their culture allowed them not simply to amass greater wealth and greater knowledge but to inculcate in their people greater *virtu*. Thus for Roosevelt, the answer to America's problem of declining *virtu* did not come in immigration control or preservation of a superior socio-economic or political status for the "old Americans." The solution was not to be found in breeding. It was to be found in training. And the key to training men of *virtu* was to set before them difficult tasks and charge them with heavy duties, tasks and duties that would demand that they find and strengthen within themselves their very best. It was in taking on these tasks and in doing one's duty that *virtu* was built.

To Roosevelt's way of thinking, earlier American generations had in fact been blessed by the challenges that history placed before them. Repeatedly in his addresses Roosevelt referenced two of these challenges. The first was nature. For generations, the American frontier had offered a test of manhood, the possibility of developing the qualities encompassed in *virtu* by pitting oneself against nature in its raw form. The second was war. For the men of Roosevelt's parents' generation, the Civil War had served as an ultimate test of manhood. In war the virile physical, mental, and moral toughness that fitted a man for his place in the republic could be developed by facing the daily hardship of the campaign or the immediate prospect of violent death in battle.

Indeed it is worth stressing that for Roosevelt, the great republican triumph of the American Civil War, and the enormous *virtu* of the soldiers of that era's "greatest generation," came not only in asserting the higher principle of liberty over the individual's self-interest in holding fellow men as slaves, but in the sacrifice made by the combatants, Southern as well as Northern, as they fought for a communal cause. This hardship, this commitment, this willingness to die for something outside one's immediate self-interest, this heroism is what trained that generation's souls and taught that generation *virtu*.

If Roosevelt's mind turned often to thoughts of war and of military or naval service – and it indeed did – this is hardly surprising. While Roosevelt himself could still find nature to challenge him – he could live the life of a rancher, hunt big game in Africa, and explore the dangerous upper reaches of the Amazon – he recognized that this would not be an option for most Americans. Challenge, hardship, and duty would be increasingly difficult to find inside America's borders – especially on the democratic scale that would be necessary.

The need for "monsters to destroy"

If the domestic stage offered insufficient challenge, then the nation must look to the international stage as the venue on which to build manhood. It would be by taking up the burden of leadership on the international stage that Americans would build their character and preserve the capacity for republican government at home.

Roosevelt loathed "the cosmopolitan." For him, the nation, not some global community, was the natural locus and focus of civic life and attachment. But Roosevelt also saw concentric circles of duty, creating a sort of Maslowian hierarchy of responsibilities. Real men – virile men, strong men, moral men – were called first and foremost to do their duty to their family; this accomplished, they were called upon to do their duty to their nation. If industrialization and urbanization reduced the physical, mental, and moral challenge of providing for one's family, and if technology and prosperity did the same with regard to doing one's duty to one's nation, then Americans of the twentieth century were called upon to do their duty to their fellow men around the world.

In charting a course of Progressive Imperialism as a route to national *virtu*, Roosevelt saw in Britain an example:

> England's rule in India and Egypt has been of great benefit to England, for it has trained up generations of men accustomed to look at the larger and loftier side of public life. It has been of even greater benefit to India and Egypt. And finally, and most of all, it has advanced the cause of civilization. So, if we do our duty aright in the Philippines, we will add to that national renown which is the highest and finest part of national life, we will greatly benefit the people of the Philippine Islands, and, above all, we will play our part well in the great work of uplifting mankind.
>
> *Roosevelt 1899*

It was in finding and destroying monsters abroad – anarchy, backwardness, disease, injustice, poverty, tyranny – that Americans could develop the qualities that would make them great and would save and preserve America's republic. The harder and the more selfless the task, the better.

Roosevelt's search for monsters to destroy was of course controversial. It provoked four objections, all arguing that in one way or another Progressive Imperialism was incompatible with the principles of either liberalism or republicanism.

First, opponents argued, what of the people who were to be the paving stones of America's pathway to greater national *virtu*, those who were to be the object of governance? Did not the logic of liberalism argue that any government in, say, Puerto Rico or the Philippines should exist only with the consent of the governed? And did not America's own republican logic demand that Puerto Ricans and Filipinos, like Americans, exercise the self-governance necessary for them to become fully achieved human beings? The American Anti-Imperialist League[5] put the case like this:

> We regret that it has become necessary in the land of Washington and Lincoln to reaffirm that all men, of whatever race or color, are entitled to life, liberty, and the pursuit of happiness. We maintain that governments derive their just powers from the consent of the governed. We insist that the subjugation

of any people is "criminal aggression" and open disloyalty to the distinctive principle of our government.

American Anti-Imperialist League 1899

Roosevelt's view on this was clear. The problem — and the reason that America had a duty to intervene and rule over these peoples — was that these people had not yet developed the *virtu* necessary for self-government. The options realistically open to them given their limited *virtu* were barbarism and savagery, despotic self-rule, rule by an oppressive European empire that would deny them the capacity to develop *virtu*, or American tutelage.

Geography and the fact of Filipino insurrection made the US occupation of the Philippines more difficult to justify than that of Puerto Rico and Cuba — but it also made it a greater test for American manhood and a more compelling monster to destroy. In 1899, with the worst of the Philippine situation still lying in the future, Roosevelt let loose his oratory, reveling in the difficulty of the challenge facing Americans:

> The Philippines offer a yet graver problem [than Puerto Rico or Cuba]. Their population includes half-caste and native Christians, warlike Moslems, and wild pagans. Many of their people are utterly unfit for self-government, and show no signs of becoming fit. Others may in time become fit, but at present can only take part in self-government under a wise supervision, at once firm and beneficent. We have driven Spanish tyranny from the islands. If we now let it be replaced by savage anarchy, our work has been for harm and not for good. I have scant patience with those who fear to undertake the task of governing the Philippines, and who openly avow that they do fear to undertake it, or that they shrink from it because of the expense and trouble; but I have even scanter patience with those who make a pretence of human-itarianism to hide and cover their timidity, and who cant about "liberty" and the "consent of the governed," in order to excuse themselves for their unwill-ingness to play the part of men.

Roosevelt 1899

The second objection to Progressive Imperialism was not about what American overseas engagement did to the target of that engagement — people like the Filipinos and Puerto Ricans — but about what it did to those Americans actively engaged in this imperialism. How could the acts of brutality, cruelty, and torture that were reported in the American press be consistent with the inculcation of *virtu*?

To this, Roosevelt offered two responses — one dismissive but the other an intriguing and deeper assertion of republican logic. First, he argued that while the instances of brutality by American soldiers were to be condemned and deplored, these cases of American loss of self-control needed to be considered in the context both of the success of most American troops in restraining their violent animal passions and of the far more brutal acts being committed by the insurrectionists – acts that would have been even more widespread had not the American troops mastered the violence of the situation and imposed order. But second, he argued, it was necessary to realize that this sort of brutality was not caused by American presence in the Philippines: it was latent in American society. It was, for example, the same animal brutality that one saw in lynchings. While inexcusable whatever its cause and wherever it occurred, this sort of evil could not be blamed on Progressive Imperialism, Roosevelt contended. It reflected the decline of the individual American's moral character and manly self-control, a decline that had come about as a consequence of rampant liberalism and materialism in American society. Eliminating this sort of evil from the American character required restoration of the average American's individual *virtu*. And of course it was precisely to build such *virtu* that Americans needed challenges of the sort the Philippines posed. However counterintuitive the logic, if Americans committed heinous crimes against Filipinos, this was evidence that Americans needed to intervene abroad *more*, not less.

The third objection was a broader one, about the consequences of imperialism for America. Did not the occupation and imposition of colonial rule over the Philippines, regardless of how cruelly or kindly this rule was imposed, corrupt American political institutions? The indictment leveled by the American Anti-Imperialist League was that Progressive Imperialism was fundamentally inconsistent not simply with the republic's constitution but with the very principles of republicanism as well as of liberalism. Because it involved rule *over* people, rather than self-rule *by* a people, imperialism by its nature transformed a republic into a despotism:

> A self-governing state cannot accept sovereignty over an unwilling people … Much as we abhor the war of "criminal aggression" in the Philippines, greatly as we regret the blood of the Filipinos on American hands, we more deeply resent the betrayal of American institutions at home. Whether the ruthless slaughter of the Filipinos shall end next month or next year is but an incident in a contest that must go on until the Declaration of Independence and the Constitution of the United States are rescued from the hands of their betrayers.
>
> *American Anti-Imperialist League 1899*

Roosevelt's response was that because the *capacity* for self-government (presumably unlike the *right* to self-government) did not exist by nature but needed to be developed, assuming the burden of preparing others for self-government was a republican duty, not a betrayal of republicanism. As for liberalism, the American occupation offered the Filipino people for the first time in their history a protection of their individual natural rights to life, liberty, and the pursuit of happiness. The protection of these rights would disappear were the United States to withdraw and hand the governance of the islands over to the Filipino people themselves or to a foreign power. The Philippines was not a case, Roosevelt reasoned, of one people denying self-government and freedom to another, but of one people doing its duty to humanity by laying the foundations for self-government and by protecting, for the first time, fundamental natural rights.

The final objection to Progressive Imperialism was that it would militarize American society by creating a substantial standing army, expanding state power, and eroding individual liberties. As the anti-imperialists put it: "We hold that the policy known as imperialism is hostile to liberty and tends toward militarism, an evil from which it has been our glory to be free" (American Anti-Imperialist League 1899).

For this objection, Roosevelt had no patience whatsoever, and it was per-haps only on this point that he explicitly disagreed with Hamilton, Washington, Madison, and the other founders of the republic. It was, in his view, a fallacy to see a well-regulated republican army as a danger to freedom and republicanism at home. America had grown wealthy enough and its political institutions strong enough that it could easily sustain a quite substantial army without endangering its institu-tions. Quite the opposite, in Roosevelt's view military service inculcated important republican virtues.[6] Speaking in Chicago in 1899, Roosevelt was unapologetic in his support for increasing the size of America's military:

> Our army has never been built up as it should be built up. I shall not discuss with an audience like this the puerile suggestion that a nation of seventy millions of freemen is in danger of losing its liberties from the existence of an army of one hundred thousand men, three-fourths of whom will be employed in certain foreign islands, in certain coast fortresses, and on Indian reservations. No man of good sense and stout heart can take such a proposi-tion seriously. If we are such weaklings as the proposition implies, then we are unworthy of freedom in any event. To no body of men in the United State is the country so much indebted as to the splendid officers and enlisted men of the regular army and navy. There is no body from which the country has less to fear, and none of which it should be prouder, none which it should be more anxious to upbuild.
>
> *Roosevelt 1899*

Staying true to "the traditional policy of the country"[7]

While Roosevelt's embrace of Progressive Imperialism and his willingness to build a significant, though by European standards still very modest, standing army mark significant policy departures, what should be equally clear is that Roosevelt was by no means rejecting America's liberal tradition. The pursuit of "monsters to destroy" and a willingness to countenance the tools that would make this pursuit possible were not the sum total of Roosevelt's foreign policy, and Roosevelt's other pol-icy goals and the strategies used to pursue them were very much consistent with traditional American policy – although admittedly Roosevelt sometimes pursued these with more vigor and enthusiasm than had his predecessors.

Two of these foreign policy goals deserve particular comment, if for no other reason than the frequency with which they are misunderstood. The first is the

US pursuit of overseas markets. As much as Roosevelt warned against the pursuit of profit, he did not actually object to it. To the contrary, he saw wealth and its accumulation as positive goals for a society. His concern was that these not be the *only* goals of society or that they become its ultimate ones.

For Roosevelt, therefore, it was entirely natural and appropriate that the US government should seek to open markets for American products and manufactures and should seek to insure opportunities for American capital abroad. In some cases protective tariffs might be desirable, and in other cases, not. The general principle of pursuing access to global markets, however, was as obviously correct to Roosevelt as it had been to the presidents who had preceded him.

Marxist scholars and Wisconsin-school historians of this period who note that in its foreign policy the US government served the interests of America's capitalist system and that US governments routinely used their power on behalf of American capital and American products are certainly correct. But where they go wrong is in assuming that because this is true, it must explain the turn to Progressive Imperialism. Roosevelt sought monsters to destroy in order to inculcate *virtu* in American life; he also sought markets and opportunities abroad in order to promote American prosperity. These were, however, entirely separate and at times conflicting objectives.

We see a similar picture in the second key area of continuity: maintenance of the Monroe Doctrine. As different as their views were with regard to imperialism, Roosevelt and the anti-imperialists – for example, President Grover Cleveland and his secretary of state, Richard Olney – saw largely eye-to-eye on policies aimed at preventing any expansion of European influence in the New World that might force the United States to take sides in European politico-military affairs.

The Venezuela Crisis of 1895 is illustrative. Cleveland and Olney took a hard line against Britain, arguing the importance of upholding the Monroe Doctrine and of deterring any possible future infringement (Cleveland 1895; Olney 1895). As Olney explained, the United States could not tolerate Britain pressing claims to what the United States regarded as Venezuelan territory because:

> What one power was permitted to do could not be denied to another, and it is not inconceivable that the struggle now going on for the acquisition of Africa might be transferred to South America. If it were, the weaker countries would unquestionably be soon absorbed, while the ultimate result might be the partition of all South America between the various European powers. The disastrous consequences to the United States of such a condition of things are obvious. The loss of prestige, of authority, and of weight in the councils of the family of nations, would be among the least of them. Our only real rivals in peace as well as enemies in war would be found located at our very doors. Thus far in our history we have been spared the burdens and evils of immense standing armies and all the other accessories of huge warlike establishments, and the exemption has largely contributed to our national greatness and wealth as well as to the happiness of every citizen. But, with

the powers of Europe permanently encamped on American soil, the ideal condition we have thus far enjoyed can not be expected to continue. We too must be armed to the teeth, we too must convert the flower of our male population into soldiers and sailors, and by withdrawing them from the various pursuits of peaceful industry we too must practically annihilate a large share of the productive energy of the nation.

Olney 1895

Roosevelt and his Progressive allies fully embraced this logic and applauded the Cleveland administration's defense of the doctrine (Lodge 1897: 243–251). As much as they may have condemned the administration for its unwillingness to march down the road of Progressive Imperialism, Roosevelt and his friends saw eye-to-eye with Cleveland and the Mugwumps on the continued cardinal importance of the Monroe Doctrine.

Indeed, of course, Roosevelt was prepared to be more aggressive and more proactive than Cleveland or Olney in defending the Monroe Doctrine. For example, for Roosevelt the Monroe Doctrine logically implied the acquisition of the Hawaiian Islands, given their dominating position *vis à vis* the Pacific approaches to any isthmian canal, something Cleveland resolutely resisted. Similarly, Roosevelt was more concerned than Cleveland or Olney that the bad behavior of Caribbean states might give European powers a legitimate, legal basis for occupying them and for demanding, as indemnity, bases or concessions that would threaten the US Navy's dominance of the Caribbean. Particularly given plans for some sort of isthmian canal – which would change the Caribbean from a quiet *cul de sac* into a global highway and vital American jugular – the danger of a German naval presence in the Caribbean appeared to Roosevelt to be a fundamental threat, one that would force the United States into European politics. Cleveland's relatively restrained policy was thus replaced by the Roosevelt Corollary to the Monroe Doctrine. In this, Roosevelt explicitly warned both the American republics and the European powers of US intentions to intervene in Caribbean states if their misgovernment promised to offer European powers the legal basis for European occupation:

> Chronic wrong-doing, or an impotence which results in a general loosening of the ties of civilized society, may in America, as elsewhere, ultimately require intervention by some civilized nation, and in the Western Hemisphere the adherence of the United States to the Monroe Doctrine may force the United States, however reluctantly, in flagrant cases of such wrong-doing or impotence, to the exercise of international police power … We would interfere with them only in the last resort, and then only if it became evident that their inability or unwillingness to do justice at home and abroad had violated the rights of the United States or had invited foreign aggression to the detriment of the entire body of American nations.

Roosevelt 1904a

Again, however, to understand Roosevelt's foreign policies, it is necessary to understand that the Roosevelt Corollary was exactly what it claimed to be: a logical corollary to the long-standing Monroe Doctrine, not part of America's Progressive Imperialist agenda.

The trumpet's summons: *virtu* and the struggle against the common enemies of man

Though Progressive Imperialism was never the entirety of America's foreign policy, neither was it an aberration. Historical observers who note that in the wake of America's painful experience in the Philippines America's Progressive Imperialist impulse quickly and quietly waned are of course absolutely correct. But to dismiss Progressive Imperialism as a historical oddity or a dead-end in America's journey as a liberal republic would be to fail to grasp both the logic that yielded it and the fact that, in different guises, the republican compulsion to go "abroad in search of monsters to destroy" remains very much with us.

While Roosevelt may have been the first American president to seek external challenges as a means of reinvigorating republican life, he certainly was not the last. In the 1960s, for example, with the "baby boomers" coming into adulthood, President John F. Kennedy and his New Frontiersmen called on Americans using appeals not dissimilar to Roosevelt's. In his Inaugural Address Kennedy proclaimed the need to go abroad to slay the world's monsters:

> Since this country was founded, each generation of Americans has been summoned to give testimony to its national loyalty. The graves of young Americans who answered the call to service surround the globe. Now the trumpet summons us again – not as a call to bear arms, though arms we need; not as a call to battle, though embattled we are – but a call to bear the burden of a long twilight struggle, year in and year out, "rejoicing in hope, patient in tribulation" – a struggle against the common enemies of man: tyranny, poverty, disease, and war itself … Will you join in that historic effort? In the long history of the world, only a few generations have been granted the role of defending freedom in its hour of maximum danger. I do not shrink from this responsibility – I welcome it. I do not believe that any of us would exchange places with any other people or any other generation.
>
> *Kennedy 1961*

Although they may have enunciated specific goals – for Roosevelt (1899), for example, it was "bringing order out of chaos in the great, fair tropic islands from which the valor of our soldiers and sailors has driven the Spanish flag" – for Kennedy as for Roosevelt the real objective was to challenge the American citizen to develop his "capacity to care for what is outside himself" (Roosevelt 1902) and to aspire to a historic greatness that could be achieved only if the individual and nation developed their fullest capability.

Obviously, the monsters threatening civilization are many, and come in an almost unimaginable range of shapes and forms. For republicans and from the perspective of building national *virtu*, the particular monster or enemy selected matters little and the strategy for slaying it matters little more, so long as the undertaking demands the moral, intellectual, and physical toughness required to achieve mastery over circumstances – over *fortuna* – and over oneself. It is in undertaking great tasks that individuals and nations become great. As Roosevelt argued:

> Our place as a Nation is and must be with the nations that have left indelibly their impress on the centuries. Men will tell you that the great expanding nations of antiquity have passed away. So they have; and so have all others. Those that did not expand passed away and left not so much as a memory behind them. The Roman expanded, the Roman passed away, but the Roman has left the print of his law, of his language, of his masterful ability in administration, deep in the world's history, deeply imprinted in the character of the races that came after him. I ask that this people rise level to the greatness of its opportunities. I do not ask that it seek for the easiest path.
>
> *Roosevelt 1903b*

"The age of crusades"

Any discussion of Roosevelt, Progressive Imperialism, and overseas intervention necessarily comes full circle, back to where we began, with a comparison of Adams's vision – an America that "goes not abroad in search of monsters to destroy" – with Roosevelt's – an America that, like Rome, imprints its character on the world. A century after Roosevelt's presidency, the conflict between these two visions remains exactly as clear and exactly as fundamental as it was in the days of Progressive Imperialism.

Indeed, for two reasons there is a timeless quality to this debate. The first is that the arguments have changed remarkably little. Secretary of State Olney's observations in 1895, condemning crusades as a dangerous anachronism and warning against the popular passions that might be whipped up, might equally well be written today:

> The people of the United States have a vital interest in the cause of popular self-government. They have secured the right for themselves and their posterity at the cost of infinite blood and treasure. They have realized and exemplified its beneficent operation by a career unexampled in point of national greatness or individual felicity. They believe it to be for the healing of all nations, and that civilization must either advance or retrograde accordingly as its supremacy is extended or curtailed. Imbued with these sentiments, the people of the United States might not impossibly be wrought up to an active propaganda in favor of a cause so highly valued both for themselves and for

mankind. But the age of the Crusades has passed, and they are content with such assertion and defense of the right of popular self-government as their own security and welfare demand.

Olney 1895

The second reason the Adams–Roosevelt debate seems timeless is because it remains timely. The debate whether overseas politico-military interventions inevitably destroy the liberal character of the American polity or whether they are necessary to make Americans fit for republican life is not simply a historical one, but rather one that, in one guise or another, is constantly revisited. Does a liberal republic in a modern world *require* an "Age of the Crusades"? Or would even a glorious and successful crusade – one that made an American liberal republic "the dictatress of the world" – simply extinguish "the ineffable splendor of freedom and independence"?

Notes

1 On British interest in using the hostility between Mexico and the Republic of Texas, and Texas's consequent need for an external guarantor of security, as a means of creating in Texas a British counterweight to the United States, see for example Smith (1844). Jones was the Republic of Texas's secretary of state; Smith was the Texas Republic's representative in London.

2 The phrase was Jefferson's, predating the creation of the American federal republic (Jefferson 1780).

3 The opposite view has been advanced most strongly by Robert Kagan, who interprets the territorial expansion and aggressive pursuit of foreign markets during the early republican period as part of the same tradition as America's post-1890 Progressive Imperialism, implicitly arguing that there was never a politico-military "isolationist" tradition in America, but only a period of American weakness. This interpretation is, I would argue, fundamentally anachronistic: it fails to understand the Founders and their immediate heirs in terms of the Calvinist and eighteenth-century liberal traditions that so clearly – and explicitly – shaped their thinking about political institutions and policies (Kagan 2006).

4 "The sinews of virtue lie in man's capacity to care for what is outside himself" (Roosevelt 1902).

5 The American Anti-Imperialist League cut across party and class lines, and included both Progressives and advocates of more limited government. Headed by George Boutwell, a former governor of Massachusetts, US representative, US senator, and US secretary of the treasury, the League also included in its leadership former president Grover Cleveland, industrialist Andrew Carnegie, labor leader Samuel Gompers, and Mugwump reformer Carl Schurz.

6 This said, Roosevelt's 1904 correspondence with his son Theodore, Jr., discouraging him from seeking an appointment to West Point or Annapolis reveals Roosevelt's real ambivalence about whether *virtu* could be adequately developed in a peacetime army. See Roosevelt's letters to his son Ted, 21 January 1904, 6 February 1904, and 19 February 1904 (published in Bishop 1919: 83–92).

7 In this case, the reference is to an essay by Roosevelt's close colleague and confidant Henry Cabot Lodge, published in 1897. Lodge applauds and embraces President Grover

Cleveland's foreign policies in the Caribbean, arguing for the maintenance of key elements of America's foreign policy tradition, most particularly the Monroe Doctrine (Lodge 1897: 250).

References

Adams, J.Q. 1821. *An Address, Delivered at the Request of the Committee of Arrangement for Celebrating the Anniversary of Independence at the City of Washington on the Fourth of July 1821, upon the Occasion of Reading the Declaration of Independence.* Hilliard and Metcalf.

Adams, J.Q. 1823. Instructions to Richard Rush. Reprinted in Bartlett, R.J., ed., 1960, *The Record of American Diplomacy.* Knopf, pp.179–181.

American Anti-Imperialist League. 1899. Platform of the American Anti-Imperialist League. October 18. Reprinted in Bartlett, R.J., ed., 1960, *The Record of American Diplomacy.* Knopf, p.389.

Bishop, J.B., ed. 1919. *Theodore Roosevelt's Letters to His Children.* Charles Scribner's Sons.

Canning, G. 1823. Private and Confidential to Richard Rush. August 20. Reprinted in Bartlett, R.J., ed., 1960, *The Record of American Diplomacy.* Knopf, pp.173–174.

Cleveland, G. 1895. Annual Message to Congress. December 2. Reprinted in *American Foreign Policy.* Carnegie Endowment for International Peace, 1920, p.18.

Jefferson, T. 1780. Letter to George Rogers Clark. December 25. http://wiki.monticello.org/mediawiki/index.php/Empire_of_liberty. Accessed 2 June 2016.

Jefferson, T. 1823. Letter to President Monroe. October 24, November 29. Reprinted in Bartlett, R.J., ed., 1960, *The Record of American Diplomacy.* Knopf, pp.174–175.

Kagan, R. 2006. *Dangerous Nation: America's Place in the World from Its Earliest Days to the Dawn of the Twentieth Century.* Knopf.

Kennedy, J.F. 1961. Inaugural Address. January 20. http://avalon.law.yale.edu/20th_century/kennedy.asp. Accessed 2 June 2016.

Lodge, H.C. 1897. Our Foreign Policy. In Lodge, H.C., *Certain Accepted Heroes and Other Essays in Literature and Politics.* Harper and Brothers, pp.243–251.

Madison, J. 1787. The Federalist no. 10. November 22. http://avalon.law.yale.edu/18th_century/fed10.asp. Accessed 2 June 2016.

McDougall, W.A. 1997. *Promised Land, Crusader State.* Houghton Mifflin.

Olney, R. 1895. Letter to Thomas F. Bayard. July 20. Reprinted in Bartlett, R.J., ed., 1960, *The Record of American Diplomacy.* Knopf, pp.341–345.

Polk, J. 1845. Annual Message to Congress. December 2. www.presidency.ucsb.edu/ws/index.php?pid=29486. Accessed 2 June 2016.

Roosevelt, T. 1899. The Strenuous Life: Speech before the Hamilton Club, Chicago. April 10. Reprinted in Roosevelt, T., *The Strenuous Life.* P.F. Collier, pp.19–20.

Roosevelt, T. 1902. Speech at Bangor, Maine. August 27. Reprinted in Roosevelt, T., 1904, *Presidential Addresses and State Papers, Volume 1.* Review of Reviews Company, pp.126–133.

Roosevelt, T. 1903a. Speech at the Dedication Ceremonies of the Louisiana Purchase Exposition, St. Louis. April 30. Reprinted in Roosevelt, T., 1904, *Presidential Addresses and State Papers, Volume 1.* Review of Reviews Company, pp.352–353.

Roosevelt, T. 1903b. Speech at Mechanics' Pavilion, San Francisco, California. May 13. Reprinted in Roosevelt, T., 1904, *Presidential Addresses and State Papers, Volume 1.* Review of Reviews Company, pp.395–396.

Roosevelt, T. 1904a. Annual Message to Congress. December 6. Reprinted in *American Foreign Policy.* Carnegie Endowment for International Peace, 1920, p.20.

Roosevelt, T. 1904b. *Presidential Addresses and State Papers, Volume 1.* Review of Reviews Company, pp.126–132.

Shalhope, R.E. 1990. *The Roots of Democracy: American Thought and Culture, 1760–1800.* Rowman & Littlefield.

Smith, A. 1844. Letter to Anson Jones. June 24. Reprinted in Bartlett, R.J., ed., 1960, *The Record of American Diplomacy.* Knopf, pp.195–196.

Tilly, C. 1975. *The Formation of National States in Western Europe.* Princeton University Press.

Washington, G. 1796. Farewell Address. http://avalon.law.yale.edu/18th_century/washing.asp. Accessed 2 June 2016.

9

BETTER BALANCING THE MIDDLE EAST

Emma M. Ashford

There is perhaps no better illustration of the scope of America's commitment to the Middle East than the simple fact that US pilots have flown bombing missions in the skies over Iraq during each of the last twenty-six years. For the last quarter-century, from the Gulf War to 9/11, to the wars in Iraq and Afghanistan and the complexity of the Arab Spring, to today's fight against ISIS, the United States has been an integral player in the region. And the region has itself dominated American foreign policy; as Andrew Bacevich notes, "From the end of World War II to 1980, virtually no American soldiers were killed in action while serving in that region … Since 1990, virtually no American soldiers have been killed in action anywhere *except* in the Greater Middle East" (Bacevich 2016).

US troop levels in the region have been high for two decades, the cost of a grand strategy which argues that regional presence can help to prevent conflict. Yet this period has in fact proved a costly lesson in the folly of trying to shape a region through the use of military force. Despite the deaths of over 6,500 US service members (and an estimated 300,000 civilians) in Iraq and Afghanistan, as well as costs of more than $3.4 trillion, the Middle East is no more stable, democratic, or prosperous than it was two decades ago (Crawford 2015a, 2015b).

In fact, it is hard to argue that US involvement in the Middle East, though well intentioned, has not worsened regional outcomes. The war in Iraq not only destabilized that country – creating a decade-long insurgency that provided fertile ground for the rise of ISIS – but fundamentally altered the regional balance of power. Even America's intervention in Libya, initially hailed as a humanitarian triumph, spiraled out of control, resulting in a lengthy civil war. Certainly, not all of today's turmoil in the Middle East can be laid at the feet of US policymakers. Yet America's attempts to reshape the region have rarely actually achieved US goals.

Nor is it often clear what goals our military presence is intended to achieve, other than vague invocations of the need for 'engagement.' Two of America's biggest

Cold War-era interests in the region – anti-communism and energy security – have been rendered largely irrelevant by geopolitical and technological advances, while military force has consistently proven ineffectual at tackling more modern interests like counterterrorism. Yet throughout the post-Cold War period, US policymakers have continued to pursue a strategy of regional predominance, meddling in every key aspect of Middle Eastern affairs. Even the Obama administration, which came into office eager to complete a 'pivot' towards more pressing strategic concerns in Asia, largely maintained this stance.

As the regional strategic environment shifts, however, this all-encompassing approach to the region comes with increasing risks: it enables dangerous behaviors by US allies, engenders moral hazard in local non-democratic states, and ignores the regional interests of other great powers like China. This chapter explores the strategic challenges facing the United States in the Middle East today and the problems inherent in our current approach to the region, before discussing the benefits of a return to offshore balancing. A more restrained approach to the Middle East has the potential to bring American commitments and interests in the region back into balance after a period of over-commitment. It is a change that is long overdue.

Growth in America's Middle East commitments

Today's high force posture in the Middle East is a historical anomaly, at odds with America's traditionally light presence in the region. In fact, US presence in the region prior to 1991 can be divided into two distinct periods, a period of hegemonic absence from 1972 to 1979 when neither Britain nor the United States maintained troops in the region, and a period of extremely light force presence from 1980 to 1990 (Rovner and Talmadge 2014; Macris 2010; Gause 2009). It is in many ways ironic that this period of low troop presence coincided with America's most important historical interest in the region: the prevention of Soviet domination. But Cold War dynamics were themselves a key cause of the low troop presence prior to 1991; the Soviet Union would have resisted American efforts to interfere in the region.

It is notable, therefore, that the United States successfully managed its Cold War-era interests in the Middle East without any substantial military presence, pushing back against Soviet dominance by partnering with and funding local states. During this era, the US employed an effective strategy of offshore balancing, first relying on the 'twin pillars' of Iran and Saudi Arabia as its regional enforcers, and then 'tilting' towards Iraq during the Iran–Iraq war. In both cases, the goal was not to end all strife, but rather to maintain the regional balance of power and ensure key US interests. Troop growth since the end of the Cold War has come despite the fact that this "defense of the Middle East has succeeded, and America has achieved hegemony" (Hudson 1996).

Notwithstanding the disappearance of this vital regional interest, US military involvement in the Middle East since 1991 has been a growth industry (Haas 2013). The initial impetus for this shift was the Gulf War. Though documents suggest

Saddam Hussein believed the United States would not respond to his unwise invasion of Kuwait, he was proved wrong by the rapid deployment of a massive United Nations-approved military force to first defend Saudi Arabia, and then push Iraqi troops out of Kuwait. American policymakers, fearful of the consequences of allowing Iraqi aggression to go unanswered, and of the risks to Saudi Arabia's oil fields, responded with a massive influx of men and material. As part of operations Desert Shield and Desert Storm, over 500,000 US troops, 700 tanks, two carrier battle groups, and various air and associated forces poured into the region (Center of Military History 2010; Englehardt 1991).

But though most of these troops departed after the end of the war, a sizable cohort remained. The Clinton administration's new strategy of 'dual containment' called for military operations – Provide Comfort, Southern Watch, Desert Fox – focusing on containment of both Iraq and Iran, and requiring the continued presence of a substantial number of US personnel. Naval and aerial patrols, bombing raids, and the management of a no-fly zone inside Iraq were all deemed necessary to prevent either state from dominating the region. As a result, between 1991 and 2003, the United States maintained around 5,000 ground troops, more than 5,000 airmen, and more than 10,000 naval personnel in the region, stationed at naval regional headquarters in Manama and Bahrain and on fifteen naval vessels, including a carrier (Rovner and Talmadge 2014).

Yet this policy of dual containment – and the effective abandonment of offshore balancing – was at best weakly justified. Iraq's armed forces had been crushed during the Gulf War, while Iran was still suffering the horrendous costs of the eight-year Iran–Iraq war. There was little reason to expect that either state could muster a strong enough force to dominate the region, or that other regional powers would not resist such a move. Nor was there any good explanation for why dealing with these two militarily crippled states now required substantial US forward deployments in the region, when they had been effectively dealt with during the 1970s–1990s through adroit balancing of aid and a swift military response to Iraqi aggression.

Indeed, a point often overlooked by critics is that the Gulf War itself was not a failure of offshore balancing (Mearsheimer and Walt 2016). A strategy of offshore balancing does not imply intervention will never be necessary, simply that it will be rare and restricted to specific scenarios. Saddam's invasion of Kuwait – featuring an aggressive state that threatened to dominate the region, and to disrupt global energy supplies – easily meets such criteria (Gholz, Press, and Sapolsky 1997). Once such a threat is dealt with, however, the United States should return to its role as an offshore balancer. Unfortunately, this did not happen. Perhaps, as some scholars have noted, the domestic political benefits of increasing US commitments in the Middle East were simply too strong for the Clinton administration, providing the "US military a needed and not-too-costly new mission" in the aftermath of the Cold War (Hudson 1996).

America's military entanglements in the region increased again after the 9/11 attacks. Troop numbers swelled in 2002 as Middle Eastern bases were used to support the US campaign against the Taliban in Afghanistan, and more substantially in 2003 as the Bush administration's occupation of Iraq became increasingly troop-intensive. Thus while only 15,200 US troops were committed to the campaign in Afghanistan in 2004, there were 130,600 boots on the ground in Iraq in the same year (Belasco 2009). US deployments in Iraq and Afghanistan peaked in 2008 at 187,900, totals that do not include support staff on other Middle Eastern bases (which in 2008 raised that total to 294,355), or US-national contractors (as high as 45,000 during the same year) (Peters, Schwartz, and Kapp 2015).

Though the Obama administration drew down these troop levels from their peak during the so-called surge – US forces in Iraq declined by more than an order of magnitude between 2009 and 2011 – troop presence remained generally high. In 2015, there were still over 12,000 troops in Iraq and Afghanistan (Peters, Schwartz, and Kapp 2015). Anti-ISIS campaign Operation Inherent Resolve, begun in August 2014, again increased these numbers. Though the Department of Defense has been reluctant to release comprehensive figures, there are at least 5,000 US troops engaged in fighting ISIS in Iraq (Ryan 2016). US presence throughout the broader region also remained high, with Central Command (CENTCOM) report-ing around 33,000 troops stationed in various Middle Eastern countries during 2016, a total that included Iraq, but not Afghanistan (International Institute for Strategic Studies 2016).

Outside of active war zones, it can be difficult to ascertain exactly where these personnel are stationed, as the Department of Defense often withholds this infor-mation at the request of host governments. Nonetheless, information is publicly available about a variety of permanent military installations, ranging from small radar bases in Turkey and Israel to major installations such as Al Udeid air base in Qatar, home to thousands of US personnel and to CENTCOM's forward head-quarters. The US Fifth Fleet is headquartered in Bahrain, while the Air Force main-tains facilities at bases in Kuwait (including Al Salem Air Base, Camp Buehring, and Camp Arifjan), Turkey (Incirlik Air Base), and the United Arab Emirates (Al Dhafra Air Base). US troops at these facilities are engaged in a variety of endeavors, including support for the campaigns against ISIS (and Al Qaeda), training for allied militaries, and the protection of trade routes.

Mismatch between strategy and interests

Proponents of a heavy American presence in the Middle East often point to a variety of US interests in the region to justify this force posture, chief among them energy security and counterterrorism. Yet energy security is far less problematic today than in the past, and a large forward-deployed military is in reality less helpful than commonly assumed in seeking to achieve US regional goals.

Though it seems logical to assume that growing domestic shale production has ended American reliance on Middle Eastern oil and gas, it is unfortunately inaccu-rate. Fracking has certainly helped to diversify supply and reduce vulnerability, but it cannot insulate us entirely from potential oil price shocks. And while only around

15% of American oil imports come from the Persian Gulf, oil's status as a globally traded commodity means that supply shortages can create price shocks, potentially harming the global economy, and the economies of the United States and its allies (US Energy Information Administration 2016). Nonetheless, protecting American energy security is not nearly as problematic as is often asserted. As Gholz and Press illustrate, global oil markets actually adapt well to oil shocks, typically replacing lost supply within three to six months. At the same time, the infrastructure innovations put in place after the oil shocks of the 1970s, such as the Strategic Petroleum Reserve and private company reserves, mitigate and minimize economic damage during this adjustment period (Gholz and Press 2010; see also Posen 2014).

These developments leave only a few scenarios with the potential to undermine American energy security: conquest of Middle Eastern oil fields by one country, the closure of key transit routes, or a civil war inside the world's largest oil-producing state, Saudi Arabia. The first of these is extremely improbable, while the second and third are unlikely, and in any case could not be easily prevented by US military presence (Al-Ubaydli 2016). Indeed, in the case of Saudi civil strife, substantial US regional troop presence and strong Saudi–US ties are more likely to incite domestic unrest among the Kingdom's religious conservatives than they are to prevent it. Nor does history suggest that substantial US forces in the region are necessary for energy security; the energy shocks of the 1970s were politically motivated and could not have been prevented by military force, while the oil supply remained relatively secure throughout the 1980s, even without substantial US troop presence (Rovner and Talmadge 2014).

More surprisingly, given America's current force posture, this observation – that military presence may not be helpful in achieving US policy goals – is actually true for a wide variety of issues. The US commitment to Israel, and policymakers' long-running attempts to resolve the Israel–Palestine conflict, for example, have by necessity always been focused more on diplomacy and on arms sales than on military force. US policymakers have also tended to rely on diplomacy and on the tools of economic statecraft in their attempts to prevent nuclear proliferation in the region. While the threat – or even the application – of force is sometimes necessary in this regard, such a threat requires neither the presence of large numbers of US troops, nor that they be based in the region. This is also the case with counterterrorism, whether we focus on non-state terrorist groups, or on their state sponsors. The 1986 US bombing of Libya's Muammar Gaddafi, for example, was undertaken by American air forces from bases in the United Kingdom and from aircraft carriers, rather than from any Middle Eastern base (Endicott 2000).

It is significant that even when military action is required, there is simply no need for the large forward-deployed forces that characterize America's commitment to the Middle East today. If the lessons of Iraq and Afghanistan can teach us anything, it is that large-scale ground campaigns are of limited utility in responding to terrorist campaigns (Pillar and Preble 2010). The Obama administration's late shift to a 'light footprint' approach for counterterrorism – the combination of small numbers of special operations forces with standoff strike capabilities – reflected this shifting understanding of counterterrorism tactics. Though the 'light footprint' approach is not without its own issues, chief among them the lack of any cohesive overarching strategy for the War on Terror, it remains far more useful and less costly than large-scale military deployments (Stapleton 2016).

Perhaps for this reason, many arguments in favor of US forward presence in the Middle East today tend to rely on much vaguer rationales to make their case. The withdrawal of US forces from the region could create a security spiral, some warn, and without US troop presence, regional leaders will tend to pick strategies that exacerbate conflicts and instability (Pollack 2016). Yet there are key problems with these assertions. First, this argument relies on the ability of the United States to credibly commit to defend the territory of other states, an always problematic assumption. Secondly, it assumes that in the absence of American military might, states would not simply balance against one another to find a stable regional equilibrium (Layne 1997). Finally, there is little evidence that US troop presence actually serves to prevent regional states from making destabilizing choices; the region-wide free-for-all that characterized the latter stages of the Arab Spring suggest that such choices can occur even with substantial US involvement. Though such arguments effectively contend that the regional security environment *might* be worse if the United States drew down its regional military presence, it is a contention based on extremely shaky assumptions.

Ultimately, proponents of heavy US presence contend simply that no regional state or combination of states can act as a guarantor of regional stability. This view is widely held, even among top officials. US Director of National Intelligence James Clapper, for example, recently acknowledged that the U.S cannot 'fix' the Middle East, but argued that it was necessary for the United States to be present in the region nonetheless (Ignatius 2016). As one recent paper argues, "Only the United States can secure the shipping lanes of the Persian Gulf, contain or rollback Iran's nuclear program … bring Israelis and Arabs to the negotiating table, and effectively coordinate responses to regional issues like counterterrorism and counter-proliferation" (Cook, Stokes, and Brock 2014). But in playing such a role, not only do we conflate military presence with diplomatic influence, we allow regional allies to free-ride on American military spending. Many of America's regional allies are among the world's richest states, with access to vast oil wealth. As Marc Lynch recently pointed out, Arab states have good reason to oppose the US drawing down its regional military presence: "For all their complaints about Bush, the regimes had found his eagerness to use military force and expend massive financial resources on their behalf quite congenial" (Lynch 2016: 20).

The failures of US preponderance in the Middle East

Arguments in favor of US preponderance in the Middle East often point to what they term the past 'failures' of offshore balancing, in particular the need for US intervention in the region during the 1987–1988 Tanker War, the 1991 Gulf War, and the 2003 Iraq War. If the strategy had been successful, they argue, these interventions would have been unnecessary (Pollack 2003). Yet in addition to mis-characterizing the 2003 US invasion of Iraq – portraying it as a necessary intervention, rather than a war of choice – such arguments ignore the much larger and more numerous failures of American regional policy since 1991. The Middle East today is more complex and conflict-ridden than it has been at any time since the collapse of the Ottoman Empire, and while not entirely to blame, US foreign policy choices have contributed to that chaos.

Osama bin Laden sought to justify his barbaric terrorist attacks through a narrative of resistance to occupation, charging the United States with "occupying the lands of Islam in the holiest of places, the Arabian Peninsula," and calling for every Muslim to kill Americans until US troops withdrew from Saudi Arabia (Bacevich 2016: 202). It is a terrible irony that while bin Laden's words were widely abhorred by Muslims, US military involvement in the region since 9/11 has helped to reinforce this narrative and breed popular discontent. Polls show a steady and dramatic decline in favorability towards the United States in almost every country over the last decade: in Turkey, for example, favorability declined from 52% to 19% between 2000 and 2014, while in Egypt the proportion of the population favorable to the United States has dropped from 30% to 10% since 2006 alone (Pew Research Center 2014).

Yet the most visible failure – and perhaps the most well-worn critique of US foreign policy since the Cold War – has undoubtedly been the long-term effects of the US invasion of Iraq in 2003. Apparently anticipating an overnight transition to flourishing liberal democracy inside Iraq, the Bush administration appears to have simply assumed that the new Iraqi government would align with the United States. In doing so, they failed to consider even the most basic domestic or international consequences of failing in their quest, ignoring Iraq's sectarian divides and long-standing regional dynamics. The key consequence of the invasion, as numerous scholars have noted, was to upend the regional balance of power, destroying an uneasy Iran–Iraq–Saudi Arabia triangle by pulling Iraq inexorably into the Iranian sphere (Lynch 2016; Gause 2015).

Though sectarian politics played a role, it was largely the weakness of Iraqi governance in the aftermath of the intervention that provided the opening for Iranian influence. It is truly ironic given the animosity towards Iran of many neoconservatives within the Bush administration that their main accomplishment has been the strengthening of Iran's position in the region. Yet it should have been easy to predict: Middle Eastern states have often hashed out their differences by intervening in the politics of weak neighboring states. One only has to look at Lebanon's tumultuous history, or at the first so-called Arab Cold War – which pitted Nasserism against conservative monarchies in states like Syria and Iraq – to see this dynamic at work (Ryan 2012; Gause 2014). The US invasion and occupation of Iraq turned one of the Middle East's most populous states into a weakly institutionalized battleground for regional power struggles.

Though the context for the 2011 US intervention in Libya was far different than for Iraq, the results were similar. In the context of the broader Arab Spring

186 Emma M. Ashford

movements and growing violence by the region's embattled regimes, the intervention was described initially as humanitarian necessity, a narrative that undoubtedly helped to convince not only the intervention-skeptical President Obama, but also enabled the Russian and Chinese UN Security Council abstentions which made it legal. Yet the NATO mission quickly and without explanation morphed into air support for the rebel campaign to overthrow Gaddafi. As Alan Kuperman illustrates, not only did the intervention, and subsequent civil wars result in a substantially higher death toll than the potential humanitarian costs of non-intervention, it also allowed Libya to become a battleground for regional rivalries. As in Iraq, US intervention created a weakened state, in which regional powers – in this case, Qatar and the United Arab Emirates – sought to play out their differences and alter the balance of power (Lynch 2016).

The effects of US foreign policy choices in Iraq and Libya have been a worsening of regional stability, with a flow of small arms emanating particularly from Libya in recent years into other regional conflicts. Nor is it accurate to argue, as some critics do, that the Syrian conflagration only arose because the US chose not to intervene. State weakness can certainly arise in the absence of US intervention. Yet in the Syrian case, the United States did intervene, arming and training Syrian rebels as early as 2013. These actions did not prevent other states from pouring arms and equipment into Syria, inflaming the conflict and contributing to the country's destruction (Ashford 2015). In a similar way, arguments that ISIS arose because of the Obama administration's decision to withdraw most US troops from Iraq are misleading (Brennan 2014). The rise of ISIS resulted from an interaction of external factors – particularly the Syrian civil war – with the lingering effects of the US invasion and occupation of Iraq. As various accounts show, the US military had failed to completely destroy Al Qaeda in Iraq (AQI), ISIS' predecessor, while many of the group's key members actually met in US prisons during the occupation (McCants 2015; Gerges 2016; Lister 2016).

Just as the United States is not entirely to blame for the rise of ISIS, the regional conflagration that constitutes today's Middle East cannot be entirely attributed to US foreign policy. Today's conflicts are rooted in the aftermath of the Arab Spring uprisings, and in decades of economic malaise and chronic authoritarianism. Yet even here, US policy has at times played a conflicting role. Active American military involvement in the region and the exigencies of the War on Terror require strong partnerships with authoritarian regimes (and often, with their repressive security services). At the same time, the United States actively promotes regional democratization, working with regime opponents and civil society through programs like the Middle East Partnership Initiative (MEPI). The inherent contradiction of these policies has long been visible to US policymakers; in a memo written shortly before the start of the Arab Spring, President Obama himself spoke of the need to weigh US interests in the region against the desire for economic and political reform (Kitchen 2012; Lizza 2011). The Arab Spring brought this tension to the fore, but its failures offer no solution going forward. Put simply, an activist foreign policy in the Middle East requires the United States to cooperate with authoritarian regimes, a move which not only undercuts our desire for regional democratization, but undermines America's image globally (Carpenter and Innocent 2015).

The risks of perpetuating a flawed strategy

Opponents of a more hands-off approach to the Middle East often cite the many failures that could result if America were not present. Yet in continuing to advocate for a 'business as usual' approach – or even increased US military engagement – in the region, they too rarely acknowledge the failures that have resulted from our primacy-based approach to the region.

Indeed, many attempt to paper over such failures, painting the chaos in the Middle East today not as the result of America's regional overreach, but instead as the result of American 'weakness' and withdrawal from the region. One recent report co-authored by former senior officials from both the Bush and Obama administrations made such an argument, noting that despite past failures, "the United States has no choice but to engage itself fully in a determined, multi-year effort to find an acceptable resolution to the many crises tearing the region apart," including "an appropriately designed no-fly zone" in Syria, a determined effort to "undermine and defeat Iran's hegemonic ambitions," and a demand that "the United States should show a new resolve by increasing significantly its military contribution across the board" in the fight against ISIS (Campbell et al. 2016).

Unfortunately, not only would this approach be extremely costly, it also carries a number of dangers. First, commitments to regional states have the potential to entrap America in conflict, particularly if US forces on the ground act as a 'tripwire' force. While some recent academic work questions the extent to which alliances can entangle or entrap states, many scholars still contend that entrapment is indeed possible (Beckley 2015; Lind 2016; Edelstein and Itzkowitz Shifrinson this volume). In theory, this risk is lower in the Middle East than in other regions simply because the US has no formal legal alliances in the region. Despite various proposals over the years to create some form of Arab NATO, the regional states most commonly described as US allies, including Saudi Arabia, are merely long-standing partners. Yet in practice, heavy US military presence in the region and pressure from these partners can weigh strongly on American decisions to intervene in local conflicts. It is extremely questionable, for example, whether the United States would have engaged with the Syrian conflict in the absence of pressure from states like Saudi Arabia or Turkey.

Likewise, there is little question that US involvement in the Saudi-led campaign in Yemen is driven by fears about the long-standing (and deteriorating) US–Saudi relationship. By providing logistical and intelligence support for the Saudi-led coalition against the Yemeni Houthis, the United States is, for the sake of loosely defined Saudi interests, directly undermining a long-standing US counterterrorism campaign against Al Qaeda in the east of that country (Council on Foreign Relations 2015). The campaign is also an excellent example of the ways in which American commitments enable allies to engage in dangerous activities, increasing the risk of US entrapment in unnecessary conflicts. US support helped to enable the Yemen conflict: without American logistical support it is doubtful the war would have been feasible for the Gulf Cooperation Council (GCC) coalition. In general, if they believe the United States will come to their rescue militarily, regional states are liable to engage in more dangerous behavior than they would otherwise. This may even lead to a curious form of security spiral, as US attempts at engagement with Iran bolster Saudi paranoia, leading the U.S to support their potentially reckless partners even more strongly.

Somewhat ironically, the evidence suggests that a primacy-based approach also encourages states which are not friendly to the United States to build up their military capacity. Such states exist in a state of "radical uncertainty," effectively unable to guarantee their own security (Monteiro 2014). In the context of the Middle East, this suggests that many of the choices made by Iran over the last few decades – to invest heavily in military power, to act aggressively, to seek nuclear weapons – were shaped at least in part by their own weakness and fear of US power. Scholars have long noted that security concerns are a key reason for states to seek nuclear weapons (Sagan 1996; Jo and Gartzke 2007). In the Iranian case, both the existence of Israeli nuclear weapons and the threat of US conventional military power likely contributed to the decision. If the US were instead to take a more hands-off approach to the region, it is likely that Iranian revisionism would actually subside rather than increase. In effect, US military presence in the Middle East can encourage dangerous behavior by both friendly and unfriendly states, increasing tensions.

US humanitarian intervention in civil conflicts such as Syria and Libya raises other concerns. As Alan Kuperman has illustrated, humanitarian intervention can itself produce moral hazard, fostering rebellion among groups who cannot defend themselves, but who nonetheless believe that the international community will intervene to protect them (Kuperman 2008a, 2008b). As the Arab Spring unfolded across the region in 2011, events in one country influenced domestic political movements in other states; the twisted incentives created by international intervention in Libya undoubtedly contributed to the decision of groups elsewhere, notably in Syria, to take up arms against their repressive governments (Lynch 2016; Kuperman 2013). This in turn placed pressure on the United States to step in again, and to overthrow the Assad regime for humanitarian reasons. Thanks to moral hazard, humanitarian intervention can beget future intervention, in the Middle East or elsewhere.

Proponents of increased or status quo US commitments to the Middle East also tend to ignore the issues raised by the growing involvement of other states in the region. Indeed, though the United States has been the undisputed hegemon in the region since 1991, the expanding interests of other major powers are gradually altering the regional strategic picture. The most obvious of these is Russia, whose sudden intervention in the Syrian conflict on behalf of the Assad regime in 2015 took many observers by surprise. Russia had long had a naval presence inside Syria, based at Tartus, and it is likely that Russia's intervention had as much to do with protecting this strategically valuable Mediterranean port as it did with the protection of the Assad regime (Synovitz 2016; Delman 2015). At the same time, Russia has been able to effectively use its brief military intervention to bolster its role as a key player in Syria's peace talks, a role that both boosts Russia's international standing and bolsters the Putin regime's domestic legitimacy.

In contrast to Russia, China has shown little interest in military involvement in the Middle East, other than its role in international anti-piracy efforts. Yet its interests in the region are substantial and rapidly growing. Today, over half of Chinese oil imports come from the Persian Gulf, making them far more reliant on the region than the United States. As China's energy needs grow, it is shifting from its historical alignment with Iran and moving closer to Saudi Arabia, signing a recent deal with the Kingdom to provide nuclear reactors as well as various weapons systems. Sino–Saudi trade is also growing, rising from $24.5 billion to $64.32 billion in 2007–2011 (Saab 2016). It remains unclear whether these growing ties pose a strategic problem for the United States. While some regional states certainly might prefer a more robust Chinese presence in the region – Chinese leaders often speak of "energy interdependence" with the Gulf rather than independence, and are unlikely to push regional states to enact democratic or economic reforms – China has given every indication that it remains reluctant to play a military role in the Middle East (Alterman 2013).

Even close US allies have shown interest in recent years in expanding their role in the region. After more than forty years, the United Kingdom has returned to Bahrain, opening a new naval base at Mina Salman. France is also increasing its military presence in the region, with troops in Djibouti, and air forces at Al Dhafra air base and a naval base at Mina Zayed, both in the United Arab Emirates (Alterman 2013). Such growing regional commitments have diverse sources, yet whether they come from allies or adversaries, it is clear that the future of the region is multipolar, not unipolar. Unfortunately, proponents of greater Middle East engagement rarely consider either the benefits or the pitfalls of this process. While growing engagement by other states may have positive effects, if it occurs at the same time as increasing US presence it has the potential to raise the risk of conflict, particularly in situations like Russia's Syrian misadventure.

Yet perhaps the biggest problem with maintaining or increasing America's Middle East involvement is the way in which it undermines natural regional balancing dynamics. As many scholars have noted, the Middle East has typically exhibited 'underbalancing,' meaning that states which might be expected to form alliances – such as the anti-Iranian axis of Turkey, Israel, and Saudi Arabia – have rarely done so. Nor has the GCC been able to successfully build joint military infrastructure or agree on political goals in many cases. The most likely explanation is that ideological factors, such as the ongoing Israeli–Palestinian conflict or intra-Sunni disagreements, are inhibiting closer alliances between regional states. While threat levels remain low, in effect, while the United States continues to act as a regional security guarantor, theory suggests that states will be unlikely to overcome these ideological factors (Gause 2014; Haas 2005).

In fact, though the Obama administration's pivot away from the Middle East was in many ways more rhetoric than reality, it did encourage various tentative attempts to build better regional alliances. Rapprochement and cooperation between Saudi Arabia and Israel on the issue of Iran – though largely kept quiet to avoid a public opinion backlash – has been growing in recent years. Certainly, the two countries disagree on a variety of issues, the most problematic of which is the Israeli–Palestinian conflict. Yet when retired top Saudi and Israeli officials spoke openly about the issue at a forum in May 2016 in Washington, they were keen to highlight that cooperation is possible even if these issues go unresolved (Rosenblum 2016a, 2016b). Informal meetings on security issues are now regularly held between the two states; even the relative lack of criticism expressed by the Gulf States during the 2006 Israeli war against Iranian-backed Hezbollah may be indicative of shifting opinion within the region (Ryan 2012). Yet in providing security guarantees, and by providing a third party cut-out which inhibits direct military cooperation and intelligence sharing, US regional military involvement can serve to inhibit such balancing behavior.

A challenging regional environment

Acknowledging the failures and successes of past US policy towards the Middle East – as well as the risks posed by continuing these policies – is the key to a robust debate on future involvement in the region. Though this debate began under the Obama administration, it remains unresolved, with many of Washington's foreign policy elites effectively endorsing either a status quo approach to the region, or an increase in US military engagement. Yet regional context is also important. Today's Middle East poses a variety of unique challenges for American policymakers. Taken as a whole, they raise a key question: Is it possible to reshape the region in line with American interests? Or, as one observer notes, is it time for US policymakers to realize that "Washington no longer holds most of the cards in the region, if it ever did?" (Kitchen 2012: 57).

The most visible of these challenges is the Islamic State (ISIS), which emerged from the wreckage of Al Qaeda in Iraq, seizing major cities in both Iraq and Syria, and declaring a "caliphate." Following the group's barbaric slaughter of several Americans in August 2014, the Obama administration authorized an open-ended military campaign against the group. Though a nominal anti-ISIS coalition now includes more than sixty states, the United States has borne the brunt of the military effort, launching over 24,000 airstrikes, at a cost of more than $14.3 billion. The United States also has around 6,500 troops on the ground in Iraq and 2,000 special operations forces in Syria, providing support and training for Iraqi government and Syrian rebel forces. Three years into the campaign against ISIS, the group is in retreat. Yet it remains unclear what will take its place; fragmented local militias offer little hope of a stable and long-lasting peace.

ISIS itself presents a challenging concept for US policymakers: while not unheard of, it has been uncommon in the past for jihadi groups to attempt to hold territory. The decision of ISIS leaders to provide social services and other state-like functions in areas that they hold is unusual, leading ISIS to resemble a proto-state more than a traditional terror group. Various scholars have even speculated that ISIS itself could develop into a weak state if given enough time, though its revolutionary ideology presents enough of a threat to surrounding states that this remains unlikely (Rubin 2015). But the extent to which ISIS actually threatened the United States is extremely questionable. Despite rapid growth and effective publicity, ISIS itself was no more threatening to the United States than other terrorist groups: potentially capable of carrying out tragic attacks against soft targets as it did in Brussels and Paris, but unable to fundamentally damage the United States (Byman and Shapiro 2014). The regional spread of ISIS is also somewhat of a mirage: while it is true that the group claims affiliates in various countries, the majority of these already existed as local or regional terrorist groups. The ISIS affiliate credited with bringing down a Russian airliner in Egypt began life as the separatist group Province of Sinai, for example, while Nigeria's Boko Haram was active more than a decade before the rise of ISIS. In Libya, the rare case where ISIS has a substantial presence, as in Syria, the group's survival is dependent on the outcome of the ongoing civil war.

Indeed, the US campaign against ISIS is nested within the context of the Syrian civil war, itself a product of the broader regional turmoil of the post-Arab Spring revolutions. This goes a long way towards explaining its failures. The Syrian civil war, though notable for extreme suffering, is itself a garden-variety example of a civil war worsened by the interference of neighboring states; Iran and Russia have primarily backed the Assad government, while Saudi Arabia, Qatar, Turkey, and others have funneled weapons and arms to opposing insurgent groups. In the context of broader regional turmoil, Syria has become a proxy battlefield. Much of the early fragmentation among anti-Assad rebels and the resultant extremism of opposition groups was the result not of Sunni–Shi'a contestation, but of contradictory funding streams from the nominally allied Gulf States and Turkey, as each state attempted to ensure that their own proxies would come out on top after the overthrow of Assad (Lynch 2016). Thus, though ISIS itself is perhaps the only major player in the Syrian civil war that has no external backer, animosity, fragmentation, and regional rivalries – such as decades of Turkish–Kurdish struggle – prevent cooperation by states on the creation of an effective force to fight it on the ground.

It is these broader regional concerns – a confrontation that has been widely framed as a Cold War-style conflict between Sunni states (led by Saudi Arabia) and Shi'a ones (led by Iran) – which pose the biggest challenge in formulating US policy towards the Middle East. Indeed, regional dynamics are often framed in sectarian terms, relying on 'ancient hatreds' to explain today's tensions. But while both Iranian and Saudi leaders have in recent years resorted to nakedly sectarian language, sectarianism itself is better understood as a tool of a more traditional balance-of-power struggle (Gause 2014; Lynch 2016). Sectarian narratives often lump widely dissimilar sects, such as the Alawites or the Houthis, together in order to fit a convenient narrative. In fact, the Arab Spring raised many fears for different states: the specter of Iranian influence for Saudi Arabia and the United Arab

Emirates, concerns about the Muslim Brotherhood for the U.A.E. and Jordan, worry about Salafist influence for Jordan, and fears of the loss of regional influence for Iran (Ryan 2015). Each of these fears reflects the strong link between domestic political outcomes and international relations.

Throughout the Arab Spring, intervention from regional states shaped domestic outcomes: in Egypt, for example, Qatari money helped to support Mohammed Morsi's Muslim Brotherhood government, while Saudi and Emirati money has since helped to ensure the survival of the Sisi regime. At the same time, international outcomes were often the result of domestic tensions: many regimes undertook interventions out of fear for their own stability or safety – such as the 2011 GCC military intervention in Bahrain, which was primarily motivated by the fear of the neighboring Al Saud monarchy for domestic stability. Elite-to-elite networks tie many countries together, often in ways that are not obvious; Jordan, for example, is heavily dependent on financial aid from the Gulf States, making domestic stability in those states a security concern for Jordan. Such incestuous ties crisscross the region.

In this light, many have portrayed today's regional tensions as pitting a conservative monarchical block of states against more revolutionary states and movements, effectively dividing the region into status quo defenders and revisionist spoilers. There is certainly some truth to this, particularly in the extent to which Saudi Arabia tried to prevent the destruction of ancien régimes in countries from Bahrain to Yemen and Egypt to Jordan. Yet even this is a substantial oversimplification. At various points in the last five years, so-called status quo states have acted in distinctly revolutionary ways, while traditionally revolutionary states have sought to defend the status quo where it meets their interests. This dynamic is perhaps most visible in Syria, where Iran was forced into the unlikely role of opposing a revolutionary uprising aimed at Bashar al Assad's government.

Nor are there truly two monolithic blocks, Sunni-conservative and Shi'a-revolutionary, struggling against each other. In spite of Saudi efforts to act as a regional Sunni leader, other states have challenged their influence in various theatres, highlighting broad schisms, or what some have described as an 'intra-Sunni' conflict. This split – which primarily separates regimes friendly to Muslim Brotherhood-oriented groups from those favoring more Salafist groups – was perhaps most visible in Libya, where continued fighting between Qatari and Emirati proxies helped to undermine a fragile post-conflict settlement. The general defeat of Muslim Brotherhood-oriented factions in Egypt and elsewhere, and the victory of various Salafi-jihadi-rebel groups has grave implications for the future of peaceful democratic change in the region, yet this conflict played out almost entirely among Sunni states. Still other states defy easy classification: tiny Oman has consistently avoided aligning with either bloc. More generally, the influence of smaller 'swing states' on the region during the last few years cannot be overstated; Qatari and Emirati influence and finance played a major role in conflicts from Libya to Syria.

In part, this is due to the Cold War-like nature of today's conflict, as the struggle for regional power and influence is contested through a series of proxy wars in weakened states. Today's Middle East bears a strong resemblance to what Malcolm Kerr (1971) termed the "Arab Cold War," a struggle between Nasser's Egypt and various conservative monarchies for control of the region during the 1950s and 1960s. Today, patronage of proxies is often more effective than any exercise of military might, a fact clearly illustrated by Turkey's limited regional influence over the last few years, particularly when compared to the outsized influence of tiny, gas-rich Qatar (Gause 2014). It is notable that in the limited cases where military power has been used – primarily Yemen – it has been largely ineffectual in achieving the desired results.

Downsizing America's Middle East commitments

As the Middle East undergoes this period of turmoil, US policymakers must decide on the extent of American involvement in the region. As this chapter has illustrated, since 1991, US policymakers have effectively rejected America's Cold War approach to the Middle East – offshore balancing and astute diplomacy – in favor of unilateralism and a reliance on military means. And while troop levels have fallen substantially from their War on Terror peak – when over a quarter-million US troops were stationed in the region – they remain high. US regional goals are often unclear: some traditional regional interests (i.e., anti-communism) are no longer relevant, some (i.e., energy security) are less pressing than in previous years, and still others (i.e., counterterrorism or state stability) are not easily achievable with large-scale military presence. In fact, it is increasingly clear that US Middle East policy – though made with the best of intentions – has actually contributed to today's regional instability. Maintaining the status quo or increasing US involvement in the region has the potential to entrap the United States in conflict, and to encourage destabilizing behavior by both US allies and adversaries.

It is time for a more restrained approach: a return to offshore balancing. As it did during the Cold War, offshore balancing would define US interests much more narrowly than today's approach, focusing on key interests and on the potential for regional hegemons to arise. It assumes that other states can (and will) balance against each other, even without direct US involvement. By relying on over-the-horizon capabilities rather than onshore military capabilities, offshore balancing has the potential to increase burden sharing and reduce blowback (Layne 1997; Posen 2014, but see Brands 2015 for a counterpoint). And while it cannot entirely negate the need for military involvement in certain scenarios – as the case of the first Gulf War shows – the situations in which this is necessary are far fewer than called for by today's primacy-based approach.

Indeed, under offshore balancing, US force posture in the Middle East would look substantially different than it does today, and much more like it did during the Cold War. It would remove the need to maintain thousands of ground forces at bases across the region, as such troops are primarily there to reassure small states like Kuwait. They are certainly not necessary to secure energy resources, and may even be counterproductive with regard to domestic state stability (Rovner and Talmadge

2014). Though small numbers of US troops will likely need to remain in-region for training, advising, and cooperation purposes, as well as small groups of Special Operations Forces engaged in counterterrorism activities, the bulk of America's troop presence in the region would no longer be required; major bases like Al Udeid could be closed or dramatically downsized.

As Rovner and Talmadge (2014) note, there are benefits to leaving certain capabilities in-region, in particular aerial intelligence, surveillance, and reconnaissance (ISR) capabilities, as well as coastal patrol vessels. Retaining and maintaining the naval base at Manama, Bahrain, as well as various stocks of pre-positioned materiel, is a sensible strategic hedge against potential future conflict in the region. At the same time, however, the United States would be able to remove the vast majority of its air and naval forces from the region, including aircraft carriers, which have been regularly stationed in the region for much of the last fifteen years. In short, offshore balancing would allow for US military presence in the region to be dramatically reduced. At the same time, this approach does not imply that the United States would (or should) disengage diplomatically or economically from the Middle East. Indeed, US policymakers may well find that US diplomatic influence on difficult issues like the Israel–Palestine conflict is actually improved when it is less entangled with the need to keep local partners happy for the sake of basing rights and military access.

A change in America's approach to the Middle East is long overdue. While major military involvement in the region may have seemed like the right answer in response to the tragic attacks of September 11, 2001, the period since that time has proven that America simply cannot reshape the region to meet its needs. Neither US interventions nor a heavy troop presence have increased the stability of the region or the security of the United States; instead, far too often, American involvement in the Middle East has done exactly the opposite. Continuing to take a hegemonic approach to the region is unlikely to yield better results in the future. Instead, US strategic interests can be more effectively managed by taking a more restrained approach to the region. It is time for the US military to largely exit the Middle Eastern stage.

References

Al-Ubaydli, O. 2016. Iran's Threat to Block Hormuz: A Game Theory Analysis. Middle East Centre Blog, London School of Economics and Political Science, May 16. Accessed from http://blogs.lse.ac.uk/mec/2016/05/16/irans-threat-to-block-hormuz-a-game-theory-analysis.

Alterman, J.B. 2013. China's Balancing Act in the Gulf. *Center for Strategic and International Studies* Gulf Analysis Paper (August). Accessed from https://www.csis.org/analysis/chinas-balancing-act-gulf.

Ashford, E.M. 2015. Friends Like These: Why Petrostates Made Bad Allies. Cato Institute Policy Analysis No. 770 (March). Accessed from www.cato.org/publications/policy-analysis/friends-these-why-petrostates-make-bad-allies.

Bacevich, A.J. 2016. *America's War for the Greater Middle East: A Military History.* Random House.

Beckley, M. 2015. The Myth of Entangling Alliances: Reassessing the Security Risks of US Defense Pacts. *International Security,* 39(4), pp.7–48.

Belasco, A. 2009, July. Troop Levels in the Afghan and Iraq Wars, FY2001-FY2012: Cost and Other Potential Issues. Library Of Congress Congressional Research Service.

Brands, H. 2015. Fools Rush Out? The Flawed Logic of Offshore Balancing. *The Washington Quarterly*, 38(2), pp.7–28.

Brennan, R. 2014. Withdrawal Symptoms: The Bungling of the Iraq Exit. *Foreign Affairs*, November/December, p.25.

Byman, D., and Shapiro, J. 2014. *Be Afraid. Be a Little Afraid: The Threat of Terrorism from Western Foreign Fighters in Syria and Iraq.* Brookings Institution.

Campbell, K., Edelman, E., Flournoy, M., Fontaine, R., Hadley, S.J., Kagan, R., Rubin, J.P., Smith, J., Steinberg, J., and Zoellick, R. 2016. *Extending American Power.* Center for a New American Security, 16.

Carpenter, T.G., and Innocent, M. 2015. *Perilous Partners: The Benefits and Pitfalls of America's Alliances with Authoritarian Regimes.* Cato Institute.

Center of Military History. 2010. War in the Persian Gulf: Operations Desert Shield and Desert Storm, August 1990–March 1991. Center of Military History, United States Army. Accessed from www.history.army.mil/html/books/070/70-117-1/cmh_70-117-1.pdf.

Cook, S.A., Stokes, J., and Brock, A.J. 2014. *The Contest for Regional Leadership in the New Middle East.* Middle East Security Series. Center for New American Security.

Council on Foreign Relations. 2015, June. Al-Qaeda in the Arabian Peninsula (AQAP). Council on Foreign Relations Backgrounder. Accessed from www.cfr.org/yemen/al-qaeda-arabian-peninsula-aqap/p9369.

Crawford, N.C. 2015a. *US Costs of Wars Through 2014: $4.4 Trillion and Counting.* June 25. Watson Institute, Brown University. Accessed from http://watson.brown.edu/costsofwar/figures.

Crawford, N.C. 2015b. *War Related Death, Injury and Displacement in Afghanistan and Pakistan 2001–2014.* May 22. Watson Institute, Brown University. Accessed from http://watson.brown.edu/costsofwar/files/cow/imce/papers/2015/War%20Related%20Casualties%20Afghanistan%20and%20Pakistan%202001–2014%20FIN.pdf.

Delman, E. 2015. The Link between Putin's Military Campaigns in Syria and Ukraine. *Atlantic*, 2(10).

Endicott, J. 2000. Raid on Libya: Operation ELDORADO CANYON. In Warnock, A.T. (ed.), *Short of War: Major USAF Contingency Operations, 1947–1997.* Air Force Historical Research Agency Maxwell AFB, pp.145–156.

Englehardt, J. 1991. *Desert Shield and Desert Storm: A Chronology and Troop List for the 1990–1991 Persian Gulf Crisis.* Strategic Studies Institute, US Army War College. Accessed from www.dtic.mil/dtic/tr/fulltext/u2/a234743.pdf.

Gause III, F.G. 2009. *The International Relations of the Persian Gulf.* Cambridge University Press.

Gause III, F.G. 2014. Beyond Sectarianism: The New Middle East Cold War. Brookings Doha Center Analysis Paper, 11, pp.1–27.

Gause, F.G. 2015. Ideologies, Alliances and Underbalancing in the New Middle East Cold War. In *International Relations and a New Middle East.* Project on Middle East Political Science. Accessed from http://pomeps.org/2015/07/09/ir-theory-and-a-new-middle-east-memos/.

Gerges, F.A. 2016. *Isis: A History.* Princeton University Press.

Gholz, E., and Press, D.G. 2010. Protecting "the Prize": Oil and the US National Interest. *Security Studies*, 19(3), pp.453–485.

Gholz, E., Press, D.G., and Sapolsky, H.M. 1997. Come Home, America: The Strategy of Restraint in the Face of Temptation. *International Security*, 21(4), pp.5–48.

Haas, M.L. 2005. *The Ideological Origins of Great Power Politics, 1789–1989.* Cornell University Press.

Haas, R. 2013. The Irony of American Strategy. *Foreign Affairs*, May/June.

Hudson, M.C. 1996. To Play the Hegemon: Fifty Years of US Policy toward the Middle East. *The Middle East Journal*, 50(3), pp.329–343.

Ignatius, D. 2016. The US Can't Fix It: James Clapper on America's Role in the Middle East. *The Washington Post*, May 10. Accessed from www.washingtonpost.com/opinions/the-us-cant-fix-it-james-clapper-on-americas-role-in-the-middle-east/2016/05/10/377666a8-16ea-11e6-9e16-2e5a123aac62_story.html.

International Institute for Strategic Studies. 2016. *The Military Balance, 2016*. Routledge.

Jo, D.J., and Gartzke, E. 2007. Determinants of Nuclear Weapons Proliferation. *Journal of Conflict Resolution*, 51(1), pp.167–194.

Kerr, M. 1971. *The Arab Cold War: Gamal 'Abd al-Nasir and His Rivals, 1958–1970*, 3rd ed. Oxford University Press.

Kitchen, N. 2012. After the Arab Spring: Power Shift in the Middle East? The Contradictions of Hegemony: The United States and the Arab Spring. IDEAS Reports. London School of Economics and Political Science.

Kuperman, A.J. 2008a. Mitigating the Moral Hazard of Humanitarian Intervention: Lessons from Economics. *Global Governance: A Review of Multilateralism and International Organizations*, 14(2), pp.219–240.

Kuperman, A.J. 2008b. The Moral Hazard of Humanitarian Intervention: Lessons from the Balkans. *International Studies Quarterly*, 52(1), pp.49–80.

Kuperman, A.J. 2013. A Model Humanitarian Intervention? Reassessing NATO's Libya Campaign. *International Security*, 38(1), pp.105–136.

Layne, C. 1997. From Preponderance to Offshore Balancing: America's Future Grand Strategy. *International Security*, 22(1), pp.86–124.

Lind, J. 2016. Review Article. *H-Diplo ISSF Article Review*, 52 (April 13). Accessed from https://issforum.org/ISSF/PDF/ISSF-AR52.pdf.

Lister, C.R. 2016. *The Syrian Jihad: Al-Qaeda, the Islamic State and the Evolution of an Insurgency*. Oxford University Press.

Lizza, R. 2011. The Consequentialist: How the Arab Spring Remade Obama's Foreign Policy. *The New Yorker*, 2 May.

Lynch, M. 2016. *The New Arab Wars: Uprisings and Anarchy in the Middle East*. PublicAffairs.

Macris, J.R. 2010. *The Politics and Security of the Gulf: Anglo-American Hegemony and the Shaping of a Region*. Routledge.

McCants, W. 2015. *The ISIS Apocalypse: The History, Strategy, and Doomsday Vision of the Islamic State*. Macmillan.

Mearsheimer, J.J., and Walt, S.M. 2016. The Case for Offshore Balancing. *Foreign Affairs*, 95(4), p.22.

Monteiro, N.P. 2014. *Theory of Unipolar Politics*. Cambridge University Press.

Peters, H., Schwartz, M., and Kapp, L. 2015. Department of Defense Contractor and Troop Levels in Iraq and Afghanistan: 2007–2015. Library of Congress Congressional Research Service.

Pew Research Center. 2014. *Global Opposition to US Surveillance and Drones, but Limited Harm to America's Image*. Pew Research Center. Accessed from www.pewglobal.org/2014/07/14/chapter-1-the-american-brand.

Pillar, P., and Preble, C.A. 2010. Don't You Know There's A War On? Assessing the Military's Role in Counterterrorism. In Friedman, B.H., Harper, J., and Preble, C.A. (eds.), *Terrorizing Ourselves: Why US Counterterrorism Policy is Failing and How to Fix It*. Cato Institute, pp.61–82.

Pollack, K.M. 2003. Securing the Gulf. *Foreign Affairs*, July/August.

Pollack, K.M. 2016. Fight or Flight: America's Choice in the Middle East. *Foreign Affairs*, March/April.

Posen, B.R. 2014. *Restraint: A New Foundation for US Grand Strategy*. Cornell University Press.

Rosenblum, T. 2016a. A Conversation on Security and Peace in the Middle East: Featuring HRH Prince Turki al-Faisal and Maj. Gen. Yaakov Amidror (Ret). Washington Institute, May 5. Accessed from www.washingtoninstitute.org/uploads/Documents/other/alFaisal-Amidror-FINAL2.pdf.

Rosenblum, T. 2016b. Improving Saudi–Israeli Relations Offers an Opportunity for the US – and a Big Risk. *Politico*, May 18. Accessed from www.politico.eu/article/middle-east-security-improving-saudi-israeli-relations-offers-an-opportunity-for-the-us-and-a-big-risk

Rovner, J., and Talmadge, C. 2014. Hegemony, Force Posture, and the Provision of Public Goods: The Once and Future Role of Outside Powers in Securing Persian Gulf Oil. *Security Studies*, 23(3), pp.548–581.

Rubin, L. 2015. Why the Islamic State Won't Become a Normal State. In *International Relations and a New Middle East*. Project on Middle East Political Science. Accessed from http://pomeps.org/2015/07/09/ir-theory-and-a-new-middle-east-memos/.

Ryan, C. 2012. The New Arab Cold War and the Struggle for Syria. *Middle East Report*, 262, pp.28–31.

Ryan, C. 2015. Regime Security and Shifting Alliances in the Middle East. In *International Relations and a New Middle East*. Project on Middle East Political Science. Accessed from http://pomeps.org/2015/07/09/ir-theory-and-a-new-middle-east-memos.

Ryan, M. 2016. The US Military Has a Lot More People in Iraq than It Has Been Saying. *The Washington Post*, March 21. Accessed from www.washingtonpost.com/news/checkpoint/wp/2016/03/21/the-u-s-military-has-a-lot-more-people-in-iraq-than-it-has-been-saying.

Saab, B. 2016. After Hub-And-Spoke: US Hegemony in New Gulf Security Order. *The Atlantic Council Policy Report*, April. Accessed from www.atlanticcouncil.org/images/publications/Hub_and_Spoke_0414_web.pdf.

Sagan, S.D. 1996. Why Do States Build Nuclear Weapons? Three Models in Search of a Bomb. *International Security* 21(3), pp.54–86.

Stapleton, B.I. 2016. The Problem with the Light Footprint: Shifting Tactics in Lieu of Strategy. Cato Institute Policy Analysis No. 792. Cato Institute.

Synovitz, R. 2016. Explainer: Why is Access to Syria's Port at Tartus So Important to Moscow? *Radio Free Europe Radio Liberty*, May 27. Accessed from www.rferl.org/content/explainer-why-is-access-/24619441.html.

US Energy Information Administration. 2016. Petroleum and Other Liquids Dataset. Accessed from www.eia.gov/petroleum/.

10

EMBRACING THREATLESSNESS

US military spending, Newt Gingrich, and the Costa Rica option

John Mueller

> One way of keeping people out of trouble is to deny them the means for getting into it.
>
> *Bernard Brodie (1978: 81)*

It is often said, even by many of his admirers, that at any one time Newt Gingrich will have 100 ideas of which five are pretty *good*. Falling into the latter category was his remark when running for the Republican presidential nomination in 2012 that "defense budgets shouldn't be a matter of politics. They shouldn't be a matter of playing games. They should be directly related to the amount of threat we have" (PBS NewsHour, January 26, 2012).

This chapter is something of a thought experiment. It applies Gingrich's sensible test and is determinedly "bottom-up." Instead of starting with things as they are and looking for places to trim, it assesses the threat environment—problems that lurk in current conditions and on the horizon.[1] Then, keeping both the risks and opportunities in mind, it considers which of these threats, if any, justify funding.

In *Overblown*, a book published in 2006, I argued that, with the benefit of hindsight, "every foreign policy threat in the last several decades that has come to be accepted as significant has then eventually been unwisely exaggerated" (Mueller 2006: 10). That is, alarmism, usually based on a worst-case approach, has dominated thinking about security.

This process seems to be continuing. After examining an important US Defense Department policy document, Benjamin Friedman observed in 2008 that rather than estimating the varying likelihood of potential national security threats and then coming up with recommendations on that basis following the Gingrich approach, it "contends simply that 'managing risk' compels the United States to prepare for all of them" while concluding that we should "retain the weapons and forces we have, with a few tweaks" (Friedman 2008: 35; see also Thrall and Cramer 2009). And

Gregory Daddis, a military historian at West Point, looking over the 2015 National Security Strategy, notes that the document stresses the "risks of an insecure world" and the "persistent risk of attacks" suggesting that "we live in a dangerous world... one in which only vigilant nations—led, naturally, by the United States—preemptively rooting out evil can survive" (Daddis 2015: 48; see also Zenko and Cohen 2012; Preble and Mueller 2014).

Greg Jaffe, Pentagon correspondent for the *Washington Post*, quotes a former planner at the Pentagon whose job, he says, "was to look for all the bad stuff. Scanning for threats is what we get paid to do." In contrast, notes Jaffe, "no one is rushing to discuss the implications of a world that has grown safer" (Jaffe 2012). While this chapter may not start the rush that Jaffe calls for, it may help to provide a useful first step.

Pacifism, isolationism, and comparative risk

The conclusion of this thought experiment is that, although there are certainly problem areas and issues in the world, the United States is, not unlike Costa Rica, substantially free from security threats that require the maintenance of large numbers of military forces-in-being.

This conclusion does not arise from pacifism, nor is it isolationist. The argument is not that large military forces are inherently evil or that there are no conditions under which they should be instituted or deployed. Indeed, some armed interventions have actually been quite successful. Rather, it simply seems that, applying Gingrich's wise and sensible test to present military spending, large military forces-in-being fail to be required in the current and likely threat environment.

And there is no suggestion in this that the United States should withdraw from being a constructive world citizen. The generally desirable processes of increasing economic inter-connectivity and of globalization make that essentially impossible anyway. Relevant is the policy perspective Eric Nordlinger once proposed: "minimally effortful national strategy in the security realm; moderately activist policies to advance our liberal ideas among and within states; and a fully activist economic diplomacy on behalf of free trade" (Nordlinger 1995: 4; see also Posen 2014)

However, it must be acknowledged at the same time that there is risk in extensively reducing the American military as will be proposed below. Although the proposal developed here does concede that some small military and nuclear capacity should be retained to hedge against unlikely contingencies and that a capacity to rebuild should be retained, these would not necessarily be enough to deal with the very sudden emergence of another major threat—a Hitler on steroids. But it really seems that it is up to the alarmists to explain how such a sudden emergence could happen (it would have to be sudden because otherwise the United States would have time to rearm) and where it would come from. As Robert Jervis (1984: 156) points out, "Hitlers are very rare."

It is most important, however, that this concern be balanced against the risk attendant on maintaining large forces-in-being that can be impelled into action with little notice and in an under-reflective, and very often counterproductive, manner (Preble 2009).

If the United States had not had the soldiers to move around on the global game board after 9/11, it might have employed responsive measures that were less likely to be self-destructive and more likely to have been more effective at far lower cost. And, of course, if it had had no military in 2003, it would never have initiated the Iraq War, and its treasury would now be trillions of dollars greater while several thousand Americans and over a hundred thousand Iraqis would not have been killed.

Looking forward, if Japan and China do manage somehow to get into an armed conflict over who owns which tiny uninhabited island in the sea that separates them, a substantially unarmed America will have a good excuse for not getting involved (Bandow 2015).

And looking back, had the country had no military in 1965, it could not have gone into Vietnam and the lives of 58,000 young Americans would not have been taken from them. Of course, the Communists might have taken over, but that seems to have happened anyway, and the losers and winners have since become quite chummy.

During the current century, in fact, American military policy, in its most dynamic aspects, has been an abject, and highly destructive, failure. Two misguided and failed wars of aggression and occupation have been launched in which trillions of dollars have been squandered and well over a hundred thousand people have perished, including more than twice as many Americans as were killed on 9/11. And there has also been a third war—the spillover one in Pakistan, which the United States has avidly promoted. Even though Pakistan receives $2–$3 billion in American aid each year, large majorities of Pakistanis—74 percent in the most recent tally—have come to view the United States as an enemy (Pew Research Center 2012). As negative achievements go, that foreign policy development is a strong gold-medal contender.

This consideration of comparative risks should be kept in mind as potential threats are assessed and evaluated in this chapter. Overall, as many military people have come increasingly to appreciate, many problems simply cannot be solved by military means.

Assessing the threats

It is important, then, to examine the array of threats that the US military is designed to, or expected to, deal with. If, in Gingrich's words, defense budgets "should be directly related to the amount of threat we have," what, and how dire, are the threats?

Major war

A sensible place to begin an evaluation of the security threat environment is with an examination of the prospects for a major war among developed countries, one like World War II. As Christopher Fettweis (2010) has argued, it really seems time to consider the consequences of the fact that leading or developed countries, reversing the course of several millennia, no longer envision major war as a sensible method for resolving their disputes. Although there is no physical reason why such a war cannot recur, it has become fairly commonplace to regard such wars as obsolescent, if not completely obsolete (Mueller 1989; Ray 1989).

World War III, then, continues to be the greatest nonevent in human history (Mueller 1989: 3). Or, as Jervis puts it, "the turning off" of the fear of, and the preparation for, war among leading countries "is the greatest change in international politics that we have ever seen" (Jervis 2011: 412).

And that condition seems very likely to persist. There have been wars throughout history, of course, but the remarkable absence of the species' worst expression for nearly three-quarters of a century (and counting) strongly suggests that realities may have changed, and perhaps permanently (Luard 1986: 395–399; Sheehan 2008; Pinker 2011: 249–251). Indeed, in the last decades international war even outside the developed world has become quite a rarity: there has been only one war since 1989 that fits cleanly into the classic model in which two states have it out over some issue of mutual dispute, in this case territory: the 1998–2000 war between Ethiopia and Eritrea. (The Ukrainian conflict of 2014 is discussed later.)

Accordingly it seems time to consider that spending a lot of money preparing for an eventuality—or fantasy—that is of ever-receding likelihood is a highly questionable undertaking.

Potential major war challenges

The remarkable absence of major war, some suggest, may be punctured some day either by the rise of China as a challenger country or by excessive assertiveness by Russia backed by its large nuclear arsenal. Both countries seek wider acceptance as major players on the world scene, and this drive, some worry, could lead them to provoke major war.

Neither state, however, seems to harbor Hitler-like dreams of extensive expansion by military means. Both do seem to want to play a larger role on the world stage and to overcome what they view as past humiliations—ones going back to the opium war of 1839 in the case of China and to the collapse of the Soviet empire and then of the Soviet Union in 1989–1991 in the case of Russia. They want to be treated with respect and deference.

To a considerable degree, it seems sensible for other countries, including the United States, to accept, and even service, such vaporous, even cosmetic, goals. If the two countries want to be able to say they now preside over a "sphere of influence," it scarcely seems worth risking world war to somehow keep them from doing so—and if the United States were substantially disarmed, it would not have the capacity to even try.

The rise of China and the issue of dominance

After a remarkable period of economic growth, China has entered the developed world. In a globalized economy, it is of course better for just about everyone if

China (or Japan or Brazil or India or Russia or any other country) becomes more prosperous—for one thing, they can now buy more stuff overseas (including debt). However, eschewing such economic logic, there has been a notable tendency to envision threat in China's rapidly increasing wealth on the grounds that it will likely invest a considerable amount in military hardware and will consequently come to feel impelled to target the United States or to carry out undesirable military adventures somewhere (Mearsheimer 2011: 3; Walt 2011a).

China's oft-stated desire to incorporate (or re-incorporate) Taiwan into its territory and its apparent design on other offshore areas do create problems—though the intensity of the Taiwan issue seems to have faded considerably in recent years (Kastner 2016). Although this could conceivably lead to armed conflict for which American military forces might appear relevant, it is also conceivable, and far more likely, that the whole problem will be worked out over the course of time without armed conflict. The Chinese strongly stress that their perspective on this issue is very long-term, that they have a historic sense of patience, and that they have reached agreement with Russia on their northern border, giving up some territory on which they had historical claims. In time, if China becomes a true democracy, Taiwan might even join up voluntarily and, failing that, some sort of legalistic face-saving agreement might eventually be worked out.

Above all, China has become a trading state, in Richard Rosecrance's phrase (Rosecrance 1986). Its integration into the world economy and its increasing dependence on it for economic development and for the consequent acquiescence of the Chinese people are likely to keep the country reasonable. Armed conflict would be extremely—even overwhelmingly—costly to the country, and, in particular, to the regime in charge. And Chinese leaders, already rattled by internal difficulties, seem to realize this. The best bet, surely, is that this condition will essentially hold.

Aaron Friedberg is quite concerned about "balancing" against China. He warns rather extravagantly (and inspecifically) that "if we permit an illiberal China to displace us as the preponderant player in this most vital region, we will face grave dangers to our interests and our values throughout the world" and that "if Beijing comes to believe that it can destroy US forces and bases in the western Pacific in a first strike, using only conventional weapons," there is "a chance" that it might "someday try to do so." However, even he concludes that China is "unlikely to engage in outright military conquest," and he notes that "it is important to remember that both China's political elites and its military establishment would approach the prospect of war with the United States with even more than the usual burden of doubt and uncertainty," that "the present generation of party leaders has no experience of war, revolution, or military service," and that the Chinese army "has no recent history of actual combat." Moreover, "even if it could somehow reduce its reliance on imported resources, the vitality of the Chinese economy will continue to depend on its ability to import and export manufactured products by sea"—something, obviously, that an armed conflict (or even the nearness of one) would greatly disrupt (Friedberg 2011: 7–8, 275, 279).

In addition, analysts point to a large number of domestic problems that are likely to arrest the attention of the Chinese leaders in future years. Among them: slackening economic growth, endemic corruption, a brain drain to the West, major environmental degradation, severe imbalances in the age distribution, an inadequate legal system, and the widespread nature of domestic opposition with particular concerns about Muslim rebellion in the western part of the country.

There is also a danger of making the issue of China's rise into a threat by treating it as such, by refusing to consider the unlikelihood as well as the consequences of worst-case scenario fantasizing, and by engaging in endless metaphysical talk about "balancing." In this respect, special consideration should be given to the observation that, as Susan Shirk puts it, "although China looks like a powerhouse from the outside, to its leaders it looks fragile, poor, and overwhelmed by internal problems." Provocative "balancing" talk, especially if military showmanship accompanies it, has the potential to be wildly counterproductive. In this respect, special heed should be paid to Shirk's warning that "historically, rising powers cause war not necessarily because they are innately belligerent, but because the reigning powers mishandle those who challenge the status quo" (Shirk 2007: 255, 261; see also Friedman and Logan 2012: 181–182; Lebow and Valentino 2009). Moreover, China's efforts at geopolitical assertiveness with its neighbors in recent years have often been counterproductive, and Chinese leaders, at least most of the time, seem to realize this (Ross 2011; Shirk 2007: 190; Johnston 2013).

John Mearsheimer criticizes what he calls "the US commitment to global dominance since the Cold War" which, he concludes, "has had huge costs and brought few benefits." He also worries that the country could be transforming itself into a "national-security state." Nonetheless, he deems it important that the US remain "the most powerful country on the planet" by "making sure a rising China does not dominate Asia in the same way the United States dominates the Western hemisphere." This he considers to be one of a very few "core strategic interests" for which the country should "use force" (Mearsheimer 2014: 12, 26, 30).

Actually, it is not clear in what way the US "dominates" the Western hemisphere— except perhaps economically. The country's neighbors do not seem to quake in fear of America's nuclear weapons or of the prowess of its Marines (whose record in Latin America during the last century was less than stunning). But their attention can be arrested if the US credibly threatens to stop buying their sugar, coffee, oil, bananas, or beer. It is in that sense that China may someday come to "dominate" Asia. But the clear implication of Mearsheimer's perspective is that American military power should be applied to keep that from coming to be. A minimally armed US wouldn't be so tempted.

From time to time, China may be emboldened to throw its weight around in its presumed "area of influence." Such weight-throwing (much of it rather childish in character) is unpleasant to watch, as well as counterproductive to China's economic goals (Bandow 2015). But, as noted, it does not seem to harbor Hitler-style ambitions about extensive conquest as even Friedberg acknowledges.

In particular, China may decide to become more assertive about controlling tiny piles of rocks, sometimes known as "islands," in the South China Sea. But even if it comes to imagine that it "controls" that body of water, it will still have an intense interest in the free flow of ships through it. At any rate, it seems unlikely that the maintenance of a huge and costly military force by the distant United States will be a credible deterrent to localized assertive behavior by China because there is likely to be little enthusiasm in the United States for sending large numbers of combatant troops abroad to directly confront such limited and distant effronteries.

Russian assertiveness and the economic doomsday machine

The notion that a major war among developed countries is wildly unlikely is also challenged by the experience of the armed dispute between Russia and Ukraine that began in 2014. It resulted in the peaceful, if extortionist, transfer of Crimea from Ukraine to Russia and then in a sporadic civil war in Ukraine in which secessionist groups in the east were supported by Russia.

Obviously, this is an unsettling development. However, unlike Hitler's acquisition of the Sudetenland in 1938, it does not seem to be a prologue to major war. It is impressive that the United States and Western Europe never even came close to seriously considering the use of direct force to deal with the issue—that is, they would have behaved much the same way even if they did not possess their great and expensive military capacity. Indeed, President Barack Obama, who presided over the episode, is given to taunting his hawkish critics: "Now, if there is somebody in this town that would claim that we would consider going to war with Russia over Crimea and eastern Ukraine, they should speak up and be very clear about it" (Goldberg 2016).

And, counter to early alarmist concerns, Russia's Vladimir Putin has not been inspired by the Ukrainian development to push further on his periphery, at least militarily. Parallels with the situation in Europe in the 1930s were repeatedly drawn during the 2014 crisis. However, one key missing element in the comparison was Adolf Hitler, who harbored great expansionist objectives and without whom the war in Europe would likely never have taken place (Mueller 1989: chapter 4, 2004: 54–69).

Russia's recent experience in the Ukraine conflict and crisis suggests an additional consideration. Countries cannot engage in such enterprises without paying a substantial economic price (a lesson not likely to be lost on the Chinese). Because of its antics, Russia has suffered a substantial decline in the value of its currency, a decline in its stock market, a decline in foreign investment, and, perhaps most importantly, a very substantial drop in confidence among investors, buyers, and sellers throughout the world, a condition that is likely to last for years, even decades (Galpin 2015; Nemtsova 2014, 2015). As part of this, its behavior has set off a determined effort by Europeans to reduce their dependence on Russian energy supplies—a change that could be permanent.

Other economic costs, like sanctions, have been visited intentionally by other states, or, like the drop in oil prices, have mainly occurred for other reasons. And the costs of the conflict itself, and of making its new dependencies something other than a long-term economic drain have been visited by Russia on itself.

But it is important to note that a substantial portion of the punishment Russia has received for its venture has, like the nuclear doomsday machine, been visited automatically—in this case, by the international market. Russia may be willing to bear that cost, but its awareness of the longer-term costs of—and perhaps its disillusion with—its new conquests is likely to increase with time. Thus far at least, the Ukrainian venture, contrary to much initial speculation, does not seem to be a game-changer (Bandow 2016; Kinzer 2016).

Assessing attacks on Taiwan and the Baltic states

It may be useful to look specifically at a couple of worst-case scenarios: an invasion of Taiwan by China (after it builds up its navy more) and an invasion of the Baltic states of Estonia, Lithuania, and Latvia by Russia.

In the wildly unlikely event that China or Russia were to carry out such economically self-destructive acts, it appears likely that the United States might well be unable to stop them under its current force levels (Shlapak and Johnson 2016; Heginbotham et al. 2015). And if it cannot credibly deter them with military forces currently in being, it would not be able to do so, obviously, if its forces were much reduced.

In either condition, however, the United States, as with expansionary Japan in the early 1940s, would have years to rearm in the rather unlikely event that it decides to wage something like World War III to turn back such expansion. And if it were substantially disarmed, the United States would have more time to reflect on whether waging a massive war in an effort to do so makes much sense.

Actually, the most likely response in either eventuality would be for the United States to wage a campaign of military and economic harassment and to support local—or partisan—resistance as it did in Afghanistan after the Soviet invasion there in 1979 (Mueller 1991, 1995b: chapter 7).[2] Such a response does not require the United States to have, and perpetually to maintain, huge forces in place and at the ready to deal with such improbable eventualities.

Rogue states

Over the course of the last several decades, alarmists have often focused on potential dangers presented by "rogue states," as they came to be called in the 1990s. Since such states can cause problems, it might make some sense to maintain a capacity to institute containment and deterrence efforts carried out in formal or informal coalition with concerned neighboring countries.

However, this would not necessarily require the United States to maintain large forces-in-being for the remote eventuality. This is suggested by the experience with the Gulf War of 1991 when military force was successfully applied to deal with a rogue venture—the conquest by Saddam Hussein's Iraq of neighboring Kuwait. It certainly appears, to begin with, that Iraq's pathetic forces needed the large force thrown at them in 1991 to decide to withdraw: over a period of half a year, they did not erect anything resembling an effective defensive system and, when the chips were down, they proved to lack not only defenses, but strategy, tactics, leadership, and morale as well (Mueller 1995a).

In addition, in a case like that, countries opposed to provocative rogue behavior do not need to have a large force-in-being because there would be plenty of time to build one up should other measures, such as economic sanctions and diplomatic forays, fail to persuade the attacker to withdraw.

It should also be pointed out that Iraq's invasion was rare to the point of being unique: it was the only case since World War II in which one United Nations country has invaded another with the intention of incorporating it into its own territory (Zacher 2001).

Proliferation

For decades there has been almost wall-to-wall alarm about the dangers supposedly inherent in nuclear proliferation.

However, the proliferation of nuclear weapons has been far slower than has been commonly predicted over the decades, primarily because the weapons do not generally convey much advantage to their possessor. And, more importantly, the effect of the proliferation that has taken place has been substantially benign: those who have acquired the weapons have "used" them simply to stoke their egos or to deter real or imagined threats (Mueller 2010: chapters 7–11, forthcoming; Hymans 2012). This holds even for the proliferation of the weapons to large, important countries run by unchallenged monsters who at the time they acquired the bombs were certifiably deranged: Josef Stalin, who in 1949 was planning to change the climate of the Soviet Union by planting a lot of trees, and Mao Zedong, who in 1964 had just carried out a bizarre social experiment that had resulted in artificial famine in which tens of millions of Chinese perished (Mueller 1989: 123; Dikötter 2010).

Despite this experience, an aversion to nuclear proliferation continues to impel alarmed concern, and it was a chief motivator of the Iraq War, which essentially was a militarized anti-proliferation effort. The war proved to be a necessary cause of more deaths than were inflicted at Hiroshima and Nagasaki combined.

The subsequent and consequent Iraq syndrome strongly suggests there will be little incentive to apply military force to prevent, or to deal with, further putative proliferation. Thus, despite nearly continuous concern—even at times hysteria—about nuclear developments in North Korea and Iran, proposals to use military force (particularly boots on the ground) to deal with these developments have been persistently undercut. Thus, maintaining huge forces-in-being to deal with the proliferation problem scarcely seems sensible. What seems to be required in these cases, as generally with the devils du jour of the Cold War era, is judicious, watchful, and wary patience.

Terrorism

Any threat presented by international terrorism has been massively inflated in the retelling (Mueller 2006; Mueller and Stewart 2016a: chapters 1, 3, and 4, 2016b).

Al-Qaeda

For almost all of the period since 9/11, the chief demon group has been al-Qaeda. It has consisted of perhaps a hundred or two hundred people who, judging from information obtained in Osama bin Laden's lair when he was murdered in May 2011, have been primarily occupied with dodging drone missile attacks, complaining about the lack of funds, and watching a lot of pornography (Mueller and Stewart 2016a: chapter 4).

It seems increasingly likely that the reaction to the terror attacks of September 11, 2001, was greatly disproportionate to the real threat al-Qaeda has ever actually presented. On 9/11, a miserable, ridiculous, tiny group of men—a fringe group of a fringe group—with grandiose visions of its own importance managed, heavily because of luck, to pull off by far the most destructive terrorist act in history (Sageman 2008; Gerges 2011). Both before and after 9/11, in war zones or outside them, there has been scarcely any terrorist attack that visited even one-tenth as much destruction.

There has been a general reluctance to maintain that such a monumental event could have been pulled off by a trivial group, and there has consequently been a massive tendency to inflate the group's importance and effectiveness (Mueller 2002a, 2002b, 2003; Seitz 2004; Gerges 2005). At the preposterous extreme, the remnants of the tiny group have even been held to present a threat that is "existential." Yet, since 9/11, al-Qaeda Central's record of accomplishment has been rather meager, even taking into consideration that it has been isolated and under siege. It has issued videos filled with empty, self-infatuated, and essentially delusional threats; may have served as something of an inspiration to some Muslim extremists; may have done some training; may have contributed a bit to the Taliban's far larger insurgency in Afghanistan; and may have participated in a few terrorist acts in Pakistan. Even though something like 300 million foreigners enter the United States legally every year, virtually no foreign al-Qaeda operative has been able to infiltrate (Mueller 2006; Mueller and Stewart 2016a; Sageman 2008).

Other groups

Terrorist groups variously connected to al-Qaeda may be able to do intermittent mischief in war zones in the Middle East and in Africa, but likely nothing that is sustained or focused enough to inspire the application of military force by the United States in the wake of its experiences in Iraq and Afghanistan. Overall, until the rise of ISIS, extremist Islamist terrorism claimed some 200–400 lives yearly worldwide outside war zones, about the same as bathtub drownings in the United States (Mueller and Stewart 2011, 2016a: 306n4).

Outrage at the tactics of ISIS is certainly justified. But fears that it presents a worldwide security threat are not. The vicious group certainly presents a threat to the people under its control and in its neighborhood, and it can contribute damagingly to the instability in the Middle East that has followed serial intervention there by the American military. However, not only does it scarcely present an existential threat to the United States, but it seems to be in considerable decline in the Middle East. ISIS is also finding that actually controlling and effectively governing wide territories is a major strain. And it has to work hard to keep people from fleeing its brutal lumpen Caliphate (Mueller and Stewart 2016c).

Responding to terrorism

The main military efforts to deal with terrorism have been the ventures in Iraq and Afghanistan. Both of these were much disproportionate to the supposed danger presented, and they have been, in their own terms, and in the long run, very considerable failures. In result, that kind of military approach to terrorism has been substantially discredited (Mueller and Stewart 2016a: chapter 3). To the degree that terrorism requires a response—including one involving militants returning from, or inspired by, terrorism in the Middle East—this does call not for large military operations, but for policing and intelligence work and perhaps for occasional focused strikes conducted from the air and by small ground units while relying on local forces to furnish the bulk of the combat personnel. This is substantially the approach the Obama administration developed to deal with ISIS (Goldberg 2016). It seems likely to prevail.

Given the decidedly limited capabilities of terrorists, a concern that they may go atomic seems to have been substantially overwrought (Mueller 2010: chapters 12–15; Lieber and Press 2013). And efforts useful for dealing with the danger mainly require policing and intelligence, international cooperation on locking up and cataloging fissile material, and sting operations to disrupt illicit nuclear markets. They do not require large military forces-in-being.

Policing wars

One possible use of American military forces in the future would be to deploy them to police destructive civil wars or to depose regimes that, either out of incompetence or viciousness, are harming their own people in a major way. Many international law authorities agree that, if such actions are mandated by the Security Council of the United Nations, they are legal and acceptable (Gray 2002: 3–7; Mueller 2004: chapter 7; Menon 2016).

And, indeed, more than twenty military interventions or policing wars have been carried out (with or without UN approval) by individual countries or by coalitions of them since the end of the Cold War. Table 10.1, appended to this chapter, provides a summary accounting (see also Miller 2013). All of these interventions were successful in the short term. Moreover, most were successful in the longer term in that they ended civil conflicts and/or deposed contemptible regimes at low cost after which the intervening forces withdrew in short, or fairly short, order, turning the countries over to governments that were very substantial improvements. In several cases, however, the venture succeeded in the short term but failed in the longer term in that the country soon devolved into costly civil armed conflict (Somalia, Afghanistan, Iraq, Libya) or in that the new governments established proved to be scarcely better than the ones that had been deposed (Haiti and probably Kosovo). The interventions were successful in that they were conducted by disciplined military forces against ones that usually were substantially criminal or criminalized (On this distinction see Mueller 2004, chapter 1).

However, policing wars are likely to be unusual because there is, overall, little stomach for such operations due to at least three key problems. To begin with, there is little or no political gain from success in such ventures. In addition, there is a low tolerance for casualties in such applications of military force. And the experience with policing wars has been accompanied by an increasing aversion to the costs and difficulties of what is often called nation-building. Indeed, in its defense priority statement of January 2012, the US Department of Defense (2012) firmly emphasized (that is, rendered in italics) that "*US forces will no longer be sized to conduct large-scale, prolonged stability operations.*" Or, as David Sanger puts it, America is "out of the occupation business" (Sanger 2012: 419).[3]

Finally, even if there is some stomach for putting American troops into humanitarian policing ventures, this would not require a large number of troops. Most of the successful ventures in Table 10.1 were accomplished by inserting a few hundred to a few thousand disciplined troops. History suggests that, should the situation deteriorate, the calls would be for removing the troops as in Somalia, not for sending in more.

Protecting allies

Some argue that a substantial force-in-being is required to protect allies and friends. However, the most important allies, those in Europe, not only seem to face little threat of a military nature, but are likely to be capable of dealing with any that should emerge (Friedman and Logan 2012: 180–181, 187; Preble 2009: 94–96).

The threat environment for some other friends and allies, in particular Taiwan and Israel, is more problematic. However, whatever the conditions of military spending, it would be foolish for either to assume, particularly in an era when the Iraq syndrome holds sway, that the United States would come riding to its rescue should the country come under severe military pressure, though it can probably count on moral and financial support in a pinch. Meanwhile, the Taiwan/China issue remains only a fairly remote concern as suggested earlier. The Palestine/Israel dispute may or may not be resolved by the end of the millennium, but the value of maintaining large American military forces seems to be irrelevant to that resolution. Israel's primary problems with violent opposition derive from the actions of sub-state groups, not from the potential for international warfare, and it seems quite capable of handling these on its own.

International crime

In 2011 a White House report proclaimed that transnational organized crime "poses a significant and growing threat to national and international security, with dire implications for public safety, public health, democratic institutions, and economic stability" (Andreas 2013: 330).

However, as Peter Andreas points out in a study of the issue, it is not at all clear that international crime is increasing as an overall percentage of global commerce. In fact, trade liberalization "has sharply reduced incentives to engage in smuggling practices designed to evade taxes and tariffs, which were historically a driving force of illicit commerce." More importantly, he continues, "the image of an octopus-like network of crime syndicates that runs the underworld through its expansive tentacles is a fiction invented by sensationalistic journalists, opportunistic politicians, and Hollywood scriptwriters." In contrast, international crime tends to be defined "more by fragmentation and loose informal networks rather than concentration and hierarchical organization" (Andreas 2013: 334).

Thus, like a parasite, international crime works best when it keeps a low profile and best of all when no one even notices it is there. Thus, *by its very nature* it does not want to take over the international system or threaten national security. It has no incentive to kill or dominate its host.

Policing the "global commons"

In an age of globalization and expanding world trade, many, particularly in the Navy, argue that a strong military force is needed to police what is portentously labeled the "global commons." However, there seems to be no credible consequential threat in that arena.

There have been attacks by pirates off Somalia, exacting costs in the hundreds of millions of dollars a year to a multi-billion dollar shipping industry which, surely, has the capacity to defend itself from such nuisances—perhaps by the application on decks of broken glass, a severe complication for barefoot predators.

There are routes around most choke points should they become clogged. And any armed cloggers are likely to be as punished and inconvenienced as the clogged. Huge forces-in-being are scarcely required because, in the unlikely event that the problem becomes sustained, newly formulated forces designed to deal with it could be developed (Friedman and Logan 2012: 183–184).

Cyber

There is also great concern about an impending invasion by cybergeeks. For the most part, however, such ventures are essentially forms of crime or vandalism, and do not require military preparations. Any military disruptions are likely to be more nearly instrumental or tactical than existential, and they call far more for a small army of counter-cybergeeks than for a large standing military force.

Other issues

In addition to these considerations, various other potential problems, or "threats," have been advanced from time to time. But these, singly or in groups, scarcely justify massive expenditures to maintain a large military force-in-being.

One of these is the ever-reliable concept of "complexity" and its constant companions, "instability" and "uncertainty." These concepts, if that is what they are, get routinely trotted out as if they had some tangible meaning, as if they had only recently been discovered, and as if they somehow necessitate more military spending (US Department of Defense 2010: 5; for critiques, see Zenko 2013; Fettweis 2013; Mueller 1995b: 13–24). Whatever their meaning, however, they can be used to justify decreases in military expenditures in favor of expenditures on intelligence, diplomacy, or soft power.

The developed world's dependence on oil imports from the Middle East has been an issue for a half-century now. However, unless the United States plans to invade other countries to seize their oil, the need for a military force-in-being to deal with this problem is far from obvious (Rosecrance 1986: 9–16; Friedman and Logan 2012: 184). Any oil disruptions are likely to be handled by the market: if supply diminishes, prices will increase, and people will buy less. Not much fun, but much more likely, especially after Iraq, than imperial invasion. Moreover, the problem seems to be in remission as, aided in part by a major technological breakthrough, fracking, domestic supplies grow and oil prices plummet worldwide—a phenomenon likely to last for a considerable amount of time.

The potential for, and the consequences of, global warming are of great concern to many, and some have envisioned security issues (Bender 2013; Posen 2014: chapter 3). The need to maintain a military force to deal with climate change is scarcely evident, however. Overall, any damage to national security that might be expected to come from climate change is likely to require defense spending adjustments that are far from significant (Stewart 2014).

The country (and the world) certainly face major problems of an economic nature, but the military is of little importance here either. Actually, large cuts in military budgets would temper the budget problem some.

There are many other issues that are frequently, if questionably, promoted as national security threats—AIDS in Africa, for example. The value of maintaining large military forces-in-being scarcely seems relevant to problems like these.

Hedging

On the chance that there is some occasional misjudgment in the arguments arrayed above, it may be sensible to hedge a bit by judiciously keeping some limited military capacities on line and viable to cover remote contingencies.

First, it appears that the maintenance of some small rapid-response or commando forces might make some sense.

Second, there may be instances in which it would be useful to be able to send troops to maintain peace where a civil war has subsided or to help maintain order in places where a despot has been removed. As discussed earlier, these ventures do not require large numbers of troops—a few thousand would surely do—and they are likely to be deployed only when the atmosphere on the ground is "permissive," or substantially so. If either of those conditions changes and substantial violence once again erupts, the troops are likely to be removed as happened in Lebanon after 1983 and Somalia after 1993.

Third, it would remain potentially wise to maintain a capacity to provide air support for friendly ground troops who are engaged in combat.

Fourth, it would likely be prudent to maintain a small number of nuclear weapons. These should be secure, hardened, and deliverable, but not numerous. It certainly seems that nuclear weapons have been essentially irrelevant to world history since 1945 (Mueller 2010: chapter 3). However, there are still imaginable, if highly unlikely, contingencies—such as the rise of another Hitler—in which they might be useful (Mueller 1995b: 75, 2010: 41).

Fifth, while it appears that standing military forces can safely be substantially reduced, maintaining an adept intelligence capacity probably remains a priority. However, studies should be made to determine whether, on balance, the benefit of a massive intelligence apparatus justifies its very considerable cost (for example, see Mueller and Stewart 2016a).

And sixth, it seems sensible to maintain something of a capacity to rebuild quickly should a sizable threat eventually materialize. The United States was very good at that in the early 1940s when global threats emerged (Mueller 1995b: 67–68, 87–94). And something similar, on a substantial, but less massive, scale happened when the Korean War broke out suddenly in 1950. In most (but not all) cases, there is likely to be time to rebuild in the unlikely event that substantial threats actually materialize, though there is inevitably waste in crash programs.

Concluding reflections

It certainly seems that, given the essential absence of any substantial security threats to the United States (and to most of the developed world), to spend huge sums on the military to cover unlikely threats (or fantasies) borders, indeed considerably oversteps, the profligacy line. It is often pointed out that defense spending, even in the United States, constitutes only a fairly small percentage of government spending and a quite small percentage of the country's gross national product (Brooks, Ikenberry, and Wohlforth 2012: 17–19). Nevertheless, the saving of several hundreds of billions of dollars each year soon adds up even in that comparison. In total, US expenditures on defense since the end of the Cold War have been about the size of the entire national debt.

Some analysts worry that a minimally armed United States would suffer a hugely damaging decline in "influence" and would become less able to order the world—to be the "American Pacifier" with "leverage to restrain partners from taking provocative action." They speculate that Europe "might" become "incapable of securing itself from various threats" materializing from somewhere or other, and that this "could be destabilizing within the region and beyond" while making the Europeans potentially "vulnerable to the influence of outside rising powers." They also worry that Israel, Egypt, and/or Saudi Arabia might do something nutty in the Middle East and that Japan and South Korea might get nuclear weapons (Brooks, Ikenberry, and Wohlforth 2012: 34–35; but see Jervis 2011: 415).

The United States can certainly take credit for being an important influence in establishing a Western order in which the losers of World War II came to view the world in much the same way as those who had bombed Dresden and Hiroshima, emerging as key contributors to that order in the process. This was one of the most impressive instances of enlightened self-interest in history. However, the United States hardly *forced* that to happen. It may have nudged, persuaded, and encouraged the process to move along, but it had a highly responsive audience in devastated peoples who were most ready to embrace the message and to get back on the road to prosperity. Indeed, it seems entirely possible that the United States was not strictly *necessary* for these developments at all—that much the same thing would have happened if it had retreated into truculent isolationism.

Over the course of the decades, the US has provided added value to the international order at various points. But, as Simon Reich and Richard Ned Lebow forcefully point out, it has also routinely embraced error and engaged in fiasco. For example, it "grossly exaggerated" the threat presented by the Soviet Union; promulgated and then wallowed mindlessly and parochially in messianism and in such self-infatuated characterizations as "exceptionalism" and "indispensability"; bullied other countries self-defeatingly; reneged on its own liberal trading rules; and has often been "unable to impose solutions consistent with hegemony" (Reich and Lebow 2014: 2, 134, 168, 23).[4]

An enormous military capacity can also impel foolish arrogance in the strong as suggested in an oft-quoted declaration of the mighty Athenians (who later went down to ignominious defeat) as reported by Thucydides: "the strong do what they can and the weak suffer what they must" (Thucydides 2009 [431 BCE]: Book 5, chapter 89). The fatuous modern-day update was supplied by American Secretary of State Madeline Albright in 1998: "If we have to use force, it is because we are America; we are the indispensable nation. We stand tall and we see further than other countries into the future" (*The Today Show*, NBC, February 19, 1998). That self-obsessed phraseology was routinely echoed, even expanded, by Barack Obama when he proclaimed, "The United States is and will remain the one indispensable nation"—rather suggesting that the United States considers all other nations to be, well, dispensable (Obama 2014).

To the degree that such arrogance continues to persist, Bernard Brodie's wistful reflection in the wake of the Vietnam War bears repeating: "One way of keeping people out of trouble is to deny them the means for getting into it" (Brodie 1978: 81; see also Walt 2011b; Bacevich 2014). A third of a century later, that sage admonition continues to be relevant. There seem to be no threats to the security of the United States that require the maintenance of a large military force-in-being. But having one at hand tempts leaders to use it in an effort to solve problems for which military force is an inappropriate, inadequate, and often counterproductive remedy.

TABLE 10.1 Military interventions or policing wars after the Cold War that worked, at least for a while

Panama. 1989. US forces invade, depose the government, return an elected one to power, and then leave. Civil peace is maintained. The venture is similar to one conducted by the United States against Grenada in 1983.

Gulf War. 1991. A large, but low-casualty, intervention ousts Iraq's (unimpressive to the point of being nonexistent) occupying army in Kuwait. It proved to be the mother of all bug-outs. Kuwait's government returns from exile, and civil peace is maintained. US troops return home and various victory parades are staged, the only time this has happened since World War II.

Iraq. 1991. US forces aid Kurds in the north, establishing a safe zone and pushing back Iraqi military forces. Little is done, however, when Iraqi forces brutally put down a Shia rebellion in the south of the country.

Somalia. 1992. UN forces, including from the US, intervene, stop a famine caused by civil warfare. Later, things deteriorate as efforts to set up a government fail and armed opposition arises. When occupying troops get killed in small numbers, they are withdrawn. Civil war chaos continues for decades.

Rwanda. 1994. An invasion by a fairly effective (by African standards) Tutsi army brings the government-ordered genocide to a close—the Rwandan army collapses and most génocidaires simply flee. The Hutu government is toppled in the process, and the Tutsis set up a new one. Civil peace is maintained, and in many cases victims and perpetrators of the genocide have lived side by side without violence.

Haiti. 1994. US sends troops to depose a military coup and to return an elected one to power. It meets no real armed resistance; this is partly due to the fact that, because of the threatening invasion, the offending government had been successfully pressured to leave. Civil peace, but not competent governance, is maintained.

Croatia. 1995. Over a few years, the newly independent Croatian government creates an effective army. It ousts the mostly criminalized forces from Serb-held areas in the country, which mostly flee to Bosnia and Serbia. It had previously liberated other Serb-held areas and enclaves in Croatia in 1993. Civil peace is maintained.

Bosnia. 1995. A continuation of the Croatian military offensive into Serb areas of Bosnia with additional attacks by newly decriminalized Muslim forces from the Sarajevo government. US works to halt the joint offensive from completely ethnically cleansing Bosnia of Serbs. NATO's bombing of Serb positions in Bosnia probably helps to concentrate the Bosnian Serb mind. However, before the bombing began, the Bosnian Serbs had already asked Milošević to negotiate for them knowing that he had previously strongly (and ineffectively) supported accepting a division like the one eventually accepted at Dayton in 1995. After the Dayton agreement, civil peace is maintained: for more than 20 years there have apparently been no episodes (even small ones) of ethnic violence in the country.

Sierra Leone. 1995. Under siege in a chaotic civil war, the government hires a mercenary group, Executive Outcomes, which sends 200 troops to fight and to train. By 1996, the country is stable enough to hold elections. In 1997, the new government refuses to renew EO's contract, and civil warfare quickly returns.

Kosovo. 1999. NATO bombing causes anti-Albanian depredations by Serb militias massively to increase. However, the persistence of the bombing over three months (initial

TABLE 10.1 (*Cont.*)

underexamined anticipations had been that Milošević would break after a few days of bombing) finally does lead Milošević to withdraw and to allow Kosovo to become effectively independent. No ground troops are sent. There are some revenge attacks by Albanians, but, overall, civil peace is maintained.

East Timor. 1999. Operating under a UN mandate, Australian troops invade, and rampaging militia groups supported/encouraged by the Indonesian army fade away without fighting. A new government is set up. Civil peace is maintained.

Sierra Leone. 2000. Britain sends a few hundred troops to join UN forces in a civil war-like, chaotic situation and is able to stabilize the country and set up a new government. Civil peace is maintained.

Afghanistan. 2001. In alliance with anti-Taliban elements in the north of the country, US bombing contributes considerably to the fall of the Taliban. Except for some foreign fighters, no one seems to be willing to fight for them. Members of the CIA and Special Forces on the ground are effective at directing the bombing and at hiring local combatants. The Taliban flees to Pakistan for several years, eventually regroups, and returns to wage an extended insurgency. But for about five years they commit little violence in Afghanistan beyond some isolated terrorist attacks.

Ivory Coast. 2002. The French send troops to help police a civil war situation.

Iraq. 2003. US military forces invade and conquer the country, sending Saddam Hussein fleeing and setting up a new government. The invasion is of Iraq itself—rather than, as in 1991, simply of an area Iraq had conquered earlier. Nonetheless, the US suffers even fewer casualties in the venture. Civil conflict grows, and anti-invader terrorism eventually rises to the level of insurgency.

Liberia. 2003. In a civil war situation in which semi-coherent rebel groups are bombarding Monrovia, Charles Taylor agrees under pressure to leave the country. African troops, mainly Nigerian, invade and face little resistance. Fighting stops, a new government is formed, and civil peace is maintained.

Ivory Coast. 2011. France sends in troops to pacify the country when a civil war breaks out.

Libya. 2011. European and North American countries, under a UN mandate, intervene, particularly by air, in a civil war in which armed rebels seek the removal of the country's long-time leader. With that help, the rebels eventually succeed, but the country then descends into civil war chaos.

Syria. 2011. When the government seems to be falling to armed rebels, Russia, Iran, Iraq, and Hezbollah send assistance and combatants to prop it up. The government survives, but the civil war continues as the country is effectively partitioned.

Mali. 2013. Under a UN mandate, France sends troops to quell a civil war that emerged after weapons arrived in the country from Libya when that country descended into civil war.

Central African Republic. 2013. France sends troops to try to help pacify a civil war situation.

Other possibilities:
Russian interventions against Georgia in Abkhazia and in Ossetia
Russian intervention against Ukraine
US, Russian, and other interventions against ISIS in Iraq and Syria

Notes

1 On his 95% side, Gingrich does imagine many dire threats and dangers (Mueller 2011).
2 On the possibility that such a strategy might have been used against the Japanese after Pearl Harbor, see Mueller (1991); also in Mueller (1995b: chapter 7).
3 My thanks to Christopher Preble for pointing me to these references. For additional evidence of reticence in the military, see Martinez (2013). One popular argument is that the American public has slumped into an isolationist mood as a result of Iraq/Afghan syndrome. But there has always been a deep reluctance to lose American lives or to put them at risk overseas for humanitarian purposes. An examination of the trends on poll questions designed to tap "isolationism" does not suggest a surge either of isolationism or of militarism. Instead, there was something of a rise in wariness about military intervention after the Vietnam War and then, thereafter, a fair amount of steadiness punctured by spike-like ups and downs in response to events including 9/11 and its ensuing wars. In the wake of the disastrous military interventions in Iraq and Afghanistan, it has gone back to about where it was in the aftermath of Vietnam (Mueller and Stewart 2016a: chapter 2).
4 Reich and Lebow argue that "it is incumbent on IR scholars to cut themselves loose" from the concept of hegemony (2014: 183). It seems even more important for the foreign policy establishment to do so. After that, perhaps we can quietly abandon other scholarly concepts that are often vacuous, usually misdirecting, and singularly unhelpful. These would include not only concepts like "hegemony" and "primacy," but also "polarity," "system," "power transition," and, eventually perhaps, "power" itself. See Mueller (1995b: chapter 2).

References

Andreas, P. 2013. *Smuggler Nation: How Illicit Trade Made America*. Oxford University Press.

Bacevich, A.J. 2014. Do We Really Need a Large Army? *Washington Post*, February 27.

Bandow, D. 2015. The Ultimate Irony: Is China the "America" of Asia? nationalinterest.org, May 27. Viewed March 21, 2017, from http://nationalinterest.org/feature/the-ultimate-irony-china-the-america-asia-12976.

Bandow, D. 2016. Why on Earth Would Russia Attack the Baltics? nationalinterest.org, February 7. Viewed March 21, 2017, from http://nationalinterest.org/blog/the-buzz/why-earth-would-russia-attack-the-baltics-15139.

Bender, B. 2013. Chief of US Pacific Forces Calls Climate Biggest Worry. *Boston Globe*, March 9.

Brodie, B. 1978. The Development of Nuclear Strategy. *International Security*, 2(4), pp.65–83.

Brooks, S.G., Ikenberry, G.J., and Wohlforth, W.C. 2012. Don't Come Home, America: The Case against Retrenchment. *International Security*, 37(3), pp.7–51.

Daddis, G.A. 2015. America: Addicted to War, Afraid of Peace. *The National Interest*, July–August.

Dikötter, F. 2010. *Mao's Great Famine: The History of China's Most Devastating Catastrophe, 1958–1962*. Walker & Co.

Fettweis, C.J. 2010. *Dangerous Times? The International Politics of Great Power Peace*. Georgetown University Press.

Fettweis, C.J. 2013. *The Pathologies of Power: Fear, Honor, Glory, and Hubris in US Foreign Policy*. Cambridge University Press.

Friedberg, A.L. 2011. *A Contest for Supremacy: China, America, and the Struggle for Mastery in Asia*. W.W. Norton & Company.

Friedman, B.H. 2008. The Terrible Ifs. *Regulation*, winter.

Friedman, B.H., and Logan, J. 2012. Why the US Military Budget is "Foolish and Sustainable". *Orbis*, 56(2), pp.177–191.

Galpin, R. 2015. Russians Count the Cost a Year after Crimea Annexation. *BBC News*, March 20. Viewed March 21, 2017, from www.bbc.com/news/world-europe-31962156.

Gerges, F.A. 2005. *The Far Enemy: Why Jihad Went Global*. Cambridge University Press.

Gerges, F.A. 2011. *The Rise and Fall of Al-Qaeda*. Oxford University Press.

Goldberg, J. 2016. The Obama Doctrine. *The Atlantic*, April.

Gray, C. 2002. From Unity to Polarization: International Law and the Use of Force against Iraq. *European Journal of International Law*, 13(1), pp.1–19.

Heginbotham, E., Nixon, M., Morgan, F.E., Hagen, J., Heim, J.L., Engstrom, J., Li, S., DeLuca, P., Libicki, M.C., Frelinger, D.R., and Brady, K. 2015. *The US–China Military Scorecard: Forces, Geography, and the Evolving Balance of Power, 1996–2017*. RAND Corporation.

Hymans, J.E. 2012. *Achieving Nuclear Ambitions: Scientists, Politicians, and Proliferation*. Cambridge University Press.

Jaffe, G. 2012. The World Is Safer. But No One in Washington Can Talk About It. *Washington Post*, November 2.

Jervis, R. 1984. *The Illogic of American Nuclear Strategy*. Cornell University Press.

Jervis, R. 2011. Force in Our Times. *International Relations*, 25(4), pp.403–425.

Johnston, A.I. 2013. How New and Assertive is China's New Assertiveness? *International Security*, 37(4), pp.7–48.

Kastner, S.L. 2016. Is the Taiwan Strait Still a Flash Point? Rethinking the Prospects for Armed Conflict between China and Taiwan. *International Security*, 40(3), pp.54–92.

Kinzer, S. 2016. The Inestimable Importance of Strategic Depth. *Boston Globe*, March 5. Viewed March 21, 2017, from www.bostonglobe.com/ideas/2016/03/04/the-inestimable-importance-strategic-depth/FCqTtIF5eyDlOtkFUd5K3N/story.html.

Lebow, R.N., and Valentino, B. 2009. Lost in Transition: A Critical Analysis of Power Transition Theory. *International Relations*, 23(3), pp.389–410.

Lieber, K.A., and Press, D.G. 2013. Why States Won't Give Nuclear Weapons to Terrorists. *International Security*, 38(1), pp.80–104.

Luard, E. 1986. *War in International Society: A Study in International Sociology*. IB Tauris.

Martinez, L. 2013. Gen. Martin Dempsey Lays Out US Military Options for Syria. abcnews.go.com, July 22.

Mearsheimer, J.J. 2011. Imperial by Design. *The National Interest*, 111, pp.16–34.

Mearsheimer, J. 2014. America Unhinged. *The National Interest*, 129, pp.9–30.

Menon, R. 2016. *The Conceit of Humanitarian Intervention*. Oxford University Press.

Miller, P.D. 2013. *Armed State Building: Confronting State Failure, 1898–2012*. Cornell University Press.

Mueller, J. 1989. *Retreat from Doomsday: The Obsolescence of Major War*. Basic Books.

Mueller, J. 1991. Pearl Harbor: Military Inconvenience, Political Disaster. *International Security*, 16(3), pp.172–203.

Mueller, J. 1995a. The Perfect Enemy: Assessing the Gulf War. *Security Studies*, 5(1), pp.77–117.

Mueller, J. 1995b. *Quiet Cataclysm: Reflections on the Recent Transformation of World Politics*. HarperCollins.

Mueller, J. 2002a. False Alarms. *Washington Post*, September 29.

Mueller, J. 2002b. Harbinger or Aberration? A 9/11 Provocation. *The National Interest*, 69, pp.45–50.

Mueller, J. 2003. Blip or Step Function? Paper presented at the Annual Convention of the International Studies Association, Portland, OR, February 27.

Mueller, J. 2004. *The Remnants of War*. Cornell University Press.

Mueller, J. 2006. *Overblown: How Politicians and the Terrorism Industry Inflate National Security Threats, and Why We Believe Them*. Free Press.

Mueller, J. 2010. *Atomic Obsession: Nuclear Alarmism from Hiroshima to al-Qaeda*. Oxford University Press.

Mueller, J. 2011. Newt Gingrich and the EMP Threat. nationalinterest.org, December 13.

Mueller, J. Forthcoming. "At All Costs": The Destructive Consequences of Antiproliferation Policy. In Sokolski, H., ed., *Stopping the Bomb's Further Spread: Should We Bother?*

Mueller, J., and Stewart, M.G. 2011. *Terror, Security, and Money: Balancing the Risks, Benefits, and Costs of Homeland Security*. Oxford University Press.

Mueller, J., and Stewart, M.G. 2016a. *Chasing Ghosts: The Policing of Terrorism*. Oxford University Press.

Mueller, J., and Stewart, M.G. 2016b. Conflating Terrorism and Insurgency. lawfare.com, February 28.

Mueller, J., and Stewart, M.G. 2016c. Misoverestimating ISIS: Comparisons with al-Qaeda. *Perspectives on Terrorism*, August.

Nemtsova, A. 2014. How Crimea Crashed the Russian Economy. thedailybeast.com, December 17. Viewed March 21, 2017, from www.thedailybeast.com/articles/2014/12/17/how-crimea-crashed-the-russian-economy.html.

Nemtsova, A. 2015. Can Putin Afford to Keep East Ukraine? thedailybeast.com, July 25. Viewed March 21, 2017, from www.thedailybeast.com/articles/2015/07/25/can-putin-afford-to-keep-east-ukraine.html.

Nordlinger, E.A. 1995. *Isolationism Reconfigured: American Foreign Policy for a New Century*. Princeton University Press.

Obama, B. 2014. Remarks by the President at the United States Military Academy Commencement Ceremony. US Military Academy-West Point, West Point, NY. Viewed September 11, 2017, from www.whitehouse.gov/the-press-office/2014/05/28/remarks-president-united-states-military-academy-commencement-ceremony.

Pew Research Center. 2012. Pakistani Public Opinion Ever More Critical of US: 74% Call America an Enemy. Pew Research Global Attitudes Study, June 27.

Pinker, S. 2011. *The Better Angels of Our Nature: The Decline of Violence in History and Its Causes*. Penguin UK.

Posen, B.R. 2014. *Restraint: A New Foundation for US Grand Strategy*. Cornell University Press.

Preble, C.A. 2009. *The Power Problem: How American Military Dominance Makes Us Less Safe, Less Prosperous, and Less Free*. Cornell University Press.

Preble, C.A., and Mueller, J., eds. 2014. *A Dangerous World? Threat Perception and US National Security*. Cato Institute.

Ray, J.L. 1989. The Abolition of Slavery and the End of International War. *International Organization*, 43(3), pp.405–439.

Reich, S., and Lebow, R.N. 2014. *Good-bye Hegemony! Power and Influence in the Global System*. Princeton University Press.

Rosecrance, R.N. 1986. *The Rise of the Trading State: Commerce and Conquest in the Modern World*. Basic Books.

Ross, R.S. 2011. Chinese Nationalism and Its Discontents. *The National Interest*, 116, pp.45–51.

Sageman, M. 2008. *Leaderless Jihad: Terror Networks in the Twenty-First Century*. University of Pennsylvania Press.

Sanger, D.E. 2012. *Confront and Conceal: Obama's Secret Wars and Surprising Use of American Power*. Crown.

Seitz, R. 2004. Weaker Than We Think. *American Conservative*, December 6.

Sheehan, J.J. 2008. Where Have All the Soldiers Gone. In Sheehan, J.J., *The Transformation of Modern Europe*. Houghton Mifflin.

Shirk, S.L. 2007. *China: Fragile Superpower: How China's Internal Politics Could Derail Its Peaceful Rise*. Oxford University Press.

Shlapak, D.A., and Johnson, M. 2016. *Reinforcing Deterrence on Nato's Eastern Flank:* Wargaming the Defense of the Baltics. RAND Corporation.

Stewart, M.G. 2014. Climate Change and National Security. In Preble, C.A., and Mueller, J.E., eds., *A Dangerous World? Threat Perception and US National Security*. Cato Institute.

Thrall, A.T., and Cramer, J.K., eds. 2009. *American Foreign Policy and the Politics of Fear: Threat Inflation since 9/11*. Routledge.

Thucydides. 2009 [431 BCE]. The History of the Peloponnesian War. Viewed September 11, 2017, from http://classics.mit.edu/Thucydides/pelopwar.html.

US Department of Defense. 2010, February. Quadrennial Defense Review Report.

US Department of Defense. 2012. Sustaining US Global Leadership: Priorities for 21st Century Defense. Viewed March 21, 2017, from www.defense.gov/news/Defense_ Strategic_Guidance.pdf.

Walt, S.M. 2011a. Explaining Obama's Asia Policy. Foreignpolicy.com, November 18.

Walt, S.M. 2011b. Is America Addicted to War? The Top 5 Reasons We Keep Getting Into Foolish Fights. foreignpolicy.com, April 4. Viewed March 23, 2017, from http://foreign-policy.com/2011/04/04/is-america-addicted-to-war/.

Zacher, M.W. 2001. The Territorial Integrity Norm: International Boundaries and the Use of Force. *International Organization*, 55(2), pp.215–250.

Zenko, M. 2013. Most. Dangerous. World. Ever. foreignpolicy.com, February 26. Viewed March 21, 2017, from http://foreignpolicy.com/2013/02/26/most-dangerous-world-ever/.

Zenko, M., and Cohen, M.A. 2012. Clear and Present Safety: The United States Is More Secure Than Washington Thinks. *Foreign Affairs*, March/April, pp.79–93.

11

UNRESTRAINED

The politics of America's primacist foreign policy

Benjamin H. Friedman and Harvey M. Sapolsky

Primacy, the grand strategy that says that US security requires a preponderance of military power to manage global security, dominates US security policy. Policymakers and those who seek that title treat its tenets as gospel and deviations, especially advocacy of the strategy of restraint, as near heresies (Friedman and Logan 2016). In this chapter, we argue that primacy has achieved this position not through intellectual merit or public opinion, but rather due to US power's effect on its domestic political interests.[1] Over its history, the United States' wealth, technological prowess, and martial capability increasingly fueled ambitious uses of the military. Tempered by human and financial costs that have grown lower with time, these ambitions created dependent interests that promote primacy to promote themselves.

The Cold War's end opened new parts of the world to US bases and military interventions. Without the Soviet Union's resistance, the risk of US military action triggering cataclysmic war plummeted. The United States embraced the role of the world's self-appointed, self-financed sheriff, spending on its military at a Cold War pace in the name of a concept of security expanded nearly into a synonym for national ambition. US policymakers mostly saw this job as a reward for victory, one they had engineered through their obvious mastery of world politics and their unyielding and admirable commitment to global leadership. They dismissed arguments, axiomatic to the generation that launched the Cold War, that the collapse of the enemy that originally justified US forces and defense commitments should occasion their withdrawal.

More than two decades later, US security policy is fundamentally unchanged. The failures in Iraq and Afghanistan limited the nation's willingness of pay heavy war costs without much curtailing its willingness to launch wars. Technological advances, especially in airpower, have made military action ever easier. Though policy mandarins in both parties decry what they describe as Trump's isolationism, his administration has not substantively changed the nation's security policies. He has cuddled autocratic allies and irritated European ones but abandoned none. US wars—in some cases consisting just of drone strikes—continue in Syria, Iraq, Yemen, Libya, Somalia, Afghanistan, and Pakistan, in several cases expanded under Trump, and get little sustained opposition, or even much interest, from Congress and the public.

This bipartisan consensus reflects primacy's ideological success in Washington and a nearly total reversal of the nation's approach to security (McDougall 1997). Early American leaders feared that aggressive foreign policies, especially permanent war and defense alliances that embroiled the United States in Europe's rivalries, would cause militarization and growth of federal and especially executive power. This corrosion of liberalism here, they claimed, would damage its global prospects by denying others an example to emulate. Early US political institutions restricting the growth of a military establishment, and the President's discretionary use of it largely reflected those fears.

Today Democratic and Republican leaders generally argue that aggressive US foreign policies, especially permanent alliances that embroil the United States in sustained foreign rivalries, are essential to global stability and trade, and ultimately to the spread of liberal government. Democrats are more dovish than Republicans, but are generally supportive of several ongoing wars, and quite hawkish by historical standards. Congressional leaders in both parties fight to maintain high levels of military spending, supporting a vast military establishment held in a state of readiness to fight various wars, while generally deferring to the President's assertions of war powers (Sapolsky, Gholz, and Talmadge 2017: 158–172).

This chapter explains this shift to primacy. We argue that, over time, with the growth of US power, the benefits of expansive military policies became more concentrated and their costs more distributed. That change enhanced support for primacy while undermining rival approaches. Before explaining this theory, we first address alternative explanations for primacy's success: that it came by out-arguing alternatives and that it reflects democratic will. The final section discusses how events and policy changes might corrode primacy's support. Unpopular wars and entitlement spending, in combination with resistance to tax increases, heighten the perceived cost of expansive foreign policies, which can encourage foreign policies more in line with majority interests. Policies like budgetary competition and war taxes can enhance those effects. Still, as long as the United States' geopolitical good fortune continues, primacy's support is unlikely to collapse. The costs of managing global security, wasteful and foolish though they may be, are just not high enough to force a change. The United States is likely to remain as global security boss because it is easy.

Primacy's primacy

A common lament among foreign policy commentators is that the United States lacks an effective strategy. But mostly these complaints are not about the failure to have a grand strategy, but rather the lack of discernable progress in America's current wars and conflicts. The complaints are really about tactics. Should we bomb more or less in Syria to defeat ISIS? Should we deploy more of our own ground forces there or make peace with the Syria regime? Should we add new allies, like Ukraine, to the NATO alliance or deploy more forces in the Baltics to deter Russia? Was the nuclear deal with Iran the right way to control its threat to other states? These questions are important but operational; they take strategic goals as a given and ask how to best achieve them (Friedman and Logan 2016).

The United States does have the makings of a grand strategy, one so widely shared in Washington that it is practically implicit (Posen 2014). That is primacy, sometimes called liberal hegemony, which reflects a peculiar interpretation of the nation's experience in the world wars and the Cold War (Kristol and Kagan 1996; Campbell and Flournoy 2007). This view sees far more danger in US foreign policy inaction than action. It holds that the United States erred by withdrawing from Europe after World War I and was too slow in returning to help combat Nazi Germany. It assumes that the United States was right not only to change tack after World War II by forming NATO to defend West Europe and integrate Germany into it, but to expand the Cold War into a global struggle for liberalism by freely dispersing forces and defense commitments. With the exception of Vietnam and some covert acts, this take sees nearly every aspect of Cold War policy as vital to success over communism. It says that Cold War policies are worth continuing even in the absence of a rival of similar potency. This interpretation of history obscures a less heroic take on the Cold War common to advocates of restraint: that the Soviet threat was overrated and its empire always liable to collapse under the weight of economic malpractice, and that much US military activism in the Cold War was a useless or tragic overreaction that is even less sensible when conducted today (Gholz, Press, and Sapolsky 1997).

Primacy's peculiar interpretation of history underlies its major premises. As discussed in this volume's introduction, these start with the claims that US global leadership plays a crucial role in maintaining global stability and trade and that such leadership is comprised largely of military commitments—allies, overseas bases, naval patrols, and threats or acts of war (Ikenberry 2011; Brooks and Wohlforth 2016). Other core tenets of primacy, at least in Washington, say that internal problems abroad—civil wars, governmental collapse, even autocracy—spread easily and are amenable to repair by US military efforts.[2] Because of the value it places on alliances and US military preeminence, even vis-à-vis allies, primacy's backers tend to worry more than others about US credibility and nuclear proliferation (Craig et al. 2013). These fears translate into high military spending and continuous uses of force (Friedman and Logan 2012; Monteiro 2011).

Advocates of primacy claim that its ideological dominance in Washington results from its success during the Cold War and that debate proved to leaders that changing course would be risky (Cohen 2012). One response is that the Cold War containment strategy of defensive alliances in Europe and Asia is not equivalent to primacy. Most of today's advocates of restraint would back something similar if an enemy like Nazi Germany or the early Cold War Soviet Union emerged (Layne 2007). To critics of primacy, like us, US security comes largely from geography and wealth and in spite of primacy, which courts avoidable trouble. Had the United States adopted something closer to restraint during the Cold War, especially its second half, it would have avoided much suffering, starting with Vietnam, and saved funds that would have produced more welfare in non-military uses.

Nor is there much evidence that primacy's prominence in Washington is the result of its success in debate. Were that so, its advocates would build their arguments on scholarship and contend with critics.[3] Instead, with few exceptions, they ignore even scholarship favorable to their cause and works supportive of restraint, except to attack "isolationist" straw men.

Democracy is another possible explanation for primacy's success. Because it gives people what they want, you might say, primacy must be the people's choice. But voters do not demand primacy. Studies of US public opinion show the US public to be persistently less enthusiastic about the burdens of global leadership and war than the leaders it elects and the policies they enact (Bouton and Page 2006; Drezner 2008). That gap is especially evident of late. According to a 2014 Chicago Council on Global Affairs study (Smeltz et al. 2014), the public is far less enthusiastic about taking an "active" role in global affairs and global leadership than elites.[4] That holds across partisan lines—elites identifying as Democratic, Republican, and Independent are all consistently more hawkish than the public in those groups. The public also lacks elites' support for using force to defend allies and long-term US military bases, and is less likely to agree that those garrisons produce stability. A more recent Chicago Council study likewise finds that normal voters are more skeptical than party elites about the value of defending allies and managing global politics (Smeltz et al. 2017).[5]

Recent wars show similar divides. In polls of the public and Council on Foreign Relations members taken in November 2009 (Pew Survey of Council on Foreign Relations Members 2009), just before President Obama announced the surge of US troops in Afghanistan, Pew found 32 percent of the US public wanted more US troops there, versus 50 percent of CFR members, while 40 percent of the public and 24 percent of CFR members preferred a decrease.[6] The 2014 Chicago Council study found even wider gaps between elites and the public on keeping troops in Afghanistan and substantial gaps with regard to deploying US peacekeepers to Syria (Smeltz et al. 2014). All this suggests that leaders push the public toward primacy, not the other way (Berinsky 2007).

Donald's Trump's election further undermines primacy's populist pretensions. Trump was never the non-interventionist some took him as, but his skepticism about allies showed that he was not a good primacist either (Friedman 2016). He seems to have exploited an opportunity long evident in polling of the right to tap its public's relatively low esteem for foreigners, free trade, and alliances as compared to GOP foreign policy elites. Their feckless denunciations of Trump further make the point.

Primacy and interest groups

The persistence of this gap between US foreign policy and public opinion seems to defy the logic of democracy until one accounts for salience (Bouton and Page 2006). Most people care a lot about only a few things, generally those that directly affect their personal well-being, while remaining rationally ignorant about other matters (Downs 1957). In our democracy, things that a lot of people care about a little do not count for much. With so many issues and so few candidates to choose from, elections are a poor tool for aggregating preferences. Unlike in markets, where even a low-price demand generates supply, there is no good reason to expect a democratic majority that wants something a little to get its way. Because more salient issues will drive ballot choices, representatives face little sanction for ignoring the public on low-tier issues. Primacy is democratic in the limited sense that voters tolerate it because the issues it impacts are rarely salient to them (Knecht 2010).

What people care deeply about—what issues are salient—varies according to their work, heritage, geography, and lots of other factors. These differences create special interests: minorities of people interested enough in a policy area to form organizations that advocate for particular policy outcomes (Wilson 1974). Special interests eager to broaden support for their cause are also likely to produce much of the information the public gets about these issues (Sapolsky 1990). But because the public is disinterested in most things, we should not expect it to be easily swayed by these efforts (Mueller 1973).

Motivated special interests and apathetic majorities are why "minorities rule" on most issues in democracies, as opposed to dictatorships, where a minority rules (Dahl 1956). In this mode of analysis, which can be called pluralism, what drives policy outcomes is how special interests are aligned and where they clash. An optimistic take on this competition begins with *Federalist 10*, where James Madison argues that faction checks faction in large republics, preventing narrow interests from dominating public policy. Madison's essay (1787) reflects a classically liberal idea—one manifest in the checks and balances in the Constitution—that competition among self-interested actors serves the general interest. A school of pluralism builds on this view to argue that interest groups spark the creation of rival interest groups, creating balanced policy competition and energizing a marketplace of ideas that vets alternative policies (Truman 1951; Lindblom 1965).

A more pessimistic view says that many societal goods will lack interest-group protection and, therefore, public policies that serve them. Mancur Olson argues that no one has an incentive to organize to provide public goods—those that no one can be excluded from enjoying and where one person's consumption of the good does not reduce availability of the good for consumption by others (Olson 1965). Those characteristics encourage people to free-ride—to try to enjoy the good without contributing to its provision. Small groups overcome the free-rider problem by enforcing participation and providing benefits to members for participation. Governments provide a facsimile of public goods, like defense, only by creating special interests that benefit from their provision, like military bureaucracies and contractors. These interests have no incentive to limit defense spending even if threats are slight, meaning the public good of the socially optimal amount of defense remains underprovided (Lee 1990).

To understand how interest groups drive policy outcomes, in our view, the question of whether a good is public is less useful than how public it is—who it affects enough to spur their political organization. Different policies create different economies of interests conducive to different patterns of conflict and collaboration. We rely here on James Q. Wilson's division of policy areas into four categories based on whether they create concentrated costs and benefits (Wilson 1974: 327–337).[7] Policies that produce concentrated benefits and distributed costs yield what Wilson calls "client politics," where agencies tend to serve special interests. He offers agricultural subsidies and veterans' benefits as examples and notes that volunteer groups, like the Veterans of Foreign Wars, tend to develop in these areas to mediate relations between the beneficiary group and agencies.[8] Policies that create concentrated costs and diffuse benefits Wilson calls entrepreneurial because they tend to reflect public-minded regulatory goals, like food safety. Policies that create concentrated costs and benefits create interest-group politics: well-organized conflict, for example between corporate groups and labor. Majoritarian politics result from distributed costs and benefits. This circumstance might seem to produce apathy, but Wilson has in mind broadly provided benefits like Social Security and Medicare, which he says quickly generate institutional support, producing regular benefit increases and broad public support.

Note that the accumulation of costs is no obstacle to maintaining these policies so long as those costs remain distributed. That means that society will persist in policies that it loses out on massively if they continue to serve concentrated interests and do not concentrate costs. A recent study suggests that large chunks of US public policy probably have this attribute (Gilens and Page 2014).

Policies are not permanently fixed in these categories (Wilson 1974). Ideological fervor can mellow with age and generational shift, slowly enfeebling a powerful interest, as is arguably occurring with the anti-Castro Cuba lobby in Florida. A concentrated interest enjoying client politics might promote a policy that concentrates costs, creating a powerful opposition and interest-group politics. An example is Boeing provoking the opposition of the pro-Israel lobby in its ultimately successful efforts to sell AWACS aircraft to Saudi Arabia (Laham 2002). Similar shifts can occur when economic trouble leads to lower budgets and heightened resource competition or when new interests emerge due to new concerns, like new environmental organization to oppose fracking or liquefied natural gas terminals. A tragedy or crisis can rapidly awaken public interest, shifting sleepy interest-group competition into a majoritarian public brawl (Schattschneider 1960). On the other hand, revenue increases and new technologies can reduce opposition to policies, quieting interest-group competition and generating client policies. Economic change might reduce industry's reliance on a regulated practice, shifting entrepreneurial politics to a majoritarian sort.

That said, policies may not shift as quickly as their support structure. That is because of information costs and ideology, which lets people develop a lot of policy preferences from a few beliefs (Converse 1964). A person's belief that they are conservative, for example, is a kind of crib sheet for policy preferences in specific areas, as provided by conservative intellectual elites. In that sense, ideologies are efficient for their users. That does not mean, however, that all the policy preferences that go along with ideologies serve the interests of their adherents as well as some alternative, only that those alternatives are far more costly to pursue (Zaller 1992: 18).

This take helps explain why ideologies are so hard to change, even among those that would benefit materially from the success of a different set of ideas. Established ideas about politics, including foreign policy, profit from what economists call increasing returns, where organization around the current set-up makes people dependent on it, and from the transaction cost of establishing and promoting new ideas (North 1990: 95). Those that benefit from the current approach oppose change and have good reason to convince others to take their side (North 1993; Moe 2005; Acemoglu and Robinson 2012).

Still, once a policy's cost becomes concentrated enough, those paying have incentive to inform themselves, even it means ideological reevaluation. That means that the shifts in political terrain discussed above should occur gradually as the new conditions are sustained. Faster change will occur if sudden shocks suddenly concentrate the costs of the status quo—like a war or crisis that endangers a lot of people. Those likely to be drafted into Vietnam, for example, had to worry about being killed there and became more informed about the war and more likely to oppose it (Erikson and Stoker 2011). The Vietnam War's galvanization of anti-war interests led to lasting restraints on presidential war powers, and other institutional changes that made wars harder to start (Sapolsky, Gholz, and Talmadge 2017: 76).

Change is easier when people adhere to belief systems out of social conformity without truly believing in them. If many people are hiding their beliefs, political events might create swift change where people cast off their public, phony ideologies (Kuran 1995). This is particularly likely in autocratic societies that limit dissent. But something similar is possible in democratic societies in areas, perhaps including national security, where pressures for conformity among elites can be considerable.

US security policy has, over time, moved from majoritarian toward client politics.[9] We attribute the shift to complementary results of US military power (Friedman and Logan 2012; Friedman 2014). First, it reduced the financial burden and human cost of expansive military policies—distributing the costs of defense policy. Second, power allowed the country to undertake expansionary policies that created various concentrated beneficiaries. In other words, the marshalling of military power, particularly for World War II and the Cold War, created a military establishment interested in maintaining a large military establishment and in promoting a foreign policy ideology that justifies it. That circumstance helps explain the paradox where increased US wealth and military power, indicators of security, produced an increased sense of insecurity (Thompson 1992). It also explains why the United States has long persisted in a grand strategy that is generally bad for

Americans, despite predictions that primacy's flaws would be its undoing—basically the country is so well off that primacy has not enough concentrated harm to produce change (Friedman and Logan 2012).

How US military power generates primacy

US military power comes from technological capability, wealth, and geographic protection, among other things. These factors protect the US public from the consequences of US security policy, including wars, and thus make them generally disinterested, even as they make war less burdensome and thus more attractive. Support for primacy stems from these dual effects of power.

To understand how that happens, consider a facet of the American "way of war"—the US tendency to replace soldiers on the battlefield with technology (Weigley 1977). In the United States, labor was historically scarce while capital—along with the technical proficiency to employ it in making ships and aircraft—was relatively abundant (Roland 1991). Geography meanwhile meant that US battlefields were generally remote and their stakes only vaguely related to Americans' security, making it difficult to demand that Americans sacrifice their lives in those fights (Sapolsky and Shapiro 1996). These factors gave the United States a unique ability and desire to limit the costs of war through technology, though it rarely worked as well as advertised (Cohen 1994).

The United States has increasingly succeeded in shielding its citizens from the cost of its military actions, even as they have grown more frequent and prone to failure in recent years. The Cold War, where a powerful rival restricted US military options by threatening escalation to potentially devastating war, obscures this general trend, which reflects wealth creation, military prowess, especially technological capability, and a dearth of powerful enemies. Primacy is not becoming more rewarding for Americans; but it has gotten cheaper for most Americans. That makes it less burdensome and more desirable, or, at least less worth making a fuss about. Meddling abroad rarely affects those at home enough for them to object.

Changes in warfare and US military superiority have dramatically reduced the human costs of wars for the US military. US combat deaths in World War II, which were far lower than those of European nations per capita, were eight times higher than in Vietnam and 83 times higher than the recent Iraq War's toll (DeBruyne 2017). Today, with precision airpower, including drone strikes, the United States can totally avoid military casualties in most of the seven nations where it now bombs at least on occasion and sometimes daily.

US wealth creation, meanwhile, spreads the economic burden of US security policies. For example, US defense spending authority was about $600 billion in the fiscal year 2016 versus $674 billion in 1952 (inflated to today's prices), the year of the highest annual total of the Cold War (US Department of Defense 2016: 140–146). In 1952, that spending amounted to nearly 14 percent of gross domestic product and 69 percent of federal spending, whereas today those percentages are 3.3 and 15.3, respectively (US Department of Defense 2016: 264–266). US spending on the Iraq War never took more than one percent of GDP (Belasco 2014). Drone strikes and air campaigns, like the 2011 bombing of Libya, which cost $1–2 billion, require small fractions of that (Baron 2011). Today's spending to generate military capability is similar to the past's, but the economic sacrifice required to produce it is far reduced.

Policy choices add to the insulation most Americans feel from war's costs. Taxes were generally used to fund past wars, whereas the wars in Iraq and Afghanistan commenced along with tax cuts (Daggett 2006). The current wars are funded with borrowing and today are exempt from the budget caps put in place by the 2011 Budget Control Act, which capped the rest of the defense budget (Belasco 2015). The end of the draft after Vietnam means that war's casualties now fall only on the volunteer military, buttressed by reservists and contractors. More than almost any people in history, Americans today can support wars without worrying about themselves or their children dying in them, which naturally reduces opposition (Horowitz and Levendusky 2011).

By making primacy less risky to Americans and less economically demanding, power discourages Americans from organizing against it. US defense policies require a smaller portion of taxes and less painful tradeoffs from other government programs. Interest groups associated with low taxes and groups defending domestic spending programs have less reason to object (Friedberg 2000). Because few Americans worry about going to war, peace groups wither, and debate about wars suffers.[10]

The allies of primacy

Primacy has many allies, some knowingly collaborating and some perhaps unknowingly (Betts 2005). Historically, the United States demobilized after major wars. But after the World War II, with the quick start of the Cold War and the belief that the nation had to meet aggression far from its shores, the nation stayed mobilized, keeping large standing forces, its network of overseas bases acquired during the war, many of the allies acquired for the war, and many of its investments in military-related technologies. A network of national laboratories and research centers exclusively focused on national security problems was created, including policy organizations to help the Defense Department and component agencies to analyze complex operational and strategic issues (Sapolsky 2003). Weapons contractors, normally intent on returning to civilian production after wars, remained busy with defense work, took over the task of developing equipment for the military from government arsenals and shipyards, and spread production facilities out across the states (Markusen 1991; Gholz and Sapolsky 2006).

With these developments, large groups of Americans had their fortunes tied to military spending and became personally interested in the nation's defense posture. These entities, often including the military services, still had competing interests. But especially after the cessation of the 1950s inter-service fights, they had more in common (Cote 1996).That is the basic idea of the military-industrial complex, or iron triangle, which notes a confluence of interest among military weapons buyers, their manufacturers, including the employees and others they contract with, and the Representatives elected in districts heavily invested in defense through bases or production (Lindsay 1990). Military spending created a host of smaller dependents and triangles of mutual support with research institutes, universities, and other recipients of obscure subsidies and so on (Sapolsky, Gholz, and Talmadge 2017: 158–172).

Representative's and Senators' role in defense matters is largely to maximize the portion of defense spending gained by their district. The average Representative who has no large interests in his or her district is unlikely to join a defense committee. Generally these committees, in both houses, take little interest in truly overseeing weapons programs, let alone wars and strategy, unless there is an unusually large audience to impress (Sapolsky, Gholz, and Talmadge 2017: 159–163).There is rarely reward in such oversight beyond the accolades of a few good government organizations. Members prefer to celebrate programs, pleasing some concentrated interest, rather than evaluate them, even when their own constituents are not involved. Attacking a program may upset a colleague whose support may be needed for an issue useful to the district. Representatives and Senators are intense but opaque expressions of parochialism—their local advocacy is often obscured in soaring rhetorical commitment to the national interest.

Presidents have the power to set an independent course on security matters and often do. But mostly they tend to reflect the wishes of defense interests because they have limited time and political capital and must pick their fights (Neustadt 1960). They are presented with a status quo conducive to these interests and, generally, no great political imperative to oppose them. Once they compromise, for example by signing a defense budget, they identify themselves with the standard set of primacy policies and tend to repeat the standard arguments for them.The power of the status quo is arguably evident in President Trump's failure to buck standard Republican foreign policy, despite his nonstandard rhetoric.[11]

Few of Washington's foreign policy experts have incentive to buck the primacy consensus (Friedman and Logan 2016). Jobs and grants and their prospects of getting more tie them to the existing power structure. Most are eager to serve presidents one way or another, and thus anticipate and defer to their views, creating a foreign policy establishment careful to avoid offending future patrons by disparaging primacy. Journalists meanwhile are kept from bucking the standard view by their dependence on government sources and the limits on their time, which generally keep them from doing the research needed to sustain contrarian views.

The low cost of America's recent wars in terms of their public burden quieted much of the leftist political agitation against a meddling foreign policy prominent throughout the Cold War. Some political liberal groups whose goals might seem to set them against primacy have in practice embraced it. An example is the arms control movement, especially its anti-nuclear component. Anti-proliferators' main goal is stopping the spread of nuclear weapons. They also may want the elimination of all nuclear weapons, including American nuclear weapons, but their first

concern is keeping the number of nuclear states frozen. That makes them support-
ers of America's alliances and nuclear guarantees. In the absence of such guarantees,
Germany, Japan, and South Korea, among others, might acquire nuclear weapons of
their own, fearing powerful neighbors who have them.

Ironically, America's nuclear guarantees are really America's conventional warfare
protections. With nuclear guarantees to allies, the fear is of being tested. Allies can
provoke nuclear armed neighbors over small issues, forcing the United States to
risk having to trade Washington for Berlin or San Francisco for Tokyo. America's
protection then must extend to lower levels of conflict so as to avoid escalation to
a nuclear confrontation (Snyder 1965). US troops are then seen as global salves to
temper the risks of nuclear blackmail, the possibility of nuclear war and the spread
of nuclear capabilities. Anti-proliferation advocacy is then really advocacy for primacy (Sapolsky 2016).

A similar story applies to human rights activists, at least the vocal subset that sees
the US military as a useful tool. On the strength of limited success in halting mass
slaughter, as in the Bosnian War, and the failure to prevent others, most prominently
in Rwanda, many liberal foreign policy thinkers and officials became advocates
of more aggressive US interventions to protect human rights in places like Libya,
Syria, and even Iraq, and of maintaining US forces in others, like Afghanistan (Osnos
2014). The problem is that US interventions in the name of one group's protection
often involve stoking or prolonging insurgencies and wars that ultimately endanger
many others (Betts 1994).

The allies are generally supportive of primacy. They are fairly shameless in
exploiting America's domestic political vulnerabilities through lobbying and funding friendly studies at think tanks (Lipton, Williams, and Confessore 2014). They
under-invest in their own defenses, wondering loudly to the press where America's
leadership is when trouble appears: knowing the American political party out of
power will be quick to repeat the accusation of leadership failure. The allies never
challenge the primacists' notion that they cannot fend for themselves militarily. The
South Koreans, for example, continue to delay the date, now years postponed, at
which they will be in command of their own troops in event of an attack by the
North. And the Europeans happily host American troops and provide bases and the
use of airspace and port facilities for US forces, long after the end of the Cold War
and even longer since they regained the resources to fully fund their own militaries.

America's political parties both have an interest in reflecting the views of the
domestic consensus supporting primacy. The Republicans, long ago champions of
an isolationist foreign policy, converted to internationalism in the aftermath of
World War II, allowing for a bipartisan stance against the Soviet Union's push into
Eastern Europe and support of the Communist revolution in China. One reason
for the shift was that the cost of the Cold War came to seem more manageable as
the economy grew and Keynesian ideas took root (Gaddis 2005). Wealth lubri-
cated friction between fiscal conservatives, who once might have agitated about
the tax burden of defense, and Cold War hawks (Friedberg 2000). There was also
an electoral reason for this shift: when the Democrats began to turn dovish during

the Vietnam War, Republicans became correspondingly more hawkish and reaped electoral reward, at least according to the conventional wisdom that convinced many. The Iraq War damaged this perception, but the habit had grown so strong among Republicans that few doves have emerged.

Although public opinion suggests an opening for Democrats, especially in a crowded presidential primary field, to stake out an anti-war stance, prominent Democrats remain only occasional and tentative doves. Peace groups find an audience when wars go sour, but opposition to some wars has not led any major party figures to question alliances or call for a re-evaluation of US grand strategy to emphasize peace as a major campaign issue. President Obama moved tentatively towards elements of restraint in office, but never questioned an alliance and left the nation at war in seven nations. Party leaders like Hillary Clinton and Charles Schumer reliably align with neoconservatives, while more radical figures, like Senators Elizabeth Warren and Bernie Sanders (technically an Independent) have preferred to emphasize other issues. With war costs generally low, the Democratic base, despite its relatively dovish views, has more pressing concerns and nowhere better to turn.

Primacy is a big tent

These disparate entities supportive of relatively hawkish parties and high military spending are not much of a complex. Politicians compete bitterly, as do agency heads, at times. Defense contractors compete in spite of industry associations. The military services compete in certain ways despite being under joint management and their zealous devotion to "jointness" in operations (Sapolsky, Gholz, and Talmadge 2017: 36–38). But US military power limits these fissures. National wealth obviates the sharper choices austerity encourages (Friedman 2011). The absence of a large enemy demanding the concentration of resources has a similar effect (Posen 1984). The result is a security policy that leaves room for a lot of interests to get their wishes, through a log-roll of objectives collectively so broad that they amount to a kind of disparate global management (Snyder 1991).

In Washington, primacy serves as less a guide to particular objectives than a justification for limiting choices among them. US policymakers strain for compromise because they divide power in a system that is open to the influence of diverse interest groups (Schilling 1962). This division of power militates against strategic coherence (Jervis 1998). By voting for budgets, as they generally must, politicians essentially endorse the whole package, including items of no direct importance to them. In explaining their votes, procedural rationales that admit of the need for compromise among agendas do not suffice, especially for presidents. Those arguments offend the notion that even leaders elected by states or districts should serve the national interest, especially in the security realm.

Grand strategies, or the simpler versions of them politicians express, can serve that rationalization function. Primacy is especially useful in this regard because it discriminates so little. By justifying activist US military policies virtually anywhere, primacy accommodates a host of agendas. These interests would compete more if the United States had less power. Primacy results from the luxury to avoid choices among programs, dangers, and regions. Really it is a pretense of strategy, helping avoid the choices that true strategy entails.

There is a feedback mechanism here (Pierson 2000). As a result of being unrestrained and rich, the United States, in the course of its history, became more active abroad. To promote activist policies and justify their cost, leaders hyped their benefits, renovating ideas about foreign policy by adopting elements of primacy. Over time, others, including new leaders, embraced these ideological arguments without recognizing their functional origins. Left unchallenged, these beliefs have become a kind of social convention, especially among informed elites, because people either are convinced or want to seem convinced (Sunstein 2004: 78–99). That problem is particularly acute in Washington's security debates, where ambition checks dissent.

On the other side, as a future secretary of defense once wrote, there is no other side (Aspin 1980). A few interest groups, favoring low taxes or good government work to counterbalance the power of the defense establishment, but not very many, and none is very powerful.[12] Taxpayers all have an interest in these groups' goals, but their individual interest—a few tax dollars—is too small to spur action on materialistic grounds; the collective action problem prevents people from even learning about these issues, let alone aiding these particular groups. So only a passionate few who care deeply about government accounting or taxes support these organizations.

They are allied with a larger group of people motivated to oppose the defense industry for non-material reasons, namely a dislike for militaristic policies. These are Americans who abhor arms races, weapons, or wars for moral reasons, or believe the United States to be driven by industrial interests. But arms control and peace groups face collective action problems maybe more daunting than tax warriors and good government types. Their goals are likely to be more diffuse and abstract. President Eisenhower was worried about this asymmetric kind of debate when he warned of the potential "unwarranted influence" of the military-industrial complex in his famous Farewell Address (Ledbetter 2011). The military-industrial complex may create a tendency for profligate defense spending without being a conspiracy executing a nefarious plan. It is just the result of normal interest-group politics, American citizens expressing their political preferences, a fundamental tenet of our democracy.

Sources of restraint

Despite the support for primacy, all is not lost for restraint. Various routes might lead to the restoration of interest groups willing to take on primacy or the weakening of primacy's support base. Unfortunately many of these paths require bad events, like another unpopular war or recession.

Soldiers are often accused of fighting the last war, but it is the public and politicians who remember the last foreign misadventure best and who use its experience to inhibit policy. Casualties tend to make the potential cost of wars more salient, discourage military deployments even short of war, and pressure Congress to restrain presidential war powers, sometimes just in anticipation of political trouble (Howell and Pevehouse 2011). They generate anti-war lobbying groups and sentiment that lasts, creating incentives for leaders to oppose the next war. They create more savvy and skeptical journalism (Western 2005). Vietnam lingered over US policy for decades whenever the use of ground forces was under consideration (Mueller 1973). Iraq and Afghanistan serve a similar but less powerful purpose today, by making it harder for leaders to take risks at war, but not much harder to launch wars via drone strikes or special operations forces' activities. These wars were not tragic enough force a fundamental reconsideration of US strategy, but they have produced a generation of new voters considerably more restrained in their views than their elders (Thrall and Goepner 2015).

Because the military bears the human cost of war, it has a unique ability to constrain it. Military leaders worry that new commitments will strand them in some distant place, degrading the readiness of the force to meet the peer competitor just over the horizon by keeping it tied down in small missions (Recchia 2015). They want the participation of allies, particularly in the peacekeeping and nation-building phases following initial entry and any intense combat. While limited by law and custom from lobbying against wars, military leaders can tip their hand in testimony sure to make headlines, in back-channel complaints to lawmakers, and by creating rules of deployment or unofficial doctrines that make it tougher for civilians to start wars, like the Weinberger-Powell doctrine (Sapolsky, Gholz, and Talmadge 2017: 45). In dragging its heels in this way, the military can tap into a great well of public support.

The public is sympathetic to the military's desire for the participation of allies, as such involvement provides reassurance of the wisdom of American action (Bouton and Page 2006). This need for reassurance pushes intervention advocates to seek United Nations or NATO approval for the intervention, as most allies require such approval to gain their own public support. Delays and complications in getting international organizations' approval then become part of the intervention process, constraining action.

The military might also constrain primacy by thinking more productively about the demands put on the force. Today the Pentagon complains loudly about the strains of deployments and wars on its readiness to fight. This is a reasonable, if frequently exaggerated, complaint that is undermined by a refusal to reallocate funds to improve readiness rather than use readiness problems as a ploy to get higher total spending. Pentagon leaders could request that Congress reprogram funds to operations and maintenance for training and material vital to readiness. But like Congress, the Pentagon now seems to prefer being less ready and asking for more funding to trying this solution. A more honest approach to readiness would lead to an assault on primacy, given its exaggerated notion of all the missions for which units might need to be ready. A less taxing strategy would produce more readiness at less cost. If demands grow and the military's size does not keep pace, which seems a strong possibility in the next several years, the strains on the force might lead some service leaders and even Congressional allies to push for reprioritization of resources under a new strategy.

An effort to stir inter-service competition would encourage strategic review. Jointness encourages the services to avoid targeting each other's budgets and instead to grow together. That produces log-rolls conducive to primacy. Strategies promoted by the services individually would serve their particular skills and platforms and presumably downgrade the importance of other services. Those sorts of fights would empower savvy decision-makers looking to find cheaper doctrines and hidden tradeoffs (Sapolsky 1996). The Navy in particular is well suited to advocate an offshore balancing strategy where war is made from the sea. Note also that budget pressure and caps that group together multiple departments can heighten interagency competition, in turn heightening debate about what the best use of tax dollars is to produce welfare—regulation, defense, deficit reduction, and so on.

A draft could cut against primacy by making more people care about military deployments. On the other hand, by flooding the military with cheap labor, a draft might create shortfalls in personnel and facilitate a more expansive US security policy. It would also reduce the military incentive to innovate to save on personnel. And by taking people out of the labor market and putting them on the public payroll, it would impose terrific costs on the government while robbing it of tax revenue. That and the effect on people's freedom is why we oppose a draft, even though it would probably make wars somewhat harder to start.

Potential enemies are always a constraint. The Soviet Union was a long-lived check on US foreign policy ambitions. Today, the only real contender for that job is China (Russia's belligerence in Ukraine and election meddling notwithstanding, its long-term prospects are poor). But various obstacles to its continued growth and capacity to generate military power, along with the Pacific Ocean, limit the extent to which China is likely to take on a global balancing role (Brooks and Wohlforth 2016: 14–47). In the coming decades, US military hegemony seems likely to last. Note, however, that primacy is limited by the spread of firepower, missile, and surveillance capability to smaller states. The United States already would have to pay a steep cost for close-in fights with those states, let alone occupational wars (Posen 2003). A war with Iran could prove costly enough, particularly if it involved US ground forces, to produce lasting aversion to primacy or at least to the wars against proliferation that it encourages. Enemies will remain a check on primacy's ambitions, but are an unlikely source of strategic reappraisal.

Financing remains an obstacle to primacy. Economic troubles led to the 2011 Budget Control Act, which imposed initial defense cuts of almost 10 percent. Had the Pentagon adhered to the cap, it might have elected to find the savings by pushing for more modest strategy (Friedman 2011). Indeed, over the following several years, one of the many ways Pentagon officials complained about austerity was to say that they could not execute the nation's defense strategy without more funds. (Friedman 2015). As with readiness complaints, however, this was a way to demand more money, which the Pentagon has gotten even since the imposition of caps, as Congress has raised each annual cap and provided the Pentagon with tens of billions more, annually, through the uncapped Overseas Contingency Operations "war account" (Belasco 2015; Heeley and Wheeler 2016). These steps released pressure on the Pentagon to adopt a more affordable budget, allowing it to muddle through with minor trims and great complaint. Although both the Trump administration's proposed defense budget for 2018 and existing Congressional alternatives would vastly exceed the present cap, triggering sequestration if enacted, complying with it, especially after another Congress plus up, as is likely, will not cause strategic bankruptcy.

The continued growth of the federal debt does offer some rather unfortunate hope for restraint (Williams 2011). The Congressional Budget Office estimates that publicly held debt exceeds $14 trillion, or 77 percent of gross domestic project, and that those numbers will grow to $23 trillion and 89 percent in the next decade (Congressional Budget Office 2017). Unless that growth slows, pressure to cap spending or raise taxes will remain, possibly requiring the extension of the Budget Control Act into the mid-2020s. Republicans, if recent history is a guide, will refuse to raise taxes, and Democrats will protect most entitlement programs from cuts (See Figure 11.1). That means the pressure for savings will remain on discretionary spending, of which defense is a majority. The savings offered by a strategy of restraint might make it attractive to more budget hawks, given these pressures.

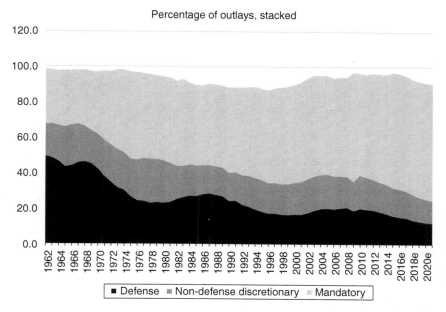

FIGURE 11.1 US government outlays by category (note that the missing area up to 100 percent is interest payments)

Source: Office of Management and Budget 2017, chart 8.3, https://obamawhitehouse. archives.gov/omb/budget/Historicals

Budget policies might also be imposed to encourage restraint, or least to discourage wars, in several ways. First, Congress could extend the budget caps to cover "overseas contingency operations," so these funds cannot be used as a slush fund to bail out defense accounts. Second, Congress could impose a "pay for the wars" bill requiring war funds be deficit-neutral—paid for by either a tax or an offsetting spending cut. Even given the small costs of the current wars, either funding source would create a rival interest—another program or anti-tax groups—that would lose out from the war, at least creating a more fulsome debate about its merits. Third, Congress could lower defense caps, ideally while stopping the Overseas Contingency Operations (OCO) scam, to force harder choices on the Pentagon and encourage a strategic review that prioritizes goals that avoid competition.

In the longer term, health care and entitlements are the main threat to primacy (Sapolsky 2010). There is always a degree of competition between federal spending priorities, and the growth in entitlement's share has long been a limit on military spending. The portions of national wealth spent on health and defense have roughly flipped spots over the last fifty years, with health costs now around 20 percent of GDP (See Figure 11.2). One way or another, that squeezes other priorities, including defense. Given the political salience of the transfer payments, which make up a substantial chunk of health care spending, they are unlikely to

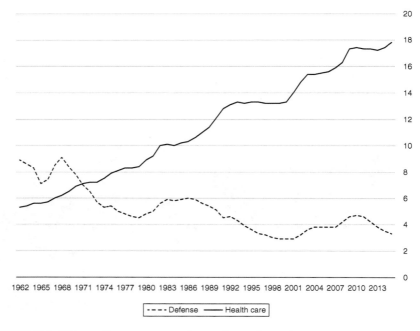

FIGURE 11.2 US spending as percent of gross domestic product

Source: Congressional Budget Office 2017

give way to fund defense or anything else (Wilson 1974). The question is whether economic growth and debt can cover their cost, without requiring big discretionary spending cuts. The alternative, however unappealing, could be a long-term boon for restraint.

Conclusion: prospects for balance

The concentration of US power abroad has concentrated it at home. Military power has made the United States more able to go forth and do things with its military. That is an enviable circumstance that has also skewed debate about security and led to the crowning of a deeply flawed idea of what security requires. Wealth and safety limited exposure to international danger that might have aided political interests that prefer military restraint. The military actions that power allowed, meanwhile, spawned political interests that prefer ambitious military policies abroad. Those interests make arguments to convince everyone else that those policies serve the national interest. They do not sing together exactly, but their collective voices produce a powerful chorus. As in other less prominent areas of US foreign policy, a motivated minority, a sort of oligarchy or confederacy of interested parties, rules over a rationally apathetic minority.

Democracy functions better, producing better outcomes, or at least more informative debate, when rival interests engage in fair fights. A variety of mechanisms, some bad, and some public policies might encourage more rivalry in US defense. The bad includes bad wars, more powerful enemies, economic downturn, more debt, and entitlement and health costs squeezing defense spending. The public policies include military reforms as self-protection, a war tax or offset requirement, more effective spending caps, and heightened inter-service or inter-agency competition. All these developments would produce greater opposition to primacy. Likewise, bad public memories of the wars in Iraq and Afghanistan will tie future policymakers' hands somewhat in fighting the wars that primacy encourages.

Besides that, a revival of the anti-militarist brand of liberal ideology could help. That ideology serves to assemble and frame the costs of primacy—in terms of liberties, economic health, and security—in ways that might otherwise escape people's minds. That is not likely to produce immediate results, but in the long term might shift the terms of debate.

Despite these threats, primacy's elite support is not obviously eroding. And the wealth creation, safety, and military superiority that let the public indulge primacy's costs are likely to continue, while bad memories of recent wars fade. The most likely future seems one where the gap between the pro-primacy elite making policy and the more restrained public grows, while the public remains mostly indifferent given low costs, but liable to turn against wars. Happily, the sort of calamity that might produce a sea change is unlikely. There is a lot of ruin in our nation, and it may take a good bit more of it before our leaders give up on the idea that they can run the world.

Notes

1 Primacy is sometimes called liberal hegemony (Posen 2014) or "deep engagement" (Brooks, Ikenberry, and Wohlforth 2012). These advocates of "deep engagement" now differentiate it from the more hawkish Beltway version, which they call "deep engagement plus" (Brooks and Wohlforth 2016). Our focus here is on that Washington take on primacy.
2 It is true that elite support for regime change ebbed considerably due to US troubles in Iraq and Afghanistan (Mueller 2005), but the general idea that foreign internal trouble is amenable to forceful correction remains strong, at least in comparison to the US public's view and that of academics (Friedman and Logan 2016).
3 We will not engage primacy's theoretical flaws here, as they are covered in various other works (Gholz, Press, and Sapolsky 1997; Craig et. al. 2013; Gholz 2014; Posen 2014, Friedman and Logan 2016), as well as elsewhere in this book.
4 The elites are "leaders" the pollsters identified and polled in various fields. The authors describe these results as follows:

> Large majorities of leaders and the public say that strong US leadership in the world is at least somewhat desirable. But there is a great difference between leaders and the public in degree or emphasis. At least six in ten leaders (57% of Independent leaders, 70% of Democratic leaders, and 90% of Republican leaders) say it is "very desirable" for the United States to exert strong leadership in world affairs, compared to just over one-third of the public (37%). Similarly, a much larger portion of leaders (94% Republicans, 97% Democrats, and 92% Independents) than of the public (58%) thinks it will be best for the future of the country if the United States takes an active part in world affairs.

5 The authors do not dwell on this gap, preferring to portray the results as a public repudiation of Trump.
6 The poll does show, on the other hand, a public more willing than CFR members to bomb Iran should it acquire nuclear weapons.
7 Wilson developed his classification from Theodore Lowi's (Lowi 1964).
8 The category labels we use here come from Wilson's later work on bureaucracy, where he slightly refined these concepts (Wilson 1989: 79–83).
9 A recent book by Rebecca Thorpe explains the nation's adoption of a large, permanent military establishment using similar analysis, but argues that the benefits have been widely distributed (Thorpe 2014: 4–6).
10 This absence of economic obstacles to primacy essentially reverses some of the processes that some scholars see as a cause of "capitalist peace" (Gartzke 2007; McDonald 2007).
11 It is unclear to what extent the President really wants to buck that standard (Friedman 2016).
12 This section roughly follows Sapolsky, Gholz, and Talmadge (2017: 165).

References

Acemoglu, D., and Robinson, J.A. 2012. *Why Nations Fail: The Origins of Power, Prosperity, and Poverty*. Crown Business.
Aspin, L. 1980. Foreword. In Koistinen, P., *The Military Industrial Complex: A Historical Perspective*. Praeger.
Baron, K. 2011. For the US, War against Qaddafi Cost Relatively Little: $1.1 Billion. *The Atlantic*, October 21, www.theatlantic.com/international/archive/2011/10/for-the-us-war-against-qaddafi-cost-relatively-little-11-billion/247133/, accessed July 25, 2017.

Belasco, A. 2014. The Cost of Iraq, Afghanistan, and Other Global War on Terror Operations Since 9/11. Library of Congress Congressional Research Service.

Belasco, A. 2015. Defense Spending and the Budget Control Act Limits. Library of Congress Congressional Research Service.

Berinsky, A.J. 2007. Assuming the Costs of War: Events, Elites, and American Public Support for Military Conflict. *Journal of Politics*, 69(4), pp.975–997.

Betts, R.K. 1994. The Delusion of Impartial Intervention. *Foreign Affairs*, 73(6), pp.20–33.

Betts, Richard K. 2005. The Political Support System for American Primacy. *International Affairs*, 81(1), pp.1–14.

Bouton, B.I., and Page, M.M. 2006. *The Foreign Policy Disconnect: What Americans Want from Our Leaders but Don't Get*. University of Chicago.

Brooks, S., and Wohlforth, W. 2016. *America Abroad: The United States' Global Role in the 21st Century*. Oxford University Press.

Brooks, S., Ikenberry, G.J, and Wohlforth, W. 2012. Don't Come Home, America: The Case against Retrenchment. *International Security*, 37(3), pp.7–51.

Campbell, K.M., and Flournoy, M.A. 2007. *The Inheritance and the Way Forward*. Center for a New American Security.

Cohen, E.A. 1994. The Mystique of US Air Power. *Foreign Affairs*, January/February, pp.109–124.

Cohen, M.A. 2012. Can't We All Just Not Get Along? Why the Push for Bipartisan Consensus in Foreign Policy is a Dumb Idea. *Foreign Policy*, http://foreignpolicy.com/2012/06/22/cant-we-all-just-not-get-along-2/, accessed July 26, 2017.

Congressional Budget Office. 2017. The 2017 Long-Term Budget Outlook. www.cbo.gov/system/files/115th-congress-2017-2018/reports/52480-ltbo.pdf, accessed July 25, 2017.

Converse, P.E. 1964. The Nature of Belief Systems in Mass Publics. In Apter, D.E., ed., *Ideology and Discontent*. Free Press of Glencoe.

Cote, O.R. 1996. *The Politics of Innovative Military Doctrine: The US Navy and Fleet Ballistic Missiles*. Doctoral dissertation, Massachusetts Institute of Technology.

Craig, C., Friedman, B.H., Green, B.R., Logan, J., Brooks, S.G., Ikenberry, G.J., and Wohlforth, W.C. 2013. Debating American Engagement: the Future of US Grand Strategy. *International Security*, 38(2), pp.181–199.

Daggett, S. 2006. Military Operations: Precedents for Funding Contingency Operations in Regular or in Supplemental Appropriations Bills. Library of Congress Congressional Research Service.

Dahl, R.A. 1956. *A Preface to Democratic Theory*. University of Chicago.

DeBruyne, N.F. 2017. American War and Military Operations Casualties: Lists and Statistics. Library of Congress Congressional Research Service, https://fas.org/sgp/crs/natsec/RL32492.pdf, accessed July 25, 2017.

Downs, A. 1957. *An Economic Theory of Democracy*. Harper and Row.

Drezner, D.W. 2008. The Realist Tradition in American Public Opinion. *Perspectives on Politics*, 6(1), pp.51–70.

Erikson, R.S., and Stoker, L. 2011. Caught in the Draft: The Effects of Vietnam Draft Lottery Status on Political Attitudes. *American Political Science Review*, 105(2), pp.221–237.

Friedberg, A.L. 2000. *In the Shadow of the Garrison State: America's Anti-Statism and Its Cold War Grand Strategy*. Princeton University Press.

Friedman, B.H. 2011. How Cutting Pentagon Spending Will Fix US Defense Strategy. *Foreign Affairs*, November/December.

Friedman, B.H. 2014. Alarums and Excursions: Explaining Threat Inflation in US Foreign Policy. In Preble, C., and Mueller, J., eds., *A Dangerous World? Threat Perception in US National Security*. The Cato Institute.

Friedman, B.H. 2015. The Pentagon's Bloat. *Boston Globe*, February 17.

Friedman, B.H. 2016. The Trump Administration Will Be Hawkish. *War on the Rocks*, November 18, https://warontherocks.com/2016/11/the-trump-administration-will-be-hawkish/, accessed July 25, 2017.

Friedman, B.H., and Logan, J. 2012. Why the US Military Budget is "Foolish and Sustainable." *Orbis*, 56(2), pp.177–191.

Friedman, B.H., and Logan, J. 2016. Why Washington Doesn't Debate Grand Strategy. *Strategic Studies Quarterly*, 10(4), pp.14–45.

Gaddis, J.L. 2005. *Strategies of Containment: A Critical Appraisal of American National Security Policy during the Cold War*. Oxford University Press.

Gartzke, E. 2007. The Capitalist Peace. *American Journal of Political Science*, 51(1), pp.166–191.

Gholz, E. 2014. Assessing the "Threat" of International Tension to the US Economy. In Preble, C., and Mueller J., eds., *A Dangerous World? Threat Perception and US National Security*. The Cato Institute.

Gholz, E., and Sapolsky, H.M. 2006. Restructuring the US Defense Industry. *International Security*, 24(3), pp.5–51.

Gholz, E., Press, D.G., and Sapolsky, H.M. 1997. Come Home, America: The Strategy of Restraint in the Face of Temptation. *International Security*, 21(4), pp.5–48.

Gilens, M., and Page, B.I. 2014. Testing Theories of American Politics: Elites, Interest Groups, and Average Citizens. *Perspectives on Politics*, 12(3), pp.564–581.

Heeley, L., and Wheeler, A. 2016. Defense Divided: Overcoming the Challenges of Overseas Contingency Operations. Stimson Center, www.stimson.org/sites/default/files/file-attachments/DefenseDivided_OCO.pdf, accessed July 26, 2017.

Horowitz, M.C., and Levendusky, M.S. 2011. Drafting Support for War: Conscription and Mass Support for Warfare. *Journal of Politics*, 73(2), pp.524–534.

Howell, W.G., and Pevehouse, J.C. 2011. *While Dangers Gather: Congressional Checks on Presidential War Powers*. Princeton University Press.

Ikenberry, G.J. 2011. *Liberal Leviathan: The Origins, Crisis, and Transformation of the American World Order*. Princeton University Press.

Jervis, R. 1998. U.S Grand Strategy: Mission Impossible. *Naval War College Review*, 51(3), pp.22–36.

Knecht, T. 2010. *Paying Attention to Foreign Affairs: How Public Opinion Affects Presidential Decision-Making*. Pennsylvania State University Press.

Kristol, W., and Kagan, R. 1996. Toward a Neo-Reaganite Foreign Policy. *Foreign Affairs* 75(4), pp.18–32.

Kuran, T. 1995. *Private Truth, Public Lies: The Social Consequences of Preference Falsification*. Harvard University Press.

Laham, N. 2002. *Selling AWACS to Saudi Arabia: The Reagan Administration and the Balancing of America's Competing Interests in the Middle East*. Praeger.

Layne, C. 2007. *The Peace of Illusions: American Grand Strategy from 1940 to the Present*. Cornell University Press.

Ledbetter, J. 2011. *Unwarranted Influence: Dwight D. Eisenhower and the Military-Industrial Complex*. Yale University Press.

Lee, D.R. 1990. Public Goods, Politics, and Two Cheers for the Military Industrial Complex. In Higgs, R., ed., *Arms, Politics, and the Economy: Historical and Contemporary Perspectives*. Holmes and Meier.

Lindblom, C.E. 1965. *The Intelligence of Democracy: Decision-Making through Mutual Adjustment*. Free Press.

Lindsay, J.M. 1990. Parochialism, Policy, and Constituency Constraints: Congressional Voting on Strategic Weapons Systems. *American Journal of Political Science*, 34(4), pp.936–960.

Lipton, E., Williams, B., and Confessore, N. 2014. Foreign Powers Buy Influence at Think Tanks. *New York Times*, September 6.

Lowi, T.J. 1964. American Business, Public Policy, Case-Studies, and Political Theory. *World Politics*, 16(4), pp.677–715.

Madison, J. 1787. Federalist 10: The Same Subject Continued: The Union as a Safeguard against Domestic Faction and Insurrection. *New York Packet*, http://thomas.loc.gov/home/histdox/fed_10.html, accessed August 3, 2017.

Markusen, A.R. 1991. *The Rise of the Gunbelt: The Military Remapping of Industrial America.* Oxford University Press.

McDonald, P.J. 2007. The Purse Strings of Peace. *American Journal of Political Science*, 51(3), pp.569–582.

McDougall, W.A. 1997. *Promised Land, Crusader State: The American Encounter with the World since 1776.* Houghton Mifflin Harcourt.

Moe, T.M. 2005. Power and Political Institutions. *Perspectives on Politics*, 3(2), pp.215–233.

Monteiro, N.P. 2011. Unrest Assured: Why Unipolarity Is Not Peaceful. *International Security*, 36(3), pp.9–40.

Mueller, J.E. 1973. *War, Presidents, and Public Opinion.* Wiley & Sons.

Mueller, John. 2005. The Iraq Syndrome. *Foreign Affairs*, 84(6), pp.44–54.

Neustadt, R.E. 1960. *Presidential Power: The Politics of Leadership.* Wiley & Sons.

North, D.C. 1990. *Institutions, Institutional Change and Economic Performance.* Cambridge University Press.

North, D.C. 1993. Economic Performance through Time. Nobel Prize Lecture, December 9.

Olson, M. 1965. *The Logic of Collective Action: Public Goods and the Theory of Groups.* Harvard University Press.

Osnos, E. 2014. In the Land of the Possible. *The New Yorker*, December 15, pp.90–107.

Pew Survey of Council on Foreign Relations Members. 2009, October 2–November 16. Question: "Over the next year, do you think the number of US troops in Afghanistan should be—increased, decreased, or kept as it is now?" www.people-press.org/files/legacy-pdf/569.pdf, accessed August 3, 2017.

Pierson, P. 2000. Increasing Returns, Path Dependence, and the Study of Politics. *The American Political Science Review*, 94(2), pp.251–267.

Posen, B.R. 1984. *The Sources of Military Doctrine: France, Britain, and Germany between the World Wars.* Cornell University Press.

Posen, B.R. 2003. Command of the Commons: the Military Foundation of U.S Hegemony. *International Security*, 28(1), pp.5–46.

Posen, B.R. 2014. *Restraint: A New Foundation for US Grand Strategy.* Cornell University Press.

Recchia, S. 2015. *Reassuring Reluctant Warriors: US Civil Military Relations and Multilateral Interventions.* Cornell University Press.

Roland, A. 1991. Technology, Ground Warfare, and Strategy: The Paradox of American Experience. *The Journal of Military History*, 55(4), pp.447–465.

Sapolsky, H.M. 1990. The Politics of Risk. *Daedalus*, 11(4), pp.83–96.

Sapolsky, H.M. 1996. The Interservice Competition Solution. *Breakthroughs*, 5(1), pp.1–3.

Sapolsky, H.M. 2003. Inventing Systems Integration. In Prencipe, A., Davies, A., and Hobday, M., eds., *The Business of Systems Integration.* Oxford University Press.

Sapolsky, H.M. 2010. The Enemy the Pentagon Should Fear the Most. *National Defense*, March 1.

Sapolsky, H.M. 2016. Getting Past Nonproliferation. In Sokolski, H., *Should We Let the Bomb Spread?* Army War College.

Sapolsky, H.M., and Shapiro, J. 1996. Casualties, Technology, and America's Future Wars. *Parameters*, 26(2), pp.119–126.

Sapolsky, H.M., Gholz E., and Talmadge, C. 2017. *US Defense Politics: The Origins of Security Policy*, 3rd ed. Taylor & Francis.

Schattschneider, E.E. 1960. *The Semisovereign People: A Realist's View of Democracy in America*. Holt, Rinehart and Winston.

Schilling, W. 1962. The Politics of National Defense: Fiscal 1950. In Schilling, W., Hammond, P.Y., and Snyder, G.H., eds., *Strategy, Politics, and Defense: Budgets*. Columbia University Press.

Smeltz D., Busby, J., Holyk, G., Kafura, C., Monten, J., and Tama, J. 2014. United in Goals, Divided on Means: Opinion Leaders Survey Results and Partisan Breakdowns from the 2014 Chicago Survey of American Opinion on US Foreign Policy. Chicago Council on Global Affairs, www.thechicagocouncil.org/sites/default/files/2014%20Chicago%20Council%20Opinion%20Leaders%20Survey%20Report_FINAL.pdf, accessed August 2, 2017.

Smeltz, D., Friedhoff, K., Kafura, C., Busby, J., et al. 2017. The Foreign Policy Establishment or Donald Trump: Which Better Reflects American Opinion? Chicago Council on Global Affairs, www.thechicagocouncil.org/publication/foreign-policy-establishment-or-donald-trump-which-better-reflects-american-opinion, accessed August 2, 2017.

Snyder, G.H. 1965. The Balance of Power and the Balance of Terror. In Seabury, P., ed., *The Balance of Power*. Chandler, pp.184–201.

Snyder, J. 1991. *Myths of Empire: Domestic Politics and International Ambition*. Cornell University Press.

Sunstein, C. 2004. *Risk and Reason: Safety, Law, and the Environment*. Cambridge University Press.

Thompson, J.A. 1992. The Exaggeration of American Vulnerability: the Anatomy of a Tradition. *Diplomatic History*, 16(1), pp.23–43.

Thorpe, R.U. 2014. *The American Warfare State: The Domestic Politics of Military Spending*. University of Chicago.

Thrall, T., and Goepner, E. 2015. *Millennials and US Foreign Policy: the Next Generations's Attitudes toward Foreign Policy and War (and Why They Matter)*. Cato Institute White Paper.

Truman, D.B. 1951. *The Governmental Process: Political Interests and Public Opinion*. Knopf.

US Department of Defense, Under Secretary of Defense (Comptroller). 2016. National Defense Budget Estimates for FY2017. http://comptroller.defense.gov/Portals/45/Documents/defbudget/fy2017/FY17_Green_Book.pdf, accessed July 26, 2017.

Weigley, R.F. 1977. *The American Way of War: a History of United States Military Strategy and Policy*. Indiana University Press.

Western, J. 2005. *Selling Intervention and War: The Presidency, the Media, and the American Public*. Johns Hopkins University Press.

Williams, C. 2011. The Future Affordability of US National Security. Tobin Paper, October 28, http://web.mit.edu/ssp/people/williams/Williams_Tobin_paper_102811.pdf, accessed September 13, 2017.

Wilson, J.Q. 1974. *Political Organizations*. Princeton University Press.

Wilson, J.Q. 1989. *Bureaucracy: What Government Agencies Do and Why They Do It*. Basic Books.

Zaller, J. 1992. *The Nature and Origins of Mass Opinion*. Cambridge University Press.

12

IDENTIFYING THE RESTRAINT CONSTITUENCY

A. Trevor Thrall

Introduction

For most of the past hundred years isolationism has been the bogeyman for the American foreign policy establishment. Before World War II and throughout the Cold War pundits decried the public's disinterest in the world and worried about how to ensure that the public would be willing to support the massive defense spending and global system of military bases and alliances designed to confront the Soviet Union. After the Cold War those concerns did not fade away but instead shifted toward maintaining public support for ever-increasing levels of military intervention both for humanitarian purposes and, after 9/11, to combat terrorism (Dunn 2005; Kull and Destler 1999).

Despite a broad bipartisan consensus in Washington about the need for sustained intervention abroad, however, today there is a growing sense among many foreign policy experts that it is time for a more restrained foreign policy. Other chapters have outlined the case against the existing interventionist tradition and articulated many of the potential benefits of restraint. At this point several questions loom. If the United States were to pivot toward a foreign policy of restraint, would public opinion follow? Is there a large enough restraint constituency to make it possible for presidents to resist the political pressures that encourage military intervention abroad? Who, exactly, are the "restrainers," those segments of the population who might support a foreign policy of restraint?

In this chapter I take up these questions and make three related arguments. First, I estimate that the core restraint constituency comprises somewhere between 35% and 40% of the public. This core exhibits a reliable predisposition toward restraint, opposing the use of force in all but a few cases. Perhaps surprisingly to many, its members are not simply liberals or democrats but instead come from across the political spectrum.

Second, in view of public behavior and historical polling data, I argue that we should consider the public "reasonably restrained" in its attitudes toward foreign policy in general and the use of military force in particular. Though a majority of the public defaults toward caution under most circumstances, a persistent susceptibility to elite rhetoric provides regular challenges to the maintenance of restrained opinions. The balance between restraint and interventionist views, moreover, ebbs and flows with international events and recent experiences. As a result, the public's predispositions do indeed provide an opening for presidents to adopt restrained foreign policies, but they also make it possible for them to do the opposite with some frequency.

Finally, thanks to fatigue from more than a decade of war in the Middle East the American public expresses more restrained views today than at any point in the history of polling. Even so, I argue that the political heft of the restraint constituency will only increase over time thanks to steady replacement of older and more hawkish Americans by the Millennial Generation, which is emerging as the most restrained generation of Americans.

To develop these arguments I begin by situating restraint within the broader literature on foreign policy attitudes. I then analyze data from national surveys to generate two independent estimates of the restraint constituency and to assess its demographic correlates. The following section draws on a range of previous research and survey data to make the case for the reasonably restrained public, identifying the factors that encourage and discourage support for restrained foreign policies. I conclude by assessing the appeal of restrained foreign policy today and its prospects in the future.

Hawk, dove ... restrainer?

What is restraint?

Before we attempt to measure the restraint constituency we need to define restraint more carefully. This volume makes clear that the restraint paradigm is not monolithic but its basic principles are relatively straightforward. The restraint perspective begins with the assertion that although the United States has many foreign policy goals, only one – national security – merits the potential use of military force. Happily, the United States inhabits an extremely favorable security environment in the post-Cold War world. Thanks to its geography, friendly (and weak) neighbors, large and dynamic economy, and secure nuclear arsenal, the United States faces very few real threats to its security (Ravenal 1973; Nordlinger 1995; Gholz, Press, and Sapolsky 1997; Preble 2009; Posen 2014).

From this perspective, the United States enjoys what Nordlinger called "strategic immunity" – most of what happens in the rest of the world is simply irrelevant with respect to US national security. The outcomes of civil conflicts in the Middle East, the balance of power in Asia, or whether Russia annexes Crimea may be morally and politically significant for many reasons, but they do not threaten the ability of the United States to defend itself.

Similarly, American prosperity is the result of participation in, not control of, the international economic system. American military might is not required to ensure the ability of American companies to sell their goods around the world, not even to ensure the flow of oil on which much of its economy relies (Gholz and Press 2010; Drezner 2013). It is true that the United States played the leading role in establishing the liberal institutions that make globalization possible. It does not follow, restrainers argue, that the United States must play the role of hegemon to maintain them.

In short, because the United States enjoys assured security and because its prosperity follows from its citizens' everyday economic activity, the restraint paradigm asserts that the use of military force is rarely necessary.

Restraint proponents further argue that although military power is useful for self-defense, its effectiveness is decidedly limited with respect to achieving non-security-related national interests. Spreading democracy, promoting liberal values, nation-building, counterterrorism, and resolving civil wars are all well beyond the capabilities even of a military as powerful as the American one. Thus, even in cases where the United States identifies important non-security- or non-prosperity-related foreign policy goals, the use of force is an ineffective policy choice (Mandelbaum 1996; Luttwak 1999; Byman and Seybolt 2003; Pickering and Peceny 2006; Peic and Reiter 2011; Downes and Monten 2013; Lynch 2013).

Reinforcing this argument is the belief that military activism can actually work against national interests by creating new enemies, by making large conflicts out of smaller ones, by drawing the US into more conflicts, and by necessitating the expenditure of large sums of national treasure (Mearsheimer 2014; Posen 2014; Gholz, Press, and Sapolsky 1997; Preble 2009; Bacevich 2009, 2016; Mandelbaum 2016).

The final pillar of the restraint perspective is that the United States should not make ambitious efforts to control the behavior of other nations. Attempts to micro-manage other nations or the global system display the same fatal conceit as governmental efforts to guide economies through central planning (Hayek 1988). Despite its formidable power and capabilities, not even the United States has the ability to remake the world into something it is not. Attempting to control the rest of world is likely to go particularly poorly when military means are used. Regime change, democracy promotion, and nation-building at gunpoint are all bad ideas not just because they wrongly presuppose such an ability but also because they lead inevitably to death and suffering and a wide range of unintended consequences, some of which may be worse than the original conditions prompting the action (Bacevich 2016; Mandelbaum 2016; Menon 2016).

Restraint and the literature on foreign policy attitudes

The early literature on foreign policy attitudes produced what came to be known as the "Lippmann-Almond" consensus, which offered two central arguments about the American public. The first was that the public had little concern for and even less knowledge of the international arena, leading to a decided tendency towards isolationism. The second was that public attitudes lacked ideological structure. At the individual level, studies found that people very often took a mix of liberal and conservative positions on policy questions, and often answered the same survey questions differently from one year to the next. At an aggregate level, scholars like Gabriel Almond argued that the public was "moody," cycling between a preference for isolationism and a preference for internationalism without any rational explanation (Lippmann 1927,1946; Almond 1950; Campbell, Converse, Miller, and Stokes 1960; Rosenau 1961; Converse 2006 [1964]).

By the 1980s, however, new scholarship began to challenge this consensus. Eugene Wittkopf (1981, 1986, 1990, 1994) was the first to identify an enduring structure underlying American foreign policy attitudes. Wittkopf's central insight was that internationalism has both cooperative and militant dimensions. Support for using military force to pursue national interests, he recognized, did not lead necessarily to support for using cooperative means to do so, or vice versa. Accordingly, Wittkopf organized survey respondents into a two-by-two matrix based on their preferred approach to engaging the world, resulting in what Wittkopf called the four "faces of internationalism": groups supportive only of cooperation (accomodationists), only of military force (hardliners), supportive of both approaches (internationalists), or exhibiting low support for both (isolationists). Wittkopf went on to illustrate that these foreign policy orientations, or postures, were quite consistent over time both in terms of their distribution among the public and in terms of their ability to reliably predict people's positions on specific issues.

Wittkopf's work spawned numerous replications and extensions and the cooperative internationalism/militant internationalism framework has become the most common organizing framework for foreign policy attitude research (see, e.g., Holsti 1996; Kertzer et al. 2014; Rathbun et al. 2016). Reinforcing the argument that foreign policy attitudes have meaningful structures, recent studies have revealed that these general foreign policy orientations map, in turn, to predictable patterns of more abstract moral values. Building on the work of psychologists (Haidt 2007; Schwartz, Caprara, and Vecchione 2010; Schwartz et al. 2012), scholars like Kertzer et al. (2014) and Rathbun et al. (2016) have shown that high levels of concern for the moral values of harm/care and fairness/reciprocity are correlated with support for cooperative internationalism, while concern for authority, in-group loyalty, and purity are correlated with support for militant internationalism.

In light of the existing research, two important questions emerge for the study of restraint. The first question is whether restraint is a foreign policy orientation in the same sense as militant or cooperative internationalism, i.e. a predisposition that exists over time independent from the immediate context and that affects people's positions on specific policy questions in predictable ways. Or, alternatively, is restraint simply the result of calculations that are contingent on the interplay of various external factors like interests, risk, or casualties? The second important question is whether restraint represents something distinct from isolationism or whether, as some critics of restraint claim, restraint is just a modern repackaging of an old worldview.

Since both questions deserve an entire chapter I will not resolve either debate here. Instead, with respect to whether restraint is an orientation or the product of calculation, I will simply assert that we should think of restraint in both ways. The data, I believe, provide support for viewing restraint as an orientation, since we can use relatively abstract measures of support for restraint to predict support for more specific policy positions involving the use of military force. At the same time, of course, it is also true that many people support restrained positions in specific situations without ascribing to the broader paradigm. Since this group of "contingent restrainers" often determines the difference between majority support and majority opposition to a policy, contingent restraint is in fact no less important than categorical restraint.

With respect to the relationship between restraint and isolationism I will make two points. First, the previous literature on isolationism suffers from a serious lack of conceptual clarity, making clear comparisons difficult (Dumbrell 1999; Braumoeller 2010). Isolationism has been variously described as a context-driven mood (Almond 1950; Kertzer 2013), a general desire to disengage from the world (Urbatsch 2010), or opposition to any of the specific elements of the post-World War II internationalist project of which the United States has been the leader (Dunn 2005). In the same vein, the poll question used most often to measure isolationist preferences in academic studies[1] is so vague that even the polling organizations that have asked the question since World War II have recently acknowledged that it doesn't actually measure support for isolationism (Pew Research Center 2013: 4; Smeltz, Daalder, and Kafura 2014: 8).

Second, scholars working from the restraint perspective have defined restraint and isolationism as two very different things (Friedman and Preble 2013). To restrainers, isolationism is defined by its preferred end state: isolation. According to this view, true isolationism is a belief that the United States would be better off by cutting off relations with the rest of the world across all fronts, economic, cultural, and military. Restraint as articulated in this volume, on the other hand, is defined by its preferred approach to engaging the world. Restrainers favor strategic independence, eschew meddling in the affairs of other nations, and support restraint regarding the use of force, while still embracing all kinds of international engagement including trade and diplomacy.

Identifying the restraint constituency

Though most Americans' foreign policy attitudes are more structured than the early scholarship suggested, recent work acknowledges that people rely on a heavily streamlined version of the idealized paradigms academics have constructed (Drezner 2008; Kertzer and McGraw 2012). Thus, we first need to reduce the restraint orientation to a limited and more digestible set of principles in order to find survey questions that will then provide reasonable measures of people's support for restraint.

For practical purposes we can identify two major principles of restraint. The first principle is that the United States should use military force infrequently because it is rarely necessary for national security and because using military force to promote other foreign policy goals is usually a bad idea. The second principle is that the United States should be limited in its ambitions to control the behavior of other nations and the outcomes of conflicts that do not involve American national security.

Even with two relatively concise concepts in hand, however, using old surveys to answer new questions is challenging. Not only do surveys often simply fail to ask questions of interest, they often ask questions on the right topics but in ways that make them difficult to use effectively. In our case, the minimum requirement for assessing the size, composition, and policy positions of the restraint constituency is a survey that contains both measures of the core principles and a range of questions asking about specific foreign policy positions, in addition to the standard demographic background questions.

Unfortunately, this requirement is rarely met in the case of restraint. As a result the analysis that follows relies on just two surveys that manage to ask questions that allow us to measure both principles of restraint – and even then with far less precision than we would like. Despite this, as I will show, the two surveys manage to provide very similar estimates of the restraint constituency and allow us to create attitude clusters that do a good job at predicting preferences on specific foreign policies.

Profiling the restraint constituency

Restraint constituency estimate one: CNN/ORC 2014

The CNN/ORC survey provides a very straightforward measure of the first principle concerning the use of force: "If you had to choose, would you describe yourself more as a hawk, that is someone who believes that military force should be used frequently to promote US policy, or as more of a dove, that is someone who believes the US should rarely or never use military force?" As Figure 12.1 shows, CNN/ORC have asked this question a number of times (though, as noted, only once when also asking a question allowing us to measure support for the second principle). With the exception of the rally immediately following the ground war in Iraq in 2003, there has been a fairly steady division between hawks and doves among the public, with doves slightly outnumbering hawks. The steadiness over time supports the position that restraint is a persistent characteristic of people's attitudes – a foreign policy orientation – rather than a calculation based on current events and conducted anew each time the pollsters call.

The same survey measures support for restraint with respect to controlling outcomes abroad with the following question: "Do you think the United States should or should not take the leading role among all other countries in the world in trying to solve international problems?" The results appear in Table 12.1. There is some difference in the results between the 2014 and 2015 surveys – likely thanks to the emergence of the Islamic State. Other surveys that have asked very similar questions, however, have regularly found results in much the same range, suggesting again a fairly stable division of views over time.

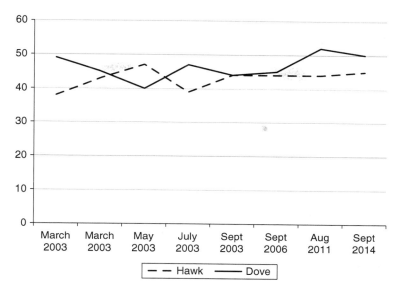

FIGURE 12.1 Percentage of people who call themselves hawks and doves
"If you had to choose, would you describe yourself more as a hawk, that is someone who believes that military force should be used frequently to promote US policy, or as more of a dove, that is someone who believes the US should rarely or never use military force?"

Source: CNN/ORC via PollingReport.com.

TABLE 12.1 Views on United States' leadership in international affairs
% who say the United States _____ take the leading role …

Date	Should	Should not	Unsure
Nov. 2015	45	54	1
Sep. 2014	39	58	3

"Do you think the United States should or should not take the leading role among all other countries in the world in trying to solve international problems?"
Source: CNN/ORC 2014.

To identify the restraint constituency and its counterparts we then combine people's answers to the two questions, resulting in the four attitude clusters displayed in Figure 12.2. Those who responded that they considered themselves a dove and that the United States should not take the leading role among all nations in solving international problems I have labeled Restrainers. Restrainers comprise 37% of the sample while Interventionists, the cluster of self-described hawks who want the United States to take the leading role in solving problems, make up about 24%.

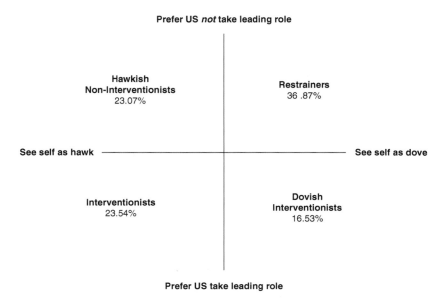

FIGURE 12.2 The Restraint Matrix – CNN/ORC
Source: CNN/ORC 2014.

Figure 12.3 provides initial validation of our definition of the restraint constituency by comparing each cluster's opinions on several questions regarding possible US intervention in Syria. Consistent with the position of the restraint paradigm, the restraint constituency identified through this analysis exhibits the lowest support for intervention, in stark contrast to the interventionist constituency. The gap in support for the three policies between the two groups is between 35 and 45 percentage points. This suggests that, whatever their imperfections, the survey questions we have used to measure support for the principles of restraint may well be capturing at least some of what we have been hoping to capture.

Restraint constituency estimate two: Chicago Council on Global Affairs 2014

Table 12.2 summarizes the responses to the Chicago Council on Global Affairs (CCGA) (Smeltz, Daalder, and Kafura 2014) question measuring the principle about the use of military force: "How effective do you think each of the following approaches have been to achieving the foreign policy goals of the United States? … Maintaining military superiority." The question wording here clearly raises concerns about whether it measures the concept of interest. Most obviously, it does not ask about the use of military force directly, nor is it clear exactly which foreign policy goals someone might be considering when answering the question. Respondents could be thinking about protecting the homeland, or about defeating

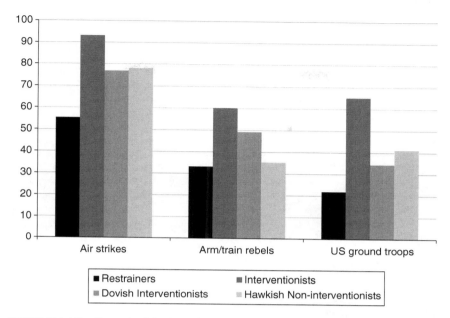

FIGURE 12.3 The Restraint Matrix and support for military intervention in Syria
"Do you favor or oppose ... air strikes ... sending arms and training rebels ... sending US ground troops ..."

Source: CNN/ORC 2014.

TABLE 12.2 The effectiveness of maintaining military superiority

% who say that maintaining US military superiority is ...

Year	Very effective	Somewhat effective	Not very effective	Not effective at all	Not sure
2012	43	42	12	3	1
2014	47	37	12	2	1

"How effective do you think each of the following approaches have been to achieving the foreign policy goals of the United States – very effective, somewhat effective, not very effective, or not effective at all? ... Maintaining US military superiority."

Source: Smeltz, Daalder, and Kafura 2014.

terrorism abroad, or even about promoting democracy. There is simply no way to know for sure.

One fairly simple way to interpret the results, however, is to consider them in relation to the hawk/dove question from the CNN/ORC survey. If we imagine that most of the hawks would answer "very effective" to this question, while most doves would not, then we might conclude that this question offers a reasonably similar estimate of 43% hawks and 57% doves that likely underestimates the numbers of

TABLE 12.3 Views of US leadership

% who say it is …

Date	Very desirable	Somewhat desirable	Somewhat undesirable	Very undesirable	Not sure
2002	41	42	9	5	2
2010	35	49	12	4	1
2012	36	46	14	4	1
2014	37	46	13	3	1

"From your point of view, how desirable is it that the US exert strong leadership in world affairs? Very desirable, somewhat desirable, somewhat undesirable, or very undesirable?"

Source: Smeltz, Daalder, and Kafura 2014.

hawks by a bit. Admittedly, this is speculative, but the question does appear on the most useful foreign policy survey and, as I will attempt to illustrate below, further analysis indicates that this question probably captures the spirit of the first principle.

As a measure of people's attitudes towards American ambitions to control outcomes around the world the CCGA asks a question fairly similar to that asked by CNN/ORC: "From your point of view, how desirable is it that the US exert strong leadership in world affairs?" Table 12.3 reports the trend over time. Even though the vague question wording makes it difficult to interpret (i.e. leadership toward what ends?), we can look at the responses and imagine once again that most interventionists would answer "very desirable," while most restrainers would not, suggesting at least tentatively that it may capture the spirit of the second principle.

Figure 12.4 reveals that despite relying on different measures of the key concepts, the CCGA estimate of the four clusters is very similar to the CNN/ORC estimate. For this survey I defined Restrainers as those who responded that strong US leadership was something other than "very desirable" (i.e. not at all, somewhat undesirable, or very undesirable) *and* who responded that maintaining US military superiority was something other than "very effective" (i.e. not at all effective, not very effective, or somewhat effective). Interventionists answered that strong leadership was "very desirable" and that military superiority was "very effective," with the other two groups offering the other two alternative combinations.

In the case of the CCGA survey, a host of questions regarding the potential use of military force allow us to inspect this strategy for identifying the restraint constituency in some detail. Figure 12.5 summarizes the gap between Restrainers and Interventionists across twenty-one different scenarios of all types. Restrainers' support averaged 39% and a majority supported the use of force in just five cases (and in no case was the majority greater than 65%). Interventionists, on the other hand, averaged 60% support and a majority supported the use of force in sixteen cases, eight of those at rates between 70% and 88%. Those who felt military superiority was a "very effective" tool but did not support strong US leadership averaged 51% support (majorities in ten cases) while those who felt strong US leadership was very

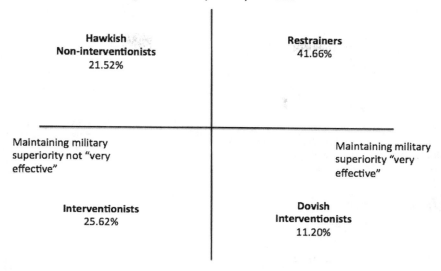

FIGURE 12.4 The Restraint Matrix – Chicago Council
Source: Smeltz, Daalder, and Kafura 2014.

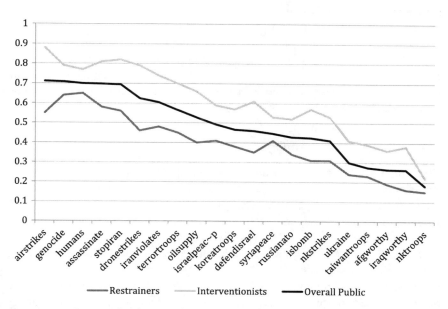

FIGURE 12.5 Support for the use of military force: Restrainers vs. Interventionists
Source: Smeltz, Daalder, and Kafura 2014.

desirable but did not believe military superiority was very effective averaged 54% (majorities in twelve cases).

Who are the Restrainers?

The question "Who are the Restrainers?" requires two answers. The first concerns the partisan composition of the restraint constituency and the other groups. This is important because partisanship affects the mobilization of opinions during campaigns by presidents to build support for war and foreign policies. The second has to do with the underpinnings of restraint. What demographic factors and other beliefs make people more or less likely to adopt the restraint orientation? Knowing this can help us understand how many people might be "contingent" Restrainers and what sorts of arguments or factors might make them more or less likely to support restrained foreign policy positions. The following analysis relies on the CCGA 2014 survey.

Partisanship and restraint

Panel A of Table 12.4 shows the breakdown of partisans across each of the four foreign policy postures; Panel B flips the table and shows the partisan composition of each orientation. Perhaps surprisingly, restraint is not quite as partisan an orientation as one might imagine given the rancor that now accompanies most foreign policy debates in Washington. Even though Republicans in the survey were considerably more likely than either Democrats or Independents to believe that military superiority was very effective (by 11 and 15 percentage points, respectively) and somewhat more likely to think exerting strong US leadership was very desirable (by 5 points and 12 points), more Republicans fall into the restraint constituency than any other category. Of course it is also true that Democrats and Independents are far more likely to be Restrainers than to be Interventionists, almost twice as likely in fact.

The correlates/underpinnings of restraint

Though the CCGA survey does not contain any questions about moral values that would help us connect the restraint constituency to more fundamental psychological foundations, we can nonetheless make use of a wide range of background variables to assess how important various factors are for predicting who will support restraint.

Table 12.5 displays the results of a logistic regression analysis that includes standard demographic variables as well as several other measures identified in previous work as relevant to foreign policy attitudes. The analysis finds that threat perceptions, partisanship, ideology, nationalist pride, and age all have a significant effect on a person's likelihood of adopting the restraint perspective. Restrainers, on average, are younger, feel less threatened by the world, are more likely to be

TABLE 12.4 Partisanship and restraint

Panel A. Distribution of attitudes by partisanship

	Restrainers	Interventionists	Hawkish Non-interventionists	Dovish Interventionists
Republicans	33.6	31.36	22.74	12.3
Democrats	42.64	23.63	19.29	14.43
Independents	46.12	24.65	22.05	7.18

Panel B. Partisan composition of each attitude cluster

	Republicans	Democrats	Independents
Restrainers	21.85	37.27	39.47
Interventionists	33.16	33.59	30.78
Hawkish non-interventionists	28.63	32.64	34.99
Dovish interventionists	29.76	46.94	23.03

Source: Smeltz, Daalder, and Kafura 2014.
Note: Rows do not sum to 100% because table does not include respondents who refused to answer the partisan identification question.

liberal, are less likely to be Republicans than Democrats or Independents, and are less likely to believe that the United States is the greatest country in the world. Income, education, gender, and race, on the other hand, did not exhibit a statistically significant influence on the adoption of a restrained orientation.

We should be cautious, however, about drawing final conclusions about the restraint constituency at this point. Even though the findings to this point follow fairly closely with expectations, the analysis thus far relies on just two surveys and our identification of foreign policy orientations rests on just two questions from each, none of which was designed expressly to measure support for restraint. Moreover, the lack of any time series data means we have no way to compare the relative importance of individual predispositions to the ebb and flow of world events. As with most things, more data is better, and more research is necessary before we can make more concrete statements about the size and composition of the restraint constituency and how it might be changing over time.

How restrained is the American public?

Having estimated the size of the restraint constituency we turn now to ask the practical question: how restrained is the American public when it comes to the real world? Under what conditions should presidents expect to have an easy (or difficult) time building support for military intervention?

TABLE 12.5 The correlates of restraint

	Coefficient	Z-score	p-value
Patriot	−1.139	−10.83	0
	(.105)		
Foreign policy goals	−0.342	−10.5	0
	(.033)		
Threat perceptions	−0.147	−5.65	0
	(.026)		
Education	0.013	0.48	0.632
	(.026)		
Income	−0.016	−1.22	0.221
	(.013)		
Age	−0.019	−5.77	0
	(.003)		
Female	0.055	0.52	0.601
	(.105)		
Ideology	−0.144	−3.91	0
	(.037)		
Republican	−0.275	−1.94	0.053
	(.142)		
Democrat	−0.007	−0.06	0.956
	(.126)		
White	0.100	0.85	0.397
	(.118)		
Constant	3.445	9.58	0
	(.360)		

Source: Smeltz, Daalder, and Kafura 2014.

The answer is complicated. At any given time, the "restraint coalition" includes both fixed and variable components. The first group contains the restraint constituency – those who have embraced the restraint orientation and who provide the base of support for restraint on any given issue. The second group consists of people who do not hold the same basic pattern of beliefs in the basic principles of restraint, but who exhibit contingent support for restraint from time to time based on their interpretation of various contextual cues. Which contextual cues matter will vary across issues and individuals. Hawks who tend to support the use of military force, for example, might reluctantly oppose an operation to prevent Iran from building nuclear weapons simply because they don't believe it will be successful. Doves with strong feelings about resolving humanitarian crises might, in similar fashion, oppose action in Syria because they don't believe it is possible to avoid getting engaged in major combat operations. Since neither the restraint constituency nor any other general orientation (including political parties for that matter) encompasses a majority of the public, the battle for public support in foreign policy is all about building a winning coalition.

The reasonably restrained public

Overall, however, I argue that the public should be considered "reasonably restrained."[2] Although the default majority position is a set of preferences aligned fairly well with the restraint perspective, the public remains susceptible to elite cues, threat inflation, and threat framing, all of which can significantly affect support for restraint. Below I justify this assessment and consider some of the most important contextual cues affecting support for restraint.

The clearest evidence of the public's support for restraint is that there are simply very few scenarios under which a majority of the public supports military intervention when American national security is not directly at stake. Jentleson (1992) has persuasively argued that in the "post-post-Vietnam" era the public adopted what he calls a "pretty prudent" stance on military intervention, supporting policies based on the principal policy objective (PPO) they are designed to meet. Jentleson argues that the public lends far greater support to initiatives in which the primary goal is restraining aggressive nations and actors than they do to nation-building and efforts to instill social or political change within other nations. In Jentleson's words (which echo the restraint perspective quite closely), "The key distinction is between force used to coerce *foreign policy restraint* by an adversary engaged in aggressive actions against the United States or its interests, and force used to engineer *internal political change* within another country whether in support of an existing government considered an ally or seeking to overthrow a government considered an adversary" (1992: 50).

Following Jentleson's line of argument, the restraint coalition will be at its largest when US foreign policy is at its most explicitly unrestrained, that is, when it seeks to intervene militarily in the internal politics of other nations. And indeed, for ten cases between 1992 and 1996 Jentleson and Britton (1998) found average levels of public support of 64% for humanitarian intervention, 55% for foreign policy restraint missions, and 36% for internal political change missions. In an extension of Jentleson's work, Eichenberg (2005) found that public support for interventions focused on internal political change averaged just 48% across almost 500 poll questions between 1980 and 2004.

Table 12.6 echoes these findings using data from the 2014 Chicago Council survey. Of the eight scenarios that do generate majority support, six of them are what Jentleson would categorize as foreign policy restraint. Four of the cases deal with terrorism, an issue of obvious relevance to American homeland security and the safety of individual Americans. Two of the cases deal with a potentially nuclear-armed Iran, which a majority of the public views as a significant security threat to the United States, and the final two cases concern extreme levels of humanitarian crisis. Thus, though not as restrained as some in the restraint camp might prefer, this

TABLE 12.6   Public support by principle policy objective

	% public support
Foreign policy restraint	
Air strikes on terrorist bases	71
Assassinate individual terrorist leaders	70
Drone strikes on terrorist bases	62
Send US troops to attack terrorist bases	56
"Military action" to stop Iran from developing nuclear weapons	69
"Military action" if Iran violates nuclear deal	60
Air strikes on North Korea to stop nuclear program	41
Send US troops if Russia invades more of Ukraine	30
Send US troops to North Korea to stop nuclear program	18
Average	*53*
Humanitarian intervention	
Send US troops to prevent genocide	71
Send US troops to deal with humanitarian crises	70
Average	*71*
Defending allies	
Send US troops if Russia invades a NATO ally like Latvia	43
Send US troops to defend Israel from its neighbors	46
Send US troops if North Korea invades South Korea	47
Send US troops if Israel attacks Iran and Iran strikes back	42
Send US troops if Russia expands Ukraine invasion	30
Send US troops if China attacks Taiwan	27
Average	*39*
Internal political change/peacekeeping	
Send US troops to keep peace between Israel and Palestinians	49
Send US troops to keep peace in Syria	45
Average	*47*

Source: Smeltz, Daalder, and Kafura 2014.

pattern of support suggests that the public is reasonably restrained regarding the use of force.

A second piece of evidence for the generally restrained nature of public opinion is the fact that Americans routinely choose diplomacy over the use of military force when given a choice. Figure 12.6 illustrates the general preference for diplomacy over military strength. Figure 12.7 shows that this preference holds even in specific cases like Iran when the prospect of nuclear proliferation by a "rogue state" looms.

The second set of factors affecting restraint relates to the implementation of foreign policy, including costs, especially casualties, and the likelihood that an operation will end successfully. Even once moved to support intervention, as it turns out, the public does not lose its preference for restraint.

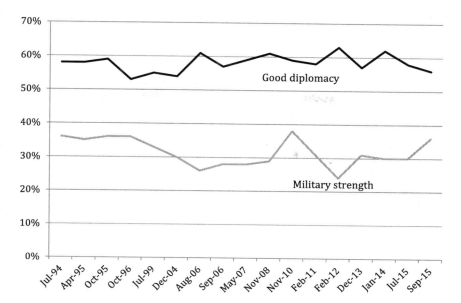

FIGURE 12.6 Best way to ensure peace

"In your view what is the best way to ensure peace – good diplomacy or military strength?"

Source: Pew Research Center.

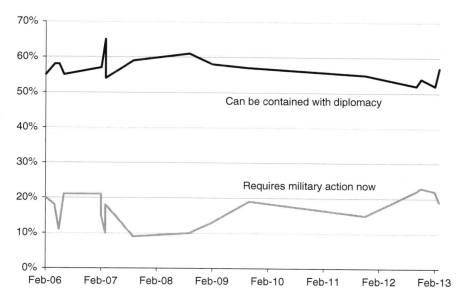

FIGURE 12.7 Best way to deal with Iran

"Is Iran a threat that requires military action now, a threat that can be contained with diplomacy, or not a threat at this time?"

Source: CBS/New York Times.

The most popular explanation for public support of war (and its decline) is the public's sensitivity to how many casualties America has suffered. John Mueller (1973) found that support for war in Korea and Vietnam fell at the same rate in response to rising casualties – a drop of 15 percentage points in support for every factor-of-ten increase in casualties (dead and wounded). In light of the radically different contexts of the two wars, Mueller hypothesized that the effect of casualties on public support did not depend on other factors. The war in Vietnam, Mueller noted, featured far more intense political and social polarization including a large anti-war movement as well as vivid television news coverage of the horrors of war. And yet public support dropped at the same rate in each case. Thus Mueller wrote, "The relevant measure then becomes the amount of pain caused by the war – as reflected in the total casualty figures – rather than simply the amount of time the war has been going on. The assumption is that people react more to the cumulative human costs of the war than to its duration"(Mueller 1973: 59).[3]

Gelpi, Feaver, and Reifler (2006, 2009) argue, on the other hand, that "overall the general public expresses a remarkable willingness to accept casualties (that is, combat fatalities) when necessary for victory. The public appears to be defeat phobic, not casualty phobic" (Feaver and Gelpi 2004: 149). From a related perspective, Jentleson (1992) acknowledges what he calls a "halo of success" effect in his study, suggesting that when presented with a quick victory the public worries far less about the original justification. Eichenberg (2005: 147), meanwhile, agrees with Gelpi, Feaver, and Reifler, and concludes "Successful military operations enjoy high support even when the objective is unpopular and casualties are suffered."

The steady evaporation of public support for the wars in Afghanistan and Iraq is consistent with both lines of argument and suggests that the restraint coalition will grow whenever wars become costly and go poorly.

Challenges to restraint

On the other hand, however, there are limits to the public's restraint. Majorities have emerged in support of several interventions that most people later turned out to believe were mistakes and that should have been opposed from a restrained perspective, with Afghanistan and Iraq being the two most significant recent cases. Part of this dynamic can be assigned to what John Mueller called the "rally effect," the tendency of the public to support the troops and the nation during crises and once the nation goes to war (Mueller 1973). As Mueller and others have noted, rally effects tend to fade in relatively short order (see, e.g., Baker and Oneal 2001). Nonetheless, the political importance of even temporary majorities can be critical, especially given the president's ability to generate crises and to set the nation on a path towards conflict in the first place.

At another level, however, these temporary majorities emerge thanks to the public's reliance on elite cues. A healthy literature now attests that since most people do not know enough about foreign policy to interpret world events on their own, they rely heavily on cues from political elites, delivered through the news media, in order to develop opinions on specific policy issues (Zaller 1992; Berinsky 2007; Baum and Groeling 2009).

In theory, the news media encourage a robust marketplace of ideas in which competing policy arguments must duel one another for support. In practice, however, few believe that the news about American politics provides such a service. In the case of foreign policy, in particular, most scholars believe the president enjoys significant communication advantages that allow him to set the news agenda, frame issues, and manipulate information in an effort to build support for his policies (Entman 2004; Bennett, Lawrence, and Livingston 2008). Chaim Kaufmann, among others, has argued that these advantages combined with an apathetic news media to enable President Bush to convince many Americans that Iraq had or was actively seeking to acquire weapons of mass destruction in 2002–2003 (Kaufmann 2004).

Similarly, elite threat inflation and framing efforts have encouraged many Americans to view certain problems as existential national security threats when in fact they are not, leading to less restrained opinions than would otherwise be the case. The most obvious example of this dynamic is elite rhetoric about terrorism since 9/11. As scholars like Brigitte Nacos (Nacos, Bloch-Elkon, and Shapiro 2011) and John Mueller (2006) have shown, elite discourse has wildly oversold the nature and extent of the terrorist threat to the United States. The result, as Table 12.6 shows, is that, despite little evidence that such efforts have done anything to reduce the threat of terrorism against the United States, majorities continue to support a wide range of aggressive counterterrorism measures.

Third, the public's support for humanitarian intervention shows mixed tendencies toward restraint. On the restrained side, Americans clearly do not believe they are responsible for fixing other countries' problems as a general rule. Pollsters never reported majority approval of the American-supported intervention in Libya in 2011 (Jones 2011), for example, and almost 70% of the public responded that the United States had no responsibility to help solve the Syrian civil war crisis before the emergence of ISIS. But on the other hand, surveys show consistent and large majorities in favor of sending troops to prevent potential genocides or to manage hypothetical humanitarian crises. And though even pundits of the restraint persuasion differ on what factors might justify military intervention on humanitarian grounds, they are quick to point out that such missions have a serious tendency toward mission creep, leading to deeper and more costly entanglement, and that many such missions fail to improve conditions in the long run (Mandelbaum 1996; Coyne 2013; Menon 2016). Thus, humanitarian intervention represents a significant potential source of support for unrestrained foreign policy action.

And finally, the public's restraint tends to go AWOL in the face of the rally effect at the launch of military operations. As noted, if the operation lengthens into a long-term war the public tends to recover its preference for restraint as the costs and casualties pile up. But in cases of quick military "successes" the public's restraint tends to remain absent even if those operations are conducted for dubious reasons. The invasions of Grenada in 1983 and Panama in 1989, for example, were both launched without public debate and with little or no national secu-rity justification. Nonetheless both operations garnered significant public support after the fact because each operation came to a quick and decisive (read: "success-ful") conclusion. That a majority of the public can support such actions suggests another less restrained aspect of public attitudes toward foreign policy.

Conclusion: today's restraint coalition, tomorrow's restraint constituency

Today a confluence of factors has produced a significant increase in the restraint coalition. Surveys by the Chicago Council, Pew, and others have all found histor-ically high levels of sentiment in favor of stepping back from the consistent inter-ventionism of the past fifteen years (Smeltz, Daalder, and Kafura 2014; Smeltz et al. 2015; Pew Research Center 2013, 2016).

There are at least three candidate explanations for this trend. The most obvi-ous is war fatigue. Large majorities are now convinced that the wars in both Afghanistan and Iraq were mistakes. And with almost 7,000 US military personnel killed and roughly one million wounded, and trillions of dollars spent killing ter-rorists and "exerting influence" in the Middle East and elsewhere, many Americans are simply convinced it is time to spend more time focusing on domestic concerns. A Pew (2016) survey found, along these lines, that 70% of the public want the next president to focus on domestic issues compared to just 17% who want to see a focus on foreign policy. One possible interpretation of this finding is that a grow-ing number of Americans may see little connection between military intervention and American security, especially given how few terrorist attacks there have been on American soil since 9/11. As a result, fewer may now believe such efforts are worth the high costs in lives, money, and the lack of attention paid to domestic issues.

A second likely reason for the shift in the restraint direction is the increase in political polarization in the United States. Research by Urbatsch (2010) and Kertzer (2013) reveals that when a president from the opposing party occupies the White House, citizens tend to judge the results of American foreign policy more harshly, which tends to lead to higher support for disengagement from interna-tional affairs. This is not because people's underlying predispositions change but simply because they now oppose whatever actions the president supports. Some of the Republican opposition to the Iran nuclear deal might fall into this category, for example.

This dynamic is at work no matter who is president, of course, but with the recent increase in polarization in Washington this effect may well be getting stron-ger, leading more people than ever toward contingent opposition to the president's foreign policies (Hill and Tausanovitch 2015). And since presidents have been pur-suing interventionist policies through this period of polarization, the upshot has been an increase in the size of the restraint coalition. Though such an increase does not increase the size of the base restraint constituency, if enhanced polarization

TABLE 12.7 The restrained millennial generation

% of each generation who fall into each camp

	Restrainers	Interventionists	Hawkish non-interventionists	Dovish interventionists	
Millennials	54.8	14.7	20.8	9.7	100%
	52.1	*15.7*	*16.3*	*16.0*	
Gen X	47.0	21.7	22.0	9.4	100%
	33.7	*27.7*	*24.8*	*13.8*	
Baby Boomers	32.7	32.6	22.7	12.0	100%
	28.8	*22.4*	*30.6*	*18.3*	
Silent Generation	23.3	41.4	18.4	16.9	100%
	23.7	*33.9*	*22.5*	*20.0*	

Source: The top number in each cell is the estimate from the 2014 Chicago Council survey. The lower number is the estimate from the 2014 CNN/ORC survey.

becomes a permanent fact of political life then the resulting increase in the contingent restraint coalition may well be permanent.

The third reason for the historic figures is, in fact, history. Looking beyond the temporary effects of global events, the situation today reflects generational shifts in public opinion. The data suggest that the restraint constituency has been growing as younger and less intervention-minded Americans start to replace older, more interventionist Americans. The Millennial Generation, born between 1980 and 1997, is the most restrained yet. Table 12.7 illustrates the generational march toward restraint.

One reason for this shift is that Millennials are decidedly more liberal than previous generations and also more likely to identify as independent or non-partisan (Jones 2015). Since liberals, Democrats, and Independents are more likely to identify as Restrainers than conservatives and Republicans, young Americans are more likely to fall into the restraint constituency.

However, as Figures 12.8a and 12.8b show, ideology and partisanship are not the only story. Young Americans of all partisan stripes have grown more restrained down the generations, though the story depends on which survey we use to interpret it. Democrats and Independents show an unbroken increase in support for restraint on both surveys, while Millennial Republicans are either the most restrained generation or the second most restrained generation.[4] Nor do these results depend on how we define the restraint constituency. As previous work has shown, Millennials are simply the generation least supportive of the use of military force (Thrall and Goepner 2015).

Though the arguments here remain preliminary, the analysis presented in this chapter strongly suggests that the restraint constituency exists, that it is larger and more politically diverse than many people might suspect, and that it is getting larger over time. Moreover, given the broad sweep of public opinion regarding foreign policy, the public can fairly be labeled "reasonably restrained." As a result, presidents

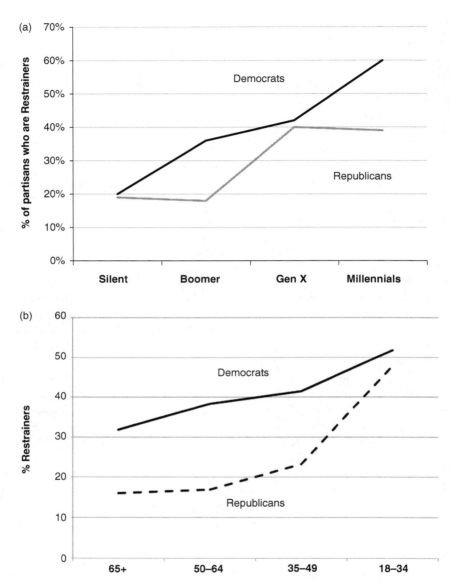

FIGURE 12.8 Restraint constituency trends by party and generation

Source: Panel A: 2014 Chicago Council Survey.
Panel B: 2014 CNN/ORC Survey

seeking to chart a foreign policy at odds with the current Beltway interventionism appear to be in good shape.

At the same time, of course, there remains a sturdy interventionist constituency, bolstered by the elite consensus on the need for muscular American internationalism. That consensus has produced a long series of unnecessary, often expensive, and sometimes counterproductive interventions since the end of the Cold War. On many occasions, despite the public's tendency to restraint, presidents have been able to generate majority support for intervention, in part thanks to a news media that seems uninterested in challenging elites on foreign policy matters. Looking ahead, the United States will continue for the foreseeable future to suffer from what Christopher Preble (2009) calls the "power problem." Thanks to the exceptional security and overwhelming power the United States enjoys, it also enjoys too great a temptation, not to mention the ability, to intervene abroad in pursuit of all kinds of foreign policy goals that have no effect on national security.

Notes

1 The wording of the Chicago Council on Global Affairs version is: "Do you think it would be best for the future of the country if we take an active part in world affairs or if we stay out of world affairs?" The Gallup/Pew version is very similar: "The US should mind its own business internationally and let other countries get along the best they can on their own."
2 With a hat-tip to Bruce Jentleson's "pretty prudent" public, obviously.
3 One can see here that Mueller is arguing against a previously popular theory of "war weariness," which held that the public would not maintain support for long wars.
4 The complication in this story is likely due to the partisan polarization that has taken place under President Obama, but more research would be necessary in order to come up with a conclusive answer.

References

Almond, G.A. 1950. *The American People and Foreign Policy*. Praeger.
Bacevich, A.J. 2009. *American Empire*. Harvard University Press.
Bacevich, A.J. 2016. *America's War for the Greater Middle East: A Military History*. Random House Trade Paperbacks.
Baker, W.D., and Oneal, J.R. 2001. Patriotism or Opinion Leadership? The Nature and Origins of the "Rally 'Round the Flag" Effect. *Journal of Conflict Resolution*, 45(5), pp.661–687.
Baum, M.A., and Groeling, T.J. 2009. *War Stories: The Causes and Consequences of Public Views of War*. Princeton University Press.
Bennett, W.L., Lawrence, R.G., and Livingston, S. 2008. *When the Press Fails: Political Power and the News Media from Iraq to Katrina*. University of Chicago Press.
Berinsky, A.J. 2007. Assuming the Costs of War: Events, Elites, and American Public Support for Military Conflict. *The Journal of Politics*, 69(4), pp.975–997.
Braumoeller, B.F. 2010. The Myth of American Isolationism. *Foreign Policy Analysis*, 6(4), pp.349–371.
Byman, D., and Seybolt, T. 2003. Humanitarian Intervention and Communal Civil Wars. *Security Studies*, 13(1), pp.33–78.

Campbell, A., Converse, P., Miller, W., and Stokes, D. 1960. *The American Voter*. University of Chicago Press.

CBS News/New York Times Poll (various dates). Available at www.pollingreport.com/iran.htm

CNN/ORC. 2014, September. CNN/ORC International Poll, USORC.092914A.R29. ORC International, Roper Centre for Public Opinion Research, Cornell University.

Converse, P.E. 2006 [1964]. The Nature of Belief Systems in Mass Publics. *Critical Review*, 18(1–3), pp.1–74.

Coyne, C.J. 2013. *Doing Bad by Doing Good: Why Humanitarian Action Fails*. Stanford University Press.

Downes, A.B., and Monten, J. 2013. Forced To Be Free? Why Foreign-Imposed Regime Change Rarely Leads to Democratization. *International Security*, 37(4), pp.90–131.

Drezner, D.W. 2008. The Realist Tradition in American Public Opinion. *Perspectives on Politics*, 6(1), pp.51–70.

Drezner, D.W. 2013. Military Primacy Doesn't Pay (Nearly As Much As You Think). *International Security*, 38(1), pp.52–79.

Dumbrell, J. 1999. Varieties of Post-Cold War American Isolationism. *Government and Opposition*, 34(1), pp.24–43.

Dunn, D. 2005. Isolationism Revisited: Seven Persistent Myths in the Contemporary American Foreign Policy Debate. *Review of International Studies*, 31(2), pp.237–261.

Eichenberg, R.C. 2005. Victory Has Many Friends: US Public Opinion and the Use of Military Force, 1981–2005. *International Security*, 30(1), pp.140–177.

Entman, R.M. 2004. *Projections of Power: Framing News, Public Opinion, and US Foreign Policy*. University of Chicago Press.

Feaver, P.D., and Gelpi, C. 2004. *Choosing your Battles: American Civil–Military Relations and the Use of Force*. Princeton University Press.

Friedman, B.H., and Preble, C.A. 2013. Americans Favor not Isolationism but Restraint. *Los Angeles Times*, December 27.

Gelpi, C., Feaver, P.D., and Reifler, J. 2006. Success Matters: Casualty Sensitivity and the War in Iraq. *International Security*, 30(3), pp.7–46.

Gelpi, C., Feaver, P.D., and Reifler, J. 2009. *Paying the Human Costs of War: American Public Opinion and Casualties in Military Conflicts*. Princeton University Press.

Gholz, E., and Press, D.G. 2010. Protecting "the Prize": Oil and the US National Interest. *Security Studies*, 19(3), pp.453–485.

Gholz, E., Press, D.G., and Sapolsky, H.M. 1997. Come Home, America: The Strategy of Restraint in the Face of Temptation. *International Security*, 21(4), pp.5–48.

Haidt, J. 2007. The New Synthesis in Moral Psychology. *Science*, 316(5827), pp.998–1002.

Hayek, F.A. 1988. The Fatal Conceit: The Errors of Socialism. In W.W. Bartley, ed., *The Collected Works of F.A. Hayek*. University of Chicago.

Hill, S.J., and Tausanovitch, C. 2015. A Disconnect in Representation? Comparison of Trends in Congressional and Public Polarization. *The Journal of Politics*, 77(4), pp.1058–1075.

Holsti, O.R. 1996. *Public Opinion and American Foreign Policy*. University of Michigan Press.

Jentleson, B.W. 1992. The Pretty Prudent Public: Post Post-Vietnam American Opinion on the Use of Military Force. *International Studies Quarterly*, 36(1), pp.49–74.

Jentleson, B.W., and Britton, R.L. 1998. Still Pretty Prudent: Post-Cold War American Public Opinion on the Use of Military Force. *Journal of Conflict Resolution*, 42(4), pp.395–417.

Jones, J.M. 2011. Americans Approve of Military Action against Libya, 47% to 37%. Gallup.com-Daily News, Polls, Public Opinion on Government, Politics, Economics, Management. Accessed June 2, 2016, at www.gallup.com/poll/146738/Americans-Approve-Military-Action-Against-Libya.aspx.

Jones, J.M. 2015. US Baby Boomers More Likely to Identify as Conservative. Gallup.com, January 29. Accessed June 2, 2016, at www.gallup.com/poll/181325/baby-boomers-likely-identify-conservative.aspx.

Kaufmann, C. 2004. Threat Inflation and the Failure of the Marketplace of Ideas: The Selling of the Iraq War. *International Security*, 29(1), pp.5–48.

Kertzer, J.D. 2013. Making Sense of Isolationism: Foreign Policy Mood as a Multilevel Phenomenon. *The Journal of Politics*, 75(1), pp.225–240.

Kertzer, J.D., and McGraw, K.M. 2012. Folk Realism: Testing the Microfoundations of Realism in Ordinary Citizens. *International Studies Quarterly*, 56(2), pp.245–258.

Kertzer, J.D., Powers, K.E., Rathbun, B.C., and Iyer, R. 2014. Moral Support: How Moral Values Shape Foreign Policy Attitudes. *The Journal of Politics*, 76(3), pp.825–840.

Kull, S., and Destler, I.M. 1999. *Misreading the Public: The Myth of a New Isolationism*. Brookings Institution Press.

Lippmann, W. 1927. *The Phantom Public*. Transaction Publishers.

Lippmann, W. 1946. *Public Opinion* (Vol. 1). Transaction Publishers.

Luttwak, E.N. 1999. Give War a Chance. *Foreign Affairs*, July/August, pp.36–44.

Lynch, M. 2013. The Political Science of Syria's War. POMPEPS Studies #5, December 13. Project on Middle East Political Science, George Washington University.

Mandelbaum, M. 1996. Foreign Policy as Social Work. *Foreign Affairs*, January/February, pp.16–32.

Mandelbaum, M. 2016. *Mission Failure: America and the World in the Post-Cold War Era*. Oxford University Press.

Mearsheimer, J.J. 2014. Why the Ukraine Crisis is the West's Fault: The Liberal Delusions that Provoked Putin. *Foreign Affairs*, 93, 77–89.

Menon, R. 2016. *The Conceit of Humanitarian Intervention*. Oxford University Press.

Mueller, J.E. 1973. *War, Presidents, and Public Opinion*. John Wiley & Sons.

Mueller, J.E. 2006. *Overblown: How Politicians and the Terrorism Industry Inflate National Security Threats, and Why We Believe Them*. Simon and Schuster.

Nacos, B.L., Bloch-Elkon, Y., and Shapiro, R.Y. 2011. *Selling Fear: Counterterrorism, the Media, and Public Opinion*. University of Chicago Press.

Nordlinger, E.A. 1995. *Isolationism Reconfigured: American Foreign Policy for a New Century*. Princeton University Press, pp.5–23.

Peic, G., and Reiter, D. 2011. Foreign-Imposed Regime Change, State Power and Civil War Onset, 1920–2004. *British Journal of Political Science*, 41(3), pp.453–475.

Pew Research Center. 2013. Public Sees Power Declining as Support for Global Engagement Slips. December.

Pew Research Center. 2016. Public Uncertain, Divided over America's Place in the World. April.

Pickering, J., and Peceny, M. 2006. Forging Democracy at Gunpoint. *International Studies Quarterly*, 50(3), pp.539–560.

Posen, B.R. 2014. *Restraint: A New Foundation for US Grand Strategy*. Cornell University Press.

Preble, C.A. 2009. *The Power Problem: How American Military Dominance Makes Us Less Safe, Less Prosperous, and Less Free*. Cornell University Press.

Rathbun, B.C., Kertzer, J.D., Reifler, J., Goren, P., and Scotto, T.J. 2016. Taking Foreign Policy Personally: Personal Values and Foreign Policy Attitudes. *International Studies Quarterly*, 60(1), pp.124–137.

Ravenal, E.C. 1973. The Case for Strategic Disengagement. *Foreign Affairs*, 51(3), pp.505–521.

Rosenau, J.N. 1961. *Public Opinion and Foreign Policy: An Operational Formulation* (Vol. 35). Random House.

Schwartz, S.H., Caprara, G.V., and Vecchione, M. 2010. Basic Personal Values, Core Political Values, and Voting: A Longitudinal Analysis. *Political Psychology*, 31(3), pp.421–452.

Schwartz, S.H., Cieciuch, J., Vecchione, M., Davidov, E., Fischer, R., Beierlein, C., Ramos, A., Verkasalo, M., Lönnqvist, J.E., Demirutku, K., and Dirilen-Gumus, O. 2012. Refining the Theory of Basic Individual Values. *Journal of Personality and Social Psychology*, 103(4), p.663.

Smeltz, D., Daalder, I., and Kafura, C. 2014. *Foreign Policy in the Age of Retrenchment*. The Chicago Council on Global Affairs.

Smeltz, D., Daalder, I., Friedhoff, K., and Kafura, C. 2015. *America Divided: Political Partisanship and US Foreign Policy*. Chicago Council on Global Affairs.

Thrall, A.T., and Goepner, E. 2015. *Millennials and US Foreign Policy: The Next Generation's Attitudes toward Foreign Policy and War (and Why They Matter)*. Cato Institute.

Urbatsch, R. 2010. Isolationism and Domestic Politics. *Journal of Conflict Resolution*, 54(3), pp.471–492.

Wittkopf, E.R. 1981. The Structure of Foreign Policy Attitudes: An Alternate View. *Social Science Quarterly*, 62(1), pp.108–123.

Wittkopf, E.R. 1986. On the Foreign Policy Beliefs of the American People: A Critique and Some Evidence. *International Studies Quarterly*, 30(4), pp.425–445.

Wittkopf, E.R. 1990. *Faces of Internationalism: Public Opinion and American Foreign Policy*. Duke University Press.

Wittkopf, E.R. 1994. Faces of Internationalism in a Transitional Environment. *Journal of Conflict Resolution*, 38(3), pp.376–401.

Zaller, J. 1992. *The Nature and Origins of Mass Opinion*. Cambridge University Press.

INDEX